OXFORD EC LAW LIBRARY

General Editor: F. G. Jacobs
Advocate General, The Court of Justice
of the European Communities

THE LAW OF MONEY AND FINANCIAL
SERVICES IN THE EC (2nd Edition)

OXFORD EC LAW LIBRARY

The aim of this series is to publish important and original studies of the various branches of European Community Law. Each work will provide a clear, concise and critical exposition of the law in its social, economic and political context, at a level which will interest the advanced student, the practitioner, the academic, and government and Community officials.

Other Titles in the Library

The European Union and its Court of Justice
Antony Arnull

The General Principles of EC Law
Takis Tridimas

EC Company Law
Vanessa Edwards

EC Sex Equality Law
second edition
Evelyn Ellis

European Community Law of State Aid
Andrew Evans

EC Competition Law
third edition
Daniel G. Goyder

External Relations of the European Community
I. MacLeod, I. D. Hendry and Stephen Hyett

Directives in European Community Law
Sacha Prechal

EC Tax Law
Paul Farmer and Richard Lyal

The European Internal Market and International Trade
Piet Eeckhout

Trade and Environmental Law in the European Community
Andreas R. Ziegler

The Law of Money and Financial Services in the EC

SECOND EDITION

J. A. USHER

OXFORD
UNIVERSITY PRESS

This book has been printed digitally and produced in a standard specification in order to ensure its continuing availability

OXFORD
UNIVERSITY PRESS

Great Clarendon Street, Oxford OX2 6DP

Oxford University Press is a department of the University of Oxford. It furthers the University's objective of excellence in research, scholarship, and education by publishing worldwide in

Oxford New York

Auckland Bangkok Buenos Aires Cape Town Chennai Dar es Salaam Delhi Hong Kong Istanbul Karachi Kolkata Kuala Lumpur Madrid Melbourne Mexico City Mumbai Nairobi São Paulo Shanghai Singapore Taipei Tokyo Toronto

with an associated company in Berlin

Oxford is a registered trade mark of Oxford University Press in the UK and in certain other countries

Published in the United States by Oxford University Press Inc., New York

Reprinted 2002

ISBN 0-19-829877-3

General Editor's Foreword

On 1 January 1999 Europe acquired its single currency. Although that currency is for the time being confined to eleven of the fifteen Member States of the European Union, there are indications from the governments of the other Member States of preparations to adhere to the new currency, which will become a tangible reality for the peoples of Europe on 1 January 2002 when the new coins and notes enter their purses and pockets.

The emergence of a single currency has been seen as a development likely to transform the economic character of the European Union and perhaps even its political character. In economic terms such a transformation, which was merely a prediction when the first edition of this book was published, is already under way; the currency seems to be acting as a catalyst for change within the Eurozone.

The new edition of this book takes full account of the legal aspects of this transition to the third and final stage of Economic and Monetary Union, and situates the whole subject in the new context. The first edition focused on three areas: the free movement of capital, financial services, and developments towards monetary union. The achievement of the final stage of monetary union has of course profound implications for the free movement of capital and for freedom of financial services, and the book examines those implications. At the same time it considers the substantial new developments in these areas both in Community legislation and in the case-law of the Court of Justice.

Subjects of much practical importance are fully explored. These include the application of the competition rules to financial services; the Treaty rules on cross-border financial services; and the Community legislation on banking, investment and loans.

Two features of the new edition are of particular interest. First, one of the significant implications of the introduction of the single currency, and the correspondingly greater ease of cross-border investment, has been the drive for greater harmonisation in the field of tax. A new chapter dealing with taxation relates the developments in this field both to monetary movements and to the Treaty freedoms generally.

Secondly, the achievement of monetary union has important institutional implications. That would be so even if all Member States were within the Eurozone; but the fact that the union is for the time being only partial raises additional institutional questions. Both aspects of this topic are discussed.

The author thus succeeds in providing, within a reasonable compass, a comprehensive guide to the legal and institutional dimensions of what may come to be seen as the most significant innovation in European economic integration since the foundation of the European Communities in the nineteen-fifties.

December 1999 Francis G. Jacobs

Author's Preface

The first edition of this book was written when the Maastricht Treaty, with its detailed timetable for economic and monetary union, was entering into force. The 1992 deadline for the completion of the internal market programme, which laid particular emphasis on financial service legislation, had also recently expired, and a particular aim of the book was to relate the development of economic and monetary union in the EC to the development of the single market. It was also, however, a time at which the exchange rate mechanism of the European Monetary System was widely perceived as having collapsed, carrying with it the hopes for economic and monetary union, although I concluded the first edition with the view that there was a continuing political will to proceed to the third stage of economic and monetary union. The actual achievement of economic and monetary union in 1999, within the timescale laid down in the Treaty of Maastricht, albeit an economic and monetary union between 11 of the 15 Member States, has therefore necessitated a new edition which fully reflects the institutional and legal consequences of this situation, while taking account also of the continuing flow of Community legislation and case-law in the wider area of financial services.

The question was asked in the first edition of this book whether in fact an integrated market for financial services or the movement of capital could in reality be achieved without a form of control of currency fluctuations between the exchange rates of the currencies of Member States, or indeed without the development of a common currency. It may be suggested that such an integrated market is becoming more of a reality for the 11 Member States which now participate in monetary union, since exchange risks between these countries have been eliminated, and there can no longer be national governmental interference with interest rates as a matter of monetary policy, the definition of Community monetary policy being a matter for the European System of Central Banks. The removal of those risks for the 11 participants, making it practicable even for private investors to move their money from Member State to Member State, has raised the profile of issues such as tax evasion and tax competition and brought them onto the Community agenda, and the new edition contains a new chapter on these issues of taxation. On the other hand, the fact that four Member States do not participate in economic and monetary union makes this an area in which variable geometry has become a legal reality, and this also is reflected in a new chapter of the book.

Like its predecessor, this edition reflects ideas developed in the series of seminars on the law of money and financial services in the EC which I have continued to lead at the College of Europe in Bruges. I am also very grateful to the Universities of Stockholm and Helsinki for a continuing series of conference invitations which have enabled me to discuss, and test reaction to my thoughts in this rapidly developing area. It is furthermore a tribute to the administrative efficiency of the faculty of Law of the University of Edinburgh that I was able to complete most of this edition while holding office as the Dean of that Faculty. This book is however dedicated to Jean, Richard and Helen, and Alastair.

John A. Usher
Edinburgh, October 1999

Contents

Table of Cases

Table of Legislation

A. European Community

Treaties and Conventions

Decisions

Directives

Opinions

Regulations

B. National Legislation

France

United Kingdom

1

Money in the context of the EC Treaty

1. Introduction: the Treaty framework

The Treaty on European Union signed at Maastricht made detailed and complex amendments and additions to the EC Treaty for the purpose of creating Economic and Monetary Union. By contrast, the Treaty of Amsterdam, signed in 1997 and entering into force in May 1999, just after the start of the third stage of Economic and Monetary Union, did not amend any of the provisions relating to Economic and Monetary Union. There were, however, contemporaneous important non-Treaty developments, notably the enactment of Council Regulation 1103/97[1] on certain provisions relating to the introduction of the euro. The term 'euro' is nowhere to be found in the EC Treaty, but at the meeting of the European Council in Madrid on 15 and 16 December 1995, the decision was taken that the term 'ECU' used by the Treaty to refer to the European currency unit was a generic term, and the Governments of the fifteen Member States reached a common agreement that this decision was 'the agreed and definitive interpretation of the relevant Treaty provisions' and that the name of the European currency should be the 'euro'. Thus, without changing the Treaty, the Treaty term was changed.

On the other hand, the rules of the EC Treaty relevant to the activities of private sector financial institutions have for the most part remained in force since the end of the original transitional period. The major exception is that the Maastricht Treaty introduced new provisions on capital movements and payments—the only Treaty 'freedom' to be substantively amended—and it is also the case that following the start of the third stage of Economic and Monetary Union in January 1999, the prudential supervision of financial institutions other than insurance undertakings may, in terms of the Treaty, be entrusted to the European Central Bank.[2]

In reality financial services are a matter of particular complexity in the context of the EC Treaty because they link the provisions specifically relating to movements of money, in particular the movement of capital (originally arts. 67 to 73) and current payments (originally art. 106), to the general provisions concerning establishment, services, and competition, even if in the view of the European Court a clear distinction may be drawn between 'means of payment' and goods, so that means of payment do not benefit from the principle of the free movement of

[1] OJ 1997 L162/1.

[2] Under art. 105(6) of the EC Treaty (one of the few provisions to retain the same number after the entry into force of the Treaty of Amsterdam).

goods.[3] Even here, however, the question was asked in the first edition of this book whether an integrated market for financial services or for the movement of capital could in reality be achieved without some form of control over currency fluctuations between the exchange rates of the currencies of Member States, or indeed without the development of common currency units. It may be suggested that such an integrated market could become more of a reality for the eleven Member States[4] which participate in monetary union, since exchange risks between these countries have been eliminated, and there can no longer be national governmental interference with interest rates as a matter of monetary policy, the definition of Community monetary policy being a matter for the European System of Central Banks.[5] However, such risks have not been eliminated for the four Members States[6] which do not participate in monetary union. On the other hand, the removal of those risks for the eleven participants, making it practicable even for private investors to move their money from one Member State to another, has raised the profile of issues such as tax evasion and tax competition and brought them onto the Community agenda.[7]

With regard to Economic and Monetary Union, it may be observed that the original version of the EEC Treaty stated in art. 3 that the activities of the Community should include 'the application of procedures by which the economic policies of the Member States can be co-ordinated and disequilibria in their balances of payments remedied'. This was reflected in the original art. 104, requiring each Member State to pursue the economic policy needed to ensure the equilibrium of its overall balance of payments and to maintain confidence on its currency; under the original art. 105(1), Member States were to co-ordinate their economic policies so as to facilitate the attainment of those objectives. Those obligations can hardly be said to have been universally observed, and indeed in the context of the Common Agricultural Policy the European Court held in the late 1970s that the floating of exchange rates and the underlying failure to co-ordinate divergent monetary policies constituted a breach of the obligation set out in art. 105(1).[8]

To these provisions the Single European Act, which entered into force in July 1987, added a new art. 102a (itself replaced by a new version under the Maastricht Treaty, renumbered art. 124 under the Amsterdam Treaty) which provided for the convergence of economic and monetary policies 'necessary for the further development of the Community', and added a new Chapter heading: 'Co-operation in Economic and Monetary Policy'. The effect of all this came to be considered by the European Court in 1991, when it was asked to give its Opinion under art. 300

[3] Case 7/78 *R* v. *Thompson* [1978] ECR 2247. In so far as the European Court treated krugerrands in that case as being the subject of monetary transfer falling outside the free movement of goods, it has been heavily criticized—see F. A. Mann, 'Legal Aspects of Money' (5th ed. 1992) pp. 27–8.

[4] Germany, France, Italy, Spain, Portugal, the Netherlands, Belgium, Austria, Ireland, Finland, and Luxembourg.

[5] Under art. 105(2) of the EC Treaty.

[6] The United Kingdom, Denmark, Sweden and Greece.

[7] See Chapter 3 below.

[8] See e.g. Cases 80–81/77 *Ramel* v. *Receveur des Douanes* [1978] ECR 927.

(then art. 228) of the EC Treaty on the compatibility with that Treaty of an agreement with the EFTA countries creating the European Economic Area. The Court gave its Opinion in December 1991,[9] the same month as the Maastricht Treaty was negotiated. In that Opinion, the Court found it necessary to analyse the nature and objectives of the EC Treaty and, *inter alia*, it concluded that the European Community already had the objective of achieving Economic and Monetary Union under the terms of the version of the Treaty then in force.

To some extent this merely confirmed what had already happened in the political and legislative spheres: the European Council had decided at its meeting in Madrid in June 1989 that the first stage[10] of Economic and Monetary Union should begin on 1 July 1990, and during 1990 legislation such as Council Decision 90/141 'on the attainment of progressive convergence of economic policies and performance during stage one of EMU'[11] had already been enacted. Hence it may be suggested that all Community provisions relevant to financial services and monetary movements should be viewed in this overall context, and that the detailed provisions on economic policy and monetary policy set out in the Maastricht Treaty on European Union should be seen as governing the movement towards and the operation of the second and third stages of Economic and Monetary Union.[12] Furthermore, whilst art. 2 of the EC Treaty, as amended by the Maastricht and Amsterdam Treaties, contains the express statement that the Community should achieve its objectives 'by establishing a common market and an economic and monetary union', the requirement in art. 4(2) (formerly art. 3a(2)) that the activities of the Community 'shall include the irrevocable fixing of exchange rates leading to the introduction of a single currency, the ECU, and the definition and conduct of a single monetary policy and exchange rate policy' was declared by the Protocol on Certain Provisions Relating to the United Kingdom of Great Britain and Northern Ireland not to apply to the United Kingdom once it had given notice that it would not participate in the third stage.[13] The conclusions drawn from the previous version of the Treaty may therefore be of particular importance in the legal systems of the United Kingdom. By way of example, although it was adopted before the UK gave its notice in November 1997, Council Regulation 1103/97 on certain provisions relating to the introduction of the euro[14] is concerned in particular with the change from the ECU to the euro which, as mentioned above, is a matter not expressly envisaged in the EC Treaty. However, this Regulation was adopted at a Council meeting attended by ministers from all the Member States under art. 308 (formerly 235) of the EC Treaty, which allows action to attain 'one of the objectives of the Community' where the Treaty has not provided the necessary powers. Rather unusually for a Regulation, the explanation of the need for

[9] *Opinion 1/91* [1991] ECR I–6079; the Court in fact held that version of the agreement not to be compatible with the EC Treaty, largely because of its institutional structure, but approved a revised version in April 1992 in *Opinion 1/92* [1992] ECR I–2821.

[10] See Chapter 8 below.

[11] OJ 1990 L78/23.

[12] See Chapters 8, 9, and 10 below.

[13] Protocol para. 5.

[14] OJ 1997 L162/1.

the legislation (and hence the justification for the use of art. 308) is longer than the substantive text. It is conceivable that art. 308 may be used in future in the general area of Economic and Monetary Union.

2. The concept of money in EC law

In a classic definition,[15] 'the quality of money is to be attributed to all chattels which, issued by the authority of the law and denominated with reference to a unit of account, are meant to serve as universal means of exchange in the State of issue'. Leaving aside the political nature of the Union, which in terms of art. 1 of the Treaty on European Union (formerly art. A) is founded on the European Communities, those Communities have from the outset used their own units of account,[16] and it will be seen that it is the practice of the Commission, for example, to make and require certain payments in the current form of unit of account, the ECU. However, the ECU itself was defined by reference to fixed sums of *national* currencies,[17] and although it might have been possible to hold a bank account denominated in ECU,[18] a sum in ECU had in practice to be converted into a national currency before it could be spent in ordinary commerce.

However, as envisaged in the Maastricht Treaty, from 1st January 1994 (the start of the second stage of Economic and Monetary Union) the currency composition of the ECU basket was frozen, so that it was not able to reflect the currencies of Austria, Finland, and Sweden when they joined the Community in 1995, and since the start of the third stage[19] the value of the ECU, in the form of the euro, has been irrevocably fixed.[20] It has become a currency in its own right. As expressed in Council Regulation 974/98,[21] the euro is the currency of the participating Member States, but during a transitional period lasting until 2002 the euro is to be represented by the former national currency units at the fixed conversion rates.

As far as the participating Member States are concerned, the European Central Bank has the exclusive right to *authorize* the issue of bank notes within the Community, although both the European Central Bank and national central banks may *issue* such notes. The bank notes issued by the European Central Bank and the national central banks shall, in the terms of art. 106(1) (formerly art. 105a(1)) of the EC Treaty, be the only such notes to have the status of legal tender within the Community. Under art. 10 of Council Regulation 974/98 [22] such notes will only be put into circulation from 1 January 2002: until then the former national currency notes remain legal tender within their territorial limits.[23] With regard to coins, under art. 106(2) the Member States may issue coins subject to approval by

[15] Mann, *The Legal Aspect of Money*, 5th ed. (Oxford University Press, Oxford 1992) p. 8.

[16] See Chapter 7 below.

[17] See Regulation 3320/94 (OJ 1994 L350/27).

[18] See Chapter 7 below.

[19] See Chapter 8 below.

[20] EC Treaty art. 118 (formerly art. 109g).

[21] OJ 1998 L139/1.

[22] OJ 1998 L139/1.

[23] Under art. 9 of Regulation 974/98.

the European Central Bank of the volume of the issue. By that stage, therefore, as far as the participating Member States are concerned, there can be little doubt that notes and coins authorized or approved by the European Central Bank will indeed be 'chattels which, issued by the authority of the law and denominated with reference to a unit of account, are meant to serve as universal means of exchange in the State of issue'.

In the modern world, of course, means of payment and monetary transfer are widely used and accepted which do not involve the physical use of banknotes and coins, and examples may be found where national legislation actually requires payment by cheque or bank transfer and prohibits payment in cash, often to prevent tax evasion.[24] Indeed, in a Decision concerning the production and design of the relevant cheques and cards, the Commission suggested that Eurocheques, which are guaranteed by the issuing banks for payment in other states in the local currency, were the equivalent of banknotes.[25]

3. The distinction between goods and means of payment

A key element in the definition of money given above is that coins and banknotes are chattels or goods. In European Community law the question then arises how it may be determined whether they fall under the rules relating to the free movement of goods or rules more specific to monetary movements. The matter came before the European Court in Case 7/78 *R* v. *Thompson and Others*,[26] which involved a breach of the United Kingdom rules then in force prohibiting the importation of gold coins and the export of silver alloy coins minted before 1947. The appellants had apparently exported silver coins without the licence required by the Export of Goods (Control) Order 1970, and imported gold coins without the licence required by the Import of Goods (Control) Order 1954. The appellants argued that the UK legislation at issue breached arts. 28 and 29 (then arts. 30 and 34) of the EC Treaty, which prohibits quantitative restrictions and measures equivalent to quantitative restrictions on imports and exports in trade between Member States. The UK government argued that the coins at issue were 'capital' within the meaning of the Treaty, so that the free movement of goods rules did not apply.

The judgment is of particular importance in that, rather than determining whether the transactions in question were movements of capital, the Court

[24] See e.g. French *loi* 88–1149 of 23 Dec. 1988 (modifying art. 1 of the *loi* of 22 Oct. 1940) requiring certain commercial payments above 5,000FF to be made by cheque, credit transfer, or by payment card or credit card; and art. 107 of *loi des finances* 89–935 of 29 Dec. 1989, requiring all payments above 150,000FF by private individuals to be by crossed cheque payable only to the account of the payee, or by bank transfer, postal account transfer, or card.

[25] Commission Decision 89/95 (OJ 1989 L36/16). For further analysis of the Eurocheque system see Chapter 4 below.

[26] [1978] ECR 2247.

established a distinction between 'goods' falling within the free movement of goods rules, and 'means of payment', falling within the scope of other provisions. The Court further emphasized that capital transfers were only one specific category of monetary transfer, which might be effected for a great variety of purposes, noting in particular that the Treaty provided not only for capital movements as such but also for payments related to the exercise of other Treaty freedoms.[27] It therefore concluded that means of payment were not to be regarded as goods.

In determining whether the coins at issue constituted means of payment, the basic criterion used by the Court, as suggested by A.-G. Mayras.[28] was whether they were legal tender: a criterion which has been heavily criticized.[29] On this basis it dealt with the coins in three groups. It held that such of the silver coins as were still legal tender were, by their very nature, to be regarded as means of payment. With regard to kruggerands, it was stated that although there may be doubts as to whether they were a means of legal payment, 'it can nevertheless be noted that on the money markets of those Member States which permit dealing in these coins they are treated as being equivalent to currency', and therefore their transfer constituted a monetary transfer. On the other hand, with regard to the silver alloy coins minted before 1947 which were not legal tender (notably half-crowns) the Court took the view that they were not a 'means of payment' and could be designated as goods. The question of the application of art. 30 (then art. 36) which allows restrictions on imports or exports justified, *inter alia*, on grounds of public policy[30] therefore arose. Here the Court started from the premise that it is for Member States to mint their own coins and to protect them from destruction (which of course is no longer the case for those States which participate in monetary union). Being informed that in the United Kingdom the melting down or destruction of national coins was prohibited even if they were no longer legal tender, the Court held that a ban on exporting such coins which was imposed to prevent their being melted down or destroyed in another Member State was justified on grounds of public policy under art. 30.

It may be suggested that the Court was influenced in its approach by the views of A.-G. Mayras, who referred to 'the happy days of the gold standard' and to the concept of 'monetary gold'.[31] However, in the words of Dr. F. A. Mann,[32] that 'the Court ought to have asked whether in the context of the particular transaction the coins were used as objects of commerce or currency'. On this view, what matters is not whether the coins were in law legal tender, but whether in the particular transaction they were used as a commodity to be bought and sold or as money

[27] See section 4 below.

[28] [1978] ECR 2247 pp. 2287–9.

[29] See F. A. Mann, *The Legal Aspect of Money* 5th ed. (Oxford University Press, Oxford 1992) pp. 27–8.

[30] See Green, Hartley, and Usher, *Legal Foundations of the Single European Market*, (Oxford 1991) chapter 7.

[31] [1978] ECR p. 2283.

[32] *The Legal Aspect of Money* 5th ed. (Oxford University Press, Oxford 1992) p. 27.

at their face value.[33] In other areas of Community law, it appears that gold and gold coins are in principle subject to VAT as goods, except to the extent that they benefit from specific exemptions,[34] and when sanctions were imposed on South Africa, krugerrands were treated as goods whose importation was prohibited.[35] Nonetheless, the basic distinction made by the European Court between goods and means of payment remains important.

4. Payments relating to other Treaty freedoms

It is self-evident that the free movement of goods would be nugatory if a purchaser in one Member State was not able to pay a supplier in another Member State, and the same holds true for the other Treaty 'freedoms'.[36] This was expressly recognized in art. 106 of the EEC Treaty as originally drafted, which was continued until January 1994 as art. 73h of the EC Treaty by virtue of the Maastricht amendments. Under paragraph 1 of this provision each Member State undertook to authorize, in the currency of the Member State in which the creditor or the beneficiary resided, any payment connected with the movement of goods, services, or capital, and any transfers of capital and earnings, to the extent that the movement of goods, services, capital, and persons between Member States had been liberalized pursuant to this Treaty. The second paragraph specified that in so far as movements of goods, services, and capital were limited only by restrictions on payments connected therewith, these restrictions should be progressively abolished by applying, *mutatis mutandis,* the provisions of the Chapters relating to the abolition of qualitative restrictions, the liberalization of services, and the free movement of capital. Under the third paragraph Member States undertook not to introduce between themselves any new restrictions on transfers connected with invisible transactions,[37] and agreed that the progressive abolition of existing restrictions should be effected in accordance with the general programme on freedom to provide services in so far as such abolition was not governed by the provisions contained in paragraphs 1 and 2 or by other provisions of the Chapter on the free movement of capital.

The first paragraph was of particular importance in that it was held to be directly effective, giving rise to rights enforceable by individuals before their national courts,[38] at a time when the Treaty rules on free movement of capital did not give

[33] The German suppliers of the krugerrands brought an action to recover them from Customs and Excise, claiming that they had not received payment and the coins were therefore still their property. However, the Court of Appeal held in *AGOSI* v. *Customs and Excise* [1980] QB 390 that Customs and Excise were entitled to forfeit the coins as smuggled 'goods'.

[34] Sixth VAT Directive 77/388 (OJ 1977 L145/1) art. 28(3)(b) and Annex F point 26.

[35] Council Regulation 3302/86 (OJ 1986 L305/11).

[36] Although, conversely, a restriction on the freedom to provide services, justified as being in the general good, may also justify a restriction on correlative monetary movements: Case C–148/91 *Veronica* v. *Commissariaat voor de Media* [1993] ECR I–487.

[37] Listed in Annex III to the EC Treaty.

[38] Cases 286/82 and 26/83 *Luisi and Carbone* v. *Ministero del Tesoro* [1984] ECR 377.

rise to such rights.[39] Nevertheless, the substantive rights to which it gives rise have been narrowly interpreted by the European Court. The question first arose in Case 203/80 *Casati*,[40] which arose from a breach of Italian exchange control legislation in relation to the re-export of German bank notes from Italy after their holder had failed to achieve his intention of using them to buy a piece of machinery in Italy: the factory was apparently closed for its holiday. Turning to article 106(1) as it then was, the Court took the view that this provision did not require Member States to allow the movement of bank notes if such movement was not necessary and indeed standard practice for the transaction in question, holding that the importation and exportation of banknotes was neither necessary nor standard practice in relation to commercial transactions. It is perhaps questionable whether the Court's view of standard practice in relation to the habits of small businessmen was wholly accurate.

Furthermore, the Court found that the transaction in question could not be an invisible transaction within the meaning of the old art. 106(3), where the money was in fact being re-exported from the State in which it was supposed to have been spent. The view expressed in *Casati* that there is no requirement to allow cash payments was followed in Case 308/86 *Lambert*,[41] where the Court upheld Luxembourg (and Belgian) rules requiring payments for exports to be made by credit transfer or cheque, and to be converted on the regulated market (which then still existed) rather than the free market.

With regard to the currency in which payment may be made, the European Court in Case 308/86 *Lambert*[42] applied a restrictive literal approach to the old art. 106, holding that it was not relevant to the way in which an *exporter* received payment, being concerned only to ensure that the *importer* was able to make the payment. It is respectfully suggested that both aspects are equally important to the achievement of genuine free movement of goods and services, and that this judgment takes an unduly narrow approach. However, in the leading case on the direct effect of this provision, Cases 286/82 and 26/83 *Luisi and Carbone* v. *Ministero del Tesoro*,[43] the Court had noted that the original art. 106 only applied to liberalize current payments made in the currency of the State of the creditor, which helps explain the decision in *Casati*, since in that case art. 106 would only have justified payment in lire.

A similar provision is still found in the Europe Agreements with Central and Eastern European countries.[44] However, there is an important difference: payments linked to transactions liberalized under the Agreements must be authorized in 'freely convertible currency'[45] rather than just the currency of the creditor. The aim however is the same: to ensure that to the extent that trade is liberalized, payments can be made without restrictions, even where there is no immediate

[39] Case 203/80 *Casati* [1981] ECR 2595. [40] Ibid. [41] [1988] ECR 4369.

[42] Ibid. [43] [1984] ECR 377.

[44] Art.60 in most of the Agreements, but art. 59 in the Agreements with Poland and Hungary.

[45] See e.g. art. 60 of the Agreement with Bulgaria (OJ 1994 L358/1).

obligation on the Central and Eastern European countries to liberalize capital movements as such. On the other hand, in the context of the European Economic Area Agreement with Norway, Iceland, and Liechtenstein, art. 41 simply provides that current payments connected with the movement of goods, persons, services, or capital between contracting Parties within the framework of the provisions of the Agreement shall be free of all restrictions.

It may be suggested that the substantive Treaty provisions relating to the 'freedom' at issue may themselves have a wider scope: hindrance of the payment for goods imported from another Member State may amount to a restriction on the free movement of those goods. This matter came to light in Case 95/81 *Commission* v. *Italy*[46] in relation to an import deposit scheme. Under Italian law, in order to deter currency speculation, importers paying for goods in advance of their release from customs clearance had to lodge an interest-free security or guarantee. The Court found that although the measures in question were enacted for the purpose of preventing currency speculation, they were not specific rules for the attainment of that objective, but general rules which affected normal commercial transactions where payment was made in advance. Since they were undeniably a hindrance to trade, the Italian rules were classified as measures equivalent to quantitative restrictions. The Italian government next argued that these measures could be justified under art. 30 (then art. 36) of the EC Treaty on grounds of public policy, since their objective was to safeguard a fundamental interest of the State, the defence of its currency, but the Court, following well established case-law, reaffirmed that art. 30 applied only to matters of a non-economic nature.

In effect the Italian government had also argued that the rules at issue were a matter of monetary policy, and therefore could not be subject to the free movement of goods rules. However, the Court pointed out that the Treaty contained specific provisions (then arts.108 and 109, now arts. 119 and 120) allowing for protective measures to counter difficulties in the balance of payments, and concluded that the requirement in the then art. 104 that each Member State should pursue the economic policy needed to ensure the equilibrium of its overall balance of payments and to maintain confidence in its currency did not itself permit derogations from the free movement of goods rules.

Monetary policy has also been unsuccessfully invoked to prevent the application of other general Treaty rules. In Cases 6 and 11/69 *Commission* v. *France*[47] it was alleged that a preferential rediscount rate for exports constituted a breach of the state aid rules. France argued that this system was justified under the old art. 109 as a protective measure, but the Court found that the requirements laid down by this provision had in any event not been met. Case 57/86R *Greece* v. *Commission*[48] involved the similar matter of interest rebates on exports. The Greek government argued that it was a monetary measure, designed to encourage Greek exporters to repatriate rapidly the foreign currency which they obtained. The Court stated that

[46] [1982] ECR 2187. [47] [1969] ECR 523. [48] [1986] ECR 1497.

in its judgment in *Commission* v. *France* it did not accept that the discount rate for exports fell within monetary policy, and that the principle of that judgment should apply in the Greek case; it further noted that the objective of early repatriation of foreign currency could easily be achieved by other means. The question of the relationship between monetary policy and other Treaty rules has, as will be seen,[49] caused more problems in the application of the competition rules, though even here monetary policy has not been allowed to justify conduct which would otherwise breach the Treaty.[50] In any event, for the eleven Member States participating in monetary union, monetary policy is no longer a matter of national competence: under art. 4(2) (formerly art. 3a(2)) of the EC Treaty, there is a single Community monetary policy, defined under art. 105(2) by the European System of Central Banks.

Returning to the scope of the original art. 106, notice may be taken of the early decision of the English Court of Appeal in *Schorsch Meier* v. *Hennin*[51] that art. 106 empowered a national court actually to give judgment in the creditor's currency, an interpretation which appears to go further than that of the European Court. The underlying problem was one familiar to countries with a floating exchange rate: a German company had supplied car parts to Mr Hennin at an invoice price of DM3756, which when payment became due amounted to £452; the debt was not paid, and at the date of the judgment, £452 was worth only DM2664, following a fall in the value of the pound. Following the established case-law confirmed by the House of Lords,[52] an English court could only give judgment in sterling, and the debt had to be converted at the date payment became due, and if this precedent was followed the German supplier would only receive just over 70 per cent of what it was owed in DM. The German supplier claimed that this rule was incompatible with art. 106, and the Court of Appeal held that that article could be invoked before them,[53] stating that one of the purposes of art. 106 was to ensure that a creditor in one Member State should receive payment for his goods in his own currency, if that was the currency of the contract, 'without any impediment or restriction by reason of changes in the rate of exchange'. The Court of Appeal concluded that in order to comply with the Treaty, the defendant should be ordered to pay the stated sum in DM or its sterling equivalent at the time of payment, although unfortunately it did add[54] that the plaintiffs would have to extricate themselves from the problems of exchange control—the one problem clearly overcome by art. 106 and its successors.

While the House of Lords heavily criticized the Court of Appeal in *Miliangos* v. *Frank*[55] for interpreting art. 106 in this way without making a reference to the

[49] See Chapter 4 below.

[50] See Case 267/86 *Van Eycke* [1988] ECR 4769.

[51] [1975] QB 416.

[52] Re *United Railways of Havana* [1961] AC 1007.

[53] Nine years before the European Court held it to be of direct effect, and without mentioning any of the usual criteria for determining whether a provision in the Treaty may give rise to enforceable individual rights.

[54] *Per* Lawton LJ.

[55] [1975] 3 All ER 801.

European Court, and for not following the earlier decision of the House of Lords, it did in fact reach the same result as a matter of English law,[56] reversing the previous case-law. Desirable as this may be, it illustrates the fundamental problem as to whether the Community can really constitute a single internal market if exchange risk has to be taken into account. However, in the context of trade between the eleven Member States participating in monetary union, there is no longer any exchange risk.

5. Current payments and capital movements

One of the aims of arts. 56 to 69 (formerly arts. 73b to 73g) of the EC Treaty, which by virtue of the Maastricht amendments entered into force on 1 January 1994 as a new Chapter on 'Capital and Payments', appears to be to ensure that capital movements and current payments are treated in the same way. Article 56(1) provides that, within the framework of the provisions set out in the chapter on capital and payments, all restrictions on the movement of capital between Member States and between Member States and third countries shall be prohibited, and art. 56(2) provides that, within the same framework, all restrictions on payments between Member States and between Member States and third countries shall be prohibited. However, earlier case-law distinguished; and the distinction helps to explain why restrictions tended to be authorized under what continue in force for the non-participants in monetary union as arts. 119 and 120 (originally arts. 108 and 109), rather than under other Treaty provisions.[57]

The distinction was particularly examined in Cases 286/82 and 26/83 *Luisi and Carbone* v. *Ministero del Tesoro*[58] in relation to Italian residents who had acquired more than the permitted amount of foreign currency, claiming it was to pay for various services in France and Germany. Under the capital movements Directives then in force, there was no requirement to liberalize the physical transfer of banknotes, but the original art. 106 did require current payments relating to other Treaty freedoms to be authorized in the creditor's currency.[59] The Court noted that the Treaty did not define movements of capital, and held that it was not necessarily the case that every physical transfer of financial assets constituted a movement of capital. After comparing the original arts. 67 and 106, the Court concluded that current payments are transfers of foreign exchange which constitute the *consideration* within the context of an underlying transaction, whilst movements of capital are financial operations essentially concerned with the investment of the

[56] The case involved payment in Swiss francs, so art. 106 could not be prayed in aid.

[57] See Chapter 2 below.

[58] [1984] ECR 377.

[59] Even if Council Directive 63/340 'on the abolition of all prohibitions on or obstacles to payments for services where the only restrictions on exchange of services are those governing such services' (JO 1963 p. 1609) made under art. 106(2) expressly excluded services in connection with transport and foreign exchange allowances for tourists.

funds in question rather than remuneration for a service, noting that the original art. 67(2) of the Treaty recognized that there could be current payments connected with the movement of capital. It was therefore held that the physical transfer of banknotes could not be classified as a movement of capital where the transfer in question corresponded to an obligation to pay arising from a transaction involving the movement of goods or services.

While this distinction between the consideration and the underlying transaction may seem clear, it gives rise to practical difficulties. To take the simple example of a with-profits life assurance policy, part of the premium will be used for investment purposes (presumably 'capital' in the Court's definition), and part will be used to meet expenses and to pay for the life assurance (presumably both payments for services). Although the Court sought to draw a clear distinction between movements of capital and current payments, the series of Directives on the free movement of capital enacted under the original art. 67 of the Treaty still appear to cover both types of transaction,[60] although intriguingly they require transfers in respect of capital movements to be made on the same exchange rate conditions as those governing payments relating to current transactions, a terminology which appears to recognize that there are two different concepts. In the version resulting from Directive 86/566,[61] to take a historic example, list A, a list of transactions to be liberalized, expressly included transfers in performance of insurance contracts 'as and when free movement in respect of services' was extended to them. The effect of this on the first paragraph of art. 106 concerning current payments is considered in the next Chapter, but it increased the importance of the distinction drawn in the insurance cases[62] and the subsequent Directives[63] between those types of insurance service which may be offered by companies established in another Member State, and those which may not without further authorization. Indeed, list A expressly included transfers of monies required for the provision of services, which was a clear overlap with the concept of current payments enounced in *Luisi and Carbone*.

The distinction between current payments and capital movements is continued in both the European Economic Area Agreement and the Europe Agreements with Central and Eastern European countries. In the European Economic Area Agreement, art. 40 provides that there shall be no restrictions between the Contracting Parties on the movement of capital belonging to persons resident in EC Member States or EFTA States, 'and no discrimination based on the nationality or on the place of residence of the parties or on the place where such capital is invested'. Article 41 provides that current payments connected with the movement of goods, persons, services, or capital between contracting Parties within the frame-

[60] Council Directive 88/361 (OJ 1988 L178/5), replacing Council Directive of 11 May 1960 (JO 1960 p. 921), as amended by Council Directive 63/21 (JO 1963 p. 62) and Council Directive 86/566 (OJ 1986 L332/22).

[61] OJ 1986 L332/22.

[62] Case 205/84 *Commission* v. *Germany* [1986] ECR 3755.

[63] See Chapter 5 below.

work of the provisions of the Agreement shall be free of all restrictions. As far as the Europe Agreements with Central and Eastern European countries are concerned, it is provided that payments shall be authorized in freely convertible currency to the extent that the transactions underlying the payments concern movements of goods, services, or persons between the Parties which have been liberalized pursuant to the Agreement.[64] Furthermore, the Member States of the Community have undertaken from the entry into force of the respective Agreements not to introduce any new foreign exchange restrictions on the movement of capital and current payments connected therewith between residents of the Community and the relevant Central or Eastern European State, and not to make existing arrangements more restrictive.[65] However, they have not undertaken (except to the extent of holding consultations) to eliminate pre-existing restrictions. On the other hand, the Central and Eastern European countries, with the notable exception of Estonia, benefit from transitional arrangements which impose no immediate obligation to liberalize all capital movements. The old distinctions therefore linger in this wider context.

6. Invisible transactions

The invisible transactions not connected with the movement of goods, services, capital, or persons referred to in the original art. 106(3) and listed in Annex III to the EC Treaty were expressly liberalized by Council Directive 63/474,[66] at least to the extent of imposing an obligation on Member States to grant all foreign exchange authorizations required for transfers between residents of Member States. These invisible transactions included[67] such matters as banking charges and representation expenses, and periodic settlements in connection with public transport and postal, telegraphic, and telephone services, which are in fact all arguably related to the provision of services. On the other hand, subscriptions and membership fees were included only to the extent that they did not represent remuneration for services, damages were included only to the extent that they could not be considered as capital, and sports prizes and racing earnings excluded those won by professionals. Payments in which there is a public interest feature strongly on the list, notably government expenditure, consular receipts, taxes (other than death duties), court expenses, registration of patents and trade marks, fines, and maintenance payments resulting from a legal obligation (as well as financial assistance in cases of hardship).

[64] See art. 60 of the Agreements with Bulgaria, the Czech Republic, Estonia, Latvia, Lithuania, Romania, Slovakia, and Slovenia, and art. 59 of the Agreements with Hungary and Poland.

[65] See e.g. art. 61(2) of the Agreements with Bulgaria, the Czech Republic, and Slovakia, art. 61(3) of the Agreement with Romania, and art. 60(2) of the Agreements with Hungary and Poland.

[66] JO 1963 p. 2240.

[67] Annex to the Directive.

Whatever the difficulties of these distinctions, as from 1 January 1994 all these transfers may be regarded as subsumed in the concept of 'payments' under art. 56(2) (formerly art. 73b(2)); indeed, art. 106(3), which referred to invisible transactions, only remained in force under the Maastricht amendments as part of art. 73h until that date, and has now been repealed.

2

Capital movements

1. The original Treaty provisions

Whatever may be the meaning of capital in the context of the EC Treaty,[1] the provisions relating to capital movements are distinguished by the fact that in the original version they were drafted in a style very different from that of the other Treaty 'freedoms', and by the fact that, with effect from the beginning of the second stage of Economic and Monetary Union on 1 January 1994, they were replaced by a completely new set of provisions similar in many respects to those governing the free movement of goods. The current provisions may be regarded as having been drafted with Economic and Monetary Union in mind, but it must be emphasized that in principle the same rules apply to all Member States, irrespective of their participation in monetary union. However, these rules can best be understood in the light of what went before.

The basic requirement set out in art. 67(1) of the original EEC Treaty was that during the transitional period Member States should between themselves progressively abolish all restrictions on the movement of capital belonging to persons resident in Member States and any discrimination based on the nationality or place of residence of the parties or on the place where such capital is invested, but only 'to the extent necessary to ensure the proper functioning of the common market'. With regard to transitional and standstill arrangements, the original art. 68(1) required Member States to be 'as liberal as possible' in granting exchange authorizations still necessary after the entry into force of the Treaty, and the original art. 71 required Member States to 'endeavour' to avoid introducing within the Community any new exchange restrictions on the movement of capital and current payments connected with such movements, and to 'endeavour' not to make existing rules more restrictive.

Briefly summarizing the remainder of the original version of the Title, art. 69 enabled the Council to issue Directives for the implementation of art. 67, acting by a qualified majority from the beginning of the third stage (1 January 1966). Articles 70 and 72 dealt with the question of capital movements between Member States

[1] See Chapter 1 above. In particular, it may be suggested that notions derived from national company or tax law are not relevant in this context; however, successive Directives issued under the original Treaty provisions defined the monetary movements to which their various provisions related, and it is now clear from Case C–222/97 *Trummer and Mayer* (16 Mar. 1999) that these definitions continue to be relevant in the context of the current Treaty provisions.

and third countries.[2] Article 73 enabled protective measures to be authorized by the Commission or, under art. 73(2), to be taken by the Member State itself in cases of urgency.[3]

The legal effects of art. 67 of the original version of the EEC Treaty were considered by the European Court in Case 203/80 *Casati*.[4] It has been seen that art. 67 differed from the other 'freedoms' laid down by the Treaty in that it was not drafted in absolute terms. It does not absolutely require restrictions on the movement of capital to be abolished; rather it requires them to be abolished 'to the extent necessary to ensure the proper functioning of the common market'. In *Casati* it was held that the scope of that restriction might vary in time, and depended on both an assessment of the requirements of the common market and an appraisal of the advantages and risks which liberalization might entail. It was further stated that such an assessment was 'first and foremost' a matter for the Council, and that the obligation to abolish restrictions on movements of capital could not be separated from the Council's assessment of the need to liberalize the category of transactions in question.

In other words, it was not a straightforward rule which could be applied directly by a national court, or even the European Court, but was essentially a question of policy for the Council, the role of the Court being limited to checking whether the Council had overstepped the limits of its discretion. The Court concluded that there was no reason to suppose that, by taking the view at that stage that it was unnecessary to liberalize the exportation of banknotes, the Council had in fact overstepped those limits.

With regard to the 'standstill' provision in the original art. 71, the Court again noted that the wording of the requirement for Member States to 'endeavour' to avoid introducing within the Community any new exchange restrictions on the movement of capital and current payments connected with such movements, and to 'endeavour' not to make existing rules more restrictive, departed noticeably from the more imperative terminology used in the other Treaty freedoms, and did not impose on Member States an unconditional obligation which could be relied on by individuals.

The fact that only the monetary movements listed in the Council Directives were liberalized had consequences even for current payments under the original art. 106. In Cases 286/82 and 26/83 *Luisi and Carbone* v. *Ministero del Tesoro*,[5] in the context of current payments relating to the provision of services, the Court held that since liberalization of capital movements had not yet been fully achieved, Member States retained the power to impose controls on transfers of foreign currency in order to verify that those transfers did not constitute movements of capital which had not yet been liberalized,[6] suggesting that Member States could fix flat-

[2] See Chapter 11 below. [3] See p. 28 below. [4] [1981] ECR 2595.

[5] [1984] ECR 377.

[6] The Court noted that Council Directive 63/340 on the abolition of obstacles to payments for services where the only restrictions on exchange of services are those governing such payments (JO 1963 p. 1609) had provided that Member States could verify the nature and genuineness of payments.

rate limits below which no verification was carried out (provided that the level did not affect the normal pattern of the provision of services), but could require proof if expenditure exceeded those limits that the amounts transferred had actually been used in connection with the provision of services.

The provision of services in the financial sector is also subject to the express statement in art. 51(2) (formerly art. 61(2)) that the liberalization of banking and insurance services connected with movements of capital should be effected in step with the progressive liberalization of movements of capital, which came in practice to mean that if a service related to a capital movement which had not been liberalized, the Treaty rules on freedom to provide services could not be invoked, i.e. the capital movement rules prevailed over the freedom to provide services. Case 267/86 *Van Eycke* v. *ASPA*[7] held that, since the opening of a savings account in another Member State was not at that time liberated under the capital movement Directives, it was not a breach of the Treaty provisions on freedom to provide services for Belgium to limit tax exemptions on such accounts to deposits in local currency at credit institutions having their head office (*siège social*) in Belgium. Indeed, even after liberalization of capital movements has in principle been achieved, the recitals to the Second Banking Directive[8] recognized that capital safeguard measures under the 1988 Capital Movements Directive[9] might lead to restrictions on the provision of banking services.

2. The capital movement Directives

Although the original Treaty provisions may not have been capable of giving rise to rights enforceable by individuals, the first Council Directive under the original art. 67 was enacted during the first stage of the original transitional period on 11 May 1960,[10] and was amended at the end of 1962 by Directive 63/21.[11] It may be observed that, in their recitals, these Directives claim to be made under a number of Treaty provisions, including not only arts. 67 and 69 on capital movements but also the former art. 106(2) on current payments. The basic pattern established by these Directives was to divide capital movements into four lists, with different degrees of liberalization. Member States were required to grant 'all foreign exchange authorizations' for the transactions or transfers set out in List A. These included direct investments (defined to exclude purely financial investments) in an undertaking in another Member State, investments in real estate, certain personal capital movements, short (one-year) and medium-term (one- to five-year) credits related to commercial transactions or provision of services, death duties, and

[7] [1988] ECR 4769.

[8] Council Directive 89/646 (OJ 1989 L386/1).

[9] Council Directive 88/361 (OJ 1988 L178/5).

[10] JO 921/60.

[11] JO 62/63.

damages to the extent they may be regarded as capital,[12] but they also included transfers in performance of insurance contracts 'as and when free movement in respect of services' was extended to them, authors' royalties, and 'transfers of moneys required for the provision of services', which appear clearly to involve current payments.

The transactions and transfers in List B required 'general permission' by the Member States.[13] List B consisted largely of operations in securities, notably the acquisition and liquidation by non-residents of domestic listed securities, and the acquisition and liquidation by residents of foreign listed securities. On the other hand, while in principle the transactions and transfers in List C required foreign exchange authorizations, Member States could maintain or reintroduce exchange restrictions operative at the date of entry into force of the Directive where such free movement of capital might form an obstacle to the achievement of the economic policy objectives of the Member State concerned. List C included the issue and placing of securities of a domestic undertaking on a foreign capital market and of a foreign undertaking on the domestic capital market, cross-border acquisition and liquidation of units in unit trusts, and the granting and repayment of certain long-term credits. Finally, List D set out the capital movements which did not have to be liberalized, including in particular the opening and the placing of funds on current or deposit accounts, the physical import and export of financial assets, and personal loans.

In 1986 this was amended by Council Directive 86/566,[14] which in effect merged the old lists A and B into a new List A, and added other elements from the former List C, notably the issue and placing of securities of a domestic undertaking on a foreign capital market and of a foreign undertaking on the domestic capital market, cross-border acquisitions and liquidations of units in unit trusts, and the granting and repayment of certain long-term credits noted above. However, art. 2(2) of the Directive allowed Spain and Portugal, as an ancillary measure to their Accession arrangements, to retain the power to reimpose restrictions on certain of the movements which had been transferred from the old List C to List A. What was left of List C was renamed List B, still subject to the power of the Member States to maintain or reintroduce the exchange restrictions which were operative at the date of entry into force of the Directive where free movement of capital might form an obstacle to the achievement of the economic policy objectives of the Member State concerned; it included transactions in unlisted securities, medium and long-term loans and credits not connected with commercial transactions or provision of services, and sureties and guarantees relating thereto. Finally, the old List D became List C, still not liberalized.

[12] Cf. Council Directive 63/474 (JO 1963 p. 2240) on invisible transactions, including damages which could not be considered as capital. See Chapter 1 above.

[13] Although it is only of historic interest, it might be argued that 'general permission' is in fact a wider-ranging obligation than granting 'all foreign exchange authorizations' under List A.

[14] OJ 1986 L332/22.

A new approach was followed by Council Directive 88/361,[15] which finally established the basic principle of free movement of capital as a matter of Community law, with effect for most Member States from 1 July 1990. Free movement of capital thus become the only Treaty 'freedom' to be achieved in the manner envisaged in the Treaty—by the enactment of a programme of legislation—albeit twenty years after the time-limit envisaged in the Treaty. Subject to its other provisions, art. 1(1) of the 1988 Directive provided that 'Member States shall abolish restrictions on movements of capital taking place between persons resident in Member States', and although there was still a nomenclature of capital movements annexed to the Directive, it was stated to be intended to facilitate its application, rather than to introduce distinctions in treatment. Annex I itself stated that the nomenclature was not intended to be an exhaustive list of the notion of capital movements, and should not be interpreted as restricting the scope of the principle of full liberalization of capital movements in art. 1. However, in the absence of a Treaty definition, the headings of the nomenclature (which in reality owe much to the previous lists) indicate the concept of capital underlying the Directive: direct investments, investments in real estate, operations in securities normally handled on the capital market, operations in units of collective investment undertakings, operations in securities and other instruments normally undertaken on the money market, operations in current and deposit accounts with financial institutions, credits related to commercial transactions or to the provision of services in which a resident is participating, financial loans and credits, sureties, other guarantees and rights of pledge, transfers in performance of insurance contracts, personal capital movements, physical import and export of financial assets, and 'other capital movements' (defined to include transfers of moneys required for the provision of services).

The introduction to the Annex further states that the capital movements mentioned are taken to cover all the operations necessary for the purposes of capital movements, i.e. the conclusion and performance of the transaction and related transfers, and should also include access for the economic operator to all the financial techniques available on the market approached for the purpose of carrying out the operation in question.

Two particular comments may be made about this nomenclature. First, in the continued silence of the Treaty it remains a useful illustration of the principle of the free movement of capital even after the entry into force of arts. 56 to 60 (formerly arts. 73b to 73g) under the Maastricht Treaty. This was expressly confirmed by the European Court in Case C–222/97 *Trummer and Mayer*.[16] Secondly, many of the movements listed were clearly current payments under what was then art. 106(1), even though the Court had clearly held in Cases 286/82 and 26/83 *Luisi and Carbone* v. *Ministero del Tesoro*[17] that art. 106(1) was directly effective. At first sight it might seem that to include such movements in the Directive was superfluous.

[15] OJ 1988 L178/5. [16] 16 Mar. 1999. [17] [1984] ECR 377.

However, the difficulties in distinguishing clearly between capital movements and current payments,[18] and the narrow way in which the Court read art. 106 in Case 308/86 *Lambert*,[19] holding that it was not relevant to the way an *exporter* received payment, merely being concerned to ensure that the *importer* was able to make the payment, and that it entitled the exporter only to payment in his own currency, meant that there was some practical advantage in including what were possibly current payments in the concept of liberalized capital movements.

Nevertheless, the 1988 Directive purported to be made under arts. 69 and 70(1), which related only to capital movements. However, it is now clear that borrowing money from a bank in another Member State to buy a house fell within the scope of the Directive, as was held in Case C–484/93 *Svensson and Gustavsson* v. *Ministre du Logement*.[20] Though it was subsequently suggested by A.-G. Tesauro in his Opinion in Case C–118/96 *Safir* v. *Skattemyndigheten i Dalarnas Län*[21] that a narrower concept of capital movements should be adopted, the Court confirmed that a mortgage fell within the scope of a capital movement as defined in the Directive in *Trummer and Meyer*,[22] and held that this interpretation should continue to apply to the free movement of capital under art. 56.

During the legislative process doubts were expressed about the wisdom of bringing about the liberalization of capital movements without taking a number of related measures. In its Opinion,[23] the Economic and Social Committee suggested that liberalization ought to be accompanied by efforts in such important fields as harmonizing the operating rules for financial services[24] and stock markets, the rules governing the solvency[25] and stability of financial institutions, and tax harmonization. Furthermore, they stated that liberalization could not be achieved without stabilizing exchange rates, noting that unstable exchange rates and sudden fluctuations pose considerable danger for the economies of the various Member States, and concluding that it was becoming more and more difficult to conduct a coordinated Community policy with floating exchange-rate and fixed-parity currencies existing side by side. While this may help explain the political impetus towards the Maastricht provisions on monetary union,[26] it emphasizes the point that internal market legislation in the financial sector has to be viewed in its wider context. Indeed, the adoption of the 1988 Capital Movements Directive was accompanied by the adoption of Council Regulation 1969/88[27] on medium-term financial assistance, designed to help Member States with balance of payments difficulties.

With regard to tax harmonization, Directive 88/361 expressly envisaged in its art. 6(5) that the Commission would submit to the Council by 31 December 1988 proposals aimed at eliminating or reducing the risks of distortion, tax evasion, and

[18] See Chapter 1 above. [19] [1988] ECR 4369. [20] [1995] ECR I–3955.

[21] Opinion delivered 23 Sept. 1997, [1998] ECR I–1899.

[22] Case C–222/97. [23] OJ 1988 C175/1.

[24] See e.g. the Second Banking Directive 89/646 (OJ 1989 L386/1).

[25] See e.g. Council Directive 89/647 on a solvency ratio for credit institutions (OJ 1989 L386/14) and Council Directive 89/299 on the 'own funds' of credit institutions (OJ 1989 L124/16).

[26] See Chapter 8 below. [27] OJ 1988 L178/1.

tax avoidance 'linked to the diversity of national systems for the taxation of savings and for controlling the application of these systems', and the Council was to take a position by 30 June 1989. The Commission did in fact put forward a proposal, albeit slightly late, for a Directive on a common system of withholding tax on interest income,[28] requiring the payer of interest to deduct from the amount of interest due a withholding tax at a rate of at least 15 per cent, so as at least to ensure the payment of a 'minimum taxation of interest'. However, under art. 6(5) of the Directive, the Council was required 'in accordance with the Treaty'[29] to act unanimously, and it failed to approve the proposal, with the result that the capital movements Directive entered into full effect with no corresponding Community tax legislation, with all the possibilities for tax evasion to which that gave rise.

Nevertheless, as the single market has become more of a reality, and in particular as exchange risks (and artificial interference with interest rates at the national level) have been eliminated for those Member States participating in Economic and Monetary Union, the market effects of differential tax systems have become more obvious. In the area of the free movements of goods the Community did indeed take steps to limit the range of variation in rates of VAT.[30] However, there is now clearly a political impetus in this area, exemplified by an ECOFIN meeting on 1 December 1997 which adopted a Code of Conduct for Business Taxation,[31] and reached political agreement on the need for legislation on withholding tax. The Commission then put forward a new proposal for a Directive 'to ensure a minimum of effective taxation of savings income in the form of interest payments within the Community'.[32] This is based on the 'coexistence' model under which Member States have a choice between applying a withholding tax at source (of which the suggested level is 20 per cent) or providing information on income from savings to other Member States, and its scope is limited to interest paid in each Member State to individuals resident in another Member State.

Returning to the structure of the 1988 Directive, as well as requiring the abolition of restrictions on movements of capital under art. 1(1), art. 1(2) stated that transfers in respect of capital movements should be subject to the same exchange rate as payments relating to current transactions, a measure aimed at the dual exchange rate used by Belgium and Luxembourg (noted in Annex V), which was subsequently abolished.

On the other hand, most of the remainder of the Directive noted or allowed limitations to the basic freedom. It was accepted in art. 2 that national measures to regulate bank liquidity may have an impact on capital transactions carried out by credit institutions with non-residents, and these should therefore be notified, *inter alia*, to the Commission. Art. 3 provided a limited safeguard clause, allowing the

[28] OJ 1989 C141/5.

[29] The Commission proposal was in fact put forward under the general art. 100 of the EC Treaty: art. 99 on the harmonization of certain forms of taxation refers only to *indirect* taxation.

[30] Directive 92/77 (OJ 1992 L316/1) on rates of VAT.

[31] OJ 1998 C2/3.

[32] COM(1998) 295 final (20 May 1998).

Commission, where short-term capital movements of exceptional magnitude impose severe strains on foreign exchange markets and lead to serious disturbances in a Member State's monetary and exchange rate policies, reflected especially in substantial variations in domestic liquidity, to authorize the Member State involved to take protective measures for a period not exceeding six months in respect of certain defined capital movements; under art. 3(2), the Member State itself might take such protective measures on grounds of urgency, subject to review by the Commission. In both cases the Council was given power by qualified majority to revoke or amend the Commission's decisions. The movements which may be thus restricted are listed in Annex II, which bears a remarkable resemblance to the former List C (originally List D) of capital movements which did not have to be liberalized under the previous Directives.

The wording of a more general power to take measures to prevent the breach of certain national legislation in art. 4 was copied into art. 58(1)(b) (formerly art. 73d1(b)) introduced by the Maastricht amendments, and is therefore considered below in the context of restrictions which continue to be permitted,[33] but arts. 5 and 6 made specific provision for named Member States. Art. 5 indicated the scope of the Accession derogations for Spain and Portugal using the new nomenclature introduced by the 1988 Directive, and art. 6(2) provided for the temporary continuation of other restrictions which Spain and Portugal, and also Greece and Ireland,[34] were at that stage still authorized to impose. These restrictions have now all expired.

3. The Maastricht Treaty provisions

a) Scope of the provisions

As has already been indicated, the Maastricht Treaty on European Union introduced new provisions on 'capital and payments' with effect from 1 January 1994, the date set for the start of the second stage of Economic and Monetary Union. The fundamental rules are set out in art. 56 (formerly art. 73b): paragraph 1 states that within the framework of the provisions set out in that Chapter, all restrictions on the movement of capital between Member States and between Member States and third countries shall be prohibited; paragraph 2 states that within the same framework, all restrictions on payments between Member States and between Member States and third countries shall be prohibited.

At first sight a fundamental distinction between these provisions and the original provisions—and indeed from the situation reached under the 1988 Directive—is that movements to and from third countries appear to be treated the same way as movements between Member States. With hindsight, this can be seen as antici-

[33] See section 4 below.

[34] By virtue of art. 108 (now art. 119) of the EC Treaty.

pating the need to ensure the external movement and availability of the euro. However, in reality differences remain. Under art. 57 (formerly art. 73c) the provisions of art. 56 are stated to be without prejudice to the application to third countries of any restrictions existing on 31 December 1993 under national or Community law adopted in respect of the movement of capital to or from third countries involving direct investment (including investment in real estate), establishment, the provision of financial services, or the admission of securities to capital markets; in other words, they do not require existing lawful restrictions to be abolished in these (admittedly limited) areas. Furthermore, the second paragraph of art. 57, empowering the Council to legislate on those capital movements, refers to 'endeavouring' to achieve the objective of free movement of capital between Member States and third countries to the 'greatest extent possible', language redolent of the original capital movement provisions in relation to movements between Member States. Under art. 59 (formerly art. 73f) where, in exceptional circumstances, movements of capital to or from third countries cause, or threaten to cause, serious difficulties for the operation of economic and monetary union, the Council, acting by a qualified majority on a proposal from the Commission and after consulting the ECB, may take safeguard measures with regard to third countries for a period not exceeding six months if such measures are strictly necessary. Finally, by virtue of art. 60 (formerly art. 73g), the Council may take urgent measures under art. 301 (formerly art. 228a) where Community action to interrupt or reduce economic relations with one or more third countries is required by a common position or in a joint action adopted under the European Union provisions on a common foreign and security policy, in relation to the movement of capital and on payments as regard the third countries concerned; indeed, pending such measures, Member States themselves may, under the second paragraph of art. 60, take unilateral measures against a third country with regard to capital movements and payments 'for serious political reasons'. The freedom is therefore not absolute. Be that as it may, to the extent that a payment or capital movement is not excluded, art. 56 has been held to be directly effective even with regard to capital movements to third countries such as Switzerland and Turkey. [35]

This in itself is an interesting development given the Court's reluctance in earlier case-law automatically to extend concepts developed in the context of the internal market to situations governed by similar language in relations with third countries. So, for example, in Case 270/80 *Polydor* v. *Harlequin*,[36] in the context of the free movement of goods, it was held that even where a free trade agreement does expressly prohibit both quantitative restrictions and measures having effects equivalent to quantitative restrictions, the same interpretation of that phrase need not be given in the context of trade with a non-Member State as in the context of trade between States, since there is no intention to create a single market under free trade agreements

[35] Cases C–163, 165, and 250/94 *Sanz de Lera* [1995] ECR I–4821.

[36] [1982] ECR 379.

A synthesis of the approach to the direct effect of provisions of international agreements was given in the context of an agreement between the Community and Portugal in the *Kupferberg* case.[37] The Court started from the principle that it is open to the Community and the third country to agree what effect the provisions of the agreement are to have in the internal legal order of the contracting parties, and that the matter fell to be decided by the court only in the absence of express agreement on the point, although emphasizing that it was open to the courts of one contracting party to consider that certain provisions were directly effective even if that view was not shared by courts of the other contracting party. It went on to consider whether the provision at issue could be regarded as unconditional and sufficiently precise to have direct effect in the light of the object and purpose of the agreement, concluding that the provision at issue imposed an unconditional rule against discrimination in matters of taxation, dependent only on a finding that the products affected were of like nature, so that it could be applied by a court and produce direct effects throughout the Community. However, the Court did emphasize that, despite the fact that the provision at issue had the same object as art. 95 (now art. 90) of the EC Treaty, each of these provisions should be interpreted in its own context, and that the interpretation given to article 90 could not be applied by simple analogy to the corresponding provision of an agreement on free trade. However, in *Sanz de Lera* the judgment does not discuss these issues, and simply holds art. 56 to be directly effective in itself and on its own terms.

b) Legal nature

Turning to the movement of capital and payments between Member States, it may be wondered why, given that the 1988 Directive already laid down the basic principle of unrestricted free movement of capital between persons resident in Member States, it was felt necessary to draft new Treaty provisions apparently to the same effect. One substantive difference is that by treating payments between Member States in the same way as capital movements, the new Treaty provisions remove any lingering doubts as to the precise scope of the freedom to make current payments.[38] A more fundamental reason, no doubt, is that as secondary legislation, a Directive could relatively easily be amended, and progress to Economic and Monetary Union could hardly be envisaged unless monetary movements between Member States rested on the same legal basis as the other fundamental features of that Union, i.e. provisions of the EC Treaty itself.

As argued in the first edition of this book,[39] it has been held that both art. 1 of the 1988 Directive, in Cases C–358 and C–416/93 *Bordessa and Mellado*,[40] and art. 56(1) and (2) of the EC Treaty, in Cases C–163, 165, and 250/94 *Sanz de Lera*[41]

[37] Case 104/81 *Hauptzollamt Mainz* v. *C. A. Kupferberg & Cie KG* [1982] ECR 3641, [1983] 1 CMLR 1.

[38] See Chapter 1.

[39] At p. 23.

[40] [1995] ECR I–361.

[41] [1995] ECR I–4821.

are drafted in a manner sufficiently clear, precise, and unconditional to be directly effective[42] and therefore give rise to rights enforceable by individuals before their national courts from their respective dates for implementation (1 July 1990 and 1 January 1994 respectively). However, the direct effect of a Directive is a residual concept, only relevant where a Member State has failed to comply with its obligations under the Directive in time,[43] and only available against the Member State on which that obligation is imposed,[44] although the concept of the Member State may extend to local authorities[45] or to utilities and other undertakings given special powers by the public authorities[46]—which in the present context might include banking authorities and regulators. On the other hand, the direct effect of a clear, precise, and unconditional provision of the Treaty may be invoked against any subject of the law on which it imposes obligations,[47] which raises the question whether art. 56 imposes obligations on subjects of the law other than the State itself.

Neither paragraph of art. 56 is addressed to Member States as such; they simply state, in absolute terms, that all restrictions on the movement of capital and on payments between Member States shall be prohibited. With regard to similarly drafted provisions relating to the movement of employed persons under art. 39 (formerly art. 48), the movement of the self- employed ('establishment') under art. 43 (formerly art. 52), and the freedom to provide services under art. 49 (formerly art. 59), it has long been established that their effects may be invoked against e.g. private sector employers, trade unions and professional associations.[48] Nevertheless some controversy remains as to whether the rules on the free movement of goods, notably art. 28 (formerly art. 30) prohibiting quantitative restrictions on imports and all measures having equivalent effect in trade between Member States, also drafted in similar terms, is binding on anyone other than the State.

The problem has arisen particularly in the context of the exercise of intellectual and industrial property rights,[49] and was clearly presented in the leading cases which established the principle that the Treaty rules impose on holders of

[42] Under the concept developed in the famous decision in Case 26/62 *Van Gend en Loos* [1963] ECR 1. For a more detailed discussion of direct effect, see Usher, 'The Application of Community Law in National Courts' in *Law of the European Communities* (ed. Vaughan), Butterworths 1991, pp. 3/1 to 3/206.

[43] Case 148/78 *Ratti* [1979] ECR 1629.

[44] Case 152/84 *Marshall* v. *Southampton Area Health Authority* [1986] ECR 723.

[45] Case 103/88 *Costanzo* v. *City of Milan* [1989] ECR 1839.

[46] Case C–188/89 *Foster* v. *British Gas* [1990] ECR I–3313.

[47] A concept most frequently encountered in the area of competition law: see e.g. Case 127/73 *BRT* v. *SABAM* [1974] ECR 313.

[48] See e.g. Case 36/74 *Walrave and Koch* v. *Union Cycliste Internationale* [1974] ECR 1405, where it was held that the rules on free movement of workers and those on freedom to provide services could be invoked against a professional cycling association.

[49] Analogies with the free movement of goods are complicated by the fact that art. 36 of the EC Treaty contains special rules relating to intellectual property rights. The arguments developed here are put forward in Green, Hartley and Usher, *The Legal Foundations of the Single European Market* (Oxford 1991) chapter 5.

industrial property rights the duty not to use those rights to prevent the importation into a Member State of goods lawfully marketed in another Member State by the holder of the property right himself or with his consent.[50]

While the Court has consistently maintained its case-law on the exercise of industrial and intellectual property rights, its subsequent dicta in other areas are not always easy to reconcile. In Case 58/80 *Dansk Supermarked* v. *Imerco*,[51] in the context of alleged unfair trading practices, it was stated that 'it is impossible in any circumstances for agreements between individuals to derogate from the mandatory provisions of the Treaty on the free movement of goods'. On the other hand, in Cases 177 and 178/82 *Officier van Justitie* v. *Van de Haar*[52] a comparison was made between art. 28 and art. 81 (formerly art. 85)[53] in which it was suggested that the competition rules are addressed to undertakings and associations of undertakings, whereas the free movement of goods rules seek to eliminate measures taken by Member States. A similar view was expressed in Case 311/85 *Vlaamse Reisbureaus*.[54] It may be suggested that these views were *obiter*, particularly in the second case, which involved the application of the competition rules to a supply of services, and that the situation remains that actions by an individual may be subject to arts. 28 and 29 (formerly art. 34) at least where they involve the use of legal rights and remedies. However, an individual acting outside a legal context is almost certainly not subject to those rules, as appears from Case 222/82 *Apple and Pear Development Council* v. *Lewis*.[55] It was there indicated that whilst it might be a breach of art. 28 for a publicly financed body to promote national products on the basis of their national origin, greater liberty could be enjoyed by producers themselves or producers' associations of a voluntary character with regard to their advertizing. The other necessary consequence of this, however, is that action taken, or promoted, by the public authorities may be regarded as a measure equivalent to a quantitative restriction, even though it does not take the form of legislation.

Furthermore, the actions of an association or organization which controls the activities of a particular profession may be subject to arts. 28 and 29 even if it is not a public authority and its actions are not legislative in nature. This results from Case 266/87 *R* v. *Royal Pharmaceutical Society*,[56] which concerned the compatibility with art. 28 of rules of the Society which required pharmacists, when faced with a prescription naming a branded medicine, to supply only that branded product, and not a generic equivalent. It was held that those rules did breach art. 28, since they amounted to a restriction on the importation of equivalent drugs from other Member States (although they were held to be justified under art. 30 (formerly art. 36)). The reason why they were found to be measures equivalent to quantitative restrictions appears to be that pharmacists had little option but to observe the rules,

[50] Case 15/74 *Centrafarm* v. *Sterling Drug* [1974] ECR 1147; Case 16/74 *Centrafarm* v. *Winthrop* [1974] ECR 1183.

[51] [1981] ECR 181.

[52] [1984] ECR 1797.

[53] See Chapter 4 below.

[54] [1987] ECR 3801.

[55] [1983] ECR 4083.

[56] [1989] ECR 1295.

and those rules governed the activities of the whole profession, so the effect was like that of action by the public authorities.

At the very least therefore it may be suggested that not only the public authorities but also professional associations are bound by art. 56 not to restrict the movement of capital or payments between Member States. However, it is submitted that in this area analogies may be drawn not only with the free movement of goods, but also with the freedom to provide services where, as stated above, it has long been established that the relevant Treaty rules may be invoked against private sector employers, trade unions, and professional associations,[57] and that art. 56 may therefore be invoked against operators in the private sector with regard to transactions between Member States. It is not difficult to envisage a situation in which the unilateral conduct of a financial institution, for example with regard to the terms and conditions under which it will effect monetary transfers to other Member States, may be regarded as restricting payments between Member States. Indeed, with regard to the competition rules of the Treaty, it has long been accepted that the charges levied for transferring money from one Member State to another may affect trade between Member States.[58]

4. Permitted restrictions

a) Introduction

Like all the other Treaty freedoms, the freedom of capital movements and payments between Member States is subject to permitted restrictions, set out in art. 58 (formerly art. 73d). This resembles the drafting of art. 30 (formerly art. 36) of the EC Treaty in relation to the free movement of goods in that it requires that such restrictions should not constitute 'a means of arbitrary discrimination or a disguised restriction' on the free movement of capital and payments, as defined in art. 56. While art. 58 is not the only source of such restrictions, it must be emphasized that to the extent that art. 56 applies to monetary movements to and from third countries, attempts to restrict such movements are subject to Community rules just as much as attempts to restrict monetary movements between Member States. It might also be observed that, for movements between participants in Economic and Monetary Union, restrictions on monetary movements as such are hardly compatible with that concept, and it may be suggested that the drafting of the Treaty reflects this view.

b) Market disturbances

Under the original art. 73(1), which remained in force until 1 January 1994, the Commission could, after consulting the Monetary Committee,[59] authorize a

[57] See e.g. Case 36/74 *Walrave and Koch* v. *Union Cycliste Internationale* (see fn. 48 above).

[58] Case 172/80 *Züchner* v. *Bayerische Vereinsbank* [1981] ECR 2021.

[59] See Chapter 10 below.

Member State to take protective measures in the field of capital movements if movements of capital had led or were leading to disturbances in the functioning of the capital market in that Member State. Article 73(2) further provided that a Member State which was in difficulties might, on grounds of urgency or secrecy, take such measures on its own initiative, subject to informing the Commission and the other Member States by the date of their entry into force, although the Commission could, again after consulting the Monetary Committee, decide that the measures should be amended or abolished.

In practice, this power appears not to have been used; a number of explanations may be offered. One is that under the 1960, 1962, and 1986 Directives many of the more sensitive capital movements did not have to be liberalized (List D, becoming List C after the entry into force of the 1986 Directive), and on others Member States could maintain or reintroduce restrictions which were operative on the date of entry into force of the original Directive (List C, becoming List B after the entry into force of the 1986 Directive).[60] It was pointed out by the European Court in Case 203/80 *Casati*[61] that if there was no Community law obligation to liberalize a particular capital movement, then there was no need to have recourse to art. 73 in order to impose restrictions thereon; furthermore, since such restrictions were a purely a matter of national law, there was no need to comply with principles of Community law such as proportionality or non-discrimination.

Another possible explanation for the lack of use of the original art. 73 is that it was in terms limited to capital movements, thus raising the question of the distinction from current payments, whereas there were and are alternative sources of protective measures, ostensibly to deal with balance of payments problems, in the original art. 108(3) (now art. 119(3)) and art. 109 (now art. 120), which are not so limited, authorizing the taking of 'protective measures'. Furthermore, the European Court accepted in Case 157/85 *Brugnoni and Ruffinengo*[62] that if protective measures were taken under art. 108(3), there was no need to comply with the procedural requirements of art. 73. In practice, it would therefore appear that protective measures were in general authorized under the former art. 108(3).[63]

The specific possibility of protective measures envisaged in art. 3 of the 1988 Directive was also linked to the idea of market disturbances, but only allowing the Commission, where short-term capital movements of exceptional magnitude impose severe strains on foreign exchange markets and lead to serious disturbances in a Member State's monetary and exchange rate policies, being reflected in particular in substantial variations in domestic liquidity, to authorize the Member State involved to take protective measures for a period not exceeding six months in respect of certain defined capital movements. Under art. 3(2) the Member State itself might take such protective measures on grounds of urgency, subject to review by the Commission. In both cases the Council was given power by qualified majority to revoke or amend the Commission's decisions. As was noted above,[64]

[60] See p. 18 above.
[61] [1981] ECR 2595.
[62] [1986] ECR 2013.
[63] See p. 29 below.
[64] See p. 22 above.

the movements which may be thus restricted were listed in Annex II, which bears a remarkable resemblance to the former List C (originally List D) of capital movements which did not have to be liberalized under the previous Directives. The scope of such protective measures was therefore somewhat limited.

c) Balance of payments

The powers to deal with balance of payments problems set out the original arts. 108 and 109 were continued in force following the Maastricht amendments as arts. 119 and 120, at least until the start of the third stage of Economic and Monetary Union. They remain in force thereafter for Member States which do not participate in the single currency,[65] but only for those States. From the drafting of art. 119 it appears that its chief concern is mutual assistance, and that protective measures are an exceptional fallback position. However, although it gave rise to legislation such as Council Regulation 1969/88 establishing a single facility providing medium-term financial assistance for Member States' balances of payments,[66] in its previous incarnation as art. 108 it was more frequently used as a source of protective measures. Art. 119(1) provides that where a Member State is in difficulties or is seriously threatened with difficulties as regards its balance of payments, either as a result of a overall disequilibrium in its balance of payments, or as a result of the type of currency at its disposal, and where such difficulties are liable in particular to jeopardize the functioning of the common market or the progressive implementation of the common commercial policy, the Commission shall immediately investigate the position of the State in question and the action which, making use of all means at its disposal, that State has taken or may take in accordance with the provisions of this Treaty. The Commission shall state what measures it recommends the State concerned to take. Then, if the action taken by a Member State and the measures suggested by the Commission do not prove sufficient to overcome the difficulties which have arisen or which threaten, the Commission shall, after consulting the Monetary Committee, recommend to the Council the granting of mutual assistance and appropriate methods thereof. The Commission is required to keep the Council regularly informed of how the situation is developing.

Paragraph 2 provides that the Council, acting by a qualified majority, shall grant such mutual assistance; it shall adopt directives or decisions laying down the conditions and details of such assistance, which may take such forms as:

(a) a concerted approach to or within any other international organizations to which Member States may have recourse;

(b) measures needed to avoid deflection of trade where the State which is in difficulties maintains or reintroduces quantitative restrictions against third countries;

[65] Art. 122(6), formerly art. 109k(6), and the UK and Danish Protocols.
[66] OJ 1988 L178/1.

(c) the granting of limited credits by other Member States, subject to their agreement.

Under paragraph 3, only if the mutual assistance recommended by the Commission is not granted by the Council, or if the mutual assistance granted and the measures taken are insufficient, is the Commission to authorize the State in difficulties to take protective measures, the conditions and details of which the Commission is to determine. Such authorization may be revoked, and conditions and details changed, by a qualified majority of the Council.

Art. 120 enables the Member State itself, where a sudden crisis in the balance of payments occurs and a decision within the meaning of art. 119(2) is not immediately taken, as a precaution, to take the necessary protective measures. Such measures must cause the least possible disturbance in the functioning of the common market and must not be wider in scope than is strictly necessary to remedy the sudden difficulties which have arisen. It is required that the Commission and the other Member State should be informed of such protective measures not later than when they enter into force. The Commission may recommend to the Council the granting of mutual assistance under art. 119, but it is for the Council, not the Commission, to take action with regard to the Member State's unilateral measures: the third paragraph of art. 120 provides that after the Commission has delivered an opinion and the Economic and Financial Committee (formerly the Monetary Committee) has been consulted, the Council may, by a qualified majority, decide that the State concerned shall amend, suspend, or abolish the protective measures referred to above.

In practice it is the protective measures authorized by the Commission under art. 119(3), or more accurately its predecessor, art. 108(3), which have been of importance, and which have given rise to legal debate. However, it must be emphasized at the outset that the power to take measures under this provision to protect the balance of payments is totally separate from the state of liberalization of capital movements or payments. In Cases 286/82 and 26/83 *Luisi and Carbone*[67] the European Court stated that arts. 108 and 109, as they then were, remained operative 'even after the free movement of capital has been fully achieved', which helps to explain why they have continued in operation even after the entry into force of art. 56, even if they have become redundant for countries which share a single currency.[68] Yet the Court also emphasized that they related only to 'periods of crisis', which may be contrasted with its judgment in Case 157/85 *Brugnoni and Ruffinengo*,[69] where it seemed to accept that a decision taken in 1985 under what was then art. 108 in favour of Italy could continue safeguards originally enacted in 1974 to protect the balance of payments. It is arguable whether a threat to the Italian balance of payments really continued throughout all that time, and it is of interest to note that following the interim extension of the liberalized capital movements by Directive 86/566,[70] additional safeguard measures were enacted in favour

[67] [1984] ECR 377 p. 406.

[68] This is the effect of arts. 119(4) and 120(4).

[69] [1986] ECR 2013.

[70] OJ 1986 L332/22.

of those Member States which were at that stage permitted to restrict otherwise liberalized movements,[71] to allow protective measures under art. 108(3) with regard to operations newly liberalized under the Directive.

To make a further comparison with the free movement of goods, the point may be taken that when the Commission authorized a Member State under art. 134 (formerly art. 115) not to grant Community treatment to goods in free circulation in another Member State, having been imported from a third country, the Court consistently held that since this was a derogation from one of the fundamental freedoms of the Treaty, the Commission must take great care when exercising its powers. In particular, it appears both from the *Kaufhof*[72] and *Ilford* cases[73] that the Commission must be satisfied both that the Member State is authorized as a matter of Community law to have the measure of commercial policy whose protection it is seeking, and that the threatened importations would actually be likely to endanger that policy. Unfortunately, in *Brugnoni and Ruffinengo* there appears to be no real discussion as to whether the Commission is under a duty when using what is now art. 119 to investigate the seriousness of any threat to the balance of payments of the Member State, and whether the transactions in question are likely to threaten the balance of payments. However, it has apparently subsequently interpreted its duties under this provision more strictly; indeed, no protective measures appear to have been authorized in the second half of the 1990s.

While these provisions may now only be invoked by States not participating in Economic and Monetary Union, the others may act together as the Community. The safeguard clause which may be used by the Community as opposed to its Member States in art. 60 (formerly art. 73f) relates only to movements to and from third countries, stating that where, in exceptional circumstances, movements of capital to or from third countries cause, or threaten to cause, serious difficulties for the operation of economic and monetary union, the Council, acting by a qualified majority on a proposal from the Commission and after consulting the ECB, may take safeguard measures with regard to third countries for a period not exceeding six months if such measures are strictly necessary. There is no provision for the 'ins'to take parallel measures in relation to non-participant Member States, even though such States, the 'outs', may remain entitled to take or be authorized to take measures even with regard to movements to or from other Member States to protect their balance of payments under arts. 119 and 120. However, while as a matter of legal theory there may be an imbalance between these provisions, it may be wondered how likely it is that an Economic and Monetary Union of eleven Member States would need to invoke safeguard measures against the other four.

[71] Commission Decisions 87/150 (Ireland), 87/151 (Italy) and 87/152 (Greece) (OJ 1987 L63/34, 36, and 38).

[72] Case 29/75 [1976] ECR 431.

[73] Case 1/84R [1984] ECR 423.

d) Taxation

The interaction between monetary movements and taxation is a matter of increasing legal and political importance, and is considered in more detail in the next Chapter. It has been noted that under the 1988 Directive proposals aimed at eliminating or reducing risks of tax evasion and tax avoidance were required to be put forward by the Commission and considered by the Council. However, while a proposal for a withholding tax was put forward,[74] it did not meet with approval in the Council of Ministers, a situation which left the matter in the hands of the Member States: under art. 4 of the 1988 Directive the freedom to make monetary movements between Member States is stated to be without prejudice to the right of Member States to take all requisite measures to prevent infringements of their laws and regulations, *inter alia*, in the field of taxation, provided that such measures do not impede capital movements carried out in accordance with Community law (which appears to raise a circular question as to what constitute such movements). This was repeated in art. 58(1)(b) (formerly art. 73d(1)(b)), albeit with a different caveat prohibiting arbitrary discrimination and disguised restrictions on the free movement of capital and payments, and will be considered together with the other restrictions which may be imposed under that provision.[75]

Of wider legal interest in the context of Community law is the question whether discriminatory tax treatment can be given to non-residents and foreign investments compared to that given to residents and home investments. In this context, it is of particular interest, and perhaps surprising, to note that the capital movement provisions inserted into the EC Treaty by the Maastricht Treaty with effect from 1 January 1994 include in art. 58(1)(a) (formerly art. 73d(1)(a)) a statement to the effect that the prohibition of restrictions on capital movements is without prejudice to the right of Member States to apply provisions of their tax law which distinguish between taxpayers who are not in the same situation with regard to their place of residence or with regard to the place where their capital is invested.

At first sight this might be taken as a clear authorization to discriminate in the tax system between residents and non-residents. Most of the discussion has centred on the question whether this provision allows discrimination *against* non-residents, which would clearly conflict with the fundamental Treaty freedoms relating to establishment, provision of services, and movement of workers, although the conclusion may be reached that this provision does not in fact override the basic Treaty freedoms, which clearly do prohibit adverse discrimination within the scope of their application.[76] Be that as it may, the more recent decision in Case C–118/96 *Safir* v. *Skattemyndigheten i Dalarnas Län*[77] held that it was a breach of art. 49 (for-

[74] OJ 1989 C141/5.

[75] See p. 34 below.

[76] See Usher, 'Tax discrimination under the new capital movement provisions and the basic Treaty freedoms' in *European Financial Area* ed. Rudanko and Timonen, University of Helsinki, 1998 pp. 259–275. See also Chapter 3 below.

[77] [1998] ECR I–1897.

merly art. 59) for Sweden to impose a different tax regime for insurance policies purchased from providers outside Sweden which would have the effect of deterring Swedish residents from taking out such policies, even though it was intended to achieve tax neutrality between policies purchased inside and outside Sweden. It was stated that the decision on this point made it unnecessary to determine whether the legislation was also incompatible with arts. 56 and 58 (formerly arts. 73b and 73d) even though under the express terms of art. 50 (formerly art. 60), services are only services within the meaning of the Treaty to the extent that they do not fall under one of the other Treaty freedoms.

On the other hand, it has been suggested that the aim of art. 58(1)(a) was to permit discrimination *in favour of* non-residents. However, the provision must be taken in its context: in effect it is drafted as a permission to take measures which might interfere with the free movement of capital and payments, rather than *carte blanche* to discriminate. In other words, the fact that a measure may be justifiable as a restriction on the movement of capital and payments does not necessarily make it acceptable as a state aid. In any event art. 58(1)(a) is subject both to the caveat that such measures 'shall not constitute a means of arbitrary discrimination or a disguised restriction on the free movement of capital and payments as defined in Article 56', and to a Declaration made by the Member States when the Maastricht Treaty was signed stating that: 'The Conference affirms that the right of Member States to apply the relevant provisions of their tax law as referred to in [Article 73d(1)(a)]of this Treaty will apply only with respect to the relevant provisions which exist at the end of 1993. However, this Declaration shall apply only to capital movements between Member States and to payments effected between Member States.' This at the least amounts to a political commitment not to introduce any new measures of the type at issue.

The political impetus in this area is further exemplified by a meeting of the Council of Finance Ministers (ECOFIN) on 1 December 1997 which adopted a Code of Conduct for Business Taxation,[78] and reached political agreement on the need for legislation on withholding tax. In 1998 the Commission therefore put forward a new proposal for a Directive 'to ensure a minimum of effective taxation of savings income in the form of interest payments within the Community'.[79]

e) Other restrictions

Following the wording of art. 4 of the 1988 Directive, art. 58(1)(b) allows Member States to take all requisite measures to prevent infringement of national law and regulations, in particular in the field of taxation and the prudential supervision of financial institutions, or to lay down procedures for the declaration of capital movements for purposes of administrative or statistical information, or to take measures which are justified on grounds of public policy or public security. While

[78] OJ 1998 C2/3. [79] COM(1998) 295 final (20 May 1998). See Chapter 3 below.

the reference to public policy and public security was not in the 1988 Directive, some indication of the type of measure originally envisaged may be gleaned from the original limiting clause in that Directive, which stated that the application of those measures and procedures must not have the effect of impeding capital movements carried out in accordance with Community law. It is therefore submitted that what could be imposed under art. 4 of the Directive were essentially control measures (the equivalent of e.g. health inspection measures under art. 30) rather than prohibitions against liberalized capital movements, and that even under the Treaty version it would be difficult to justify measures going beyond control measures, for reasons which will be explained.

The restrictions permitted under art. 58(1)(b) must not constitute a means of arbitrary discrimination or a disguised restriction on the free movement of capital and payments as defined in art. 56. Again, comparison with art. 30 on the free movement of goods may be useful.[80] It was made clear from a very early stage that art. 30 is concerned with protecting non-economic interests.[81] As it stated more recently in Case 72/83 *Campus Oil* v. *Minister for Industry and Energy*,[82] 'a Member State cannot be allowed to avoid the effects of measures provided for in the Treaty by pleading the economic difficulties caused by the elimination of barriers to intra-Community trade'. It may be suggested that here, the power of a Member State to take all requisite measures to prevent infringement of national law and regulations, in particular in the field of taxation and the prudential supervision of financial institutions, or to lay down procedures for the declaration of capital movements for purposes of administrative or statistical information, relates to the effective administration and enforcement of the tax system and the effective supervision of e.g. banks and insurance companies, rather than to matters of underlying economic policy. Indeed, balance of payments problems are expressly to be dealt with under arts. 119 and 120, provisions which may only be invoked by Member States which do not participate in Economic and Monetary Union.[83]

Secondly, the burden of proving that a measure falls within art. 30 rests on the party which relies on that provision, usually the national authorities.[84] It is submitted that the same rule applies under art. 58(3). Ancillary to this, a measure cannot fall within national competence under art. 30 or art. 58(3) if there is Community legislation which is intended to regulate the matter at issue in a comprehensive manner. This was clearly shown in Case 28/84 *Commission* v. *Germany*,[85] where the animal foodstuffs Directives were found to create a comprehensive system with regard to the composition and preparation of animal foodstuffs, so that Germany

[80] For a more detailed discussion of the issues, see Green, Hartley and Usher, *Legal Foundations of the Single European Market* (Oxford 1991) chapter 7.

[81] See Case 7/61 *Commission* v. *Italy* [1961] ECR 317 p. 329.

[82] [1984] ECR 2727 p. 2752.

[83] See p. 31 above.

[84] Case 251/78 *Denkavit Futtermittel* [1979] ECR 3369 p. 3392. The same rule appears to apply with regard to the invocation of 'mandatory requirements' under the *Cassis de Dijon* case-law, Case 25/88 *Wurmser* [1989] ECR 1105.

[85] [1985] ECR 3097.

could not lay down its own rules on minimum and maximum levels of certain ingredients. The relevance of that principle here is that under art. 105(6) of the EC Treaty the prudential supervision of credit institutions and other financial institutions (with the exception of insurance undertakings) may eventually be entrusted to the European Central Bank, in which case Member States could no longer invoke that aspect of art. 58(1)(b).[86]

Thirdly, in order to avoid being categorized as arbitrary discrimination, it must be shown that effective measures to protect the same interest have been taken with regard to domestic products, and not just with regard to imports or exports.[87] In the context of the similarly worded art. 30 of the EC Treaty relating to restrictions on the free movement of goods, the question has arisen how far it must be shown that effective measures are taken to deal with the problem at issue within the Member State concerned, as in Case 4/75 *Rewe-Zentralfinanz* v. *Landwirtschaftskammer Bonn*.[88] This case arose from a requirement of German law that imported apples, in this case from France, should be subject to phytosanitary inspection on entry, when no such compulsory examination was imposed on home-produced apples. The case thus posed, at a time when many commentators thought that only discriminatory measures breached art. 28 in the first place,[89] the problem of how to reconcile such a measure with the second sentence of art. 30, requiring health measures not to constitute a means of arbitrary discrimination. Indeed, the Court expressly recognized the inspections as being discriminatory within the meaning of art. 2(2) of Commission Directive 70/50[90] on the elimination of measures equivalent to quantitative restrictions. Its approach was first to investigate the objective of the inspections, which it found to be to control San José Scale, and held that this was in principle justified under art. 30. It then turned to the question whether there was nevertheless arbitrary discrimination, and reached a conclusion which is still relevant:

> The different treatment of imported and domestic products, based on the need to prevent the spread of the harmful organism could not, however, be regarded as arbitrary discrimination if effective measures are taken in order to prevent the distribution of contaminated domestic products and if there is reason to believe, in particular on the basis of previous experience, that there is a risk of the harmful organism's spreading if no inspection is held on importation.

Therefore it may be possible to justify a discriminatory measure under art. 30 on health grounds, but only if effective measures serving the same purpose are taken with regard to the equivalent domestic product. The same view has been taken with regard to public morality under art. 30: if effective measures are not taken to prevent domestic trade, then imports cannot be prohibited on grounds of public

[86] This is not a matter from which Member States with a derogation (see Chapters 8 and 9 below) or the United Kingdom are excluded.

[87] Case 4/75 *Rewe-Zentralfinanz* v. *Landwirtschaftskammer Bonn* [1975] ECR 843; Case 121/85 *Conegate* v. *HM Customs and Excise* [1986] ECR 1007.

[88] [1975] ECR 843.

[89] See Green *et al*, *Legal Foundations*, Ch. 6.

[90] JO 1970 L13/29.

morality. This issue arose in Case 121/85 *Conegate* v. *HM Customs and Excise*,[91] where it was held that the United Kingdom could not prevent the importation of life-size inflatable female dolls when (subject to certain limits) there was no prohibition on manufacturing or marketing such objects within the United Kingdom.[92]

Applying these principles by analogy to art. 58(1), the more general conclusion may be reached that not only must the measure be justified to protect an interest recognized under art. 58(1) but it must also be shown that effective measures are taken at the domestic level in the national tax system or system of prudential supervision or in relation to another recognized interest to deal with the perceived problem. Thus in Case C-439/97 *Sandoz* v. *Finanzlandesdirektion Wien*[93] it was held that Austria could require an Austrian resident borrowing money in another Member State to pay the same stamp duty as would have been payable if the transaction had taken place in Austria. However, it was a breach of art. 58(1)(b) to treat a loan contracted in another Member State as subject to stamp duty when the equivalent loan in Austria would not be subject to that duty.

Finally, under art. 30, even if a measure complies with all these requirements, it may still be regarded as a disguised restriction on trade if it goes beyond what is necessary for the effective protection of the general interest at issue, and in particular if that objective could be achieved by means less restrictive of intra-Community trade.[94] In other words, a test of proportionality or reasonableness[95] is applied. In particular, a prohibition against free movement will not be permitted where less restrictive control measures could be taken. Perhaps the clearest example of import controls being regarded as disproportionate is Case 124/81 *Commission* v. *United Kingdom*[96] which concerned the United Kingdom rules on the importation of UHT milk. In practice they meant that the milk had to be retreated in the United Kingdom. Retreatment would make importation uneconomic, so the requirement amounted to a total prohibition on imports. In the view of the Court, the United Kingdom could protect the health of consumers by a requirement that importers produce certificates issued by the competent authorities of the exporting Member States, coupled with controls by means of samples.[97] It is submitted that exactly the same criteria apply with regard to restrictions on capital movements and payments under art. 58(1). However, one of the few instances where a total prohibition on free movement was held to be justified on public policy grounds under art. 30 involved money.[98] This was Case 7/78 *R* v. *Thompson and Others*,[99] which

[91] [1986] ECR 1007.

[92] There is a clear link here with the public policy rules which affect the free movement of persons, as was recognized by Advocate General Slynn in his Opinion [1986] ECR p. 1011. See Cases 115 & 116/81 *Adoui and Cornuaille* v. *Belgium* [1982] ECR 1665.

[93] 14 October 1999.

[94] See e.g. Case 124/81 *Commission* v. *United Kingdom* [1983] ECR 203; Case 25/88 *Wurmser* [1989] ECR 1105.

[95] Case 104/75 *De Peijper* [1976] ECR 613.

[96] [1983] ECR 203.

[97] The matter of UHT milk has subsequently been regulated by Council Directive 85/397 (OJ 1985 L226/13) on health and animal-health problems affecting intra-Community trade in heat-treated milk.

[98] See Chapter 1 p. 000.

[99] [1978] ECR 2247.

involved a breach of the United Kingdom rules then in force prohibiting the importation of gold coins and the export of silver alloy coins minted before 1947. As observed above, the Court took the view that since the silver alloy coins minted before 1947 were not legal tender, they were not a 'means of payment', and could be designated as goods. The Court started from the premise that it is for Member States to mint their own coinage and to protect it from destruction. Being informed that in the United Kingdom the melting down or destruction of national coins was prohibited even if they were no longer legal tender, the Court held that a ban on exporting such coins which was imposed to prevent their being melted down or destroyed in another Member State was justified on grounds of public policy under what is now art. 30.

Even before the entry into force of the Maastricht provisions, however, the Court appears to have extended to capital movements the concept of 'mandatory requirements' developed in the context of the free movement of goods in its 1979 judgment in Case 120/78 *Rewe* v. *Bundesmonopolverwaltung für Branntwein.*[100] It stated, with regard to measures applying equally to domestic and imported products, that:

> obstacles to movement within the Community resulting from disparities between the national laws relating to the marketing of the products in question must be accepted in so far as those provisions may be recognised as being necessary in order to satisfy mandatory requirements relating in particular to the effectiveness of fiscal supervision, the protection of public health, the fairness of commercial transactions and the defence of the consumer.

Whilst *Rewe*[101] itself listed only four examples of mandatory requirements, it is clear from Case 302/86 *Commission* v. *Denmark*[102] that national legislation designed to protect the environment may also be regarded as justifying restrictions on trade between Member States. Another possible extension occurred in Cases 60 & 61/84 *Cinéthèque*[103] in the context of French legislation prohibiting the sale or hire of video-cassettes of a film within a fixed period from the film's release in the cinema, which may be regarded as authority for the proposition that cultural policy may justify restrictions on trade. Here there is a link with restrictions on capital movements: in Case C–148/91 *Veronica* v. *Commissariaat voor de Media*[104] it was found that since Dutch rules designed to ensure a pluralist and non- commercial television service were justified in the general good as a matter of cultural policy, the regulatory authority could prevent a Dutch broadcasting organization from contributing capital to and providing a bank guarantee for a Luxembourg undertaking intending to develop a commercial television station aimed at the Dutch market. Whatever may be the difficulties in drawing a dividing line between measures justified as fulfilling mandatory requirements and those justified under the express public policy provisions set out in the Treaty[105] it may at least

[100] [1979] ECR 649. [101] [1979] ECR 649. [102] [1988] ECR 4607.
[103] [1985] ECR 2605. [104] [1993] ECR I–487.
[105] On the free movement of goods see Green, Hartley, and Usher, *The Legal Foundations of the Single European Market* (Oxford 1991) Chapters 6 and 7.

be suggested that, as in the *Veronica* case, the public policy considerations may relate to the purpose for which the monetary movement is made as much as to the movement itself.

Further emphasizing the difficulty of drawing a clear distinction between monetary movements and the other Treaty freedoms, art. 58(2) provides that the provisions of the Chapter on capital and payments shall be without prejudice to the applicability of restrictions on the right of establishment which are compatible with the Treaty. Those restrictions will be considered in the context of the application of the rules relating to freedom of establishment to financial service institutions in Chapter 5 below.

3

Monetary movements, taxation, and the Treaty 'freedoms'

1. Introduction

Linkages were clearly made between monetary movements and taxation in Council Directive 88/361,[1] which finally established the basic principle of free movement of capital as a matter of Community law, with effect for most Member States from 1 July 1990. With regard to tax harmonization, Directive 88/361 expressly envisaged in its art. 6(5) that the Commission would submit to the Council by 31 December 1988 proposals aimed at eliminating or reducing risks of distortion, tax evasion, and tax avoidance 'linked to the diversity of national systems for the taxation of savings and for controlling the application of these systems', and the Council was to take a position by 30 June 1989. As stated in the previous Chapter, this initiative failed. However, the start of the third stage of Economic and Monetary Union has led to the elimination of exchange risks and differential interest rates for the eleven participants and thus made the legal theory of moving money to other Member States a realistic proposition for ordinary taxpayers. No doubt this was one reason for the resuscitation in 1998 of a proposal for withholding taxes on investment income; however, legal problems and political initiatives may be observed with regard to tax incentives, tax competition, tax evasion, and tax discrimination. Furthermore, in the context of monetary movements, possible conflicts with other substantive provisions of the EC Treaty arise from the wording of art. 58(1)(a) (formerly art. 73d(1)(a)). This states that the provisions of art. 56 (i.e. the liberalization of capital movements and payments inside and outside the Community) 'shall be without prejudice to the right of Member States: (a) to apply the relevant provision of their tax law which distinguish between tax-payers who are not in the same situation with regard to their place of residence or with regard to the place where their capital is invested; . . .'

At first sight this might be taken as a clear authorization to discriminate in the tax system between residents and non-residents. Most of the discussion has centred on the question whether this provision allows discrimination *against* non-residents, which could clearly conflict with the fundamental Treaty freedoms relating to establishment, provision of services, and movement of workers. On the other hand, it has been suggested that the aim of art. 58(1)(a) was to permit discrimination *in*

[1] OJ 1988 L178/5.

favour of non-residents, which could conflict with the State Aids rules, and which also raises the question of tax competition.

The provision must however be taken in its context: in effect it is drafted as a permission to take measures which might interfere with the free movement of capital and payments, rather than to discriminate *carte blanche*. In other words, the fact that a measure may be justifiable as a restriction on the movement of capital and payments does not necessarily make it acceptable as a state aid. However, this is a matter on which there has been no litigation, and arguments could be made for a broad interpretation. In any event, as stated above in Chapter 2, art. 58(1)(a) is subject both to the caveat that such measures 'shall not constitute a means of arbitrary discrimination or a disguised restriction on the free movement of capital and payments as defined in art. 56' and to a Declaration made by the Member States when the Maastricht Treaty was signed that: 'The Conference affirms that the right of Member States to apply the relevant provisions of their tax law as referred to in [Article 73d(1)(a)] of this Treaty will apply only with respect to the relevant provisions which exist at the end of 1993. However, this Declaration shall apply only to capital movements between Member States and to payments effected between Member States.'

It was suggested in Chapter 2 that this at the least amounts to a political commitment not to introduce any new measures of the type at issue in the context of monetary movements between Member States.

2. Tax incentives and the state aid rules

Article 87(1) (formerly art. 92(1)) of the EC Treaty prohibits 'any aid granted by a Member State or through State resources in any form whatsoever which distorts or threatens to distort competition by favouring certain undertakings or the production of certain goods shall, in so far as it affects trade between Member States'. There is no doubt that a one-off tax concession to an individual economic operator may constitute state aid,[2] and it has also long been held that a concession to a whole economic sector may do so[3] on the basis that 'the unilateral modification of a particular factor of the cost of production in a given sector of the economy of a Member State may have the effect of disturbing the existing equilibrium'. On the other hand, in its 1998 press release on the Irish preferential tax regimes,[4] the Commission accepted that it was not taking a view on what the level of corporate taxation should be in Ireland. The question is therefore where to draw the line, and guidance can be found in the Commission's decisions in relation to establishment of an offshore centre in Trieste[5] and in relation to Irish preferential tax regimes.

[2] This was the background to Case C–294/90 *British Aerospace* v. *Commission* [1992] ECR I–493.

[3] Case 173/73 *Italy* v. *Commission* [1974] ECR 709.

[4] IP 98/691 (23 July 1998). For the substance of the Commission's views see the letters to the Irish government published in OJ 1998 C/395/14 and C395/19.

[5] Commission Decision 95/452 (OJ 1995 L264/30).

In the *Trieste* decision, the Commission was concerned with the offshore banking centre established by the Italian government in Trieste. This centre, in the Italian former free port close to the Slovenian border, was established as a consequence of the break-up of the former Yugoslavia, and the sharp loss of trade from the area with that country and, more generally, Central Europe. Even though no comments were received from other Member States or interested parties, the Commission gave only conditional approval to this scheme. Under the original Italian proposal, the Italian authorities were to set up in Trieste a *Centro di Servizi Finanziari ed Assicurativi* (financial services and insurance centre) to engage in financial activities, focusing mainly on Austria and the Eastern European countries; funds would be raised on the international markets from non-residents, and would be used solely outside Italy in transactions with non-residents. The Centre would also house foreign undertakings providing intermediary and assistance services to international business. The undertakings operating at the Centre (banks, insurers, financial intermediaries, stock exchange operators, etc., admitted in accordance with the Community rules on freedom of establishment) would be deemed to be non- resident in Italy for banking and currency market purposes. They would enjoy tax concessions on revenue generated at the Centre in the form of exemption from corporation tax and from 50 per cent of local income tax. For ten years following the opening of the Centre there would be total exemption from local income tax on the incomes of undertakings belonging to the Eastern European countries and on any capital gains on acquisitions of holdings and medium- and long-term investments in those countries. There was also a provision for reduction of indirect taxes on business.

As for categorization as a state aid, the Commission took the view that the tax concessions to be allowed by Italy under these rules were caught by art. 87(1) of the Treaty. They were to be given to undertakings engaging in particular classes of business in a particular section of Italian territory, and conferred an advantage on those undertakings over competitors who did not operate in the same place. Given that this was being done in a context of extensive intra-Community trade in financial and insurance services, the concessions constituted state aid measures incompatible with the common market unless they qualified for one of the derogations provided for in the Treaty.[6]

[6] Art. 87(3) recognizes that certain aids 'may' be considered to be compatible with the common market:

(a) aid to promote the economic development of areas where the standard of living is abnormally low or where there is serious underemployment;
(b) aid to promote the execution of an important project of common European interest or to remedy a serious disturbance in the economy of a Member State;
(c) aid to facilitate the development of certain economic activities or of certain economic areas, where such aid does not adversely affect trading conditions to an extent contrary to the common interest;
(d) aid to promote culture and heritage conservation where such aid does not affect trading conditions and competition in the Community to an extent that is contrary to the common interest; and
(e) such other categories of aid as may be specified by decision of the Council acting by a qualified majority on a proposal from the Commission.

The case therefore turned on which, if any, derogation might apply. Looking first at the possibility of exemption on regional development grounds, the Commission observed that in the province of Trieste the GDP and structural unemployment figures did not justify aid under the regional provision in art. 87(3)(c). Neither did the region satisfy the tests of eligibility for regional aid pursuant to point (a) of art. 87(3).

On the other hand, turning to point (c) of art. 87(3) which allows the exemption of aid to develop a particular economic activity of interest to the Community, the Commission recognized that the development of a capital market in the countries of Eastern Europe through the mobilization of private capital was of vital importance to the Community. It accepted that the city of Trieste, with its tradition of openness to the east, its Slavic- speaking minority, and its experience of insurance and banking, was in a specially advantageous position, unique in the Community, to promote initiatives of this kind, and to facilitate the vital work of reconstruction in the regions of the former Yugoslavia which had been hardest hit by the war.

In the original proposal, the tax concessions were not confined to financial business with Eastern European countries, but were also available for business with Austria, and with any other country as long as the business which the enterprise conducted at the Centre was 'mainly with Eastern Europe and Austria'. In the Commission's view, no Community interest could have justified aid so wide in scope, and the Italian government undertook to confine the tax concessions to profits which derived from business with or concerning the countries of Eastern Europe, so that the measure would in fact be confined to securing an important Community interest. Tax inspection measures would also be taken to prevent triangular financial transactions which might in reality involve countries other than those of Eastern Europe.

With regard to the possible distorting effect of the concessions on competition, the Italian government calculated that under the domestic system of taxation the benefit would be equal to 48 per cent of profits, assuming the profits were in fact sufficiently high to bring them into the top tax bracket, a tax advantage which would enable the undertakings benefiting to reduce their interest rates by comparison with market rates. The Commission considered that such distortion would not be strong enough to be contrary to the common interest; but it required this to be kept under careful review, imposing fixed financial limits on the total amount of budgetary resources forgone and on the total amount of loans or investments in Eastern Europe to which the special scheme applied. It also required that the scheme should not be allowed to become permanent, and its duration should accordingly be restricted to five years.

On the other hand, the *Irish* measures can with hindsight be seen to have been permitted on regional aid grounds. They had three main elements. In the case of the special treatment of finance companies, they had to be established within the International Finance Service Centre (IFSC) in the Customs House area of Dublin.

If they met the conditions for establishment, they were taxed at 10 per cent rather than up to 40 per cent. They also received special tax deductions and relief from local taxes. The second element was a similar scheme in the Shannon Customs-Free Airport Zone; and the third element was the wider Irish corporation tax (ICT) system, under which companies in the manufacturing sector have been subject to a preferential rate of tax of 10 per cent throughout the country. It appears that in 1987 the Commission approved aspects of these schemes, renewing its approval most recently in 1994[7] (albeit without publishing its decision[8]), and imposing time-limits of 2005 and 2010 on the benefits.

However, in a published letter setting out its 1998 recommendations in the matter,[9] which appear to have been accepted by the Irish government, the Commission indicated that in its view the preferential tax rates constituted operating aid, i.e. aid aimed at reducing a firm's current expenses, and that under its state aid guidelines, this form of aid can be authorized only in regions qualifying as areas where the standard of living is abnormally low or where there is serious underemployment (art. 87(3)(a) of the EC Treaty). The Commission went on to point out that Ireland was due to lose this status at the end of 1999, the clear implication being that the preferential tax system was previously permitted only because Ireland did meet the criteria of art. 87(3)(a).

The Commission therefore set out the measures needed to bring the preferential regime to an end, recognizing at the same time that past Commission decisions had built up legitimate expectations. This meant that the regime needed to be phased out with transitional arrangements having an effect over a longer timescale. The Commission in effect distinguished between the two specific regimes and the manufacturing regime. The preferential regimes in the IFSC and at Shannon are to end by 2005 for existing projects, which the Commission considers to have a legitimate expectation to a preferential rate on the basis of previous Commission decisions, and by 2002 for a limited number of further projects which will be allowed under transitional arrangements provided that they are approved by the end of 1999.

However, the arrangements for phasing out the preferential rate under the ICT system[10] are spread over a longer period, reflecting in particular the legitimate expectations acquired by companies given that since 1980 the system was regarded as a general measure and thus not covered by the state aid rules. In other words, the Commission was admitting that it had changed its mind and hardened its attitude. The press release[11] stated quite simply: 'the Commission has now decided that disparate treatment of manufacturing and service companies respectively means that the system qualifies as a state aid.' As with the IFSC and Shannon regimes, the principle of phasing out the preferential rate under the ICT system was that companies with acquired rights could retain eligibility for a preferential rate for a longer time

[7] 'Rapid' on-line Press Release relating to the ECOFIN meeting on 1 December 1997.

[8] See Williams *EC Tax Law* (Longman 1998) p. 177.

[9] OJ 1998 C395/14.

[10] Proposals published in OJ 1998 C395/19.

[11] IP 98/691 (23 July 1998).

(until 2010) than those entering the system afterwards (until 2002). The precise arrangements for phasing out the ICT measures are linked to the individual approval decisions issued by the Irish Development Authority (IDA), which provided regional investment grants to foreign investors setting up business in Ireland. This link reflects, first, the automatic application of the ICT system to eligible companies (thereby reducing the possibility to limit access the system itself) and secondly, the fact that, in the Commission's view, the principal distorting effect of the system has been to cause investors in the manufacturing sector to move their operations to Ireland. Investors approved by the IDA may be eligible for the preferential tax rate until 2010 provided such approval occurred by 31 May 1998 or, for a limited number of projects already at an advanced state of negotiation at that time, by 31 July 1998. A limited number of further projects may be approved until 2002, but can benefit only until 2002.

An indication of the reasons for the Commission's change of mind may be found in its statement such that differential rates not only constituted a state aid which could not be reconciled with the state aid rules, but 'may also constitute potentially harmful tax competition, which is a matter for discussion within the Code of Conduct Group'. This is a reference to a 'Code of Conduct for Business Taxation'[12] agreed at a Council meeting of Economics and Finance ministers (ECOFIN) on 1 December 1997. The text of this Code is discussed later in this Chapter, but it does contain a specific provision on state aids in article J:

> The Council notes that some of the tax measures covered by this code may fall within the scope of the provisions on State aid in Articles [92 to 94] of the EC Treaty. Without prejudice to Community law and the objectives of the Treaty, the Council notes that the Commission undertakes to publish guidelines on the application of the State aid rules to measures relating to direct business taxation by mid-1998, after submitting the draft guidelines to experts from the Member States at a multilateral meeting, and commits itself to the rigorous application of the aid rules concerned, taking into account, inter alia, the negative effects of aid that are brought to light in the application of this code. The Council also notes that the Commission intends to examine or re-examine existing tax arrangements and proposed new legislation by Member States, case by case, thus ensuring that the rules and objectives of the Treaty are applied consistently and equally to all.

These guidelines were published as the 1998 Commission Notice on the application of the state aid rules to measures relating to direct business taxation.[13] From this, it appears that fiscal measures may be caught within the scope of Article 87 provided that:

- the beneficiaries obtain an advantage *vis-à-vis* the normal market conditions
- the benefit is allocated from state resources—e.g. by an effective loss to the state Treasury of fiscal receipts
- the measures affect fair competition in trade between Member States, and

[12] OJ 1998 C2/3. [13] OJ 1998 C384/3.

• the measures favour 'certain enterprises or certain production'.[14]

The draft apparently takes the view that only fiscal regimes which extend across the entire territory of a Member State fall outside the scope of art. 87, and indicates that the Commission now intends to apply this rule closely. For example, regional or sector-oriented taxation regimes fall by definition under the EU state aid rules and the Commission is supposed to be notified of any such measures before they enter into force. Even a preferential regime covering as broad an area as the whole of manufacturing industry must still be considered 'specific' according to the draft—an obvious, if veiled, reference to the Irish regime.

While the Commission Guidelines (and indeed the Code itself) are 'soft' law, in practice it is the Commission itself which applies the state aid rules, and it is therefore highly likely that its criteria will be followed.

3. Tax competition

'Tax competition' is a new concept for the Community lawyer; the phrase is not found anywhere in the EC Treaty. However, the Treaty has from the outset provided for 'a system ensuring that competition in the common market is not distorted'.[15] Over the years this has been very broadly interpreted, and used to justify Community action in such diverse spheres as environmental protection, consumer protection, and equal treatment of men and women. However, as the single market has become more of a reality, and in particular as exchange risks have been eliminated between those Member States participating in Economic and Monetary Union, the market effects of differential tax systems have become more obvious. In the area of the free movements of goods the Community has indeed taken steps to limit the range of variation in rates of VAT,[16] although in the Irish tax case mentioned above the Commission denied that it was taking a view on what the level of corporate taxation should be in Ireland. However, there is now clearly a political impetus in this area, exemplified by the Code of Conduct for Business Taxation adopted by ECOFIN on 1 December 1997.[17]

The Code, which is emphatically stated to be 'a political commitment'concerns those measures which affect, or may affect, in a significant way the location of business activity in the Community. Within that scope, paragraph B provides that tax measures which create a significantly lower effective level of taxation, including zero taxation, than that which generally applies in the Member State in question are to be regarded as potentially harmful and therefore covered by this Code. The Code further provides that when assessing whether such measures are harmful, account should be taken of, *inter alia*:

[14] European Information Service European Report 22 November 1997.

[15] Currently art. 3 paragraph (g).

[16] Directive 92/77 (OJ 1992 L316/1) on rates of VAT.

[17] OJ 1998 C2/3.

(1) whether advantages are accorded only to non-residents or in respect of transactions carried out with non-residents, or
(2) whether advantages are ring-fenced from the domestic market, so they do not affect the national tax base, or
(3) whether advantages are granted without any real economic activity or substantial economic presence within the Member State offering such tax advantages, or
(4) whether the basis of profit determination in respect of activities within a multinational group of companies departs from internationally accepted principles, notably those agreed upon within the OECD, or
(5) whether the tax measures lack transparency, including where statutory rules are relaxed at administrative level in a non-transparent way.

The commitments of the Member States under the Code are divided into 'standstill' and 'rollback'. With regard to the former, they commit themselves not to introduce new tax measures which are harmful within the meaning of the Code. With regard to the latter, they commit themselves to re-examining their existing laws and established practices, having regard to the principles underlying the Code and to the review process set out in it. Member States undertake to amend such laws and practices as necessary with a view to eliminating any harmful measures as soon as possible, taking into account the Council's discussions following the review process.

The review process requires Member States to inform each other of existing and proposed tax measures which may fall within the scope of the Code. In particular, Member States are called upon to provide at the request of another Member State information on any tax measure which appears to fall within the scope of the code. It also involves an element of assessment. Any Member State may request the opportunity to discuss and comment on a tax measure of another Member State that may fall within the scope of the Code, so as to permit an assessment of whether the tax measures in question are harmful, in the light of their potential effects within the Community. That assessment will take into account all the factors identified in paragraph B mentioned above. In reviewing tax measures, the Council also emphasizes the need to assess carefully the effects which they have on other Member States, *inter alia*, in the light of how the activities concerned are effectively taxed throughout the Community. However, it is also stated that 'in so far as the tax measures are used to support the economic development of particular areas, an assessment should be made of whether the measures are in proportion to, and targeted at, the aims sought. In assessing this, particular attention will be paid to special features and constraints in the case of the outermost regions and small islands, without undermining the integrity and coherence of the Community legal order, including the internal market and common policies'. Therefore, as with the legally binding state aids rules, there is clearly an element of discretion and a willingness to take account of economic circumstances.

The review process also involved the establishment of the Code of Conduct Group. This was established by the Council[18] to assess the tax measures that may fall within the scope of the Code and to oversee the provision of information on those measures. Each Member State and the Commission has appointed a high-level representative and a deputy to this group, which was established in March 1998.[19] The group is chaired by a representative of a Member State, appointed for two years, and meets regularly (defined as at least twice a year at a high level).[20] The first chairman was Mrs Primarolo, then Financial Secretary to the UK Treasury, and the Group presented an interim report to the ECOFIN meeting on 1 December 1998. It appears from this interim report that the Code of Conduct Group initially examined intra-group activities, and financial services and offshore companies, concluding that all the measures under consideration were potentially harmful, although further studies were required. It was agreed at this meeting that the future programme of the Group would aim to:

- complete the next stage of assessment of the measures in the first two categories;
- agree on the descriptions and definitions of the tax measures mentioned in the further categories: other sector-specific regimes, regional incentives, and other measures; and
- make an initial assessment of the measures in the further categories and of the reports from Member States with dependent territories.

The Council noted what it termed 'Member States' best endeavours to terminate work on this complex matter by the month of June 1999'.

While the Code of Conduct may not be a legal commitment, it is a political commitment to which new Member States will probably be expected to accede.The terms of the Code are also likely to influence the application of related binding legal rules, such as those on state aid.

For the sake of completeness, it should be observed that in April 1998 the OECD approved a Report on 'Harmful Tax Competition—An Emerging Global Issue' . Within the EC, it may be suggested that the EC's Code of Conduct is of more direct relevance; indeed one EC state, Luxembourg, abstained at the OECD Council meeting which approved the Report, particularly because of objections to the Report's approach to bank secrecy and taxation of services.

4. Tax evasion

One reason for the introduction of art. 58(1)(a) may have been the failure to deal with the question of tax evasion when capital movements were originally liberalized under the Treaty rules by Council Directive 88/361,[21] which finally established the basic principle of free movement of capital as a matter of Community law, with effect

[18] Para. H. [19] RAPID Information Service, March 16 1998. [20] Ibid.

[21] OJ 1988 L178/5.

for most Member States from 1 July 1990. Directive 88/361 expressly envisaged in its art. 6(5) that the Commission would submit to the Council by 31 December 1988 proposals aimed at eliminating or reducing risks of distortion, tax evasion, and tax avoidance 'linked to the diversity of national systems for the taxation of savings and for controlling the application of these systems', and the Council was to take a position by 30 June 1989. The Commission did in fact put forward a proposal,[22] albeit slightly late, for a Directive on a common system of withholding tax on interest income,[23] requiring the payer of interest to deduct from the amount of interest due a withholding tax at a rate of at least 15 per cent, so as at least to ensure the payment of a 'minimum taxation of interest'. However, under art. 6(5) of the Directive, the Council was required 'in accordance with the Treaty'[24] to act unanimously, and it failed to approve the proposal (largely, it would appear, as the result of opposition from the UK and Luxembourg) with the result that the capital movements Directive entered into full effect with no corresponding Community tax legislation, with all the possibilities for tax evasion to which that might give rise.

The idea that such legislation is needed has re-emerged as part of the same package which gave rise to the Code of Conduct mentioned above. The Council Conclusions relating to the meeting in December 1997 stated that 'to ensure a minimum of effective taxation of savings income within the Community and to prevent undesirable distortion of competition, the Council requests the Commission to bring forward a proposal for a Directive on the taxation of savings'. In 1998 the Commission therefore put forward a new proposal for a Directive 'to ensure a minimum of effective taxation of savings income in the form of interest payments within the Community'.[25] This is based on the 'coexistence' model under which Member States can apply a withholding tax at source or provide information on income from savings to other Member States, and its scope is limited to interest paid in each Member State to individuals resident in another Member State. In brief, the coexistence model, as presented in the proposal, foresees that each Member State has the choice between two systems: the information system (provision of information to all other Member States in which the beneficiary is resident) and the withholding-tax system (levying a withholding tax of 20 per cent). Each Member State may choose only one of these systems and apply it to all payments of interest in its territory to residents of all other Member States. Moreover, it is possible for the beneficial owner receiving a payment in a Member State which has chosen the withholding-tax system, to obtain a modification of this system by the certificate process; the beneficiary can ensure that he is taxed exclusively in the Member State where he is resident for tax purposes as if he were receiving a payment in a Member State which had opted for the information system. However, although the proposed Directive is limited to interest paid in each Member State

[22] OJ 1989 C141/5. [23] See p. 20 above.

[24] The Treaty is in fact silent on direct taxation; the Commision proposal was put forward under the former art. 100 (now art 94).

[25] COM(1998) 295 final (20 May 1998).

to individuals resident in another Member State, it would still have some external effects. This reflects the view expressed in the December 1997 Council Conclusions that 'Member States should undertake to promote the establishment of equivalent measures in third countries, at the same time as discussions on the Directive are taking place; they should also undertake to promote their adoption in territories to which the Treaty does not apply. In particular, Member States with dependent or associated territories or which have special responsibilities or fiscal prerogatives in respect of other territories should undertake, within the framework of their constitutional arrangements, to ensure that equivalent measures are applied in those territories.'

Under art. 11 the Community is to enter into negotiations with its main third-country commercial partners, on either a bilateral or a multilateral basis, in order to ensure the effective taxation of income from savings covered by the Directive which is paid to residents for tax purposes of the Member States by paying agents established in such third countries.

At the same time, the Commission put forward a linked proposal which would apply to dependent or associated territories. This would take the form of a decision of the representatives of Member States' governments, meeting within the Council, rather than an act of the Council as such. Essentially, this appears to be a proposal for joint governmental action. Indeed, article 1 is essentially a political commitment: 'Member States undertake, in accordance with their own and the Community's respective competences . . . to promote the adoption in third countries of equivalent measures relating to payments of interest to Community residents'.

However, the core of the matter lies in art. 2, by which 'Member States which have dependent or associated territories or which have special responsibilities or taxation prerogatives in respect of other territories are committed to taking appropriate measures, where appropriate within the framework of their constitutional arrangements, to ensure that provisions concerning interest payments to Community residents, equivalent to those contained in the Directive once adopted, may be applied in those territories'. While monetary movements between Community residents and paying agents in third countries clearly fall under the EC rules on the free movement of capital, the EC itself equally clearly has no competence to change domestic rules in territories outside the Community—hence the choice of the hybrid instrument of a decision of the representatives of the governments of the Member States, meeting within the Council.

5. Tax discrimination

a) The problem

As mentioned earlier in this Chapter, art. 58(1)(a) provides that in the context of free movement of capital and payments, the prohibition against restrictions on capital movements and payments is without prejudice to the right of Member States to apply provisions of their tax law which distinguish between taxpayers who are not in the same situation with regard to their place of residence or with regard to the place where their capital is invested. It may therefore be asked how this provision can be reconciled with the concept of a single market for financial services, and more particularly how it may be reconciled with the principle of non-discrimination underlying the Treaty provisions on free movement of persons and provision of services. The most straightforward approach would be to argue that it is only concerned with monetary movements as such[26] and that it does not apply to situations governed by the other Treaty freedoms. While the thesis pursued in this paper may lead to a similar result, it is submitted that this straightforward approach does not appear to take account of art. 43 (formerly art. 52) (second paragraph) or art. 51(2) (formerly art. 61(2)) of the Treaty. These provisions were not altered by the Single European Act or by the Maastricht or Amsterdam Treaties. The second paragraph of art. 43 defines freedom of establishment as including the right to take up and pursue activities as self-employed persons, and to set up and manage undertakings, 'subject to the provisions of the Chapter relating to capital', and art. 51(2) states that the liberalization of banking and insurance services connected with movements of capital shall be effected in step with the progressive liberalization of the movement of capital. This link between the Treaty rules on establishment and the provision of services and the rules relating to the movement of money was noted in the recitals to the Second Banking Directive, which recognized that capital safeguard measures under the 1988 capital movements Directive[27] may lead to restrictions on the provision of banking services. The provision of banking and insurance services therefore appears expressly to be subordinated to the rules on monetary movements. However, in Case C–118/96 *Safir* v. *Skattemyndigheten i Dalarnas Län*[28] the European Court held that the Swedish tax regime for insurance policies taken out in other Member States concerned the provision of services, so that there was no need to consider the capital movement provisions. Such an approach is difficult to reconcile with the wording of the Treaty—though the wording of the Treaty hardly appears appropriate in the context of the eleven States sharing a single currency.

More generally, the provisions of art. 56, and therefore the exception in art. 58(1)(a), relate not only to capital movements as such but also to payments which, as 'current payments' under the old art. 106(1) were defined in terms of payments or transfers relating to the exercise of the other Treaty freedoms. Indeed, it may be wondered how far payments and transfers can be separated from the substantive Treaty freedom. In Case 95/81 *Commission* v. *Italy*[29] an import deposit scheme

[26] See Vanistendael: 'The consequences of *Schumacker* and *Wielockx*: two steps forward in the tax procession of Echternach' (1996) 33 *CMLR* 255; and Wattel: 'The EC Court's attempts to reconcile the Treaty freedoms with international tax law' (1996) 33 *CMLR* 223.

[27] Council Directive 88/361 (OJ 1988 L178/5).

[28] [1998] ECR I–1897.

[29] [1982] ECR 2187.

imposed in the context of exchange control legislation was classified as a measure equivalent to a quantitative restriction on the import of goods.

Even in the context of capital movements as such, in the absence of a Treaty definition, the headings of the nomenclature annexed to the 1988 Directive (which in reality owe much to the previous lists) indicate the concept of capital underlying that Directive: direct investments, investments in real estate, operations in securities normally dealt in on the capital market, operations in units of collective investment undertakings, operations in securities and other instruments normally dealt in on the money market, operations in current and deposit accounts with financial institutions, credits related to commercial transactions or to the provision of services in which a resident is participating, financial loans and credits, sureties, other guarantees and rights of pledge, transfers in performance of insurance contracts, personal capital movements, physical import and export of financial assets, and 'other capital movements' (defined to include transfers of the moneys required for the provision of services).

The introduction to the Annex further states that the capital movements mentioned are taken to cover all the operations necessary for the purposes of capital movements, i.e. the conclusion and performance of the transaction and related transfers, and should also include access for the economic operator to all the financial techniques available on the market approached for the purpose of carrying out the operation in question. However, it is now clear that borrowing money from a bank in another Member State to buy a house fell within the scope of the 1988 Directive, even though it might also be regarded as a provision of services.[30] It was subsequently suggested by A.-G.Tesauro in his Opinion in Case C–118/96 *Safir* v. *Skattemyndigheten i Dalarnas Län*[31] that a narrower concept of capital movements should be adopted, but the Court none the less confirmed in Case C–222/97 *Trummer and Mayer*[32] that a mortgage fell within the scope of a capital movement as defined in the Directive, and further held that this interpretation should continue to apply to the free movement of capital under art. 56.

In the light of this, consideration may be given to the treatment of tax discrimination in the context of the other Treaty freedoms.

b) Tax discrimination and the free movement of goods

While the taxation of goods is not the main concern of this Chapter, it is noteworthy that art. 90 (formerly art. 95) of the Treaty expressly prohibits discrimination in this area with regard to goods imported from other Member States. Two distinct requirements are contained in the two paragraphs of art. 90 of the EC Treaty. The first paragraph states that 'no Member State shall impose, directly or indirectly, on the products of other Member States any internal taxation of any

[30] See Case C–484/93 *Svensson and Gustavsson* v. *Ministre du Logement* [1995] ECR I–3955.
[31] Opinion delivered 23 Sept. 1997, [1998] ECR I–1899.
[32] 16 Mar. 1999.

kind in excess of that imposed directly or indirectly on similar domestic products'. The second states that 'no Member State shall impose on the products of other Member States any internal taxation of such a nature as to afford indirect protection to other products'. The difference between their consequences was noted at an early stage in Case 27/67 *Fink-Frucht* v. *HZA Munchen-Landsbergerstrasse*,[33] where it was said that whilst the first paragraph only prohibits taxation in so far as it exceeds a clearly defined level, the second paragraph is based on the protective effect of the taxation in question to the exclusion of any exact standard of reference. The ease or otherwise of the calculation will depend on how close the relationship is between the competing domestic and imported goods at issue.

Community law does not in principle prohibit domestic tax laws from imposing or permitting different rates of tax on different products, or indeed on products which may serve similar economic ends.[34] It does object to differential taxation of similar or competing products where the category of goods paying the higher rate is composed largely or exclusively of imported goods. Examples include the French taxation of cars on the basis of engine size,[35] the French distinction between grain-based spirits and fruit-based spirits,[36] and the Italian distinction between sparkling wine fermented in bottle and in cask.[37]

c) Tax discrimination and the freedom to provide services

In the context of the Treaty rules on the provision of services there is, as mentioned above, an express link with the provisions governing free movement of capital in art. 51(2), which states that the liberalization of banking and insurance services connected with movements of capital shall be effected in step with the progressive liberalization of the movement of capital. This link was applied in a restrictive way by the European Court in Case 267/86 *Van Eycke* v. *ASPA*,[38] where it was held that since the opening of a savings account in another Member State was not at that time liberated under the capital movements Directives, it was not a breach of the Treaty provisions on freedom to provide services for Belgium to limit tax exemptions on such accounts to deposits in local currency at credit institutions having their head office (*siège social*) in Belgium. It might have been thought that such rules would have to be changed when a Community law right to set up savings accounts in other Member States came into operation under the 1988 capital movements Directive.[39] However, the Court did actually accept a requirement of local establishment in Case C–204/90 *Bachmann* v. *Belgium*.[40] There, the Court held that tax deductions on life and sickness insurance premiums could be limited to payments made to insurers established in Belgium, on the basis that there was no other way of preserving the

[33] [1968] ECR 223.
[34] Case 21/79 *Commission* v. *Italy* [1980] ECR 1.
[35] Case 112/84 *Humblot* [1985] ECR 1367.
[36] Case 168/78 *Commission* v. *France* [1980] ECR 347.
[37] Case 278/83 *Commission* v. *Italy* [1985] ECR 2503.
[38] [1988] ECR 4769.
[39] Council Directive 88/361 (OJ 1988 L178/5).
[40] [1992] ECR I–249.

integrity of the tax system (which required tax to be paid on the ultimate benefits).If a requirement that a provider of a financial service should be established within the jurisdiction of the Member State concerned is the only way to ensure that a Member State's tax legislation is observed, then a considerably greater degree of co-operation between the tax authorities of the Member States is probably needed. It also has the effect of making provision of services in the Treaty sense impossible.

However, that is not the end of the story. The European Court returned to the matter in Case C–80/94 *Wielockx* v. *Inspecteur der Directe Belastingen.*[41] This involved a Belgian national resident in Belgium who was a partner in a business established in the Netherlands and whose entire income was earned in the Netherlands. He paid money into a pension reserve in the Netherlands, and claimed tax relief on that part of his income. This relief was refused on the basis that it was available only to Dutch residents. The Netherlands government invoked the *Bachmann* case to argue that in the case of a Belgian resident, the Netherlands authorities would grant the tax relief on the pension contributions, but the Belgian authorities would collect the tax on the pension when it was received. However, while accepting that in principle the situations of residents and non-residents are not generally comparable, the Court held that a non-resident taxpayer who receives all or almost all of his income in the State where he works is objectively in the same situation as concerns income tax as a resident of that State. Furthermore, on the question of tax cohesion, the Court followed Advocate-General Léger in noting that the arrangements between the Netherlands and Belgium resulted from a double taxation convention following the OECD model, under which a State taxes all pensions, irrespective of their source, received by residents, but waives the right to tax pensions received abroad, irrespective of their source. It therefore held that tax cohesion was to be established, not at the level of an individual taxpayer, but in the reciprocity of the rules applicable in the Contracting States. The Netherlands could not therefore justify a discriminatory refusal of tax relief in this case.

While there may be some debate as to the Court's analysis of the double taxation agreements[42] (though they are hardly a matter of Community legislation falling within the Court's jurisdiction) this may effectively overrule the *Bachmann* judgment. Indeed, in Case C–118/96 *Safir* v. *Skattemyndigheten i Dalarnas Län*,[43] it was held that for Sweden to impose a different tax regime for insurance policies purchased from providers outside Sweden which would have the effect of deterring Swedish residents from taking out such policies, even though it was intended to achieve tax neutrality between policies purchased inside and outside Sweden, was a breach of art. 49 (formerly art. 59).

[41] [1995] ECR I–2493.

[42] See Vanistendael: 'The consequences of *Schumacker* and *Wielockx*: Two steps forward in the tax procession of Echternach' (1996) 33 *CMLR* 255; and Wattel: 'The EC Court's attempts to reconcile the Treaty freedoms with international tax law' (1996) 33 *CMLR* 223.

[43] [1998] ECR I-1897.

d) Tax discrimination and the free movement of persons

While the second paragraph of art. 43 (formerly art. 52) defines freedom of establishment as including the right to take up and pursue activities as self-employed persons, and to set up and manage undertakings, 'subject to the provisions of the Chapter relating to capital', there is a long line of case-law indicating that those falling within its scope may not be subjected to tax discrimination. In the context of freedom of establishment, if an undertaking does establish a permanent presence in another Member State then, whatever form that establishment takes, it has been clear since Case 270/83 *Commission* v. *France*[44] that Member States may not treat companies differently for tax purposes depending on the type of establishment present within their jurisdiction. It was there held, in the context of French legislation granting shareholders' tax credits to French insurance companies but not to branches or agencies in France of foreign insurance companies, that France could not treat the branches of foreign insurance companies whose main offices were in other Member States differently from those insurance companies which took the form of French-based companies which were subsidiaries of those foreign insurance companies. In other words, branches (which are a part of the foreign undertaking in another Member State) and subsidiaries (which are formed under local law but controlled by the foreign undertaking) had to be treated in the same way, both being forms of establishment recognized in what is now art. 43. Furthermore, it was made clear in that case that there was no way in which restrictions could be imposed on the freedom of establishment in order to prevent tax evasion, even though it might be legitimate outside that context to operate differential tax treatment on the basis of residence, as was subsequently held in Case C–112/91 *Werner* v. *FZA Aachen-Innenstadt*.[45]

However, when the question of residence did arise in the context of freedom of establishment in Case C-330/91 *R* v. *Inland Revenue Commissioners* ex p. *Commerzbank*[46] it was held that a German company which traded in the UK through a branch established there but fiscally non-resident in the UK, was entitled to receive interest on the repayment of tax which should not have been charged to it, if an undertaking resident in the UK would have received interest on such a repayment. It made no difference that the only reason for the repayment of the tax was the fact that the German company was not resident in the UK. A similar approach was taken in Case C–264/96 *ICI* v. *Colmer*,[47] where tax relief for a holding company depended on the residence of its subsidiaries.

With regard to free movement of workers, in Case C–279/93 *Schumacker*[48] and Case C–151/94 *Commission* v. *Luxembourg*[49] it was made clear that discrimination

[44] [1986] ECR 273; [1987] 1 CMLR 401. See also Case C-307/97 *Saint Gobain* v. *FZA Aachen-Innenstadt* (21 September 1999).

[45] [1992] ECR I–249. This case nevertheless distinguished and reaffirmed the judgment in the French tax case.

[46] [1993] ECR I–4017.

[47] [1998] ECR I–4695.

[48] [1995] ECR I–225.

[49] [1995] ECR I-3685.

cannot be justified where the taxpayer benefits from the rules on free movement of workers, and in Case C–107/94 *Asscher*[50] it was made clear that discrimination cannot be justified where the taxpayer benefits from the rules on freedom of establishment. In the *Schumacker* case it was held that where the State of residence could not take account of the taxpayer's personal and family circumstances because the tax payable there was insufficient to enable it to do so, the Community principle of equal treatment required that in the State of employment the personal and family circumstances of a foreign non-resident be taken into account in the same way as those of resident nationals, and the same tax benefits should be granted. In the *Luxembourg* case it was held to be a breach of the rules on the free movement of workers for Luxembourg to retain and not repay excess amounts of tax deducted from the earnings of Community nationals who resided or worked in Luxembourg for less than the whole tax year. In the third case, the Netherlands could not impose a higher income tax liability on a non-resident to compensate for the fact that he paid social security contributions in another Member State. On the other hand it was accepted by the European Court in Case C-336/96 *Gilly* v. *Directeur des Services Fiscaux du Bas-Rhin*[51] that a frontier worker may have to accept less than perfect equality of treatment under a double taxation agreement, at least where the family income is split between the States concerned.

e) Situations outside the Treaty freedoms

This case-law may be contrasted with the European Court's approach in Case C–112/91 *Werner* v. *Finanzamt Aachen-Innenstadt*,[52] which can be explained on the basis that no substantive EC law rights were at issue. The case involved a German citizen who had lived in the Netherlands for thirty years but who practised as a dentist just over the border in Germany. By virtue of a double taxation agreement, he was liable to the German authorities for tax on his income arising in Germany. However, as a non-resident, the German authorities denied him the benefit of certain arrangements available for married couples, and did not allow him to deduct costs which could have been deducted by a resident. It may be suggested that in effect the Court avoided the main policy issue, and held that in the case of a German citizen subject to German tax law practising in Germany by virtue of a German qualification, art. 43 did not prevent Germany imposing a heavier tax burden on those of its citizens who were non-residents than on those who were residents; in other words it was not really a question of freedom of establishment. However, it is clear from *Wielockx* that Germany could not discriminate against e.g. a Dutch citizen practising in Germany by virtue of Dutch qualifications.

[50] 27 June 1996.

[51] [1998] ECR I–2793. See also Case C-391/97 *Gschwind* v. *FZA Aachen-Aussenstadt* (14 September 1999).

[52] [1993] ECR I–429.

f) Can art. 58(1)(a) be reconciled with the Treaty freedoms?

While the present author previously suggested that art. 58(1)(a) represented a continuation of the *Van Eycke* and *Bachmann* case-law, it is now clear that there is a conflict between the Treaty rights of freedom of establishment and free movement of workers as interpreted in *Commerzbank*, *Wielockx*, *Schumacker*, *Luxembourg*, and *Asscher*, on one hand, and the discriminatory tax treatment apparently authorised by art. 58(1)(a) on the other. As indicated above, one simple explanation would be that a situation governed by another Treaty freedom does not fall within art. 58(1)(a). However, that is hardly compatible with the express terms of art. 51(2), subjecting freedom to provide services in the financial sector to the liberalization of capital movements, or with the fact that current payments will normally relate to another Treaty freedom. In the more recent Case C–118/96 *Safir* v. *Skattemyndigheten i Dalarnas Län*,[53] it was held to be a breach of art. 49 for Sweden to impose a different tax regime for insurance policies purchased from providers outside Sweden which would have the effect of deterring Swedish residents from taking out such policies, even though it was intended to achieve tax neutrality between policies purchased inside and outside Sweden, but it was stated that the decision on this point made it unnecessary to determine whether the legislation was also incompatible with arts. 56 and 58—even though under the express terms of art. 50 services are only services within the meaning of the Treaty to the extent that they do not fall under one of the other Treaty freedoms.

In any event, art. 58(1)(a) only entered into force on 1 January 1994, and as noted above, there is attached to the Maastricht Treaty a Declaration in the following terms: 'The Conference affirms that the right of Member States to apply the relevant provisions of their tax law as referred to in [Article 73d(1)(a)]of this Treaty will apply only with respect to the relevant provisions which exist at the end of 1993. However, this Declaration shall apply only to capital movements between Member States and to payments effected between Member States.'

While a mere Declaration may not amend the terms of the Treaty, it has long been established in other areas of Community law that it may be binding upon its author.[54] If the Member States are bound by their Declaration, its effect may be that with regard to monetary movements between Member States, the only discriminatory measures which may be maintained under art. 58(1)(a) are those which were lawfully in force at the end of 1993. Since the *Commerzbank*, *Wielockx*, *Schumacker*, and *Asscher* cases all relate to situations arising before the end of 1993, it is suggested that the discrimination on the basis of residence found unlawful in those cases cannot be revived under art. 58(1)(a).

Be that as it may, in those situations where it does apply (presumably where the taxpayer does not fall within a substantive Treaty provision prohibiting discrimi-

[53] [1998] ECR I–1897.

[54] In the context of declarations under Regulation 1408/71 on social security, see Case 35/77 *Beerens* [1977 ECR 2249, 2254.

nation, and where monetary movements outside the Community are involved) art. 58(1)(a) is drafted in very broad terms. It allows Member States to apply the relevant provisions of their tax law which distinguish between tax-payers (with no mention of nationality) who are not in the same situation with regard to their place of residence or with regard to the place where their capital is invested. However, it is still subject to the general requirement in art. 58(3) that the measures in question should not constitute a means of arbitrary discrimination or a disguised restriction on the free movement of capital and payments. The question then arises of to how to reconcile a provision which expressly allows differences in treatment on the basis of residence or place of investment with a provision which prohibits arbitrary discrimination.

It may be submitted that to avoid being characterized as 'arbitrary', the discriminatory tax treatment must be shown to be objectively justified, and that in this context the criteria laid down by the Court in Case C–204/90 *Bachmann* v. *Belgium*[55] continue to be relevant: the measures must be intended to protect the coherence of the national tax system, and must be shown to be necessary for the achievement of that objective. Applying the principles developed in the context of art. 30 of the Treaty on restrictions on the free movement of goods by analogy with art. 58(1)(a), it may be suggested that in order to justify differential tax treatment under that provision, not only must the measure be justified to protect the coherence of the tax system but it must also be shown that effective measures are taken at the domestic level in the national tax system to deal with the perceived problem.[56] Thus in Case C-439/97 *Sandoz* v. *Finanzlandesdirektion Wein*[57] it was held that Austria could require an Austrian resident borrowing money in another Member State to pay the same stamp duty as would have been payable if the transaction had taken place in Austria. However, it was a breach of art. 58(1)(b) to treat a loan contracted in another Member State as subject to stamp duty when the equivalent loan in Austria would not be subject to that duty.

6. Third countries

Unlike any of the other provisions governing the Treaty 'freedoms', the rules introduced by the Maastricht Treaty in relation to monetary movements in principle treat movements to and from third countries the same way as movements between Member States. This also distinguishes them from the original provisions, and indeed from the situation under the 1988 Directive. However, in reality some differences remain, as discussed in Chapter 2, and these are of particular relevance in the context of tax discrimination; for example, under art. 57 (formerly art. 73c)

55 [1992] ECR I–249.

56 Case 4/75 *Rewe-Zentralfinanz* v. *Landwirtschaftskammer Bonn* [1975] ECR 843; Case 121/85 *Conegate* v. *HM Customs and Excise* [1986] ECR 1007.

57 14 October 1999.

the provisions of art. 56 are stated to be without prejudice to the application to third countries of any restrictions which exist on 31 December 1993 under national or Community law adopted in respect of the movement of capital to or from third countries involving direct investment (including investment in real estate), establishment, the provision of financial services, or the admission of securities to capital markets; in other words, they do not require existing lawful restrictions to be abolished in these (admittedly limited) areas.

If the analysis of the situation inside the Community set out in the previous section of this Chapter is correct, and art. 58(1)(a) cannot authorize discriminatory measures which infringe the other Treaty freedoms, on the other hand it does in principle allow tax discrimination on the basis of residence or place of investment in relation to monetary movements to and from third countries, subject to the general requirement in art. 58(3) that the measures in question should not constitute a means of arbitrary discrimination or a disguised restriction on the free movement of capital and payments, in so far as those concepts are relevant in relations between the Community and third countries. How far such discrimination fits in with the Community's wider obligations is considered in Chapter 11 below in the context of external monetary relations.

4

The application of EC competition rules to financial services

1. The Treaty rules and their administration

The competition rules of the EC Treaty prohibit in art. 81(1) (formerly art. 85(1)) all agreements between undertakings, decisions by associations of undertakings, and concerted practices which may affect trade between Member States and which have as their object or effect the prevention, restriction, or distortion of competition within the common market. Article 82 (formerly art. 86) prohibits any abuse by one or more undertakings of a 'dominant position' within the common market or in a substantial part of it in so far as it may affect trade between Member States. However, under art. 81(3), exemption from art. 81(1) may be granted to such agreements, decisions, or concerted practices, and specific categories thereof, which contribute to improving the production or distribution of goods or to promoting technical or economic progress, while allowing consumers a fair share of the resulting benefit, provided they do not impose on the undertakings concerned restrictions which are not indispensable to the attainment of these objectives, and do not afford such undertakings the possibility of eliminating competition in respect of a substantial part of the products in question. Furthermore, art. 86(2) (formerly art. 90(2)), which has been frequently invoked in the financial services sector, applies the competition rules to undertakings entrusted with the operation of services of general economic interest or which have the character of a revenue-producing monopoly only 'in so far as the application of such rules does not affect the performance . . . of the particular tasks assigned to them'.

In the light of the Commission's 1992 Guidelines on the application of the competition rules at the national level,[1] which emphasize the remedies available at the national level (e.g. damages) which the Commission itself cannot give and the underlying aim of which appears to be that the Commission should be able to concentrate on those cases of Community interest, it should be recalled that, leaving aside the Merger Regulation,[2] the EC Treaty does not confer on the Commission exclusive powers with regard to the competition rules it contains. The

[1] OJ 1993 C39/6.

[2] Council Regulation 4064/89 (corrected version printed in OJ 1990 L257/14), as amended by Council Regulation 1310/97 (OJ 1997 L180/1). For the effects of the Merger Regulation in the financial services sector, see below, p. 85.

Commission's powers to enforce the competition rules alone were conferred on it by Council Regulation 17/62,[3] and although this Regulation confers exclusive power on the Commission to grant exemptions under art. 81(3) (and for this purpose requires agreements for which individual exemption or clearance is sought to be notified to the Commission) it otherwise maintains the competence of the national authorities to apply the prohibitions in arts. 81(1) and 82 unless proceeding have been initiated before the Commission itself.[4] Of further practical importance is the fact that it has been clearly established by the European Court that the prohibitions contained in arts. 81(1) and 82 of the EC Treaty produce direct effects, and hence may be invoked by parties to litigation before national courts irrespective of the terms of Regulation 17/62 (or indeed the Merger Regulation).[5] Indeed, much of the case-law on the application of the competition rules in the financial services sector has arisen from questions referred for preliminary rulings by national courts, rather than from direct actions seeking the annulment of Commission competition decisions.

Nevertheless, the role of the Commission remains of fundamental importance for those subject to the general EC competition rules. The Commission is the only body which directly enforces those rules at the Community level in the interests of Community policy, rather than national policy or private interest; it is the only body which may grant exemptions under art. 81(3); and under art. 15 of Regulation 17/62, it may impose fines of up to € one million, or 10 per cent of turnover where that is greater.

2. The Treaty rules in the financial services sector

Although the Commission put on public record at an early stage its view that in principle the EC competition rules were applicable in the banking sector, while nevertheless recognizing the problems caused by interaction with national monetary policy,[6] it took no formal decisions before the issue of principle was settled by the European Court in Case 172/80 *Züchner* v. *Bayerische Vereinsbank*,[7] and it appears that most agreements in the banking sector were not, before that judgment, notified to the Commission under Regulation 17/62 with a view to obtaining a formal exemption or clearance.[8]

Herr Züchner had drawn a cheque in the sum of DM10,000 on his account with the defendant bank in Germany in favour of a payee resident in Italy, and for carrying out that operation the bank had charged a commission of DM15, equal to 0.15 per cent of the sum involved. He considered that to levy commission at this

[3] OJ Sp. Ed. 1959–62 p. 87.
[4] Art. 9(3).
[5] Case 127/73 *BRT* v. *SABAM* [1974] ECR 51 and the second *Brasserie de Haecht* case [1973] ECR 77.
[6] *Second Report on Competition Policy 1973* points 51 to 53.
[7] [1981] ECR 2021.
[8] See Dassesse and Isaacs, *EEC Banking Law* (Lloyd's of London, 1985) pp. 18–19.

rate constituted a concerted practice followed by most, if not all, banks in Germany and in the other Member States, contrary to the EC competition rules, and brought an action to recover the DM15. With regard to that narrow objective, Herr Züchner had already won by the time the reference was determined by the European Court, the bank having repaid the commission, but the German court held that he still had an interest in continuing the proceedings, since a similar commission might be levied on him at any time in the future. The question ultimately referred to the European Court by the Amtsgericht of Rosenheim was whether the levying by banks of a uniform commission of 0.15 per cent on payments between Member States was contrary to the EC competition rules as being a concerted practice, a question based on the hypothesis that there was such a uniform rate of commission.

In its judgment, the European Court dealt first with a preliminary point taken by the bank at the oral hearing to the effect that banks should be considered to be 'undertakings entrusted with the operation of services of general economic interest' under art. 86(2), and therefore subject to the competition rules only to the extent to which they did not obstruct the performance of those services. The Court took the view that the fact that banks carried out transfers of money from one Member State to another on behalf of clients was not in itself sufficient to bring them within the definition in art. 86(2) unless it could be shown that the public authorities specifically entrusted them with carrying out such transfers as a service of general economic interest, which appears not to have been shown in this case. The Court further held that the rules on preserving the equilibrium of the balance of payments set out in the then arts. 104 *et seq.* of the EC Treaty[9] did not even purport to exempt banks from the basic competition rules.

Starting from the premise that banks were therefore subject to the normal competition rules, the Court turned to the question of concerted practices, repeating the definition it had given in Case 48/69 *ICI* v. *Commission*[10] of that term as 'a form of co-operation between undertakings which, without having reached the stage where an agreement properly so called has been concluded, knowingly substitutes practical co-operation between them for the risks of competition'. While accepting that undertakings may adapt themselves 'intelligently' to the behaviour of their competitors, the Court nevertheless took the view that they are required to act sufficiently independently not to make direct or indirect contact with their competitors so as to produce conditions of competition which do not correspond to the normal conditions of the market in question, 'having regard to the nature of the products, the size and number of the undertakings and the volume of the said market'.[11] The defendant bank apparently did not deny that the same rate of commission was charged by other banks both in Germany and in other Member States, but claimed that it was not the result of a concerted practice, and that in any event it only covered part of the real cost of effecting a transfer to another Member State.

[9] See Chapter 1 above. [10] [1972] ECR 619.
[11] This also is a quotation from the *ICI* case.

However, the Court held that even if the latter was the case, if there was such parallel behaviour it could amount to a concerted practice within the meaning of art. 81(1); furthermore, since it affected international transactions, it would by its very nature be capable of affecting trade between Member States. The Court specifically stated that 'trade' in art. 81(1) should be taken to have a wide meaning including monetary transfers, a view later developed further by the Commission: in its decision concerning agreements between Belgian banks,[12] after referring to the *Züchner* judgment, the Commission suggested that the concept of trade relates to economic activity in general, including monetary transactions and banking services. The Court added that such a practice would palpably affect competition if it crystallized established relationships and in practice prevented banks' clients from taking advantage of more favourable opportunities which might be offered under normal conditions of competition.

Examination of whether this was in fact the case was left to the national court, although the European Court indicated in considerable detail the points which the national court ought to investigate (in language more appropriate to an inquisitorial than an accusatorial form of procedure). It stated that where there was parallel conduct, the national court should examine: (i) whether there had been contacts or exchanges of information between the banks as to the rates of commission actually charged for comparable transfers either effected or envisaged; (ii) whether the uniform rate of commission differs from that which would have resulted from free competition; (iii) the number and importance of the banks participating in the practice; and (iv) the proportion of transfers between Member States on which the commission in question is charged. In an accusatorial system these are matters on which evidence will have to be produced by the parties, and with regard to which an individual customer may encounter considerable difficulties.

However, leaving aside these precise criteria of a concerted practice, the important message flowing from *Züchner* is that banks are in principle subject to the competition rules of the EC Treaty, and that even concerted practices which might appear to have the effect of reducing direct charges to customers may breach these rules if their result differs from the situation which would prevail if there were open competition.

Having held that banks are not automatically regarded as being entrusted with the operation of services of general economic interest, the Court has gone on to hold that the competition rules apply in the financial services sector even in areas which are subject to strict regulation. It also appears from the German fire insurance cases[13] that the competition rules apply at least in so far as there is scope left for competition, repeating a view which had already been taken with regard to certain agricultural sectors, for example.[14] In its judgment in Case 45/85 *Verband der*

[12] Commission Decision 87/13 (OJ 1987 L7/27).

[13] Case 45/85 *Verband der Sachversicherer* v. *Commission* [1987] ECR 405.

[14] See Cases 40–48, 50, 54–56, 111, 113, and 114/73 *Suiker Unie and Others* v. *Commission* [1975] ECR 1663.

Sachversicherer v. Commission,[15] which involved a recommendation by the German fire insurers' association intended to 'stabilize' the sector, providing for increases in the premiums charged, the Court first emphasized that there was no express exemption for the insurance sector under Community competition legislation, and that therefore arts. 81 and 82 of the Treaty, and Regulation 17/62, applied fully in that sector.

The case in fact revealed two aspects of the interface between Community competition law and national regulation of the market: the recommendation had been approved both by the German competition authority (*Bundeskartellamt*) and by the German insurance supervisory authority. With regard to these, the Court observed in general terms that by virtue of what are now art. 3 paragraph (g)[16] and the second paragraph of art. 10[17] of the EC Treaty, national administrative practices could not prevent the full application of the Community competition rules. In particular, it held that national legislation on the supervision of insurance companies pursued a different objective from Community competition law, and it had not been shown that the application of those competition rules in any way hindered the functioning of the supervisory system.

Turning to the fact that it was a recommendation which was at issue, the Court noted that it prescribed a collective increase in premiums in imperative terms, that German reinsurance undertakings treated fire insurance at a lower premium as under-insurance, and that under its constitution and that the association did have power to co-ordinate the premium policy of its members. It therefore found that, whatever its precise legal status, the recommendation represented the faithful expression of the association's desire to co-ordinate the behaviour of its members on the German insurance market, and hence constituted a decision by an association of undertakings under art. 81(1) of the EC Treaty. The Court added that the actual effects of the recommendation were not relevant if it appeared that the aim was to prevent, restrict, or distort competition.

A further problem arose with regard to whether trade between Member States could be said to have been affected, because under the German legislation then in force, considered by the Court in Case 205/84 *Commission* v. *Germany*,[18] an insurance company could not be authorized in Germany unless it was established there, which meant in practice having a branch, subsidiary or agency there, and fire insurance services could not be offered into Germany by an undertaking in another Member State. Leaving aside the question of the legality or otherwise of the German system, it might have been thought that there could not be any trade with other Member States so far as the German fire insurance market was concerned.

[15] [1987] ECR 405.

[16] Requiring the institution of a system ensuring that competition in the common market is not distorted.

[17] Requiring Member States to abstain from any measure which could jeopardize the attainment of the objectives of the Treaty.

[18] [1986] ECR 3755; [1987] 2 CMLR 69; see Chapter 5 below.

However, the Court (following the Commission) held that if the recommendation affected the branches in the German market of companies based in other Member States, it would affect the financial relationship between the branch and its parent, and may therefore be capable of affecting trade between Member States within the meaning of art. 81(1). By this reasoning there must be very few agreements and decisions in the financial services sector which cannot be regarded as affecting trade between Member States. However, the Court also noted that the increase in the level of premiums prevented foreign undertakings from offering lower premiums through their German branches. This approach may be contrasted with that more recently adopted in Cases C–215 and 216/96 *Bagnasco* v. *Banca Popolare di Novara*.[19] These cases involved a series of agreements between Italian banks, notified to the Commission in 1993, and most of which the Commission had decided not to examine on the basis, first, that they involved activities which were either carried on only in Italian territory or had a very limited influence on trade between Member States, and secondly, that the participation of subsidiaries or branches of non-Italian financial establishments was limited. Their validity was nevertheless challenged in litigation before the Italian courts, which referred to the European Court the question of trade between Member States, in particular with regard to the rules governing the provision of general guarantees. The Court accepted that it was 'conceivable' that the Italian subsidiaries or branches of banks from other Member States might be obliged to accept the national rules and forgo the possibility of applying more favourable conditions. However, the Court also stated that the Commission's findings had not been called into question during the proceedings, and concluded that standard bank conditions relating to the provision of general guarantees to secure current account facilities such as those at issue in these cases were not, 'taken as a whole', liable to affect trade between Member States within the meaning of art. 81(1).

Returning to the German fire insurance case: with regard to the Commission's assessment of whether an exemption could be granted under art. 81(3), the Court held that the Commission had been justified in finding that the disadvantages flowing from the recommendation outweighed the advantages, particularly since the increase in premiums was on a flat-rate basis and took no account of the individual costs of each company.

However, since the Court's decision in *Züchner*, the Commission has issued a number of formal decisions in the banking sector, both in relation to agreements between banks at the national level and in relation to the international 'Eurocheque' system, from which certain criteria may be drawn as to conduct which will be approved by the Commission and conduct which it will penalize.

[19] 21 Jan. 1999.

3. The Eurocheque system

The Commission has issued three formal decisions[20] in relation to the Eurocheque system, which was originally set up in 1968 on the private initiative of European financial institutions (by no means limited to those in the EC) with the aim of making available a means of payment which customers might use in both their country of origin and in other countries.[21] It is based on cheques and a cheque guarantee card, the essential feature being that the drawee bank guarantees any payee bank reimbursement of a cheque presented with the corresponding card up to a predetermined maximum amount.

The first decision[22] related to a 'package deal' agreed by the decision-making bodies of the Eurocheque system, the Eurocheque Assembly, and the Eurocheque Working Group, concerning *uniform* Eurocheques made out abroad in local currency, designed in particular to open up the trading sector to acceptance of these cheques. The agreement came into force on 1 May 1981 for a five-year period, renewable automatically from year to year. It was designed in particular to ensure that, provided the correct formalities were observed, the trader would receive payment in full (though there is a reference in para. 22 to 'experimental' practices in France which eventually gave rise to the 1992 decision). A commission of 1.25 per cent was to be applied to all uniform Eurocheques made out abroad in local currency, but this was not to be charged at the time of encashment or to be charged by a retailer; rather, it was to be paid to the payee bank by the clearing centre and debited to the drawee bank, which in turn would debit its customer, together with any supplementary clearing costs. In other words, at the time of encashment by a member of the system, or a the time of purchase of goods or services, the drawer of a Eurocheque should receive its full face value, although his account would later be debited also with the costs.

Turning to its legal assessment, the Commission first dealt with a claim made by the Eurocheque Assembly and the Eurocheque Working Group, like that made by the bank in *Züchner*,[23] that art. 86(2) applied and that they should be considered to be 'undertakings entrusted with the operation of services of general economic interest', and therefore subject to the competition rules only in so far as they did not obstruct the performance of those services. The Commission pointed out that the system was set up on the initiative of private financial institutions, and not adopted by the public authorities, and it made no difference that the system operated with the knowledge and approval of the competent authorities in the countries concerned, or even that there had been explicit legal acts in favour of the system or part of it. The decision further emphasized that even if the system had

[20] Commission Decisions 85/77 (OJ 1985 L35/43), 89/95 (OJ 1989 L36/16), and 92/212 (OJ 1992 L95/50).

[21] This description of the scheme is taken from Decision 85/77 (*supra*).

[22] Decision 85/77 (OJ 1985 L35/43).

[23] [1981] ECR 2021.

been entrusted by an international authority or a group of national public authorities with the provision of an international means of payment, the application of the Community's competition rules could not in any way obstruct the fulfilment of that hypothetical special assignment.

The next question for determination was whether the package deal breached art. 81(1). The Commission took the view that the Eurocheque system and its various governing bodies did constitute an association of undertakings, and that an agreement or decision fixing the price or conditions of a foreign cheque was by its very nature likely to affect trade between Member States, quoting the Court's decision in *Züchner* to the effect that 'trade' in art. 81(1) should be taken to have a wide meaning including monetary transfers.[24] With regard to restrictions of competition, the Commission found that an agreement fixing the price for a service, e.g. through uniform commissions, was clearly a restrictive practice, and furthermore there could be no competition with regard to the maximum guaranteed amount. However, it also took the view that the criteria for exemption under art. 81(3) were met.

It was first held that the system contributed in three ways to the improvement of payment facilities within the common market (a services analogy with improving the production or distribution of goods or promoting technical or economic progress in the terms of art. 81(3)). It enabled cheques to be drawn outside the country of the institution which issued them and cashed at banks in foreign countries including EC Member States; it enabled uniform Eurocheques to be drawn in the local currency of countries including EC Member States and to be paid in full without deduction of commission by the payee banks, thus making them more acceptable to the trading sector; and centralized clearing made it easier for payee banks to obtain reimbursement, a matter of particular importance for credit institutions in countries with a heavy tourist trade. The Commission also found that there were benefits to users of the Eurocheque system (not just the 'consumers' referred to in art. 81(3)): holders of Eurocheques could draw cash as needed from credit institutions in European Countries they were visiting, with the benefit of the guarantee provided by their own bank; holders enjoyed the benefit of a period of interest-free credit before the cheque drawn abroad was cleared; holders could make direct payments in the trading sector by cheques from which no deductions would be made and could obtain a better rate of exchange through the application of the market rate by the clearing centre in the holder's own country; and traders accepting the cheques would benefit from the guarantee by the drawee bank and would be reimbursed in full by banks in their country without commission being charged.

The Commission next had to consider whether the restrictions were indispensable for the proper functioning of the Eurocheque system. It noted that in general a cheque drawn on a foreign bank cannot be encashed unless that bank has a branch

[24] See section 2 above.

or correspondent in the place of encashment. By accepting foreign cheques, the payee banks were providing a service to holders who were not their customers nor customers of any other bank in that country, and this service was neither balanced nor reciprocal (popular tourist areas tend not to be in States whose banks issue large numbers of Eurocheques) and the Commission accepted that where such a service was provided collectively, it was indispensable that the terms and conditions for accepting and clearing the cheques concerned be determined in common between the issuing and accepting institutions involved. It further accepted that the lack of reciprocity led to a cash drain for the payee banks, and it must therefore be inherent in the system that there should be common and uniform remuneration for this service. Otherwise there would have to be bilateral negotiations between the then 15,000 banks involved: any centralized clearing system would be impossible, and the cost of processing Eurocheques would increase substantially. The obligation for payee banks not to exceed the maximum rate of commission was also held to be essential to avoid the levying of additional charges and commissions. Finally, the Commission found that the uniform fixing of the maximum guaranteed amount in a given country[25] was indispensable: the system would be unworkable if every person accepting a uniform Eurocheque, particularly in the trading sector, had to make sure each time that the specific maximum amount guaranteed by the issuing institution had not been exceeded, and centralized clearing would be virtually impossible.

However, the Commission emphasized that the decision did not cover *national* agreements between banks or decisions by *national* banking associations to fix levels of commission charged to their customers by issuing institutions, which it suggested should be an area of residual competition. On the question of the scope left for competition (the requirement under art. 81(3) that the agreement should not afford undertakings the possibility of eliminating competition in respect of a substantial part of the products in question) the Commission observed that anyone travelling to a foreign country had a choice between several means of payment, such as cash, travellers' cheques, postal payment orders, credit cards, and cards for automatic teller machines,[26] as well as Eurocheques. Also, there was scope for competition in the relationship between issuing institutions and their customers: for example, the issuing institution could decide how much of the payee's commission to pass on to its customer, as well as the level of its own charges. However, the Commission repeated that this would not be the case if there were agreements at the national level with regard to such charges, so that the customer had no real choice.

In the event, the Commission granted an exemption, but subject to certain requirements designed to ensure transparency. In particular, customers should be

[25] I.e. a Eurocheque issued anywhere by any participating bank is guaranteed up to £100 when used in the UK, up to FB7,000 when used in Belgium, and up to DM400 when used in Germany, even though those sums are not identical. Presumably a standard limit in euros will be introduced for the countries participating in Economic and Monetary Union.

[26] Which, it must be said, include Eurocheque cards themselves.

informed by notices in banks, by leaflets, or by any other suitable method of the costs involved in using uniform Eurocheques abroad, and accepting institutions should state any costs which may be incurred for encashing uniform Eurocheques, and statements should indicate the rate of exchange used and the commissions paid.

However, the exemption was granted in December 1984 only until the termination of the first five-year period on 30 April 1986. It appears that a provisional comfort letter[27] was issued in July 1986 to cover the period until the end of 1987,[28] and during 1987 a new package deal was concluded, entering into effect on 1 January 1988, which did not differ essentially from that approved in Decision 85/77, except that, following moves originally made in 1986, the maximum commission was raised from 1.25 to 1.60 per cent and a minimum commission equivalent to two Swiss francs was introduced. Although the guarantee limit remained unchanged, it was further provided that if they were to be dealt with through the Eurocheque clearing system, Eurocheques should not exceed the equivalent of 600 Swiss francs.

In 1990 the Commission sent Eurocheque International (which had become a co-operative society under Belgian law in 1988) a statement of objections[29] relating to the commissions, the maximum clearing amounts, and an alleged failure to comply with the requirements of Decision 85/77 on the information to be provided for drawers of Eurocheques. However, the Commission also raised the question of the legitimacy of the 'Helsinki Agreement' between the French financial institutions and the Eurocheque Assembly on the acceptance by traders in France of Eurocheques drawn on foreign financial institutions. Its Decision 92/212,[30] relates solely to this aspect, being the first decision to impose financial penalties for a breach of the competition rules in the financial services sector.

The Helsinki Agreement appears to date from 1983, but it was not notified to the Commission during the proceedings leading to the adoption of Decision 85/77, although the Commission did note in that decision that the banks belonging to the Groupement Carte Bleue (all the major French banks) had only opened their trader network to Eurocheques on an experimental basis and on the same terms as to Carte Bleue and Visa cardholders.[31] Following a request for information sent in 1988 as a result of complaints, a French credit institution referred expressly to the Helsinki Agreement, and following further requests Eurocheque International sent a copy of the text to the Commission in 1989, and the Groupement Carte Bleue formally notified it in July 1990; it was formally terminated in May 1991. As the Commission bluntly observed,[32] the Agreement ran totally counter to the package deal: it provided, *inter alia*, that in respect of purchases paid for by Eurocheques, the members of the Groupement Carte Bleue and

[27] An indication by the Commission that it did not propose to take any further action. See Green, Hartley, and Usher, *Legal Foundations of the Single European Market* (Oxford 1991) p. 233.

[28] Commission Decision 92/212 (OJ 1992 L95/50).

[29] The formal notice of the commencement of enforcement proceedings under Regulation 17/62.

[30] OJ 1992 L95/50.

[31] Ibid. para. 22.

[32] Ibid. para. 16.

of Eurocard would charge their affiliated traders a commission, but no greater than that applicable to payments by Carte Bleue and by Eurocard: the essence of the package deal was that traders should receive the full face value of a Eurocheque. The Commission took the view that the Agreement on its clear wording laid down an obligation to charge a commission, and whether or not all the banks applied it, it had as its object the restriction of competition; furthermore, by referring to the charges made for payments by card, the agreement was an agreement as to the amount of commission to be charged, and created an unjustified link between payment by card and payment by Eurocheque, which were two profoundly different means of payment.

The Commission emphasized that one of the grounds for its Decision 85/77 granting an exemption for the uniform Eurocheque system had been the principle that the Eurocheque was free of charge to its payee, the costs being borne by the drawer, and it stated that no multilateral interbank agreement would have been necessary if the paying bank had been free to collect a commission on foreign Eurocheques remitted to it for payment: the package deal agreement was justified precisely because the paying bank received no remuneration from the remittance of the Eurocheque, but received a commission from the issuing bank.

With regard to the effect on trade of the Agreement, the Commission held that it clearly affected trade between Member States since it involved cheques drawn in one Member State by nationals of another Member State, and the effect was appreciable because France was the principal accepting country for Eurocheques. The question of a possible exemption under art. 81(3) was held to be relevant only for the period between formal notification in 1990 and the termination of the agreement in 1991. The Commission took the view that, far from helping the development of Eurocheques in France, the Agreement seemed to be part of a mechanism to impede the growth of Eurocheques in France, the other part of that mechanism being an agreement in 1984 between the members of the Groupement Carte Bleue not to issue Eurocheques for domestic use in France, a provision eventually terminated at the end of 1989 following a decision of the Conseil de la Concurrence[33] in 1988. The Commission concluded that the effect of the Helsinki Agreement was to hamper the development of Eurocheques in France by making French traders pay for a means of payment, the Eurocheque, which was in principle free of charge to them under the package deal agreement. For similar reasons, the agreement was of no benefit to users: according to the Commission, the only category of user to benefit was the French banks, who were to be paid twice for the same service, the only banks in the Community to be so remunerated. Furthermore, the agreement tended towards the elimination of competition since French banks were not only to bill a commission to traders but were to do so at the same rate as that applied to payments by card.

In view of the seriousness of the breach of the competition rules, the Commission decided that fines should be imposed both on the Groupement and

[33] The French national competition authority, Decision No.88-D-37 of 11 Oct. 1988.

on Eurocheque International. In determining these, the view was taken that the French banks had been the instigators of the infringement, although Eurocheque International had agreed to participate, and the Commission calculated that the banks had made 5 million ECU in commissions from traders over the relevant period. It was further stated that the agreement had impeded the development of Eurocheques in France, and it was pointed out that the parties had not, of their own volition, fully informed the Commission of the situation arising from the Helsinki Agreement, a situation which would have influenced the Commission's decision with regard to the package deal itself; indeed they had repeatedly given the Commission an incorrect interpretation of the agreement. In mitigation, however, the Commission accepted that the Agreement had been terminated before it required it to be prohibited, and that it could be criticized itself for not having investigated the Agreement more vigorously at an earlier stage. It also stated that since it was the first decision imposing fines in the banking sector, 'a degree of clemency may be appropriate'. The Commission concluded that fines of 5 million ECU should be imposed on the Groupement Carte Bleue, and of one million ECU on Eurocheque International. Despite its comments on the matter in the statement of reasons for the decision, the Commission did not indicate any disavowal of the view it had taken of the package deal agreement as such.

Part of the decision relating to Eurocheque international was annulled by the Court of First Instance, largely for procedural reasons, and the fine on the Groupement Carte Bleue was reduced to 2 million ECU in Cases T–39 and 40/92 *Groupement des Cartes Bancaires* v. *Commission*.[34]

Another aspect of the Eurocheque system considered by the Commission concerned the agreements or guidelines relating to the production and finishing of Eurocheques and Eurocheque cards, and the selection and prior approval of firms authorized to take part.[35] These matters came before the Commission by way of both complaint and notification under Regulation 17/62. Starting from the premise that because of the guarantee given by the bank, a Eurocheque accompanied by a Eurocheque card is equivalent to a banknote,[36] the Commission accepted that the cheque and card must incorporate certain features and be of uniform quality to protect them from counterfeiting and forgery; the manufacturers therefore had to be able to offer a high-quality product and to comply with stringent security arrangements. On one hand, the Commission considered the prior authorization of paper manufacturers and printers to be justified, and was satisfied that the scheme ensured that those undertakings which fulfilled the necessary conditions would be authorized if they so requested. Therefore the obligation on banks and printers respectively to obtain Eurocheque instruments and paper only from authorized printers or paper producers did not amount to a restriction on competition under art. 81(1). On the other hand, the obligation to obtain finishing

[34] [1994] ECR II–49. [35] Commission Decision 89/95 OJ 1989 (L36/16).
[36] Ibid. para. 15.

services[37] only from authorized firms was held to amount to a restriction of competition under art. 81(1) because the scheme did not here ensure the elaboration of a uniform standard and the authorization of all firms which would meet that standard. Nevertheless, in the context of exemption under art. 81(3), the Commission held that the prior authorization of finishing firms did promote economic progress in that it contributed to the security of the Eurocheque system as a means of international payment, security being an essential factor in retaining user confidence, which was indispensable in payment systems. Furthermore, the users of the Eurocheque system obtained a fair share of the resulting benefit, since a high level of security reduced the risk of the heavy costs which might result from counterfeiting and forgery in payment systems, and the widespread acceptance of Eurocheques was fostered by the security of the system. An exemption was therefore granted for the finishing guidelines until June 2002.

In summary, the Commission has been prepared to accept those features of the Eurocheque system which enable the holder or a trader to obtain the full value when such a cheque is cashed or used for payment in another country, and to accept necessary security requirements in the production of Eurocheques and cards. However, it has not been willing to accept agreements at the national level which go against what it perceives to be the main aim of the system, or which remove the residual competition which might take place at the national level.

4. Other international payments systems

Although it has not taken any formal decisions in the matter, the Commission's 1997 Competition Report[38] indicates its views on the application of the EC competition rules to two international payments systems, SWIFT (Society for Worldwide International Financial Telecommunications sc) which operates a specific international telecommunications network offering secure data communication and processing to financial institutions located all over the world, and whose basic activity is the international transfer of payment messages, and TARGET (Trans-European Automated Real-time Gross settlement European Transfer system), the payments system for the euro.

a) SWIFT

The Commission received a complaint from the French Post Office (La Poste) in July 1996 against SWIFT, which it described as a co-operative owned by over 2,000 banks, and GUF, the French group of SWIFT users, i.e. French banks. SWIFT's

[37] Defined in ibid. para. 30 as the insertion of the bank's name, the personalization and encoding of cheques and cards, lamination of cards, attachment of the signature panel to the cards, and other special features such as the hologram.

[38] *XXVIIth Report on Competition Policy* 1997, pp. 142–5.

rules obliged its members to assist it in determining whether applicant members or participants fulfil the membership criteria. This was one of the roles played by GUF. La Poste had informal contacts with GUF between 1990 and 1994 to establish the terms on which it might become a member of SWIFT. It formalized these contacts by applying to GUF in 1994 to become a member. GUF replied on 29 March 1994 that La Poste did not fulfil the membership criteria because it did not carry on an activity identical to that of credit institutions in a similar competitive environment and under equivalent regulatory conditions. This rejection was confirmed by SWIFT itself. La Poste complained to the Commission, alleging in its complaint that, by denying it admission, the two bodies had infringed arts. 81 and 82 of the Treaty.

The Commission initiated formal proceedings against SWIFT for infringement of art. 82 of the Treaty, and sent a statement of objections. GUF was left out of the proceedings because in the Commission's view its role was simply to advise SWIFT on applications. The statement of objections noted that SWIFT was an essential facility for transmitting electronic payment messages. The Commission based this finding on two considerations. First, SWIFT occupied a monopoly position on the market in international payment message transfer networks. Secondly, to deny membership to an entity would in effect be to exclude it from the international transfer market, SWIFT being the only network providing connections to banks located anywhere in the world. The Commission took the view that SWIFT had abused its dominant position in two ways. First, its current membership criteria were unjustified, as they related to the overall conditions under which applicants pursued their financial activities and not to their involvement in payment systems. Secondly, SWIFT had applied its membership criteria to La Poste in a discriminatory manner.

Although SWIFT replied to the statement of objections, the matter went no further because, following an amicable agreement between La Poste on one hand and SWIFT and GUF on the other, the Commission decided to accept an undertaking proposed by SWIFT. In the undertaking, signed on 26 September 1997, SWIFT promised to grant full access to any institution in the European Union which provided cross-border payment services to the public and fulfilled the criteria laid down by the European Monetary institute (or any successor organization: in other words, now the ECB) for admission to domestic payment systems. The EMI criteria were: (i) the entity was authorized to hold accounts for customers; (ii) its direct participation in one or more EU fund transfer systems processing third-party payments had the approval of the central bank; and (iii) either its public nature ensured little risk of failure, or its financial service activities were supervised by a recognized competent authority.

In the Commission's view, access tor this category would give access, on an equivalent and non-discriminatory basis, to the networks, products, services, working groups, and documentation that were made available to SWIFT members. The Commission published the text of the undertaking[39] on the basis that the case set

[39] OJ 1997 C335.

a precedent and because a large number of entities were potentially interested in access to the SWIFT network.

b) TARGET

While the ECB would no doubt argue that, as the payments system for the euro, TARGET is a matter of monetary policy which should not be subject to competition rules,[40] the Commission set out its views in a letter sent on 23 June 1997. With regard to the applicability of art. 81(1), the letter expressed the view that TARGET could be considered an instrument of monetary policy to which art. 81(1) does not apply in so far as it handles payments directly related to monetary policy, where the ESCB is either the beneficiary or the originator of the payment. Parties involved in these payment transactions do not in its view undertake economic activities, and these activities therefore fall outside the scope of art. 81(1).

On the other hand, the Commission asserted that art. 81(1) does apply to TARGET when it handles interbank payments through which money market operations are settled (arbitrage transactions) and payment operations involving the banks' customers, be they private individuals or corporations (third-party payments). The Commission stated that parties involved in these transactions do undertake economic activities. This was said to be obvious in the case of customer payments, but it was claimed also to hold true in the case of arbitrage transactions because banks have traditionally been actively involved in this type of transaction as a normal part of their business. The Commission did accept that the integration of the euro money market, and hence the conduct of a single monetary policy as required by art. 4(2) of the Treaty, can be achieved only if interbank funds can be rapidly and reliably transferred throughout the euro area, and that TARGET provides speed and reliability, but it took the view that this did not deprive these euro transfers of their economic nature.

The Commission also accepted that the use of TARGET would not be compulsory for these payments. It noted that commercial banks may find it convenient to use TARGET, but that they remain entirely free to avail themselves of other channels. In any event, the Commission declared that even if an obligation to set up and operate TARGET could be derived from the Treaty or the ESCB Statute, such an obligation cannot alter the economic nature of the underlying transactions.

Having concluded that in principle art. 81(1) could apply, the Commission turned to the question of possible exemption under art. 81(3)—despite the fact that no application for exemption had been submitted. The Report indicates that two issues had nevertheless been examined in detail. The first issue was the envisaged uniform end-to-end price for payments handled through TARGET. The Commission stated that this went beyond what it had previously been willing to accept in relation to payment systems. However, while questioning whether in

[40] Such views were expressed privately to the author by members of the legal service of the ECB.

practice some price differentials would be a real impediment to the achievement of these objectives, the Commission's departments acknowledged that TARGET (and the uniform end-to-end price figuring therein) contributed to the fulfilment of at least two legitimate objectives:

- the smooth conduct of monetary policy and the singleness of the money market. The letter fully recognizes the merit of TARGET as an instrument for cross-border arbitrage transactions which are crucial in securing a single money market within the euro area, and
- contributing to risk-reduction policies. Use of TARGET, which is an RTGS (real time gross settlement) system, for large-value payments indeed contributes to reducing systemic risk within the euro area.

The second issue concerned the 'full cost recovery principle' according to which the end-to-end price must cover full handling costs. The Commission indicated that it fully supported the idea that full cost recovery was necessary to avoid unfair competition between TARGET and other payment arrangements. The issue was rather how the EMI and the NCBs, and later the ECB, would guarantee the proper implementation of this principle. The Commission's departments understood that observance of the full cost recovery principle could only be demonstrated *ex post*, some time after the launching of TARGET, since fully reliable figures on the volume of payments handled through TARGET would initially be unavailable. For that reason the Commission asked to be kept informed of further developments. In its view, it would be possible to evaluate within a period of two to three years whether full costs are indeed being recovered. The Commission therefore invited the EMI forthwith to adjust, if necessary, prices according to the results of the evaluation, noting that it is clearly in no one's interest that TARGET's pricing policy should become the object of complaints in the years ahead.

Whatever the precise legal status of this pre-introduction assessment of the compatibility of aspects of TARGET with the competition rules, it appears that the EMI undertook to inform the Commission of any further developments.[41]

5. National banking agreements

Agreements between banks at the national level have been considered by the Commission in the context of Community law with regard to Irish,[42] Belgian,[43] Italian,[44] and Dutch banks.[45] The Decision relating to Belgian banks makes it clear that the agreements in question were notified in October 1962, and the formal

[41] *XXVIIth Report on Competition Policy* 1997, p. 43.
[42] Commission Decision 86/507 (OJ 1986 L295/28).
[43] Commission Decision 87/13 (OJ 1987 L7/27).
[44] Commission Decision 87/103 (OJ 1987 L43/51).
[45] Commission Decision 89/512 (OJ 1989 L253/1).

decision was not adopted until December 1986, twenty four years later! Apart from a request for information in 1975, no real action apparently occurred until, as a result of Case 172/80 *Züchner*,[46] the Commission carried out a Community-wide investigation into charges levied by credit institutions in each of the Member States for the various banking services they provided. The first decision to be adopted related to the Irish banks, which applied in 1984 for negative clearance (i.e. a declaration that art. 81(1) did not apply) with regard to agreements relating to bank opening hours, clearing rules, and a direct debiting scheme, although the Commission's decision made express reference to its investigation in 1981 into bank charges, and emphasized that the notification did not relate to such charges, the agreements existing at the time of the Commission's investigation having been terminated. This indicates that formal decisions are not the only indicator of changes in conduct brought about by the EC competition rules: the other cases similarly indicate that various provisions in the agreements at issue had been terminated by the time the Commission adopted its formal decisions.

The Commission held that the clearing rules and direct debiting scheme did not contain any rules affecting competition within the common market, but perhaps more surprisingly it held also that any restriction of competition resulting from the agreement on bank opening hours was 'not appreciable'. It is respectfully suggested that it would have been more appropriate to find that such an agreement did restrict competition but that it had no appreciable effect on trade between Member States, which was the view taken with regard to an agreement on the minimum charges for safe deposit and safe custody services in the Italian case[47] and with regard to uniform conditions for the hire of safes in the Dutch case.[48] As the Commission put it in the Italian case, the very fact of depositing articles or securities in a safe or in safe custody is an indication that their owner does not intend to use them for trade, and in both cases it was found either that trade between Member States in the use of safes was unlikely to develop to an appreciable extent, or that insignificant use of such services was made by consumers from other Member States.

Similarly in the Italian case, the Commission held that the inter-bank Bancomat (automatic teller) convention, agreements on standing orders and direct debits, and an agreement on the payment of telephone bills (all of which fixed inter-bank commissions) concerned inter-bank services limited to Italy and economic activities which could only be exercised in Italy, so that they did not have an appreciable effect on trade between Member States. Also in the Dutch case, an agreement setting uniform inter-bank commissions for fund-raising transfers was held to have no appreciable effect on trade between Member States, partly because, given their predominantly charitable objective, the transfers concerned had little or no connection with trade in goods or services between Member States. The Commission's view therefore seems to be that charitable activities are not 'trade'.

[46] [1981] ECR 2021. [47] Commission Decision 87/103 (OJ 1987 L43/51) paras. 38–40.
[48] Commission Decision 89/512 (OJ 1989 L253/1) paras. 54 and 58.

The Commission further found in the Italian case that an agreement on foreign exchange and/or non-resident account lire dealings, the aim of which was to set time limits for transfers and to penalize late execution of transfers, placed no obstacle in the way of banks' competitive activity. In the Dutch case, it took the same view with regard to provisions on dealing with documentary credits (requiring compliance with the rules of the International Chamber of Commerce) and orders for acceptance and collection, with regard to circulars on own-account dealing by foreign exchange dealers and on guidelines for transfers in foreign currencies between foreign currency banks (setting the date a transfer was deemed to be received), and an agreement on open-open telephone lines, none of which concerned charges or fees. A regulation on the establishment of foreign exchange reference rates was held no longer to restrict competition appreciably since it took account of market information and was not mandatory. Other matters held not appreciably to affect competition were: an agreement with the postal authorities on charges for postage-paid envelopes, which was found to leave the banks free to decide whether to offer such a service; a decision not to sell gift vouchers, which was treated as a negligible ancillary activity; a circular on forward transactions in foreign currencies which left the banks free to negotiate with their customers; and an agreement under which gifts and bonuses offered as an incentive to savers were to be limited to banking-related gifts and services, since it left banks free to perform their normal activities.

The Belgian case involved formal exemptions under art. 81(3) for three 'conventions' relating to commissions charged in inter-bank relations with regard to transactions in securities, payments originating abroad, and the collection of cheques and commercial bills on behalf of principals abroad. The three agreements were found to restrict competition, particularly to the extent that they prevented banks from entering into alternative arrangements, and they were found to have an effect on trade between Member States, partly because two of them directly concerned foreign exchange transactions or transfers from abroad, partly because national pricing agreements covering an entire Member State may have the effect of consolidating the isolation of a national market, and partly because the Belgian branches of foreign banks were direct emanations of those banks and hence participated in trade between Member States—reasoning similar to that used in the German fire insurance case.[49] However, it was found that the convention on transactions in securities improved the supply of banking services by enabling all the banks to take on for their customers the servicing of the whole range of securities, and those customers received a fair share of the benefit by being able to contact their own bank in connection with transactions in securities with regard to which a different bank performed registrar services. It was further found to be essential to have arrangements determined jointly by the participating banks, but there was still scope for competition because the convention did not govern relations either with issuers of securities or holders of securities.

[49] Case 45/85 *Verband der Sachversicherer* [1987] ECR 405.

The conventions on payments originating abroad and on the collection of cheques and of commercial bills were both found to improve the system of payments, and to be of benefit to users in that the customer could deal with his own bank even if it was not the correspondent of the foreign bank from which the payment derived, and payments were speeded up. The restrictions imposed were held to be indispensable for such collective arrangements: again they were held not to eliminate competition to the extent that they did not govern relations between the banks and their customers.

In the Italian case a formal exemption under art. 81(3) was given to an agreement on the Italian bills and documents collection service, an agreement on the service of collecting bank cheques and similar instruments payable in Italy, and an inter-bank agreement on a new uniform type of lire travellers' cheque. These were held in principle to breach art. 81(1), in the sense of restricting competition, to the extent that they limited, or in some cases eliminated, the freedom of participants (the entire banking sector in Italy) to determine individually the remuneration for the banking services requested or offered. They were also found to affect trade between Member States, partly because they included the Italian branches and subsidiaries of foreign institutions, and the foreign subsidiaries of Italian banks—as mentioned above in the context of the Belgian decision, reasoning similar to that used in the German fire insurance case[50]—and partly because of the volume of Italian international trade and the interpenetration of the national and international capital markets, and because of the fact that some of the services related to trans-frontier operations, which was particularly the case with regard to the lire travellers' cheque.

In determining whether these agreements could benefit from art. 81(3), the Commission emphasized the benefits of standardization and rationalization, stating in para. 53 of its decision that 'as the services involved are banking services the provision of which economic operators can request anywhere in Italy and which require the intervention of one or more banks, the simplification and standardization of services contribute to improving the provision of those services'—an approach similar to that used in the Eurocheques Package Deal decision.[51] Another similarity with that decision is that the Commission observed that under the agreement travellers' cheques were paid in full, free of commission by the paying banks, which facilitated their acceptance by the non-banking sector. It was also found that there were benefits to the consumer in the speedy notification of dishonour under the bills and the document collection and acceptance service, and in the prompt availability of the amount shown on the instrument under the agreement on collecting bank cheques. In the case of the agreement on travellers' cheques, the benefit lay in the ability to obtain every European currency, the assurance for acceptors of being paid in full, and the additional safeguard of reimbursement in the case of non-use, loss, theft, or destruction.

[50] Case 45/85 *Verband der Sachversicherer* [1987] ECR 405.

[51] Commission Decision 85/77 (OJ 1985 L35/43).

The Commission took the view that the restrictions were indispensable for their purpose, and did not afford the possibility of eliminating competition, in particular because the agreements at issue did not directly govern relations between banks and their customers, leaving the possibility of competition at the level of that relationship—again a point made in the Eurocheques case.

In the Dutch case, the only matters held both to restrict competition and to affect trade between Member States were circulars on the simplified clearing procedures for cheques denominated in guilders and foreign currencies. On one hand these were found to prevent banks from entering into bilateral arrangements for even quicker and simpler procedures, but on the other it was accepted that they resulted in an improvement in the payments system, that consumers benefited to the extent that recipients of cheques were credited more rapidly than under that previous system, that the restrictions were indispensable, and that they did not eliminate competition because they did not directly govern relations between the banks and their customers.

All the decisions referred to arrangements which were terminated before the Commission granted negative clearance or a formal exemption. It appears that many of these related to charges to customers, but in the Dutch case the Commission took the unusual step of publishing in an Annex a summary of the contents of eighteen provisions which were withdrawn, perhaps with the intention of indicating more widely the practices which it was not prepared to approve. They all relate directly or indirectly to the relationship between banks and their customers, and with one exception (relating to gifts and bonuses) they all determine commissions to be charged to customers or provide for the passing on of charges to customers.

To summarize the above:

—certain banking activities are recognized as being intrinsically localized and therefore no concern of Community competition law;

—conversely, it is recognized that other banking activities are most effectively performed on a multilateral or collective basis requiring common rules, and those rules may set inter-bank commissions;

—on the other hand, agreements between banks which govern the relationship between banks and their customers are in general regarded as anti-competitive, unless they are necessary e.g. to ensure that the customer receives full face value for a cheque, and in particular agreements relating to charges to customers, breach Community law (assuming they affect trade between Member States).

The European Court of Justice has similarly accepted that certain banking activities may be regarded as essentially localized in its judgment in Cases C–215 and 216/96 *Bagnasco* v. *Banca Popolare di Novara*.[52] As explained earlier in this Chapter, these cases involved a further series of agreements between Italian banks which had

[52] 21 Jan. 1999.

been notified to the Commission in 1993 and most of which the Commission had decided not to examine on the basis, first that they involved activities which were either carried on only in Italian territory or had a very limited influence on trade between Member States, and secondly that the participation of subsidiaries or branches of non-Italian financial establishments was limited. Their validity was nevertheless challenged in litigation before the Italian courts, which referred the matter to the European Court. The question of trade between Member States arose in particular with regard to the rules governing the provision of general guarantees. The Court accepted that it was 'conceivable' that the Italian subsidiaries or branches of banks from other Member States might be obliged to accept the national rules and forgo the possibility of applying more favourable conditions. However, the Court also stated that the Commission's findings had not been called into question during the proceedings, and concluded that standard bank conditions relating to the provision of general guarantees to secure current-account facilities such as those at issue in these cases were, 'taken as a whole', not liable to affect trade between Member States within the meaning of art. 81(1).

6. Cross-border co-operation

The Commission's attitude to cross-border co-operation is shown in its decision[53] granting an exemption under art. 81(3) to a co-operation agreement between the Banque Nationale de Paris and the Dresdner Bank, providing for full and, in principle, exclusive co-operation world-wide between the two banks. The Decision grouped the areas of co-operation under four headings. The first involved co-operation in organizational matters, including joint development of data-processing instruments, and the exchange of information. The second involved co-operation in specific areas of activity: in international financing the two undertakings aimed to arrange their affairs so as to appear to the market 'as one and the same counterparty'. The two were also to co-operate with regard to merchant banking, capital markets, and the placing of securities in third countries (i.e. outside France and Germany). Finally, with regard to securities, derivatives, asset management, and investment banking, the two banks were to co-operate without geographic limits.

The third area of co-operation related more generally to activities outside France and Germany. Here, the two banks had agreed over time to group together their existing banking activities in third countries, with the exception of the United States, either through joint subsidiaries, holdings in each other's subsidiaries, or the creation of a joint holding company. It was also agreed that if one bank did not have the means to supply a customer with the appropriate service for an international transaction, it must refer the customer to the other bank. Furthermore, the

[53] Commission Decision 96/454 (OJ 1996 L188/37).

office representing the banks in third countries would be physically merged while usually retaining autonomy and their own identity.

As far as the French and German markets were concerned, each bank undertook to make available to the other all its services at the best price and in turn to offer its own customers the widest possible range of services provided by the other bank. It was further agreed that if one bank was unable to provide its home customers with an international service, it must call in the other bank or one of their joint entities in a third country. On the other hand, if one bank wished to operate on the other's domestic market by co-operating with a competitor it must obtain the consent of the other, and any co-operation agreement with a third party must be notified to the other bank. However, following negotiations with the Commission, it was agreed that there should not be an absolute right to withhold approval except where the co-operation agreement with a third party involved the utilization of know-how or business secrets received from the other bank or which resulted from their co-operation.

The Commission then analysed the status and market share of the two banks, finding that BNP held about 7 per cent of the French market (but ranked fourth on a balance sheet basis), and DB held about 5 per cent of the German market (but ranked second). Each held less that 1 per cent of the other's market, though DB had about 5 per cent of the Luxembourg market, and BNP had about 3 per cent of that market. Looking at the effects on competition in the domestic markets of France and Germany, the Commission took the view that, despite the previous lack of interpenetration on each others' markets, the agreement would restrict competition, in part because it took the view that the Second Banking Directive[54] and the advent of a single currency would considerably facilitate access to other Community markets. However, turning to third countries (i.e. countries other than France and Germany) the Commission found that because of the 'weak presence' of the two banks, competition would not be appreciably restricted. With regard to international financing, though, the Commission found the agreement to be pro-competitive 'as it will strengthen the position of the two banks internationally so that they will in future be better able to compete against the large international banks, particularly American and Asian banks'.[55] This Decision therefore shows very clearly that the same agreement may restrict competition on the domestic market but increase competition on the international market—one of the long-standing dilemmas of competition policy.

Whatever the restrictive effect on the domestic market, the Commission went on to grant an exemption under art. 81(3). It found that the co-operation would lead to an improvement in both the production and distribution of financial services provided to individuals and undertakings so that, for example, it would be possible to go into one partner's bank and debit a current account held in the other partner's bank. It would thus meet the Commission's objective of improving cross-

[54] See Chapter 6 below. [55] Para. 16.

border payment systems. It was also found that consumers, especially in France and Germany, would benefit from qualitative and quantitative improvements in banking services[56] that the restrictions, in particular the veto on co-operation with a competitor, were indispensable to attain the objectives of the agreement,[57] and that the co-operation envisaged would not enable the two banks to eliminate competition on the French and German markets.[58] Bearing in mind the complexity of the arrangements and the likely impact of European Monetary Union, the Commission granted an exemption, for 10 years, until January 2005.

7. Interest rate agreements

A feature common to all the Commission Decisions on national banking arrangements discussed above is that the agreements notified contained or had contained provisions relating to interest rates, and that the Commission expressly refrained from pronouncing upon those provisions in its decisions.[59] Before the judgment in *Züchner*, the Commission had suggested in answer to a written question in the European Parliament that inter-bank agreements on interest rates could be considered as monetary policy instruments of the Member States.[60] However, following the *Züchner* judgment, Commissioner Andriessen suggested[61] that interest rates should not be governed by inter-bank agreements even if they were approved, authorized, or promoted by the competent national authorities. Subsequently, Commissioner Sutherland was reported as having stated that 'the osmosis which sometimes exists between supervisory authorities and those they supervise blurs a distinction between genuine monetary policy and cartels'.[62]

In the decision relating to the Irish banks[63] the Commission stated that it would 'reserve its position' regarding the arrangements for interest rates. It used the same phrase with regard to deposit interest rates in the Belgian decision.[64] In the Italian case[65] the Commission stated that it maintained the reservation with regard to interest rates on loans and deposits that it had made in the statement of objections. In the Dutch case[66] it stated simply that the decision did not apply to agreements on interest rates, on which again the Commission reserved its position.

One aspect of the matter came before the European Court in Case 267/86 *Van Eycke*[67] which, as well as involving questions of the free movement of capital[68] and freedom to provide services[69] also involved Belgian legislation laying down the maximum rates of interest to be paid on deposits in order to benefit from tax relief,

56 Para. 19.
57 Para. 20.
58 Para. 21.
59 For the earlier history, see Dassesse and Isaacs, *EEC Banking Law* (Lloyds of London, 1985) pp. 37–9.
60 WQ 199/79 (OJ 1979 C213/6).
61 Speech cited in Dassesse and Isaacs, *loc. cit.* p. 38.
62 Agence Europe No. 4543, 6 May 1987, p. 9.
63 Decision 86/507 (OJ 1986 L295/28).
64 Decision 87/13 (OJ 1987 L7/27).
65 Decision 87/103 (OJ 1987 L43/51).
66 Decision 89/512 (OJ 1989 L253/1).
67 [1988] ECR 4769.
68 See Chapter 2 above.
69 See Chapter 5 below.

legislation which appeared to have replaced a previous agreement between banks limiting rates of interest. Here the Court appears to have been taken the view that it was in order for national legislation to lay down the maximum rates of interest payable on deposit accounts in order to benefit from tax exemption, but that it would be a breach of the Treaty competition rules for the legislation to require or incite deposit-holders to follow the terms of a previous agreement between credit institutions (which in practice had not been universally followed). This gives rise to a very subtle distinction: it is permissible for national legislation to lay down rules as to interest rates, but not for national legislation to order banks to follow an agreement reached between the banks. The formal distinction may be easily discerned; but it is doubtful whether such a clear distinction may drawn between the economic effects of one method and of the other.

Following this, the Commission at last committed itself: in November 1989 Sir Leon Brittan stated on record that inter-bank agreements on interest rates limit competition in the same way as price-fixing agreements, and should therefore be avoided or abandoned. On the other hand, he accepted that national administrations could still pursue monetary policy objectives provided they did not encourage the creation or strengthening of unlawful agreements.[70] This aspect of the *Van Eycke* judgment therefore also appears to have laid down policy for the future—at least until monetary policy ceases to be a matter of national concern.

However, the Court has accepted that there may be interest-rate agreements between banks which are not to be regarded as restricting competition. In Cases C–215 and 216/96 *Bagnasco* v. *Banca Popolare di Novara*[71] the question arose as to the legitimacy of an agreement between Italian banks allowing them, in contracts for current account credit facilities, to change the interest rate at any time by reason of changes on the money market. The European Court took the view that the opening of a current account credit facility is a banking transaction which by its nature is linked to the bank's right to change the agreed rate of interest by reference to factors such as the conditions for refinancing of the loan by banks. It concluded that, since any variation in the interest rate depended on objective factors such as changes occurring in the money market, a concerted practice which excluded the right to adopt a fixed interest rate could not have an appreciable restrictive effect on competition, and therefore did not have as its object or effect the restriction of competition within the meaning of art. 81(1). It was further held that it was not necessary to decide whether the banks which were members of the Italian banking association held a collective dominant position precisely because any variation in the interest rate depended on objective factors such as changes in the money market, and therefore such conduct could not under any circumstances constitute an abuse of a dominant position within the meaning of art. 82.

With regard to interest rates as a weapon of monetary policy, art. 4 (formerly art. 3a) of the EC Treaty refers to the 'conduct of a single monetary policy and

[70] Commission Press Release IP(89) 869 of 16 Nov. 1989. [71] 21 Jan. 1999.

exchange rate policy' which is to be 'in accordance with the principle of an open market economy with free competition'. For those participating in EMU after 1 January 1999, monetary policy has, by virtue of art. 105(2) of the EC Treaty, become a matter of Community competence, defined and implemented by the European System of Central Banks, with the primary objective of maintaining price stability. It will not therefore be possible for interest rates which relate to monetary policy to be fixed at the national level. It is evident from the Statute of the ESCB and from the ECB document *The Single Monetary Policy in Stage Three*[72] that the monetary policy instruments available to the ECB operate at the level of the wholesale money markets. It may conduct open-market operations, offer standing facilities, and require credit institutions to hold minimum reserves on accounts with the ESCB, and the interest rates it sets as a matter of monetary policy operate at this level. On the other hand, it is a matter of empirical experience that the interest rates charged at the retail level in relation e.g. to credit cards, store cards, or hire purchase agreements have little direct correlation to the levels of interest rates set by central banks for the purposes of monetary policy.

It may therefore be suggested that national rules governing interest rates for other purposes are not necessarily excluded provided they do not impinge upon the measures taken by the ECB. If the analogy could be taken of prices fixed by the Community under the Common Agricultural Policy, there is a line of case-law which accepts that the price system established by the Regulations in question was applicable solely at the production and wholesale stage, with the result that those provisions left Member States free to take the appropriate measures relating to price formation at the retail and consumption stages, provided they did not jeopardize the aims or functioning of the common organization of the market in question.[73]

8. Block exemptions

The first block exemption regulation to be adopted in the financial services sector involves certain agreements, decisions, and concerted practices relating to insurance.[74] Council Regulation 1534/91[75] empowered the Commission to grant block exemptions in the insurance sector with regard to co-operation concerning the establishment of common risk premium tariffs, the establishment of common standard policy conditions, the common coverage of certain types of risks, the settlement of claims, and the testing and acceptance of security devices and registers of, and information on, aggravated risks. Commission Regulation 3932/92[76] has made use of that power with regard to the first three and the fifth of those possibilities.

72 Sept. 1998.

73 Case 31/74 *Galli* [1975] ECR 47; Cases 16–20/79 *Danis and Others* [1979] ECR 3327.

74 Commission Regulation 3932/92 (OJ 1992 L398/7).

75 OJ 1991 L143/1.

76 OJ 1992 L398/7.

At first sight it might seem surprising that a block exemption should be given to agreements, decisions, and concerted practices on the establishment of common risk premium tariffs, when such hostility has been shown to agreements between banks relating to charges levied on customers. However, the recitals make clear that concerted practices on commercial premiums (i.e. the premiums actually charged to policyholders) are *not exempted*, and art. 4 of the Regulation states that the exemption shall not benefit undertakings or associations of undertakings which agree, or oblige other undertakings, not to use calculations or tables which differ from those established under art. 2 of the Regulation. Art. 3(a) further provides that in order to be exempted the calculations etc. must include an express statement that they are 'purely illustrative'. That Regulation does permit the calculation of the average cost of risk (referred to as 'pure premiums') and the preparation of tables which will yield figures on e.g. the number of claims in a particular period, the number of individual risks insured, the total amounts paid or payable as claims in that period, and the total amount of capital insured. In other words, it is permissible to act together to make available material on the basis of which an informed choice of premium may be made, but not to impose a particular premium.

With regard to standard policy conditions, under art. 5 the exemption extends both to standard policy conditions for direct insurance and to the establishment and distribution of common models illustrating the profits to be realized from an insurance policy involving 'an element of capitalization'. Again, under art. 6, the standard conditions must indicate that they are purely illustrative and must expressly mention the possibility that different conditions may be agreed, and the common models must be established and distributed only by way of guidance. A blacklist of clauses which prevent the exemption from applying is contained in art. 7. These include clauses which exclude losses normally covered by that class of insurance, or make the cover subject to certain conditions, unless in each case there is an explicit indication that each insurer remains free to extend the cover or that each insurer remains free to waive the condition. Other blacklisted clauses include those which impose unnecessary cover, which indicate excesses to be paid by the policyholder, which allow the policy to remain in force if part of the cover is cancelled or premiums are increased or to modify the policy (unless the policyholder expressly consents), which impose a contract period of more that three years in non-life insurance, which impose automatic renewals of more than one year, which require the policyholder to obtain cover for different risks from the same insurer, or which require the policyholder in disposing of the insured property to make the acquirer take over the insurance policy. Furthermore, art. 8 excludes from the exemption agreements etc. which exclude the coverage of certain risk categories because of the characteristics associated with the policyholder. Much of this seems more concerned with consumer protection than with competition policy.

With regard to the common coverage of certain types of risk, the exemption applies under art. 10 to agreements which have as their object the setting up and operation of groups of insurance undertakings or of insurance undertakings and reinsurance undertakings for the common coverage of a specific category of risks in the form of *co-insurance* or *co-reinsurance*. The exemption is subject to an overall limit in that the insurance products underwritten by the participating undertakings or on their behalf in the markets concerned must not exceed 10 per cent (in the case of co-insurance groups) or 15 per cent (in the case of co-reinsurance groups) of all the insurance products that are identical or regarded as similar from the point of view of the risks covered and of the cover provided.[77] This reference to market shares is explained in the recitals on the basis that the mechanism of co-insurance requires uniform policy conditions and commercial premiums, with the result that residual competition between members of a coinsurance group is particularly reduced.

While the exemption for agreements etc. on security devices is perhaps of rather narrow interest, it is noteworthy that the Regulation requires the criteria for evaluation to be objective and to be applied in a non-discriminatory way.[78] Finally, bearing in mind the way in which the participation of branches or subsidiaries of foreign financial service institutions in an otherwise purely national agreement has been held to mean that agreement affects trade between Member States,[79] it is of broader interest to note that the provisions of the Regulation also apply 'where the participating undertakings lay down rights and obligations for the undertakings connected with them' and that 'the market shares, legal acts or conduct of the connected undertakings shall be considered to be those of the participating undertakings'.[80] Connected undertakings are defined in terms strikingly similar to those used in the Seventh Company Law Harmonization Directive on group accounts,[81] as those in which a participating undertaking directly or indirectly owns more than half the capital or business assets, or has the power to exercise more than half the voting rights, or has the power to appoint more than half the members of the supervisory board, board of directors, or bodies legally representing the undertaking, or has the right to manage the affairs of the undertaking. It also includes undertakings which have the same rights and powers over a participating undertaking and other undertakings over which such undertakings have those rights and powers.

9. Merger control

Discussion of connected undertakings leads ineluctably to consideration of mergers. In principle, just as financial service institutions are subject to the general competition rules of the EC Treaty, so they also fall within the scope of the specific merger control legislation, although subject to certain special provisions. The EC Treaty was silent on mergers, although certain types of takeover were eventually

[77] Art. 11.
[78] Art. 15(b).
[79] See e.g. Case 45/85 *Verband der Sachversicherer* [1987] ECR 405.
[80] Art. 16.
[81] Council Directive 83/349 (OJ 1983 L193/1).

held to constitute an abuse of a dominant position.[82] More generally, in 1990 a system of merger control under the EC Treaty came into operation by virtue of Council Regulation 4064/89,[83] which has been amended by Council Regulation 1310/97.[84] Under this legislation, notably arts. 1 and 21, the EC Commission has exclusive competence with regard to 'concentrations' with a 'Community dimension' and Member States are in principle prohibited from applying their national legislation. Thus when the Portuguese authorities purported to block a concentration between a Spanish bank and a Portuguese financial sevices group, which had been approved by the Commission under the Merger Regulation, the Commission issued a decision finding the Potuguese measures to be contrary to art. 21 of the Regulation.[85]

'Concentrations' arise, according to art. 3 of the Regulation, where two or more previously independent undertakings merge, or where one or more persons already controlling one or more undertakings, acquire, whether by purchase of securities or assets, by contract, or by any other means, direct or indirect control of the whole or parts of one or more other undertakings. 'Concentrations with a Community dimension' are defined[86] as those where the aggregate worldwide turnover of all the undertakings concerned is more than €5000 million and the aggregate Community-wide turnover of at least two of the undertakings involved is more than €250 million, unless each of the undertakings concerned achieves more than two-thirds of its aggregate Community-wide turnover in one and the same Member State.

However, under the 1997 amendments, a concentration which does not meet these thresholds nevertheless has a Community dimension where: the combined aggregate world- wide turnover of all the undertakings concerned is more than €2,500 million; in each of at least *three* Member States, the combined aggregate turnover of all the undertakings concerned is more than €100 million; in each of at least three of those Member States, the aggregate turnover of each of at least two of the undertakings concerned is more than €25 million ; and the aggregate Community-wide turnover of each of at least two of the undertakings concerned is more than €100 million. There is an overall exception to these additional criteria where each of the undertakings concerned achieves more than two-thirds of its aggregate Community-wide turnover within one and the same Member State.

However, credit institutions[87] and other financial institutions[88] have been and are still treated differently. In the original version, the figure of €5000 million

[82] Case 6/72 *Continental Can* v. *Commission* [1973] ECR 215.
[83] OJ 1989 L395/1.
[84] OJ 1997 L180/1.
[85] IP/99/774 (20 October 1999).
[86] Art. 1.
[87] In the absence of a more specific definition, that in Council Directive 77/780 on credit institutions (OJ 1977 L322/30) might be taken: 'an undertaking whose business is to receive deposits or other repayable funds from the public and to grant credits for its own account'. For a more detailed discussion see Chapter 6 below.
[88] Defined in Council Directive 92/30 on the supervision of credit institutions on a consolidated basis (OJ 1992 L110/52) as 'an undertaking, not being a credit institution, whose principal activity is to grant credit facilities (including guarantees), to acquire participations or make investments'. For more detailed consideration see Chapter 6 below.

related not to aggregate Community-wide turnover but to one-tenth of their total assets, the figure of €250 million related, not to aggregate Community-wide turnover, but to 'one-tenth of total assets multiplied by the ratio between loans and advances to credit institutions and customers in transactions with Community residents and the total sum of those loans and advances', i.e. a proportion of assets related to the amount of business conducted in the Community, and total turnover within one Member State became 'one-tenth of total assets multiplied by the ratio between loans and advances to credit institutions and customers in transactions with residents of that Member State and the total sum of those loans and advances'.[89]

Following the 1997 amendments, both sets of criteria, instead of turnover, use 'the sum of the following income items as defined in Council Directive 86/635 on the annual accounts and consolidated accounts of banks and other financial institutions, after deduction of value added tax and other taxes directly related to those items, where appropriate:

(i) interest income and similar income;
(ii) income from securities;
- income from shares and other variable yield securities,
- income from participating interests,
- income from shares in affiliated undertakings;

(iii) commissions receivable;
(iv) net profit on financial operations;
(v) other operating income.'[90]

Art.3(a) of the revised regulation goes on to say that the turnover of a credit or financial institution in the Community or in a Member State shall comprise the income items, as defined above, which are received by the branch or division of that institution established in the Community or in the Member State in question, as the case may be.

For insurance companies, the figures relate respectively to the value of gross premiums written, the gross premiums received from Community residents, and the gross premiums received from residents of one Member State.[91] In the amended version, the value of gross premiums written is defined as comprising all amounts received and receivable in respect of insurance contracts issued by or on behalf of the insurance undertakings, including also outgoing reinsurance premiums, and after deduction of taxes and parafiscal contributions or levies charged by reference to the amounts of individual premiums or the total volume of premiums.

It appears that where an undertaking is engaged in more than one type of business, the figures are calculated by using the rules applicable to each type of activity in issue, and adding up the result.[92]

In the present context it may be observed that art. 21(2) of the Regulation pro-

[89] Art. 5(3)(a). [90] Art. 3(a). [91] Art. 5(3)(b).
[92] Commission Decision of 21 November 1990 *Groupe AG/Amev* (OJ 1990 C304/27).

hibits Member States from applying their national legislation to such 'concentrations'. Member States are, however, entitled under art. 21(3) to protect legitimate interests, defined as including 'plurality of the media', by measures compatible with the general principles and other provisions of Community law. This may be of particular importance in the context of the United Kingdom rules on newspaper mergers. Furthermore, by art. 9 of the Regulation, the Commission may refer a notified concentration to the national authorities with a view to the application of national competition law where it considers that a concentration threatens to create or strengthen a dominant position as a result of which effective competition would be significantly impeded on a market within that Member State which presents all the characteristics of a distinct market, whether or not it constitutes a substantial part of the common market. The reason for this convoluted terminology is that, in the context of the single internal market of the EC, the area of a particular State as such is not necessarily a relevant criterion in determining whether competition is adversely affected. Conversely, under art. 22(3) of the Regulation a Member State may request the Commission to take a decision with regard to a concentration which has no Community dimension where it creates or strengthens a dominant position as a result of which effective competition would be significantly impeded in the Member State concerned, to the extent that the concentration affects trade between Member States. Belgium seems to have referred the takeover of Dan-Air by British Airways to the Commission under this provision.[93] To put it bluntly, the effect is that for mergers falling within the scope of the Regulation, national law cannot be applied unless the Commission so determines. Thus a Portuguese decision blocking a concentration approved by the Commission was declared to be in breach of the Regulation by the Commission.[94]

[93] Agence Europe No. 5880, 16 Dec. 1992.
[94] IP/99/774 (20 October 1999).

5

Cross-border financial services: the Treaty rules

1. Introduction

The extent to which an undertaking operating in the financial services sector in one Member State may develop a business presence or sell its financial products in other Member States involves the EC Treaty rules on free movement of persons and freedom to provide services. Before its judgment in the German insurance case,[1] the Court seems generally to have avoided drawing a clear distinction between the Treaty terms free movement of workers, freedom of establishment, and freedom to provide services. However, it is suggested that there is little that is specific to financial service institutions with regard to the free movement of workers,[2] although employees sent by their employer into another Member State to help perform a contract there or to sell their employer's financial products appear to fall within the scope of the freedom to provide services rather than that of the free movement of workers.[3]

It is therefore the EC Treaty rules on freedom of establishment and freedom to provide services which are mainly at issue in the present context, although in the international context both these concepts fall within the scope of the General Agreement on Trade in Services (GATS), which treats what the EC Treaty terms establishment as the supply of services through commercial presence[4] or through presence of natural persons.[5] As far as the EC Treaty rules on establishment and provision of services are concerned, two common features may noted at the outset. The first is that art. 43 (formerly art. 52) on establishment allows activities to be pursued 'under the conditions laid down for its own nationals by the law of the country where such establishment is effected' and art. 50(1) (formerly art. 60(1)) on services states that a person providing a service may temporarily pursue his activity

[1] Case 205/84 *Commission* v. *Germany* [1986] ECR 3755.

[2] For a discussion of the Treaty rules on free movement of workers, see Green, Hartley and Usher, *The Legal Foundations of the Single European Market* (Oxford 1991) pp. 93–4.

[3] Case C–113/89 *Rush Portuguesa* v. *Office National d'Immigration* [1990] ECR I–1417. This involved the performance of a contract by a Portuguese firm in another Member State, using its own employees, at a time when under the Portuguese Act of Accession free movement of workers was still restricted but there was immediate freedom to provide services. Similarly, in Case C–43/93 *Vander Elst* v. *OMI* [1994] ECR I–3803, a Belgian firm was able to send a team of employees including Moroccans to perform a contract in France.

[4] GATS art. 1(2)(c).

[5] GATS art. 1(2)(d).

in the State where the service is provided 'under the same conditions as are imposed by that State on its own nationals'. At first sight therefore, the Treaty provisions essentially provide for the elimination of discrimination.[6] However, subsequent case-law has taken them further. In Case C–55/94 *Gebhard*[7] it was accepted that where the taking up or the pursuit of a specific activity is subject to certain conditions in the host Member State, a national of another Member State intending to pursue that activity must in principle comply with them, but it was asserted in general terms that national measures liable to hinder or make less attractive the exercise of fundamental freedoms guaranteed by the Treaty must fulfil four conditions: they must be applied in a non-discriminatory manner; they must be justified by imperative requirements in the general interest; they must be suitable for securing the attainment of the objective which they pursue; and they must not go beyond what is necessary in order to attain it. Furthermore, the Court emphasized that Member States must take account of the equivalence of diplomas and, if necessary, proceed to a comparison of the knowledge and qualifications required by their national rules and those of the person concerned. The provisions governing establishment and services thus appear to be interpreted very similarly to the rules governing the elimination of measures equivalent to quantitative restrictions in the context of the free movement of goods,[8] a matter considered in more detail later in this Chapter. Nevertheless, the Treaty provisions on establishment and services do not necessarily mean that an undertaking authorized to offer a financial service activity in one Member State will be able to establish itself or offer services into another Member State if it does not comply with the local rules. Thus in Case C–222/95 *Parodi* v. *Banque de Bary*,[9] where the loan at issue had been granted in 1984, it was accepted that before the entry into force of the Second Banking Directive[10] there were within the banking sector imperative reasons relating to the public interest capable of justifying the imposition by the Member State of destination of conditions regarding access to the activity of credit institutions and their supervision which went beyond the minimum conditions required by the First Banking Directive[11] and already implemented in the Member State of origin. Hence the completion of the internal market in the financial services sector has required the enactment of complex Community legislation.

The second common feature is that the rules on establishment and services are drafted in terms of natural persons, and are extended to companies and other legal persons by art. 48 (formerly art. 58), paragraph 1 of which provides that companies or firms formed in accordance with the law of a Member State and having their registered office, central administration, or principal place of business within the Community are to be treated in the same way as natural persons who are nationals of the Member States for the purposes of establishment and provision of services.

[6] Case 2/74 *Reyners* v. *Belgium* [1974] ECR 631.
[7] [1995] ECR I–4165.
[8] EC Treaty arts. 28–30 (formerly arts. 30–6).
[9] [1997] ECR I–3899.
[10] OJ 1989 L386/1.
[11] Council Directive 77/780 on credit institutions (OJ 1977 L32/30).

Leaving aside the conceptual problems to which this gives rise,[12] it is clearly the case that a company may be formed in accordance with the law of a Member State and yet be partly or wholly controlled by citizens of or undertakings from non-Member States, so the analogy with nationals of Member States is not perhaps wholly appropriate, and this situation has given rise to special provisions in Community implementing legislation, notably in the Second Banking Directive[13] and the Investment Services Directive.[14]

2. Establishment

a) Scope of the freedom of establishment

Quite apart from the general rules on freedom of establishment, in the original form of the Treaty there were restrictive provisions with regard to certain aspects of the establishment of financial institutions. The second paragraph of art. 57 of the original EEC Treaty required the Council to act by unanimity on measures concerned with the protection of savings, in particular the granting of credit and the exercise of the banking profession. One of the more positive results of the Single European Act was that by virtue of arts. 6 and 16 of that Act, this special provision with regard to the protection of savings etc. was deleted and this became an area where the Council could act by a qualified majority in co-operation with the European Parliament. Following the further amendments introduced by the Maastricht Treaty, measures under what is now art. 47 of the EC Treaty fall within the scope of co-decision between the Council and Parliament under art. 251 (formerly art. 189b).

Establishment as defined in art. 43 of the Treaty includes the setting up of agencies, branches, or subsidiaries and the right to set up and manage undertakings, in particular companies or firms within the meaning of art. 48(2), as well as the right, more relevant to natural persons, to take up and pursue activities as self-employed persons. In the light of this, and providing a link with the monetary provisions of Community law, it may be observed that from the outset the Directives on the movement of capital[15] enacted under the original version of the EEC Treaty required Member States to permit direct investments (defined as relating to the establishment and extension of branches of new undertakings belonging solely to the person providing the capital), and the acquisition in full of existing undertakings, or participation in new or existing undertakings with a view to establishing or maintaining lasting economic links, and also include reinvestment of profits with a view to maintaining lasting economic links.

[12] See section 2 below.

[13] Council Directive 89/646 (OJ 1989 L386/1).

[14] Council Directive 93/22 (OJ 1993 L141/27).

[15] Council Directive of 11 May 1960 (JO 1960 p. 921), as amended by Council Directive 63/21 (JO 1963 p. 62) and Council Directive 86/566 (OJ 1986 L332/22). Replaced by Council Directive 88/361 (OJ 1988 L178/5). See Chapter 2 above.

As indicated above, in this area of the law the European Court was initially rather reluctant to make a clear distinction between establishment and services.[16] However, in the 1986 insurance cases,[17] to the extent that they involved national rules requiring establishment before an undertaking could be authorized to provide services, the Court endeavoured to make a clear distinction between establishment and services, holding that if an undertaking is established in another Member State, even by means of a branch or permanent agency, it may not invoke the provisions relating to services. Whilst this may be justifiable on a literal interpretation of the provisions relating to services, which in effect define services as economic activities that do not fall within the other freedoms,[18] it hardly accorded with the assumptions on the basis of which some undertakings had established themselves in other Member States.[19] This judgment appears nevertheless to have influenced the drafting of Council Directive 88/357,[20] the second non-life insurance Directive, art. 3 of which in effect deemed any permanent presence, including a mere office managed by the undertaking's own staff or by a person who was independent but had permanent authority to act for the undertaking, to be an establishment, but art. 13 of which required that undertakings established in a Member State should be allowed to cover certain risks by way of provision of services. The assumption appears to have been that the same undertaking may be regarded as being established in another Member State for some purposes but not others, and that it may operate by way of provision of services in the context of those activities with regard to which it cannot be regarded as established. While art. 13 of the 1988 Directive has been repealed by art. 37 of the third non-life insurance Directive,[21] introducing a system of home-state control in this sector, the general legal issue remains: may an undertaking with a limited permanent presence in another Member State offer its other activities by way of provision of services?[22] It has subsequently been made clear in Case C–55/94 *Gebhard*[23] that a provider of services, within the meaning of the Treaty, may equip him or herself in the host Member State with the infrastructure necessary for the purposes of performing the services in question, and that the temporary nature of the provision of services, envisaged in the third paragraph of art. 50 of the EC Treaty, is to be determined in the light of its duration, regularity, periodicity, and continuity. On the other hand it was also stated that a national of a Member State who pursues a professional activity on a stable

[16] See e.g. Case 48/75 *Royer* [1976] ECR 497 pp. 509–10.

[17] For the purposes of this volume, reference will be made to Case 205/84 *Commission* v. *Germany* [1986] ECR 3755.

[18] Art. 50 (formerly art. 60).

[19] For example, it raised the question whether a lawyer setting up an office in another Member State could invoke the provisions of Council Directive 77/249 on the exercise by lawyers of freedom to provide services (OJ 1977 L78/17). See Usher, 'Establishment, Services and Lawyers' *Scots Law Times*, 23 Feb. 1979, pp. 69–70.

[20] OJ 1988 L172/1.

[21] Council Directive 92/49 (OJ 1992 L228/1).

[22] For an affirmative answer, see Edward, 'Establishment and Services: an Analysis of the Insurance Cases' (1987) 12 *ELRev*. 231.

[23] [1995] ECR I–4165.

and continuous basis in another Member State where he holds himself out from an established professional base to, amongst others, nationals of that State comes under the provisions relating to the right of establishment and not those relating to services. It is suggested that this makes the distinction a question of fact.

If an undertaking does establish a permanent presence in another Member State then, whatever form that establishment takes, it is clear from Case 270/83 *Commission* v. *France*[24] that Member States may not treat companies differently for tax purposes depending on the type of establishment present within their jurisdiction. It was there held, in the context of French legislation granting shareholders' tax credits to French insurance companies but not to branches or agencies in France of foreign insurance companies, that France could not treat the branches of foreign insurance companies whose main offices were in other Member States differently from French-based insurance companies which were subsidiaries of those foreign insurance companies. In other words, branches (which are a part of the foreign undertaking in another Member State) and subsidiaries (which are formed under local law but controlled by the foreign undertaking) had to be treated the same way, both being forms of establishment recognized in art. 43.[25] It was also made clear in that case that there was no way that restrictions could be imposed on the freedom of establishment in order to prevent tax evasion. Also in the context of branches, the Court held in Case C–330/91 *R* v. *Inland Revenue Commissioners* ex p. *Commerzbank*[26] that a German company which traded in the United Kingdom through a branch established there but which was fiscally non-resident in the United Kingdom was entitled to receive interest on the repayment of tax which should not have been charged to it if an undertaking resident in the United Kingdom would have received interest on such a repayment; it made no difference that the only reason for the repayment of the tax was the fact that the German company was non-resident. A similar approach was taken in Case C–264/96 *ICI* v. *Colmer,*[27] where tax relief for a holding company depended on the residence of its subsidiaries. It has also been held to be a breach of the Treaty for a Member State to refuse tax relief to a transaction within a group of companies because a company involved in the transaction was incorporated in another Member State if relief would have been granted if the company had been incorporated in the first State.[28]

On the other hand, where a non-resident taxpayer operating in a Member State through a branch is only liable for tax on the profits arising from its activities in that State, it is not regarded as discriminatory for that taxpayer only to be allowed to set off losses incurred on its activities in that State, provided resident taxpayers are not treated more favourably.[29] In this context, residents are not regarded as being

[24] [1986] ECR 273.

[25] See also Case C–311/97 *Royal Bank of Scotland* v. *Elliniki Dimosio* (29 Apr. 1999) and Case C-307/97 *Saint-Gobain* v. *FZA Aachen-Innenstadt* (21 September 1999).

[26] [1993] ECR I–4017.

[27] [1998] ECR I–4695.

[28] Case C–1/93 *Halliburton Services* v. *Staatssecretaris van Financiën* [1994] ECR I- 1137.

[29] Case C–250/95 *Futura Participations* v. *Administration des Contributions* [1997] ECR I–2471.

treated more favourably if they can set off losses on activities anywhere, but have to pay tax on the profits arising from their activities anywhere.

In the light of this apparent general principle that Member States must not discriminate between forms of establishment authorized under the Treaty, it is intriguing to note that the Second Banking Directive[30] distinguishes between branches and subsidiaries, treating the establishment of branches in the same way as the supply of services from another Member State, subject in principle to home State control, whilst the establishment of a subsidiary requires host State authorization, albeit in consultation with the home State, under art. 7 of the Directive. A similar distinction is made in the 1993 Directive on investment services in the securities field[31] and in the 1992 Directives on life assurance[32] and non-life insurance.[33] While administratively it may be convenient that a subsidiary formed under the law of the host State should be authorized in the host State, it may be wondered whether the discriminatory treatment with regard to branches, which in principle need only be authorized[34] by the home State, is justifiable in terms of general Community law.

b) Who may benefit?

While a self-employed natural person may clearly move him or herself and his or her business to another Member State under the principle of freedom of establishment, the parallel between natural and legal persons breaks down when a company or other legal person attempts to move its primary establishment. In so far as an undertaking formed in one Member State may wish to move its business activities to another Member State without re-registering as a company or firm formed under the law of the host State, this matter had long been thought by legal theorists to raise complex problems of the recognition of the artificial legal persons of another legal system,[35] and indeed art. 293 (formerly art. 220) of the EC Treaty has from the outset envisaged the need for conventions between Member States on the mutual recognition of companies or firms and on the retention of legal personality in the event of the transfer of their 'seat' from one country to another. However, the judgment of the Second Chamber in Case 79/85 *Segers*[36] stated that it was not

[30] Council Directive 89/646 (OJ 1989 L386/1). For a suggested explanation, see Brittan, 'The Internal Market for Financial Institutions: Legal implications for their secondary establishments' (1993) *JIBFL* 3.

[31] OJ 1993 L141/27.

[32] Council Directive 92/96 (OJ 1992 L360/1).

[33] Council Directive 92/49 (OJ 1992 L228/1).

[34] For details of the authorization system see Chapter 6 below.

[35] It had been held in Belgium, before UK accession, that an English company moving its primary establishment to Belgium became wholly subject to Belgian company law (Belgian Cour de Cassation, 12 Nov. 1965, *Pasicrisie Belge* 1966 I 336), and it would appear that in French law a company would in principle be regarded as a nullity if its '*siège réel*' was different from the country of incorporation. (See e.g. Renauld, 'La reconnaissance mutuelle des sociétés dans le Marché Commun', *Revue pratique des sociétés civiles et commerciales*, 1968, p. 211.)

[36] [1986] ECR 2375.

relevant that a company registered in one Member State operated solely in another Member State, requiring such a company in effect to be granted equal treatment with companies of the host State despite its registered office being in another State; admittedly, however, this case was concerned with technical matters of social security.

The views of the legal theorists appear to have been proved correct in Case 81/87 *R* v. *HM Treasury* ex p. *Daily Mail*,[37] which involved an attempt by an English- registered company to move its central management and control to the Netherlands, which as a matter of company law was perfectly feasible under both systems. However, the UK Treasury wished to subject the move to certain conditions which the Daily Mail claimed to restrict its freedom of establishment under the EC Treaty. On a reference to the European Court, broader issues were nevertheless canvassed: it was pointed out that companies exist only by virtue of national legislation and that the Treaty rules on freedom of establishment did not overcome the national law problems of retention of legal personality on the transfer of the registered office or real head office to another Member State, so that they did not confer a right to transfer central management and control to another Member State. Hence there is no Community law right for a company to move its primary establishment, so that a company incorporated under a system, such as the French, which requires the '*siège réel*' to remain in the State of incorporation, will not be able to take advantage of primary establishment, and in other systems restrictions and conditions may be imposed. It was suggested that in the case of companies the right of establishment would usually be exercised by the setting up of agencies, branches, or subsidiaries, and it was further pointed out that by virtue of art. 221 prohibiting discrimination against nationals of other Member States with regard to participation in the capital of companies or firms, a company could take part in the incorporation of a company in another Member State. On the other hand, it is now clear that a company registered in one Member State may set up a branch in another Member State even if it has never traded in the Member State of registration, and even though the practical consequence may be to escape payment of capital taxes which would have been due if the company had been registered in the host State.[38]

In the light of this, it is interesting to observe that the recitals to the Second Banking Directive[39] oblige Member States to ensure that the head office of a credit institution is situated in the same Member State as the registered office, and that authorization must be refused where it is clear that the credit institution has opted for the legal system of one Member State for the purpose of evading the stricter standards in force in another Member State in which it intends to carry on or carries on the greater part of its activities. A similar formulation was used in the recitals to the 1993 Investment Services Directive.[40] In the UK implementation in the

[37] [1988] ECR 5483.

[38] Case C–212/97 *Centros* v. *Ervhervs-og Selskabsstyrelsen* (9 Mar. 1999).

[39] OJ 1989 L386/1.

[40] Council Directive 93/22 (OJ 1993 L141/27).

Banking Co-ordination (Second Council Directive) Regulations 1992,[41] regulations 25 and 28 provide for the refusal or revocation of authorization to a credit institution incorporated in or formed under the law of the United Kingdom whose principal place of business is (or in the case of revocation, may be) outside the United Kingdom. This approach has been further reinforced by European Parliament and Council Directive 95/26,[42] which requires[43] that a credit institution which is a legal person must have its head office in the same Member State as its registered office, and that any other credit institution should have its head office in the Member State which issued its authorization and in which it actually carries on its business—which appears to limit the rights of primary establishment of credit institutions which are not legal persons. Be that as it may, the Directive also provides[44] that Member States should require the head offices of insurance undertakings to be situated in the same Member State as their registered offices.

The clear import of all this is that, particularly in the banking sector, there is to be no Delaware in Europe, even if it might be hoped that the company law harmonization programme would ensure that no Member State had an appreciably weaker system of company law than the others.

On the other hand, in the light of what has happened in the financial services sector, it is worth observing that where establishment was effected by natural persons, the European Court was for many years unwilling to enter into discussion as to whether a qualification obtained in one Member State is equivalent to the qualification required in the host Member State, unless rules of either national or European Community law provided for such recognition.[45] However, more recently, for example in Case C–55/94 *Gebhard*,[46] the European Court has asserted that Member States must take account of the equivalence of diplomas and, if necessary, proceed to a comparison of the knowledge and qualifications required by their national rules and those of the person concerned.

Where there are rules of Community law providing for the recognition of qualifications, it would appear that they may be invoked by nationals of the host State against their own public authorities as well as by nationals of other Member States.[47]

[41] SI 1992 No. 3218.

[42] OJ 1995 L168/7. This Directive was enacted as a response to the collapse of the Bank of Credit and Commerce International (BCCI).

[43] Inserting a new art. 3(2a) into Directive 77/780 (OJ 1977 L32/20).

[44] Art. 3(1).

[45] Cf. Case 136/78 *Ministère Public* v. *Auer* [1979] ECR 437, where the Court held that France could not be required to recognize an Italian veterinary qualification in the absence of any national or Community legislation to that effect, and Case 271/82 *Auer* v. *Ministère Public* [1983] ECR 2727, where it was held that France was obliged to recognize that qualification following the expiry of the time limit for implementing Council Directive 78/1026 (OJ 1978 L362/1) on the mutual recognition of qualifications in veterinary medicine.

[46] [1995] ECR I–4165.

[47] See e.g. Case 115/78 *Knoors* [1979] ECR 399, where a Dutchman who had worked as a plumber in Belgium invoked an EC Directive to be able to work as a plumber in the Netherlands despite not having the Dutch qualification, and Case 246/80 *Broeckmeulen* v. *Huisarts Registratie Commissie* [1981] ECR 2311, where a medical doctor of Dutch nationality who had qualified in Belgium invoked the EC

3. Services

a) Nature and status

Art. 49 (formerly art. 59) of the EC Treaty provides for the abolition of restrictions on freedom to provide services 'in respect of nationals of Member States who are established in a Member State of the Community other than that of the person for whom the services are intended', subject to the caveat in art. 50 that to be considered as services, activities must not be governed by the provisions relating to the free movement of goods, capital, and persons. Whilst the basic aim of the provisions on freedom of establishment may be to achieve equal treatment for somebody establishing himself in a particular Member State with the nationals or companies of that Member State, equal treatment with nationals is not necessarily the main problem with regard to provision of services. This was realized in the earliest cases, such as *Van Binsbergen*,[48] and *Coenen*,[49] which both involved the provision of services across a border by persons who were nationals of the country in which the service was to be provided, but resident in another Member State. The *Coenen* case also illustrates the difficulties of classification in this area mentioned in the context of freedom of establishment: it involved a Dutch national acting as an insurance intermediary who resided in Belgium and had an office in the Netherlands, faced with a Dutch requirement that he should reside in the Netherlands. This was treated by the Court as restricting his freedom to provide services, yet according to the criteria laid down in the German insurance case[50] the office as a permanent presence appears to constitute establishment, so that the question of freedom to provide services could not arise. However, the solution appears in Case C–55/94 *Gebhard*[51] where it was stated that a provider of services, within the meaning of the Treaty, may equip him or herself in the host Member State with the infrastructure necessary for the purposes of performing the services in question, and that the temporary nature of the provision of services, envisaged in the third paragraph of art. 50 of the EC Treaty, is to be determined in the light of its duration, regularity, periodicity, and continuity.

The legal need to distinguish establishment from services arises from the fact that under art. 50, in order to be considered as services, activities must not be governed by the provisions relating to the free movement of goods, capital, and persons. In other words, provision of services is treated as a residual category to be applied only if the situation does not fall under one of the other Treaty freedoms; implicit in this appears to be the idea that the other freedoms and provision of services are mutually exclusive. It may however be wondered whether this concept remains

Directive on recognition of medical qualifications so as to work as a general practitioner in the Netherlands, despite not having undergone the special training for general practice required for those who qualified in the Netherlands.

[48] Case 37/74 [1974] ECR 1229.

[49] Case 39/75 [1975] ECR 1547.

[50] Case 205/84 *Commission* v. *Germany* [1986] ECR 3755.

[51] [1995] ECR I–4165.

appropriate in the modern single internal market, and some of the modern case-law is difficult to reconcile with the wording of the Treaty. In Case C–484/93 *Svensson and Gustavsson* v. *Ministre du Logement*[52] it was held that loans from a bank in another Member State to buy a house fell within the scope of the 1988 Directive on capital movements,[53] but that such transactions also[54] constituted services within the meaning of what is now art. 49. This approach was subsequently criticized by A.-G. Tesauro in his Opinion in Case C–118/96 *Safir* v. *Skattemyndigheten i Dalarnas Län*.[55] He suggested that the concepts should be kept separate and that a narrower concept of capital movements should be adopted. However, in its judgment in that case[56] the Court held it to be a breach of art. 49 for Sweden to impose a different tax regime for insurance policies purchased from providers outside Sweden which would have the effect of deterring Swedish residents from taking out such policies, even though it was intended to achieve tax neutrality between policies purchased inside and outside Sweden. However, the Court added that the decision on this point made it unnecessary to determine whether the legislation was also incompatible with arts. 56 and 58 (formerly arts. 73b and 73d) on capital movements—even though under the express terms of art. 50 services are only services within the meaning of the Treaty to the extent that they do not fall under one of the other Treaty freedoms, and it might therefore have been expected that the first question should be whether the matter fell under the capital movement rules. Indeed, the Court confirmed that a mortgage fell within the scope of capital movements as defined in the Directive in Case C–222/97 *Trummer and Mayer*,[57] and further held that this interpretation should continue to apply to the free movement of capital under art. 56. However, in Case C–410/96 *Ambry*[58] it was held that for France to require the compulsory financial security provided by a travel agent to be guaranteed by a credit institution or insurance company situated in France breached the Treaty rules on freedom to provide services, although the list in the Annex to the 1988 capital movements Directive expressly includes guarantees granted by non-residents to residents.[59]

b) The scope of the freedom

Many of the basic parameters of the freedom to provide services were laid down in the *Van Binsbergen*[60] case. This involved a Dutch national residing in Belgium who acted as an unqualified legal adviser before Dutch social courts, and found himself faced with Dutch legislation requiring legal representatives to be established in the Netherlands. Apart from the direct effect of the prohibition against discrimination on the grounds of nationality or residence, three main points arise from the judgment. First, a requirement of habitual residence or establishment in the host State could deprive art. 49 of all useful effect, making it impossible to provide services

[52] [1995] ECR I–3955.
[53] OJ 1988 L178/5.
[54] Para. 11.
[55] [1998] ECR I–1897 pp. 1905–7.
[56] Ibid.
[57] 16 Mar. 1999.
[58] 1 Dec. 1998.
[59] Annex I, heading IX A.
[60] Case 37/74 [1974] ECR 1229.

within the meaning of that provision. Secondly, however, requirements[61] imposed on the person providing the service do not breach the Treaty where they are justified in the 'general good', and those rules are binding upon any person established in the State where the service is provided.[62] As further developed in Case C–55/94 *Gebhard*,[63] such rules must be applied in a non-discriminatory manner; they must be justified by imperative requirements in the general interest; they must be suitable for securing the attainment of the objective which they pursue; and they must not go beyond what is necessary in order to attain it. The third point which was laid down in *van Binsbergen* is that a Member State may take measures to prevent the exercise of the freedom to provide services by a person whose activity is entirely or principally directed towards its territory for the purpose of evading the rules which would be applicable to him if he were established within that State—a view whose practical results appear to be similar to those of the *Daily Mail* case.[64]

To the extent that freedom to provide services may, like freedom of establishment, be regarded as based on the principle of non-discrimination, similar problems of recognition of qualifications and compliance with local requirements arise. However, in Cases 110 and 111/78 *Van Waesemael*[65] it was held that Belgium could not require a French employment agency to be licensed under its legislation when it was already licensed and subject to proper supervision in France (in fact under legislation implementing the same international convention as the Belgian legislation). On the other hand, in Case 279/80 *Webb*,[66] which involved an English undertaking supplying temporary staff to undertakings in the Netherlands, it was held that, in particular given the sensitivity of the matter, the host Member State could require the undertaking to be licensed under its scheme, although it could not require proofs and guarantees already given in the State of establishment to be repeated. With regard to personal qualifications, Case C–55/94 *Gebhard*[67] makes it clear that Member States must take account of the equivalence of diplomas, and if necessary proceed to a comparison of the knowledge and qualifications required by their national rules and those of the person concerned.

However, if the aim of freedom to provide services is the removal of obstacles to the provision of services, rather than equal treatment with host State nationals, the question arises how far such freedom should go. That the Treaty provisions on freedom to provide services may be so interpreted is evidenced by the fact that they have been held to give rights not only to those who provide services in other Member States, but also to those who seek to receive services in other Member States. Cases 262/82 and 26/83 *Luisi and Carbone*[68] are perhaps chiefly remembered for having held that what was then art. 106 on current payments, providing *inter*

[61] In the case, the Court referred to 'professional rules'.

[62] An approach which appears to anticipate that taken in Case 120/78 *Rewe* v. *Bundesmonopolverwaltung für Branntwein* [1979] ECR 649, the '*Cassis de Dijon*' case, with regard to the free movement of goods.

[63] [1995] ECR I–4165.

[64] Case 81/87 [1988] ECR 5483.

[65] [1979] ECR 35.

[66] [1981] ECR 3305.

[67] [1995] ECR I–4165.

[68] [1984] ECR 377. See Chapter 1 above.

alia that payments to creditors in their own currency relating to the movement of goods or services are to be liberalized to the extent that the movement of the goods or services has been liberalized between Member States, was capable of giving rise to enforceable individual rights. However, the cases involved Italian nationals who had exported foreign currency from Italy for the purpose of tourism and to receive medical treatment; in order to find that these payments related to the provision of services, the Court expressly held that in order to enable services to be provided, the person providing the service may go to the Member State where the person for whom it is provided is established, or else the latter may go to the State in which the person providing the service is established, even though only the first situation is mentioned in art. 50(3). It concluded that 'the freedom to provide services includes the freedom, for the recipients of services, to go to another Member State in order to receive a service there, without being obstructed by restrictions, even in relation to payments and that tourists, persons receiving medical treatment and persons travelling for the purpose of education or business are to be regarded as recipients of services'.

It may be submitted that the terms of this judgment go beyond treating the freedom to provide services as requiring no more than non-discrimination. Indeed, on the facts in Case C–484/93 *Svensson and Gustavsson* v. *Ministre du Logement*,[69] non-Community nationals resident in Luxembourg taking a loan from a bank in Belgium were held to fall within the Treaty rules on freedom to provide services, although the judgment does not discuss their personal status.

c) Permitted restrictions

Despite the terms of art. 46(1), which refer to 'special treatment for foreign nationals on grounds of public policy, public security or public health', there does not appear to be any direct equivalent in the field of the provision of services of art. 30, which recognizes as legitimate certain restrictions on the movement of goods, i.e. restrictions justified on grounds of public morality, public policy, and public security, the protection of health and life of humans, animals, or plants, the protection of national artistic, historic, or archaeological treasures, and the protection of industrial and commercial property, provided of course that such restrictions do not constitute a means of arbitrary discrimination or a disguised restriction on trade between Member States. It may also be observed that this concept of measures justified on grounds of public policy was expressly extended to monetary movements with effect from 1 January 1994 by art. 58 (formerly art. 73d) of the EC Treaty, introduced by the Maastricht Treaty.[70] In the context of services, it may be submitted that art. 46(1) relates to the persons performing the service rather than to the service itself.[71] It is therefore intriguing to observe that the Court has invented

[69] [1995] ECR I–3955.

[70] See Chapter 2 above.

[71] Council Directive 64/221 (OJ 1964 p. 850) 'on the co-ordination of special measures concerning the movement and residence of foreign nationals which are justified on grounds of public policy,

permissible restrictions which parallel art. 30 and the 'mandatory requirements' recognized in the context of non-discriminatory restrictions on the free movement of goods under the *Cassis de Dijon*[72] case-law. So, for example, the Court in Case 52/79 *Debauve*[73] recognized that a Member State may enforce its public policy with regard to prohibition against advertizing on television services provided from another Member State; and in Case 67/79 *CODITEL* v. *Ciné Vog*[74] the Court recognized that intellectual property rights in a film could be protected against a television showing of that film transmitted from another Member State.

In the context of the free movement of goods, mandatory requirements may be defined as requirements which Member States may in the absence of Community rules impose on goods imported from other Member States even though that may have the effect of restricting or even rendering impossible such importation.[75] In this respect, it is suggested that the mandatory requirements doctrine had in fact been anticipated with regard to freedom to provide services in the early *Van Binsbergen* case[76] to the extent that it held that requirements imposed on the person providing the service do not breach the Treaty where they are justified in the 'general good' and those rules are binding upon any person established in the State where the service is provided; furthermore, this doctrine would appears subsequently also to have been adopted with regard to restrictions on capital movements in Case C–148/91 *Veronica* v. *Commissariaat voor de Media*.[77] It was there found that since Dutch rules designed to ensure a pluralist and non-commercial television service were justified in the general good as a matter of cultural policy, the regulatory authority could, with regard to the movement of capital, prevent a Dutch broadcasting organization from contributing capital to and providing a bank guarantee for a Luxembourg undertaking intending to develop a commercial television station aimed at the Dutch market, and with regard to freedom to provide services, could prevent it from drawing up a business plan and giving legal advice for that undertaking.

High on this list of mandatory requirements comes the protection of consumers, a matter fundamental to the judgments of the European Court in the 1986 insurance cases.[78] The policy issue which was raised is essentially whether the consumer in the context of the provision of services should have a choice between paying less and receiving fewer safeguards in return, and paying more and receiving greater protection, or whether Member States should be permitted to restrict this choice by insisting on certain minimum safeguards that must be met by every provider of

public security or public health', which was made, *inter alia*, under this provision, refers to people who reside in or travel to another Member State, and requires measures to be based exclusively on their personal conduct.

72 Case 120/78 *Rewe* v. *Bundesmonopolverwaltung fur Branntwein* [1979] ECR 649.

73 [1980] ECR 833.

74 [1980] ECR 881.

75 See Green, Hartley, and Usher, *Legal Foundations of the Single European Market* (Oxford, 1991) chapter 6.

76 Case 33/74 [1974] ECR 1299.

77 [1993] ECR I–487. See Chapter 2 above.

78 See Case 205/84 *Commission* v. *Germany* [1986] ECR 3755 paras.39 and 64.

the particular service. The response of the European Court seems to be that it depends on the economic level at which a particular activity is carried out, but it is worth noting again the special protection given to the consumer, defined in the Consumer Credit Directive[79] as a natural person acting outside the scope of his trade or profession. To summarize Case 205/84 *Commission* v. *Germany*,[80] the Court held that with regard to direct insurance effected through intermediaries, Germany was justified in requiring insurance undertakings established in other Member States to comply with its authorization requirements, in particular with regard to technical reserves (i.e. assets set aside to meet contingent liabilities) in so far as they were necessary to ensure the protection of policy-holders and insured persons,[81] irrespective of the fact that such insurance companies may be authorized in their home states, provided the insurance companies were not required to duplicate conditions already met in their home state,[82] and given a situation in which Community Law had harmonized solvency requirements but not the rules relating to 'technical reserves' or conditions of insurance.[83] However, it was expressly recognized that there may be situations where, because of the nature of the risk insured and of the party seeking insurance, there was no need to protect the latter by the application of mandatory rules of his or her national law.[84] In particular, the Court held that in the field of co-insurance there was no justification for the German requirement that the leading insurer should be authorized by the German authorities, the arguments for consumer protection not having the same force as in connection with other forms of insurance since, in the view of the Court, co-insurance arises in the context of insurance taken out only by 'large undertakings or groups of undertakings which are in a position to assess and negotiate insurance policies proposed to them'. In any event, according to the Court, Council Directive 78/473[85] already provided sufficient co-ordination and co-operation between supervisory authorities in the Member States.

This distinction was followed by the second insurance Directive,[86] which in effect provided freedom for large risks, but did not really create freedom to provide insurance services across frontiers at the level of ordinary consumers. However, the third non-life insurance Directive,[87] which introduces a system of home-state authorization giving rise to a right to provide services and establish branches in other Member States has removed this distinction, but in art. 17[88] it provides that the home Member State shall require every insurance undertaking to establish adequate technical provisions in respect of its entire business, the amount being determined under Directive 91/674[89]—i.e. technical reserves have become a matter of

[79] Council Directive 87/102 (OJ 1987 L42/48) art. 1(2)(a).
[80] [1986] ECR 3755.
[81] Ibid. para. 39.
[82] Ibid. para. 47.
[83] Ibid. paras. 37 to 40. See EC Council Directives 73/239 (OJ 1973 L228/3) and 79/267 (OJ 1979 L63/1).
[84] Ibid. para. 49.
[85] OJ 1978 L151/25.
[86] Directive 88/357, OJ 1988 L172/1.
[87] Council Directive 92/49 (OJ 1992 L228/1).
[88] Amending art. 15 of Directive 73/239.
[89] On the annual accounts and consolidated accounts of insurance companies (OJ 1991 L374/7).

Community law. In addition, art. 45[90] maintains the Member States' right to require undertakings carrying on business within their territories under the right of establishment or the freedom to provide services to join and participate, on the same terms as undertakings authorized there, in any scheme designed to guarantee the payment of insurance claims to insured persons and injured third parties.

Returning to the German insurance judgment, neither in the case of mass risks nor in the case of co-insurance and re-insurance, however, did the Court accept that a German requirement that the insurance undertakings should themselves be established in Germany had been shown to be indispensable;[91] indeed, it took the view that such a requirement would negate the freedom to provide services.[92] In fact, with one possible exception, there appears to be no example of a requirement of establishment as a condition for the provision of services being held to be justified except in the context of taxation. The possible exception is Case C–106/91 *Ramrath*[93] where, despite the contrary opinion of A.-G. Jacobs, the Sixth Chamber held that a Member State could require an auditor providing services in that State to have some permanent infrastructure and an effective presence in that State, accepting that this was objectively necessary to ensure the observance of professional rules. However, it was subsequently made clear in Case C–55/94 *Gebhard*[94] that a provider of services, within the meaning of the Treaty, may equip him or herself in the host Member State with the infrastructure necessary for the purposes of performing the services in question, and that the temporary nature of the provision of services, envisaged in the third paragraph of art. 50 of the EC Treaty, is to be determined in the light of its duration, regularity, periodicity, and continuity. A requirement to have a permanent infrastructure is therefore not necessarily incompatible with the freedom to provide services.

In the context of taxation, the Court did actually accept a requirement of local establishment in Case C–204/90 *Bachmann* v. *Belgium*.[95] There, the Court held that tax deductions on life and sickness insurance premiums could be limited to payments made to insurers established in Belgium, on the basis that there was no other way of preserving the integrity of the tax system (which required tax to be paid on the ultimate benefits). If a requirement that a provider of a financial service should be established within the jurisdiction of the Member State concerned is the only way of ensuring that a Member State's tax legislation is observed, it indicates a need for a considerably greater degree of co-operation between the tax authorities of the Member States. It also has the effect of making provision of services in the Treaty sense impossible.

However, that is not the end of the story. The European Court returned to the matter in Case C–80/94 *Wielockx* v. *Inspecteur der Directe Belastingen*.[96] This

[90] Amending art. 24 of Directive 88/357.

[91] Case 205/84 *Commission* v. *Germany* [1986] ECR 3755, para. 56.

[92] Ibid. para. 52. This view was confirmed in Case C–222/95 *Parodi* v. *Banque de Bary* [1997] ECR I–3899 para. 31.

[93] [1992] ECR I–3351.

[94] [1995] ECR I–4165.

[95] [1992] ECR I–249.

[96] [1995] ECR I–2493.

involved a Belgian national resident in Belgium who was a partner in a business established in the Netherlands and whose entire income was earned in the Netherlands. He paid money into a pension reserve in the Netherlands, and claimed tax relief on that part of his income. This was refused on the basis that relief was only given to Dutch residents, and the Netherlands government invoked the *Bachmann* case to argue that in the case of a Belgian resident, the Netherlands authorities would grant the tax relief on the pension contributions but the Belgian authorities would collect the tax on the pension when it was received. However, while the Court accepted that in principle the situations of residents and non-residents are not generally comparable, it held that a non-resident taxpayer who receives all or almost all of his income in the State where he works is objectively in the same situation as concerns income tax as a resident of that State. Furthermore, on the question of tax cohesion, the Court followed Advocate-General Léger in noting that the arrangements between the Netherlands and Belgium resulted from a double taxation convention following the OECD model under which a State taxes all pensions, irrespective of their source, received by residents, but waives the right to tax pensions received abroad, irrespective of their source. It therefore held that tax cohesion was to be established not at the level of one individual taxpayer but in the reciprocity of the rules applicable in the Contracting States. The Netherlands could not therefore justify a discriminatory refusal of tax relief in this case. While there may be some debate as to the Court's analysis of the double taxation agreements[97] (though they are hardly a matter of Community legislation falling within the Court's jurisdiction), it may be wondered whether this effectively overrules the *Bachmann* judgment.

In any event, a requirement of establishment which could not be objectively justified was treated as a prohibited restriction on freedom to provide services in Case C–484/93 *Svensson and Gustavsson* v. *Ministre du Logement*.[98] Similarly, in Case C–410/96 *Ambry*[99] it was held that there was no objective justification for France to require the compulsory financial security provided by a travel agent to be guaranteed by a credit institution or insurance company situated in France. Indeed, in Case C–118/96 *Safir* v. *Skattemyndigheten i Dalarnas Län*[100] it was held that for Sweden to impose a different tax regime for insurance policies purchased from providers outside Sweden which would have the effect of deterring Swedish residents from taking out such policies, even though it was intended to achieve tax neutrality between policies purchased inside and outside Sweden, was a breach of art. 59.[101]

Nevertheless, a requirement of residence does appear to be recognized in the 1993 Investment Services Directive[102] with regard to access to regulated markets,

[97] See Vanistendael: 'The consequences of *Schumacker* and *Wielockx*: Two steps forward in the tax procession of Echternach' (1996) 33 *CMLR* 255; and Wattel: 'The EC Court's attempts to reconcile the Treaty freedoms with international tax law' (1996) 33 *CMLR* 223.

[98] [1995] ECR I–3955.

[99] 1 Dec. 1998.

[100] [1998] ECR I–1897.

[101] For a more detailed consideration of tax issues, see Chapter 3 above.

[102] Council Directive 93/22 (OJ 1991 L141/27).

essentially defined[103] as markets listed by the Member States where conditions for the operation of the market, conditions for access to the market, and conditions governing admission to listing or dealings on the market are defined by regulations issued or approved by the competent authorities. Art. 15(3) and (4) appear to leave it to the host State to determine whether a physical presence is required to become a member of or have access to such a market: art. 15(3) requires as a matter of Community law access for local branches or subsidiaries of investment firms authorized in their home State, but art. 15(4) only allows access without an establishment in the host State where the regulated market of the host State so allows. Whether leaving it to national law meets the objective requirements laid down in the case-law remains to be seen.

4. Scope for national measures

National measures are only regarded as justified in the absence of Community legislation, and while the details of the banking and credit legislation are considered in the next Chapter, the modern approach to Community legislation in the area of financial services began with the Unit Trusts Directive.[104] This is based on the twin principles of harmonizing certain basic requirement for such institutions and of providing that authorization by the competent authorities of the home Member State is valid for all Member States. Nevertheless, the host state may apply its own marketing and advertizing rules to undertakings authorized in another Member State. The Second Banking Directive,[105] as already noted, distinguishes between the ability to provide services (and establish branches) in another Member State on the basis of home state authorization, and the requirement to obtain host state authorization for the operation of a subsidiary. Effectively it treats setting up a branch as if it were a provision of services from another Member State, rather than a form of establishment. Here again, however, the acceptance of home country control was dependant on the simultaneous entry into force of Directives on the 'own funds' of credit institutions[106] and on solvency ratios for such institutions,[107] thus harmonizing certain of the basic requirements governing credit institutions. Furthermore, the Directive allows the host State's monetary policy to be applied to a branch of a foreign credit institution or to the provision of services from another Member State.

Closer examination of the Directive also reveals that the host State may apply certain other provisions of its domestic legislation 'in the interest of the general

[103] Art. 1(13) of the Directive.

[104] Council Directive 85/611 on undertakings for collective investment in transferable securities (OJ 1985 L375/1).

[105] Council Directive 89/646 (OJ 1989 L386/1).

[106] Council Directive 89/299 (OJ 1989 L124/16).

[107] Council Directive 89/647 (OJ 1989 L386/14).

good', a term clearly derived from the line of case-law beginning with *Van Binsbergen.*[108] Under art. 19(4), before a branch commences its activities, the host State authorities may indicate the conditions under which, in the interest of the general good, those activities must be carried on in that State. Article 21(5) makes it clear that the Directive does not prevent host States taking appropriate measures to prevent or punish irregularities committed within their territories which are contrary to the legal rules they have adopted in the interest of the general good, whether those irregularities are committed by branches of credit institutions or by institutions providing services within those territories. Finally, under art. 21(11), advertisements by credit institutions established in other Member States are subject to host State rules governing the form and content of such advertizing adopted in the interest of the public good.

While the precise scope of these provisions may be a matter of debate,[109] it may be suggested that any national measure previously justifiable under Community law, e.g. to protect consumers, may continue to be applied to the extent that it is neither replaced by nor in conflict with a provision of Community law. However, a very broad view has been taken in the UK implementing legislation, the Banking Co-ordination (Second Council Directive) Regulations 1992.[110] Regulation 8(1) provides that the Financial Services Authority shall draw to the attention of an institution intending to establish a branch in the United Kingdom such of the relevant legislation as the FSA 'considers appropriate', and reg. 14(1) makes similar provision for the Securities and Investment Board with regard to the Financial Services Act and its implementing rules.[111]

It may also be wondered how far rules of the host State may still be applied where the cross-border element is provided by the movements of the recipient of the service, rather than by its provider. In Case 15/78 *Société Générale Alsacienne de Banque* v. *Koestler*[112] a French bank, acting on the instructions of a customer who was a German national resident in France at the time, carried out certain transactions on the Paris Stock Exchange. The customer suffered losses as a result, and eventually returned to live in Germany, taking with him a large overdraft with the bank which he refused to pay off. The bank sued him before the German courts, which took the view that the transactions in question amounted to gaming contracts which were not actionable in German law, and that this public policy rule applied even if the debt was contracted abroad and was valid under the law of the State where it arose.

108 Case 33/74 [1974] ECR 1299.

109 See Dassesse, '1992: An EC update', (1991) *JIBFL* p. 384; Usher, 'Is there really a Single Market for Financial Services in the European Union?' in *The Legal Structure of the European Financial Market* (ed. Bernitz and Mohamed, Juristförlaget, Stockholm, 1996).

110 SI 1992 No. 3218.

111 Dare one suggest that this reflects the worries expressed in Katz, 'The General Good and the Second Banking Directive: A major loophole?' (1993) *JIBFL* 166.

112 [1978] ECR 1971.

On a reference to the European Court, it was first held that where a recipient of services takes up residence in another Member State while the contractual relationship with the service provider continues, the rules on freedom to provide services under art. 49 of the EC Treaty are triggered, since the provider is thereafter established in a different Member State from that of the recipient. On this basis, the Court categorized the problem as the familiar one, already discussed, of determining whether Germany was able to enforce its public policy rules against a French bank providing services in Germany. It was held that it could, the Court commenting that the Treaty did not require a foreigner providing services to be treated more favourably than someone established in the Member State where the services were provided. However, it is submitted that the reality was that in this case that German public policy was applied to a contract entered into in France between parties who were both then established in France.

Whatever conclusions are reached as a matter of private international law, as a matter of Community law on the provision of services it is submitted that a distinction should be made in the application of national public policy rules between providers who actively seek to offer their services in another Member State and those whose services are sought by recipients from other Member States, only the former being subject to such host State policy rules as are still enforceable. Such a distinction was drawn in the second Directive on direct life assurance[113] between undertakings which sought to provide services in another Member State, which were to be subject to authorization by the host State, and those whose policies were sought out by a policy-holder from another Member State, which in effect would merely have had to give notice of the fact that they were authorized by their home State. In any event, providers of services need to be aware of the problems which may be caused by the subsequent movement to another Member State of the recipient of their services.

On the face of it, art. 49 does not distinguish between rules governing the import of services and rules governing the export of services, although the equal treatment rule in art. 50 is clearly addressed to the host State, and the bulk of the case-law has involved host State rules. However, in Case C–384/93 *Alpine Investments*[114] the problem of export of services arose very clearly. Dutch legislation prohibited financial intermediaries from offering their services by way of 'cold calling' to new potential clients, whether in the Netherlands or in other countries, and Alpine Investments claimed that this was a breach of art. 49 as far as the supply of services to other Member States was concerned. The Dutch government (supported by the UK) argued by analogy with the *Keck* formula in the free movement of goods that this prohibition related to selling arrangements rather than the service itself, so it could not be regarded as breaching art. 49. However, the Court asserted that because it deprived the traders concerned of a quick and direct method of advertizing their services and making contact with potential clients, it was capable of

[113] Council Directive 90/619 (OJ 1990 L330/50).

[114] [1995] ECR I–1141.

restricting the free provision of services across the frontier to another Member State. The restriction was nevertheless found to be justified on novel grounds: while the protection of consumers is well established as a justification for non-discriminatory restrictions as a mandatory requirement in the context of the free movement of goods and as an aspect of the general good in the context of the provision of services, it was held that it was not for the Dutch authorities to protect consumers in other Member States. Nevertheless, such protection had a direct incidence on the good reputation of the Dutch financial service sector, and it was held that the maintenance of the good reputation of the financial sector in a Member State did constitute a mandatory requirement in the general interest capable of justifying restrictions on the provision of financial services. It remains to be seen whether a similar view will be taken with regard to restrictions on the free movement of goods.

5. Consumer protection

The 'general good' which appears to have been most often at issue in financial services cases is that of consumer protection, whose importance is unlikely to become diminish. The Maastricht Treaty on European Union added a specific objective of 'a contribution to the strengthening of consumer protection' in art. 3(s) (now art. 3(t)) of the EC Treaty. More particularly it inserted a new art. 129a (now art. 153) into the Treaty under which the Community is to contribute to the attainment of a high level of consumer protection, both through measures adopted in the context of the completion of the internal market and by specific action which supports and supplements the policy pursued by the Member States to protect, *inter alia*, the 'economic interests of consumers' and to provide 'adequate information to consumers'. These aims appear to be of particular importance in the context of consumer credit.

It is further provided that such measures (which are adopted by co-decision between Council and Parliament) shall not prevent any Member State from maintaining or introducing more stringent protective measures, provided they are compatible with the Treaty.

As may be gleaned from these powers, consumer protection is not just simply a justification for national restrictions on the freedom to provide services; it is also an aim of Community legislation. Although the original Treaty was silent on the matter of consumer protection, an aspect of the concept of competition relevant to the internal market, that of 'fair competition', underlies much of the Community legislation in the matter. Article 94 (formerly art. 100) of the EC Treaty empowers the Council to issue Directives for the approximation of such provisions laid down by law, regulation, or administrative action in Member States 'as directly affect the establishment or functioning of the common market', and this provision was originally used to justify Community legislation in the area of consumer protection, on the basis that divergent national legislation distorted conditions of competition and so affected the functioning of the common market.[115] Thus in the 1984 Directive on misleading advertizing[116] it was stated that the laws then in force in the Member States differed widely, that since advertizing reached beyond the frontiers of individual Member States it had a direct effect on the establishment and functioning of the common market, and that misleading advertizing could lead to distortion of competition within the common market. Similarly the Directive on liability for defective products[117] asserted that existing divergencies might distort competition, affect the movement of goods within the common market, and entail a differing degree of protection of the consumer against damage caused by defective products to his health or property.

This is also the line of reasoning behind the 1987 Consumer Credit Directive.[118] Its recitals declare that the wide differences then existing in the laws of the Member States in the field of consumer credit could lead to distortions of competition between granters of credit in the common market, and could limit the opportunities consumers had to obtain credit in other Member States, affecting the volume and nature of the credit sought, and also the purchase of goods and services. The recitals therefore conclude that these differences had an influence on the free movement of goods and services obtainable by consumers on credit, and thus directly affected the functioning of the common market. This emphasis given to the prevention of distortions of competition enabled very wide use to be made of art. 94, since it could be argued that virtually any difference between national regulatory frameworks might distort competition in the Community.

Given the existence of a body of legislation on consumer protection, it is perhaps surprising that the Single European Act did not, unlike the situation with regard to environmental protection,[119] confer an express power on the Community to legislate in the area of consumer protection, particularly since at the end of 1986 the Council formally adopted a Resolution[120] setting out a policy of integration of consumer policy into other common policies of the Community. However, the Single European Act did introduce art. 100a (now art. 95) into the Treaty, derogating from certain of the terms of art. 94 for the purposes of the achievement of the internal market as defined in art. 14 (then art. 8a) by the end of 1992. This internal market is defined as an area without internal frontiers in which the free movement of goods, persons, services, and capital is ensured in accordance with the provisions of the Treaty. For this purpose, following further amendment

[115] It was thus not usually found necessary to resort to the even wider art. 308 of the Treaty in this area. Art. 308 empowers the Council to act where the Treaty has not provided the necessary powers if action by the Community is necessary to attain one of its objectives.

[116] Council Directive 84/450 (OJ 1984 L250/17).

[117] Council Directive 85/374 (OJ 1985 L210/29).

[118] Council Directive 87/102 (OJ 1987 L42/48), now amended by Council Directive 90/88 (OJ 1990 L61/14).

[119] See now arts. 174–176 (formerly arts. 130r to 130t) of the EC Treaty.

[120] OJ 1987 C3/1.

by the Maastricht Treaty art. 95 allows the Council to act by qualified majority in co-decision with the European Parliament, rather than by unanimity as required under art. 94, it allows the adoption of 'measures', rather than just the Directives which were envisaged in art. 94, and it expressly envisages that such measures may be concerned with consumer protection.

Although the prevention of distortions of competition is not mentioned among the attributes of the internal market as defined in art. 14, those who drafted art. 95 obviously envisaged that internal market legislation might affect consumers, because art. 95(3) states that the Commission, in its proposals concerning health, safety, environmental protection, and consumer protection will take as a base a high level of protection. Internal market legislation may have a major effect on consumer protection, and may even have consumer protection as its major objective, as evidenced by the Directive on the approximation of the laws of the Member States concerning the safety of toys,[121] which both sets out the standards which must be fulfilled in order for toys to be sold on the Community market, and has the intrinsic consequence of ensuring that the safety of Community consumers taken into account when a toy is put on the Community market. Indeed, consumer protection legislation has been enacted under art. 95 which hardly seems concerned with trade between Member States: the Directives on consumer protection in the indication of prices[122] are concerned with the indication of prices to the final consumer, and might be thought to concern the retail trade within a Member State rather than trade between Member States. The explanation given in the recitals is that the indication of the selling price and the unit price of the products makes it easier for consumers to compare prices at places of sale, thus increasing market transparency and ensuring greater protection for consumers; this appears to mean that consumer protection can justify Community legislation, without reference to distortion of competition.

It is therefore no surprise that the 1990 amendment to the Consumer Credit Directive[123] was enacted under what is now art. 95, and that its recitals emphasize consumer protection. It is stated to be desirable that one method of calculating the annual percentage rate of charge should be used throughout the Community 'in order to promote the establishment and functioning of the internal market and to ensure that consumers benefit from a high level of protection'.

In summary, consumer protection, particularly in the financial services sector, is an area in which the European Community now asserts competence, but that on matters not regulated by Community law, national legislation designed to protect consumers may still be enforced against credit institutions from other Member States, provided that the legislation is not discriminatory, it is necessary for its purpose, and account is taken of requirements and safeguards met by the credit institution in other Member States.

[121] Council Directive 88/378 (OJ 1988 L187/1).

[122] Council Directives 88/314 and 88/315 (OJ 1988 L142/19 and L142/23).

[123] Council Directive 90/88 (OJ 1990 L61/14). See Chapter 6 below.

6. Services and capital movements

It may finally be noted in the context of the Treaty rules on the provision of services that one specific measure which was not altered by the Single European Act or by the Maastricht Treaty is art. 51(2) (formerly art. 61(2)). This states that the liberalization of banking and insurance services connected with movements of capital shall be effected in step with the progressive liberalization of the movement of capital. Hence a clear link is expressly drawn between the Treaty rules on provision of services and the rules relating to the movement of money, a matter noted in the recitals to the Second Banking Directive, which recognize that capital safeguard measures under the 1988 capital movements Directive[124] may lead to restrictions on the provision of banking services. Such a link was applied in a restrictive way by the European Court in Case 267/86 *Van Eycke* v. *ASPA*[125] where it was held that since the opening of a savings account in another Member State was not at that time liberated under the capital movements Directives, it was not a breach of the Treaty provisions on freedom to provide services for Belgium to limit tax exemptions on such accounts to deposits in local currency at credit institutions having their head office (*siège social*) in Belgium. On the other hand, in Case C–222/95 *Parodi* v. *Banque de Bary*[126] it was found that the mortgage loan (granted in 1984) there at issue was in principle a liberalized transaction under the Council Directive of 11 May 1960 on capital movements[127] as amended by Council Directive 63/21,[128] so that the question of freedom to provide services could be considered—though in that context it was accepted that before the entry into force of the Second Banking Directive[129] there were within the banking sector imperative reasons relating to the public interest capable of justifying the imposition by the Member State of destination of conditions regarding access to the activity of credit institutions and their supervision which went beyond the minimum conditions required by the First Banking Directive[130] and already implemented in the Member State of origin.

Following the liberalization of capital movements described in Chapter 2 above, it may be suggested that art. 51(2) is of relevance, if at all, only where the current provisions on monetary movements allow restrictions to be imposed, notably in the context of tax discrimination discussed in Chapter 3 above. As suggested earlier in this Chapter,[131] it is indeed questionable whether the subordination of the provision of services to the capital movement rules remains appropriate in the modern single internal market, and some of the modern case-law is difficult to reconcile with the wording of the Treaty. Case C–484/93 *Svensson and Gustavsson* v. *Ministre du Logement*[132] held that loans from a bank in another Member State to buy a house

[124] Council Directive 88/361 (OJ 1988 L178/5).
[125] [1988] ECR 4769.
[126] [1997] ECR I–3899.
[127] JO 921/60.
[128] JO 62/63.
[129] OJ 1989 L386/1.
[130] Council Directive 77/780 on credit institutions (OJ 1977 L32/30).
[131] See pp. 97–8.
[132] [1995] ECR I–3955.

fell within the scope of the 1988 Directive on capital movements,[133] but that such transactions also[134] constituted services within the meaning of what is now art. 49. This approach was subsequently criticized by A.-G.Tesauro in his Opinion in Case C–118/96 *Safir* v. *Skattemyndigheten i Dalarnas Län*:[135] he suggested that the concepts should be kept separate and that a narrower concept of capital movements should be adopted. However, in that case[136] the Court held it to be a breach of art. 49 for Sweden to impose a different tax regime for insurance policies purchased from providers outside Sweden which would have the effect of deterring Swedish residents from taking out such policies, even though it was intended to achieve tax neutrality between policies purchased inside and outside Sweden. The Court none the less added that the decision on this point made it unnecessary to determine whether the legislation was also incompatible with arts. 56 and 58 (formerly arts. 73b and 73d) on capital movements—even though under the express terms of art. 50 services are only services within the meaning of the Treaty to the extent that they do not fall under one of the other Treaty freedoms, and it might therefore have been expected that the first question should be whether the matter fell under the capital movement rules. Indeed, the Court confirmed that a mortgage fell within the scope of a capital movement as defined in the Directive in Case C–222/97 *Trummer and Mayer*[137] and further held that this interpretation should continue to apply to the free movement of capital under art. 56. However, in Case C–410/96 *Ambry*[138] it was held that for France to require the compulsory financial security provided by a travel agent to be guaranteed by a credit institution or insurance company situated in France breached the Treaty rules on freedom to provide services—although it may be observed that the list in the Annex to the 1988 capital movements Directive expressly includes guarantees granted by non-residents to residents.[139]

7. Investment in companies and firms in other Member States

Although it is not specific to investment in financial service undertakings, mention should finally be made of art. 294 (formerly art. 221) of the EC Treaty. This is difficult to classify in terms of the basic Treaty 'freedoms', although it may be regarded as ancillary to the freedom of establishment set out in art. 43 and extended to companies and firms by art. 48, and to the free movement of capital. Article 294 required that within three years of the entry into force of the Treaty Member States should accord nationals of the other Member States the same treatment as their own nationals as regards participation in the capital of companies or firms within

[133] OJ 1988 L178/5.
[134] Para. 11.
[135] [1998] ECR I–1897 pp. 1905–1907.
[136] [1998] ECR I–1897.
[137] 16 Mar. 1999.
[138] 1 Dec. 1998.
[139] Annex I, heading IX A.

the meaning of art. 48, without prejudice to the application of the other provisions of the Treaty.

To the extent that the right of establishment is exercized by taking part in the incorporation of a company in another Member State, it was held in the *Daily Mail* case that art. 294 ensures that an investor from another Member State will receive the same treatment as nationals of the host State as regards participation in the capital of the new company.[140] Reading art. 294 with art. 43, the Court has suggested that they confer not only the rights of establishment and of participation in companies or firms but also the right to pursue an economic activity, through a company, under the conditions laid down by the legislation of the country of establishment for its own nationals.[141] The two provisions have in common a prohibition against discrimination on grounds of nationality, and it may be submitted that just as that prohibition in art. 43 has been held to be clear, precise, and unconditional, and therefore capable of enforcement by national courts, giving rise to directly effective individual rights,[142] so the prohibition in art. 294 is also directly effective.

The distinction between the two provisions appears to be that to discriminate against a national of another Member State, or a company incorporated under the law of another Member State, holding a controlling interest in a company in the host State, would infringe the controlling shareholder's freedom of establishment even if art. 294 were not in the Treaty, whereas discrimination against a foreign shareholder buying a small number of shares as an investment would not limit freedom of establishment but would infringe art. 294. Article 294 was considered separately from art. 43 in the substantive judgment in Case C–246/89 *Commission* v. *United Kingdom*.[143] UK legislation required that in order for a fishing boat owned by a company to be registered as British, 75 per cent of the shares had to be held by or on behalf of British citizens resident in the United Kingdom or by a company incorporated in the United Kingdom subject to the same shareholding rules. As well as its major arguments based on freedom of establishment, the Commission claimed that the British rules discriminated against nationals of other Member States who might wish to buy shares in companies operating British fishing boats. The Court agreed that art. 294 required Member States to give equal treatment with their own nationals to citizens of other Member States taking a financial participation in companies or firms.

To the extent that art. 294 in itself protects investors rather than those exercising the freedom of establishment, the link with the freedom of capital movements may be seen. While art. 294 was due to be implemented within the rather unusual period of three years from the entry into force of the original EEC Treaty (the original transitional period of twelve years was divided into three stages of *four* years each under the original art. 8), it is self-evident that a national of one Member State

[140] Case 81/87 *R* v. *Treasury* ex p. *Daily Mail* [1988] ECR 5483 p. 5511.

[141] Case C–246/89R *Commission* v. *United Kingdom* [1989] ECR 3125 p. 3133.

[142] Case 2/74 *Reyners* [1974] ECR 631.

[143] [1991] ECR I–4585.

resident in that state cannot invest in a company in another state if the money cannot be transferred. Although, as has been seen,[144] the earliest capital movements Directives date from the early 1960s,[145] the legislative programme was not completed until 1988,[146] with full freedom of capital movements for most Member States being required as a matter of Community law from the summer of 1990. This may well be one reason why art. 294 has been used relatively little.

[144] See Chapter 2 above.

[145] Council Directives of 11 May 1960 (JO 921/60) and 63/21 (JO 62/63).

[146] Council Directive 88/361 (OJ 1988 L178/5).

6

Banking, investment, and loans: the Community legislation

1. Introduction

It was indicated in the previous Chapter that the basic Treaty rules on establishment and freedom to provide services do not necessarily mean that a financial service undertaking trading lawfully in one Member State will be able to operate in another Member State without complying with certain of the local rules.[1] This is therefore an area where completion of the internal market has been dependent on the enactment of Community secondary legislation. It is suggested that the basic 1973 Directive on the Freedom of Establishment and Freedom to Provide Services in relation to the activities of banks and other financial institutions[2] in reality became redundant very shortly after it entered into force following the judgments of the European Court which held that the basic principles of freedom of establishment[3] and freedom to provide services[4] were in fact directly effective. However, in so far as a general comment could be made on the subsequent legislation which has particularly concentrated on what are termed 'credit institutions', it is suggested that the common feature of this legislation was initially to ensure certain common standards of supervision of credit institutions and to ensure that certain accounting principles were followed by banks and credit institutions; hence, the emphasis appears to have been on control rather than freedom. The fundamental question is, of course, how far one can exist without the other.

If the legislation on credit institutions is taken as the model,[5] the core legislation comprises the two 'Banking Directives'[6] (hereinafter respectively referred to as the 1977 and 1989 Directives) which lay down the criteria for the authorization and supervision of credit institutions, and in principle allow credit institutions authorized in one Member State to open branches or provide services in another

[1] Case C–222/95 *Parodi* v. *Banque de Bary* [1997] ECR I–3899; see Chapter 5 above.

[2] OJ 1973 L194/1.

[3] Case 2/74 *Reyners* v. *Belgium* [1974] ECR 631.

[4] Case 33/74 *Van Binsbergen* [1974] ECR 1299.

[5] Though Council Directive 85/611 on undertakings for collective investment in transferable securities (OJ 1985 L375/3) was the first to use the concept of a 'passport' issued by the authorities in the home State.

[6] Council Directive 77/780 (OJ 1977 L322/30) and Council Directive 89/646 (OJ 1989 L386/1).

Member State, together with Directives on the 'own funds'[7] and solvency ratios[8] of such credit institutions, on their accounts[9] and on their supervision on a consolidated basis.[10] To this has been added legislation on such matters as deposit guarantees[11] and cross-border credit transfers.[12] This list in itself indicates that the price of opening the Community market may well be increased Community regulation.

2. Credit institutions

a) Definition and control

The basic definition of a credit institution, followed in all the other legislation, is given in art. 1 of the 1977 Directive: 'an undertaking whose business is to receive deposits or other repayable funds from the public and to grant credits for its own account.' It should be observed that this definition relates to the nature of the business transacted, not to the nature of the entity which transacts it: the term 'undertaking' is that used in the competition rules of the EC Treaty[13] and is apt to describe not just companies and other legal persons but any form of business enterprise. However, a list of exceptions is given in art. 2(2) which *is* defined by reference to the form of the undertaking. Article 2(2) excludes the central banks of Member States, post office giro institutions, and a number of named institutions in each Member State; in the United Kingdom the excluded institutions are the National Savings Bank, the Commonwealth Development Finance Company, the Agricultural Mortgage Corporation, the Scottish Agricultural Securities Corporation, the Crown Agents for overseas governments and administrations, credit unions, and municipal banks. What the excluded bodies appear to have in common is that they are (or were at the relevant time) state-owned or controlled, or subject to special legislation.

The 1989 Directive and the consolidated supervision Directive[14] also refer to 'financial institutions', defined in a negative way as undertakings which are not credit institutions but whose principal activity is nevertheless to acquire holdings or to carry on one or more of the activities listed in the Annex to the 1989 Directive[15] other than the acceptance of deposits and other repayable funds from the public. The same term with a different definition is used in the accounts Directive,[16] where it effectively means[17] an institution other than a credit institution which

[7] Council Directive 89/299 (OJ 1989 L124/16), amended by Directive 92/16 (OJ 1992 L75/48).
[8] Council Directive 89/647 (OJ 1989 L386/14).
[9] Council Directive 86/635 (OJ 1989 L386/1).
[10] Council Directive 92/30 (OJ 1992 L110/52), replacing Directive 83/350 (OJ 1983 L193/18).
[11] Directive 94/19 of the European Parliament and of the Council (OJ 1994 L135/5).
[12] Directive 97/5 of the European Parliament and Council (OJ 1997 L43/25).
[13] See Chapter 4 above.
[14] Directive 92/30 (OJ 1992 L110/52).
[15] See below p. 128.
[16] Council Directive 86/635 (OJ 1986 L372/1).
[17] Art. 2(1)(b).

would otherwise be excluded from the scope of the basic company law accounts Directive.[18]

The essential scheme of the Directives with regard to credit institutions as such is that Member States must require credit institutions to obtain authorization before commencing their activities,[19] and that they must prohibit persons or undertakings which are not credit institutions from carrying on the business of taking deposits or other repayable funds from the public;[20] however, this prohibition does not apply to national, regional, or local authorities, or to public international bodies of which one or more Member States are members, or to cases expressly covered by national or Community legislation, 'provided that those activities are subject to regulations or controls intended to protect depositors and investors and applicable to those cases', an exemption similar in underlying philosophy to the exclusion of various publicly controlled bodies from the definition of credit institutions. While the fundamental criteria for authorization (discussed in the following sections) are now laid down by Community law, it may be observed that by virtue of art. 3(2) of the 1977 Directive, the requirements laid down by Community law are stated to be without prejudice to other conditions of general application laid down by national laws.

The prudential supervision of a credit institution remains essentially[21] the responsibility of the competent authorities of the Member State which authorized it (the 'home' State).[22] Those authorities must require every credit institution to have sound administrative and accounting procedures and adequate internal control mechanisms. Member States must also ensure that the authorities may adopt or impose penalties in respect of a credit institution which breaches laws, regulations, or administrative provisions concerning the supervision or pursuit of its activities, or take measures aimed specifically at ending such breaches or their causes.[23] Similar measures must also be available against those who effectively control the business of credit institutions. Finally, these measures are stated to be without prejudice to the procedures for the withdrawal of authorizations[24] and the provisions of criminal law.

b) Capital, own funds, and solvency ratio

Subject to possible derogations in favour of certain categories of credit institutions, the competent authorities may not grant authorization in cases where the initial capital is less than €5 million.[25] It is of interest to note that the UK

[18] Council Directive 78/660 (OJ 1978 L222/11).

[19] 1977 art. 3(1). It should also be observed that art. 13 of that Directive sets out a requirement that the authorization procedure should be subject to judicial review, and that judicial review should also be available where no decision has been taken within 6 months of the submission of an application containing all the necessary information.

[20] 1989 Directive, art. 3.

[21] The host State has certain additional responsibilities in cases of establishment of branches or provision of services. See below pp. 131–3.

[22] 1989 art. 13. [23] 1989 art. 17. [24] See below pp. 136–7. [25] 1989 art. 4.

implementation,[26] perhaps reflecting the currency fluctuations of the second half of 1992, does not convert the ECU figure (as it originally was) into pounds[27] but refers to 5 million ECU 'or an amount of equal value denominated wholly or partly in another unit of account'. Whatever way it is expressed this is not a very large sum by the standards of the financial services industry.[28] Nevertheless, an institution's own funds may not fall below the minimum capital requirement,[29] and in the UK an institution will not be regarded as conducting its business in a prudent manner unless it maintains own funds at the required level.[30] However, under the Directives, the competent authorities may allow an institution a limited period in which to rectify its situation or to cease its activities.[31]

The 'own funds' of a credit institution are also relevant to its initial authorization. Under art. 3(2) of the 1977 Directive, as well as requiring that there should be two persons of sufficiently good repute and sufficient experience who effectively direct the business of the credit institution, the competent authorities may only grant authorization where the credit institution possesses separate and adequate own funds. This concept was originally defined[32] simply as the credit institution's own capital, including items which may be treated as capital under national rules, but a Community law definition, which the national authorities are obliged to follow, was introduced by Directive 89/299.[33]

This Directive basically lists eight items of which positive account is taken, and five items which must be deducted when own funds are calculated.[34] However, these items are not in fact all treated the same way, and it is submitted that the core of the concept may be found in two of the positive items and three of the negative ones, which form a point of reference for the others.[35] The first of these two principal positive items is capital, defined in the accounts Directive[36] as all amounts, regardless of their actual designation, which in accordance with the legal structure of the institution concerned are regarded under national law as equity capital subscribed by the shareholders or other proprietors, in so far as it has been paid up, plus share premium accounts, but excluding cumulative preference shares. (This does not mean that no account is taken of preference shares: they are treated differently under another heading.) The second item is reserves as defined under the general company account harmonization Directive[37] and profits and losses brought forward as the result of the final profit or loss; interim profits may only be taken into

[26] The Banking Co-ordination (Second Council Directive) Regulations 1992 (SI 1992 No. 3218), hereinafter referred to as the UK Regs., regulation 27(4) amending Schedule 3 to the Banking Act 1987.

[27] For discussion of the ECU and the euro, see Chapter 7 below.

[28] It is the same as the fine imposed on the French banks under the competition rules in relation to the Eurocheque Helsinki Agreement (Commission Decision 92/212, OJ 1992 L95/50). See Chapter 4 above.

[29] 1989 art. 10(1).

[30] UK Regs. regulation 27(2).

[31] 1989 Directive, art. 10(5).

[32] 1977 art. 1.

[33] OJ 1989 L124/16.

[34] Art. 2.

[35] See art. 6.

[36] Council Directive 86/635 (OJ 1986 L372/1) art. 22.

[37] Council Directive 78/660 (OJ 1978 L222/11) art. 9, to which art. 23 of the bank accounts Directive refers.

account if verified by the auditors. The three main deductions are the book value of its own shares held by a credit institution, intangible assets, defined in the accounts Directive as formation expenses (in so far as national law permits their being shown as an asset) and goodwill, to the extent that it was acquired for valuable consideration, and material losses of the current financial year.

Other assets of which account may be taken comprise revaluation reserves as defined under the general company account harmonization Directive;[38] value adjustments as defined under the bank accounts Directive;[39] 'other items' defined in art. 3 of the own funds Directive as items which are freely available to the credit institution to cover normal banking risks, are disclosed in internal accounting records, and whose amount is verified by independent auditors, a concept which can also include certain securities of indeterminate duration provided *inter alia* the credit institution has the option of deferring payment of interest and the lender has no preferential claims on the credit institution; the commitments of members of credit institutions set up as co-operative societies (i.e. the uncalled capital and any legal liability to make further payments should the credit institution incur a loss)[40] and the joint and several commitments of borrowers in the case of institutions organized as funds, provided such items may be counted as own funds of institutions of this type under national law; the own funds may also include fixed-term cumulative preference shares and subordinated loan capital, provided, *inter alia*, that binding agreements exist under which, in the event of the bankruptcy or liquidation of the credit institution, they rank after the claims of all other creditors and are not to be repaid until all other debts outstanding at the time have been settled. Unlike the two principal items, capital and reserves, there are limits on the account taken of these other assets: under art. 6(1) the amount taken into account may not exceed the sum of those two main items minus the sum of the three main deductions, and the sum of the last two items taken into account (the commitments of members of credit institutions set up as co-operative societies, fixed-term cumulative preference shares, etc.) may not exceed half of that amount.

Account may also be taken of funds for general banking risks, defined in the bank accounts Directive as those amounts which a credit institution decides to put aside for that purpose, but these are treated as a separate category.[41] There is no limit on the amount which is to be included in the calculation under this heading, but no account is taken of it in determining the limits on the sum of the other assets.

In any event, two further deductions are made from the resultant sums: holdings and subordinated claims which exceed 10 per cent of the capital of other credit or financial institutions, and holdings or subordinated claims of less than 10 per cent of the capital of such institutions which taken together amount to more than 10 per

[38] Council Directive 78/660 (OJ 1978 L222/11) art. 9, to which art. 23 of the bank accounts Directive refers.

[39] I.e. adjustments to the value of certain assets which have previously, for reasons of prudence, been shown at a lower value than would normally be used.

[40] Own funds Directive art. 4(1).

[41] Art. 6(2).

cent of the credit institution's own 'own funds' resulting from the previous calculations. However, parent companies subject to supervision on a consolidated basis need not deduct their holdings in other credit institutions or financial institutions which are included in the consolidation.

The concept of a credit institution's 'own funds' is also an integral part of the calculation of its solvency ratio under Council Directive 89/647.[42] This relates back to art. 6 of the 1977 Directive, requiring the competent authorities to establish ratios between the various assets and/or liabilities of credit institutions, with a view to monitoring their solvency and liquidity, and to calculate the ratio at least every six months. Under art. 4 of the solvency ratio Directive, own funds form the numerator of the solvency ratio of credit institutions, the denominator being risk-adjusted assets and off-balance sheet items, and by virtue of art. 10 the own funds must be permanently maintained at a level of at least 8 per cent of the risk-adjusted asset items. The adjustment of risk is carried out by multiplying the balance-sheet value of each asset by the relevant weighting,[43] and the principle used is that if the risk is low, the weighting is low, so that assets which are regarded as safe have zero weighting and do not count at all against the own funds in calculating the solvency ratio, whereas high risk assets have a 100 per cent weighting and their full value therefore counts against the own funds.[44]

To give some examples: cash in hand, claims against central banks and central governments of all EC Member States and other full members of the OECD (referred to as Zone A), and claims on the European Communities are all zero-weighted. On the other hand, 20 per cent weighting is given to claims on the European Investment Bank (even though the lawyer might observe that under the original EC Treaty it was the only body with express power to borrow, and power for the Community institutions to borrow on behalf of the Community itself had to be conferred by use of the 'everything else' provision, art. 235[45]) to claims on multilateral development banks (including e.g. the International Bank for Reconstruction and Development, and the Asian, African and Caribbean Development Banks), and to claims on Zone A regional governments and local authorities (although Member States may fix a zero-weighting for these where there is no difference in risk between claims on them and claims on central government because of the revenue-raising powers of the regional governments and local authorities and because of the existence of specific institutional arrangements which reduce the chances of default[46]). EP and Council Directive 98/33[47] has extended the 20 per cent band to include claims on churches and religious communities by deeming them, under certain conditions, to be included in the concept of regional governments and local authorities.

[42] OJ 1989 L386/14.

[43] Art. 5(1).

[44] See art. 6; however, art. 6(1) does allow the competent national authorities to fix higher weightings as they see fit.

[45] See Usher, 'The financing of the Community' in: *Thirty years of Community Law* pp. 195–217 (Commission of the European Communities, Brussels, 1983).

[46] Art. 7.

[47] OJ 1998 L204/29.

Fifty per cent weighting is given *inter alia* to loans fully and completely secured by mortgages on residential property. At first sight, this might seem to make it difficult for building societies to achieve their solvency ratio, but on the other hand it gave them very favourable treatment compared with credit institutions making loans secured on commercial property, which were subject to 100 per cent weighting. However, EP and Council Directive 98/32[48] has, on a fixed-term basis until the end of 2006, extended the 50 per cent weighting to loans secured on commercial office accommodation and by multi-purpose commercial property to the extent that the loan does not exceed 50 per cent of the valuation of the property (or 60 per cent of the mortgage valuation where that is carried out under stricter rules and is lower than that basic valuation). If the loan exceeds that figure, the excess continues to be weighted at 100 per cent.

One hundred per cent weighting is given to claims on central governments and central banks in countries not in Zone A (referred to as Zone B) except where the asset items are denominated and funded in the national currency of the borrower, to claims on regional governments and local authorities in Zone B countries and, perhaps of greatest practical importance, to claims on the Zone A or Zone B non-bank sectors: in other words, all loans to commercial and private clients, for example, are counted as a risk at their full value.

The same range of weightings applies to off-balance-sheet items, depending on whether they are full-risk (100 per cent), medium-risk (50 per cent), medium/low-risk 20 per cent) or low-risk (0 per cent).[49] Full-risk items[50] include acceptances, endorsements on bills not bearing the name of another credit institution, and the unpaid portion of partly-paid shares and securities. Medium-risk items include documentary credits issued and confirmed, warranties, indemnities and guarantees not having the character of credit substitutes, irrevocable standby letters of credit not having the character of credit substitutes,[51] and undrawn credit facilities with an original maturity of more than one year. Medium/low risk items include documentary credits in which the underlying shipment acts as collateral. Low-risk items include undrawn credit facilities with an original maturity of up to and including one year, or which may be cancelled unconditionally without notice. However, the weighting is not the end of the story for off-balance-sheet items: the risk-adjusted value is then multiplied by the weighting attributable to the relevant counterparties, applying the criteria used for the risk adjustment of assets. So if the other party is a Zone A central government the weighting is 0 per cent, but if it is a commercial operator in the non-bank sector the weighting will be 100 per cent. It should be noted finally that EP and Council Directive 98/33[52] has introduced a new version of Annex II on the credit risks relating to over-the-counter derivatives in commodities. This continues to exclude contracts traded on recognized

[48] OJ 1998 L204/26. [49] Art. 6(2). [50] The classification is given in Annex I.

[51] Guarantees and standby letters of credit which do have the character of credit substitutes count as full-risk.

[52] OJ 1998 L204/29.

exchanges from the capital requirements, and until the end of 2006 Member States may waive the application of the capital requirements to contracts cleared by a recognized clearing-house.

The solvency ratio Directive deals essentially with the monitoring of credit risks; on the other hand, market risks are the concern of Council Directive 93/6 on the capital adequacy of investment firms and credit institutions[53] (hereinafter the capital adequacy Directive).[54] The requirements of this Directive with regard to provisions against risks apply to credit institutions unless[55] their trading book business[56] does not normally exceed 5 per cent of their total business and never exceeds 6 per cent, and their total trading book positions do not normally exceed €15 million and never exceed €20 million. Essentially, the capital adequacy Directive requires that a non-exempted credit institution's own funds should be at least equal to the sum required under the solvency ratio Directive plus the requirements of the capital adequacy Directive with regard to position risk,[57] settlement and counterparty risk,[58] and large exposures for their trading book business, plus the requirements of that Directive with regard to foreign exchange risk[59] for all of their business activities. In addition, art. 4(2) of the capital adequacy Directive provides that the competent authorities must require institutions to cover risks arising from business outside the scope of that Directive and of the solvency ratio Directive but which are considered to be similar to the risks covered by those Directives by 'adequate' own funds. The combination of these requirements imposes a considerable burden on the credit institutions concerned. Finally, a new Annex VII setting out methods for calculating the market risk of positions in commodities and commodity derivatives has been introduced by EP and Council Directive 98/31.[60] The resulting requirements have been described as being generally lower than those applying before the introduction of the specific provisions.[61]

Although it may technically be a matter of monetary policy, the European Central Bank's Regulation 2818/98 on the application of minimum reserves[62] also seriously affects the way in which a credit institution may use its assets. It applies to credit institutions and branches of credit institutions in the Member States which participate in Economic and Monetary Union (including branches of credit institutions 'which have neither their registered nor their head office in a participating Member State') and requires them to hold a minimum reserve in a euro account

[53] OJ 1993 L141/1. Credit risks and market risks are distinguished in the recitals to that Directive.

[54] Art. 12(1) referring to art. 31(2) of Council Directive 93/22 (OJ 1993 L141/27) on investment services.

[55] Art. 14(6).

[56] The trading book is defined in art. 2(6) as consisting of its proprietory positions in certain financial instruments, and subject to certain conditions, exposures due *inter alia* to unsettled transactions, repurchase and reverse repurchase agreements, and securities lending and borrowing, and exposures in the form of certain fees, commission, interest, and dividends.

[57] Annex I. [58] Annex II. [59] Annex III. [60] OJ 1998 L204/13.

[61] See Nielsen, 'The Recent Updating of EU Financial Market Legislation' (1998) European Business Law Review 307.

[62] OJ 1998 L356/1.

with the national central bank in each participating Member State in which they have an establishment, proportionate to their reserve base in that State.[63] The reserve base is in principle defined as deposits, debt securities issued, and money market paper,[64] subject to exceptions for debts owed to other institutions subject to this regime and for liabilities owed to the ECB or participating national central banks. The minimum reserve is calculated by multiplying the reserve base by a reserve ratio, in principle is 2 per cent. However, a ratio of 0 per cent applies to deposits with an agreed maturity over two years, deposits redeemable at notice over two years, repos, and debt securities with an agreed maturity over two years. While the reserve requirement takes the assets concerned out of the hands of the credit institution concerned, the holdings concerned are at least to be remunerated at the average of the ESCB's rate for the main refinancing operations according to a formula laid down in art. 8 of the Regulation.

However, there is a special category of credit institutions which do not have to comply with the rules on capital,[65] own funds,[66] or solvency ratios.[67] These are institutions in one Member State, permanently affiliated to a central body which supervises them and which is established in that same Member State, provided that: the central body and its affiliated institutions have joint and several liability for their commitments or the central body completely guarantees the commitments of its affiliated institutions, that the solvency and liquidity of the central body and of all the affiliated institutions are monitored as a whole on the basis of consolidated accounts,[68] and that the management of the central body is empowered to issue instructions to the management of the affiliated institutions.

The 1977 Directive also lays down one criterion which may *not* be taken into account by the competent authorities when authorizing credit institutions: subject to transitional arrangements which have expired, Member States may not require the application for authorization to be examined in terms of the economic needs of the market. In other words, authorization may not be refused on the ground that there are already enough banks serving the area in question.

c) Notifiable holdings and 'close links'

Authorization depends not only on meeting the requirements as to minimum capital, own funds, and solvency ratio, but also on approval from those persons who have, directly or indirectly, a holding in the credit institution which represents 10 per cent or more of the capital or of the voting rights or which makes it possible to exercise a significant influence over the management of the institution (referred to as a 'qualifying holding').[69] Under art. 5 of the 1989 Directive, the competent authorities must not grant authorization for the taking up of business as a credit

[63] Art. 6. [64] Art. 3(1). [65] 1989 Directive, art. 2(3).
[66] 1977 Directive, art. 2(4). [67] Solvency ratio Directive, art. 1(3).
[68] Art. 1(3) of the solvency ratio Directive also requires a consolidated solvency ratio.
[69] 1989 arts. 1(10) and 5.

institution before they have been informed of the identities of such shareholders or members, who are termed 'shareholder controllers' in the UK implementation,[70] and authorization must be refused if the competent authorities are not satisfied as to their suitability, taking into account the need to ensure the sound and prudent management of a credit institution.

In fact monitoring of qualifying holdings in credit institutions is required to continue after authorization. A person proposing to acquire[71] or dispose of[72] such a holding must inform the competent authorities, who then have three months to decide whether to oppose a proposed acquisition if they are not satisfied as to the suitability of the person involved. The same requirements apply if a person with a qualifying holding proposes to increase it so that his proportion of the voting rights or of the capital would exceed thresholds of 20 per cent, 33 per cent, or 50 per cent, or so that the credit institution became his subsidiary, or if such a person proposes to decrease his holding so that his proportion of the voting rights or of the capital would fall below thresholds of the same percentages, or so that the credit institution would cease to be his subsidiary.

A duty of notification is also laid upon the credit institution itself: it must inform the competent authorities of any acquisition or disposal of which it becomes aware that would cause a holding to exceed or fall below one of the specific thresholds, and in any event it must once a year inform the competent authorities of the names of shareholders and members possessing qualifying holdings and the sizes of such holdings as shown by the information which has come into its possession e.g. at an annual general meeting. This at first sight rather curious formulation is no doubt intended as a recognition of the fact that in many Member States the use of bearer shares is widespread, and there will not be a register of those shareholders.

Sanctions are envisaged in two situations.[73] Those who fail to give advance notice of the acquisition of a qualifying holding or of an increase in their holding which would take them above one of the specific thresholds shall be subject to 'appropriate measures', and if a holding is acquired despite the opposition of the competent authorities Member States must at least provide for the exercise of corresponding voting rights to be suspended and for votes cast to be void or voidable. Secondly, where the influence exercised by a person with a qualifying holding is likely to operate to the detriment of the prudent and sound management of the institution, 'appropriate measures' shall again be taken to end that situation. Those measures may include injunctions, sanctions against directors and managers, or the suspension of the exercise of voting rights attached to the shares held by the shareholders or members in question.

More generally, EP and Council Directive 95/26[74] adds a requirement in its new art. 3(2) that the competent authorities should refuse authorization if 'close links' with other natural or legal persons prevent the effective exercise of their supervisory functions. 'Close links' are defined as a situation in which two or more

[70] UK Regs. regulation 43(2).
[71] 1989 Directive, art. 11(1).
[72] Art. 11(3).
[73] 1989 Directive, art. 11.
[74] OJ 1995 L168/7.

natural or legal persons either by 'participation', meaning the ownership, direct or by way of control, of 20 per cent or more of the voting rights or capital of an undertaking, or by 'control', meaning the relationship between a parent undertaking and a subsidiary or a similar relationship between any natural or legal person and an undertaking; in this context, a subsidiary of a subsidiary is considered to be a subsidiary of the parent undertaking at the head of those undertakings, and what might be termed collaterals (two or more natural or legal persons permanently linked to the same person by a control relationship) are also regarded as closely linked. Directive 95/26 further requires authorization to be refused where the laws, regulations, or administrative provisions of a non-Member country governing one or more natural or legal persons with which the credit institution has close links 'prevent the effective exercise of their supervisory functions'; the same applies where 'difficulties' involved in the enforcement of such laws, regulations, or administrative provisions would similarly prevent the effective exercise of their supervisory functions.

d) Permitted activities

The Community legislation limits or sets out the activities which may be carried on by credit institutions in three particular ways. The 1989 Directive limits the extent to which a credit institution may have qualifying holdings in other undertakings; Council Directive 92/121[75] limits the 'large exposures' of credit institutions; and the 1989 Directive defines the activities which benefit from the freedom to provide services and to set up branches in other Member States under its terms.

As stated above, a 'qualifying holding' is a holding in an undertaking which represents 10 per cent or more of the capital or of the voting rights or which makes it possible to exercise a significant influence over the management of the undertaking.[76] Under art. 12(1) of the 1989 Directive, no credit institution may have such a holding in another undertaking, where the amount involved exceeds 15 per cent of its own funds, unless that undertaking falls within certain limited categories. Such a holding is only permitted where the undertaking concerned is a credit institution, a financial institution (i.e. undertakings which are not credit institutions but the principal activity of which is nevertheless to acquire holdings or to carry on or more of the activities listed in the Annex to the 1989 Directive for the purposes of provision of services or establishment of branches, other than the acceptance of deposits and other repayable funds from the public),[77] or an undertaking whose activities are a direct extension of banking or concern activities ancillary to banking, such as leasing, factoring, the management of unit trusts, the management of data-processing services, or any similar activity.[78] Member States may also permit such holdings in insurance companies.[79]

[75] OJ 1993 L29/1. [76] 1989 Directive, art. 1(10). [77] Art. 1(6).

[78] By reference to art. 43(2)(f) of Council Directive 86/635 (OJ 1986 L372/1) on the accounts of banks and other financial institutions. [79] 1989 Directive, art. 12(3).

It is further provided that the total amount of a credit institution's qualifying holdings in undertakings other than those which are permitted may not exceed 60 per cent of its own funds,[80] thus effectively limiting a credit institution's non-banking activities. However, there are exceptions[81] in favour of shares held temporarily during a financial reconstruction or rescue operation, in favour of shares held in the normal course of underwriting (here the legislation does not seem to indicate a time limit for their disposal), and in favour of shares held in an institution's own name on behalf of others (a form of words which appears to cover both trusts and the practice, common in e.g. Germany, whereby banks hold shares for investors).

While these limits may be exceeded in (undefined) exceptional circumstances, the competent authorities must then require the credit institution either to increase its own funds or to take equivalent measures.[82] More generally, however, the limits may be disapplied where a Member State provides that 100 per cent of the amounts by which a credit institution's qualifying holdings exceed the limits must be covered by own funds, and these additional own funds are not included in the calculation of the solvency ratio.[83] In any event, a transitional period of ten years is provided for those credit institutions which on the date of entry into force of the national implementation measures exceed the limits laid down by the Directive.[84] Policing of these requirements is be carried out in the context of the supervision on a consolidated basis provided for by Directive 92/30.[85]

With regard to the control of 'large exposures', Community guidelines were first introduced by a non-binding Commission Recommendation,[86] but this was replaced by a Directive adopted in December 1992[87] on the basis, according to its recitals, that in a unified banking market credit institutions are engaged in direct competition with one another and monitoring requirements throughout the Community should therefore be equivalent. Exposures are essentially defined[88] as the assets and off-balance-sheet items referred to in the solvency ratio Directive[89] but without the risk adjustment used in that Directive; a 'large' exposure is defined as an exposure whose value equals or exceeds 10 per cent of the credit institution's own funds where that exposure is to one client or to a group of connected clients.[90] There is deemed to be a group of connected clients where two or more natural or legal persons constitute a single risk because one of them, directly or indirectly, has control over the other or others, or where, without such an element of control, they still constitute a single risk because they are so interconnected that, if one of them were to experience financial problems, the other or all the others would be likely to encounter repayment difficulties.[91] It may in practice be difficult to detect the latter situation before financial problems actually occur.

[80] Art. 12(2). [81] Art. 12(4). [82] Art. 12(5). [83] Art. 12(8).
[84] Art. 12(7). [85] OJ 1992 L110/52.
[86] Recommendation 87/62 (OJ 1987 L33/10).
[87] Council Directive 92/121 (OJ 1993 L29/1). [88] Art. 1(h).
[89] Directive 89/647 (OJ 1989 L386/14) art. 6. [90] Art. 3(1). [91] Art. 1(m).

A reporting requirement is imposed with regard to large exposures: Member States may provide either for all large exposures to be reported by the credit institution at least four times a year, or for all large exposures to be reported at least once a year together with a requirement to report during the year any new large exposure and any increase of 20 per cent or more in previously notified large exposures. The Directive also lays down both individual and overall limits on large exposures: no single exposure may exceed 25 per cent of the credit institution's own funds[92] and the total of large exposures may not exceed eight times the credit institution's own funds.[93] However, special rules govern exposure to the credit institution's parent undertaking, other subsidiaries of that parent, and the institution's own subsidiaries. Under art. 4(2), the credit institution's exposure in such a case must in principle be limited to 20 per cent of its own funds, but this limit need not be applied where a Member State provides for specific monitoring of such exposures by other measures or procedures. Furthermore, by virtue of art. 4(6), such exposures may be fully or partially exempted from both the individual and overall limits in so far as the undertakings concerned are covered by the supervision on a consolidated basis to which the credit institution itself is subject in accordance with Directive 92/30.[94] In practice therefore, the stricter limits only apply to those parent and subsidiary undertakings which do not fall within the scope of full consolidated supervision.[95]

Having set the basic parameters, the Directive goes on to allow for full or partial exemption of no fewer than twenty different types of exposure.[96] These include items weighted as being of zero risk under the solvency ratio Directive,[97] items subject to collateral security,[98] holdings in insurance companies up to 40 per cent of the own funds of the credit institution acquiring such a holding,[99] and loans secured by mortgages of residential property, but only up to 50 per cent of the value of the property concerned. Finally, it is provided that where, at the time of its publication, a credit institution had already exceeded the limits set out in the Directive, a transitional period expiring no later than the end of 2001 may be permitted.[100]

With regard to activities which may be carried out by way of provision of services or establishment of a branch, art. 18(1) of the 1989 Directive provides that the activities listed in the Annex to the Directive may be carried out in the host State, provided that such activities are covered by the authorization in the home State. The activities which may be carried on by a credit institution therefore depend on the law of the home State in which it was authorized, and it is therefore possible that a foreign credit institution may lawfully carry on activities which are denied to credit institutions authorized in the host State; this hardly seems likely to eliminate distortions of competition.

92 Art. 4(1).
93 Art. 4(3).
94 OJ 1992 L110/52.
95 See below pp. 133–6.
96 Art. 4(7).
97 Art. 7(a) to 7(f).
98 Art. 7(g), (h) and (o).
99 Art. 7(m).
100 Art. 6(4).

The activities listed in the Annex are: the acceptance of deposits and other repayable funds from the public (which is intrinsic to the definition of a credit institution under the 1977 Directive[101]); lending, defined as including consumer credit,[102] mortgage credit,[103] factoring with or without recourse, and the financing of commercial transactions; financial leasing; money transmission services; issuing and administering means of payment (e.g. credit cards, travellers' cheques, and bankers' drafts); guarantees and commitments; trading for the institution's own account or for the account of customers in money market instruments (cheques, bills, etc.), foreign exchange, financial futures and options, exchange and interest rate instruments, and transferable securities; participation in share issues and the provision of services related to such issues; advice to undertakings on capital structure, industrial strategy, and related questions, and advice and services relating to mergers and the purchase of undertakings; money broking; portfolio management and advice; safekeeping and administration of securities; credit reference services; and safe custody services. This list therefore covers both retail and merchant banking activities, and appears to move into the area of investment services.[104] However, it should be observed that such activities are included only to the extent that they are performed by institutions falling within the scope of the Directive.

To the extent that the activities of credit institutions fall within the scope of Council Directive 93/22 on investment services in the securities field[105] (hereinafter referred to as the investment services Directive) they must[106] observe its requirements with regard to capital adequacy,[107] with regard to home State prudential rules, [108] with regard to host State rules of conduct,[109] with regard to information about compensation funds,[110] with regard to the requirement to use and access to regulated markets,[111] and with regard to providing certain information to host and home Member States.[112]

e) Services and the establishment of branches

As mentioned in the previous Chapter, the current versions of the Banking Directives equate provision of services and establishment of a branch in another Member State by a duly authorized credit institution, both those activities being in principle covered by the authorization in the home State, although under the original version of the 1977 Directive[113] Member States could make the commence-

[101] Art. 1.
[102] See below p. 144.
[103] It therefore seems unlikely that a separate Directive on mortgage credit, such as was proposed by the Commission in 1985 (OJ 1985 C42/4), will be adopted. Furthermore, the proposal contained some provisions which appears to give rise to questions of considerable legal complexity. For example, art. 5 appeared to require a host State to allow a credit institution to fund itself according to the techniques of financing authorized in the home Member State.
[104] See below p. 141.
[105] OJ 1993 L141/27.
[106] Art. 2(1).
[107] Art. 8(2), referring to the capital adequacy Directive.
[108] Art. 10; see below p. 130.
[109] Art. 11; see below p. 131.
[110] Art. 12(1); see below p. 146.
[111] Arts. 14(3) and (4), and 15.
[112] Arts. 19 and 20.
[113] Art. 4(1), now overridden by art. 6(1) of the 1989 Directive.

ment of business in their territory by branches of credit institutions which had their head office in another Member State subject to authorization according to the law and procedure applicable to credit institutions established on their territory. However, even under the 1977 Directive[114] authorization could not be refused to a branch of a credit institution on the sole ground that it was established in another Member State in a legal form which was not allowed in the case of a credit institution carrying out similar activities in the host country, and that by virtue of art. 5 of that Directive, which remains in force, credit institutions may, notwithstanding any provisions concerning the use of the words 'bank', 'savings bank', or other banking names which may exist in the host Member State, use throughout the Community the name they use in the Member State in which their head office is situated.[115]

While art. 13 of the 1989 Directive provides that in principle the prudential supervision of a credit institution, including the activities it carries out by way of the establishment of a branch or the provision of services in another Member State, is to be the responsibility of the competent authorities of the home Member State, art. 7 of the 1977 Directive[116] still provides that the competent authorities of the Member States concerned are to co-operate closely in order to supervise the activities of credit institutions operating in one or more Member States, in particular by establishing branches there. In such a case, the competent authorities concerned are to supply one another with all information concerning the management and ownership of such credit institutions as is likely to facilitate their supervision, and all information likely to facilitate the monitoring of such institutions, in particular with regard to liquidity, solvency, deposit guarantees, the limiting of large exposures, administrative and accounting procedures, and internal control mechanisms. Further, the home State authorities may, either themselves or through persons they appoint, carry out on-the-spot verification of that information,[117] subject to informing the authorities of the host State, and the host State authorities may themselves carry out on-the-spot 'verifications' of branches established within their territory, in performance of their responsibilities under the 1989 Directive.[118]

The 'passport' granted to a credit institution by its authorization in its home State enables it to carry on such of the activities listed in the Annex to the 1989 Directive[119] as are covered by that authorization in any other Member State by the establishment of a branch or by the provision of services.[120] However, it is not only credit institutions as such which may benefit from this system: under art. 18(2), the same rights are accorded to certain 'financial institutions', undertakings which are not credit institutions but whose principal function is the carrying on of the activities listed in the Annex other than acceptance of deposits and other repayable funds

114 Art. 4(2).
115 Subject to a requirement to add explanatory particulars where there is danger of confusion.
116 As amended by art. 14 of the 1989 Directive.
117 1989 Directive, art. 15(1).
118 Art. 15(3).
119 See above p. 128.
120 1989 Directive, art. 18(1).

from the public[121] (the exclusive prerogative of credit institutions). To qualify, such a financial institution must be a subsidiary (termed a 'European subsidiary' in the UK Regulations[122]) of a credit institution or of two or more credit institutions, its memorandum and articles must permit the activities in question. It must also comply with a series of five conditions: the parent undertakings must be authorized as credit institutions in the Member State whose law governs the subsidiary; it must actually carry out the activities in question in the territory of that State; the parent undertakings must hold 90 per cent or more of the voting rights attached to shares in the subsidiary; the parent undertakings must satisfy the competent authorities regarding the prudent management of the subsidiary and must jointly and severally guarantee the commitments entered into by the subsidiary; and the subsidiary must be effectively included, for the activities in question, in the consolidated supervision of the parent undertakings.[123] Given the need for the parent credit institutions to guarantee the commitments of their financial institution subsidiaries, it is questionable what advantage may be derived from this provision. In any event, if a financial institution ceases to fulfil any of the conditions, the home Member State is required to inform the competent authorities of the host Member State, and the activities carried on by the financial institution in the host Member State become subject to the legislation of that State.[124] In the rest of this section, therefore, reference is simply made to credit institutions, although the same rules do in general apply to qualifying financial institutions.

With regard to the formalities for establishing a branch in another Member State, any credit institution wishing to establish a branch must first notify the home State competent authorities,[125] informing them of: the Member State within whose territory it intends to establish a branch, the types of business envisaged and the structural organization of the branch in the context of a programme of operations, the address in the host State from which documents may be obtained, and the names of those responsible for the management of the branch.[126] This information must be passed to the competent authorities of the host Member State within three months of its receipt,[127] unless the home Member State authorities have reason to doubt the adequacy of the credit institution's administrative structure or its financial situation, in which case they must give reasons for their refusal during that same period of three months; it is further provided that such a refusal, or a failure to reply, must be subject to judicial review. The home State authorities must also communicate to the host State authorities the amount of the own funds of the credit institution and its solvency ratio, and (pending the enactment of Community

[121] Art. 1(6). [122] Regulation 3(3). [123] See below p. 133.

[124] Assuming the requirements of that legislation to be justifiable under general Community law: see Chapter 5 above.

[125] Art. 19(1).

[126] Any subsequent change to this information in relation to the same host State must be notified in writing both to the home State and the host State authorities, at least one month before the change is made: art. 19(6) of the 1989 Directive.

[127] Art. 19(3).

rules in the matter[128]) details of any deposit-guarantee scheme intended to ensure the protection of depositors in the branch.

On receiving this information, the host Member State authorities have two months to prepare for their role in the supervision of the credit institution, and to indicate to the credit institution the conditions under which, in the interest of the general good,[129] the activities of the branch may be carried on in the host State. In the UK implementation, as observed, the Bank of England may draw the attention of the credit institution to such provisions of the Regulations, the relevant Acts, or regulations or rules made under those Acts, as 'the Bank considers appropriate' having regard to the activities mentioned in the notice, which seems to be a broad interpretation of the general good. In any event, the branch may be established and commence its activities on the expiry of the two-month limit or on the earlier receipt of a communication from the host State competent authorities.[130]

On the other hand, a credit institution wishing to provide services in another Member State for the first time merely has to notify the home authorities of the activities which it intends to carry on, and they have one month in which to pass on that notification to the host State authorities.[131] While the Directive itself appears to be silent in the point,[132] this seems to imply that the notice must be given at least one month before the credit institution begins to provide its services in that Member State. It may be wondered how far this is compatible with the Treaty to the extent that the activity concerned is one for which no notice was previously required under national law and which could be performed by virtue of the Treaty provisions without the benefit of the Directive.

However, although no host State authorization may be required, the 1989 Directive still confers certain supervisory powers on the host State authorities. Under art. 14(2), the host State authorities retain responsibility for the supervision of the liquidity of the branches of credit institutions in their territory, albeit in co-operation with the home State authorities, and they retain complete responsibility for measures resulting from the implementation of their monetary policies while such policies remain within national competence. However, monetary policy has ceased to be a matter of national policy for Member States participating in a single currency in the third stage of Economic and Monetary Union. Furthermore, where risks arising out of open positions on markets result from transactions carried out on the financial markets of a host State, the host State authorities must collaborate with the home State authorities to ensure that the institutions concerned take steps to cover those risks.[133] In order to carry out these functions, host Member States may require branches to provide the same information as they require from national credit institutions for that purpose,[134] and may in any event require all credit institutions having branches within their territory to report periodically on their activities in those host States.

128 For the text of the proposed Directive see OJ 1992 C163/6.
129 See Chapter 5 above.
130 Art. 19(5).
131 Art. 20.
132 As is the UK implementation.
133 Art. 14(2).
134 Art. 21(1).

If a host Member State comes to the conclusion that an institution having a branch or providing services within its territory is not complying with provisions adopted pursuant to the powers of a host State under the Directive, it may require the institution to put an end to that situation,[135] and if the necessary steps are not taken by the institution the host authorities are to inform the home authorities, so that they may take all appropriate measures. If, despite such measures, the institution persists in violating the relevant provisions, the host State itself may take appropriate measures to prevent or punish further irregularities and if necessary prevent the institution from initiating further transactions within its territory.[136]

Furthermore, the host State authorities may in emergencies take any precautionary measures necessary to protect the interests of depositors, investors, and others to whom services are provided, subject to informing the Commission and other national competent authorities at the earliest opportunity. The Commission may, after consulting the national authorities concerned, decide that the host State must amend or abolish those measures;[137] this gives rise to the question whether this aspect of the Directive in fact requires national implementation or whether it is a power available directly to the Commission as a matter of Community law. Express reference is in fact made to the Commission's role in the UK implementation.[138]

In any event, the 'back-up' ability of the host State to enforce rules flowing from the Directive is in addition to its power to take appropriate measures to prevent or punish contraventions within its territory of legal rules adopted in the 'general good', i.e. those national rules not yet replaced by Community rules which are objectively justifiable in the general interest.[139] In this context it may be observed that while the Directive permits credit institutions based in other Member States to advertize their services through all available means of communication in a host State,[140] this is expressly stated to be subject to any rules governing the form and content of such advertizing adopted in the interest of the general good; in effect local marketing rules of the host State still have to be observed,[141] though it is suggested that the terminology is wide enough to cover rules governing the export of services applied by the home State.[142]

The host State therefore finds itself both obliged to enforce certain of the Directives' requirements with regard to credit institutions which operate branches or offer services within its territory, and empowered to enforce such of its own rules as are justified in the general good with regard to such institutions. These functions appear to some extent to be treated together in the UK implementation, notably in the list of grounds which empower the Financial Services Authority to prohibit a credit institution authorized in another Member State from accepting

[135] Art. 21(3).
[136] Art. 22(4).
[137] Art. 21(7).
[138] UK Regs. 11(5), 11(6), 11(7).
[139] See Chapter 5 above.
[140] Art. 21(11).
[141] For a critical view see Katz, 'The General Good and the Second Banking Directive: A major loophole?' (1993) *JIBFL* 166; Björkland, 'The Scope of the General Good Notion in the Second Banking Directive According to Recent Case-Law' (1998) *European Business Law Review* 227.
[142] As in Case C–384/93 *Alpine Investments* [1995] ECR I–1141. See Chapter 5 above.

deposits in the United Kingdom.[143] These include the situations where it appears that the branch lacks adequate liquidity, or where the Authority is informed by the home State authority that the institution has failed to take sufficient steps to cover risks arising from its open market position in the United Kingdom, which respectively relate to art. 14(2) and art. 14(3) of the 1989 Directive, and also the situation where it appears that the institution has failed to comply with any obligation imposed on it under the UK Regulations 'or by or under any of the relevant Acts', a formulation wide enough to cover such national legislation as might be claimed to be justified in the general good. More particularly, under regulation 14(2)(f) and 14(3), the FSA as a host State authority may take action against a credit institution authorized in another Member State, after having unsuccessfully requested the home State authorities to take action, as envisaged in art. 21 of the 1989 Directive, where it appears to the FSA that if the institution were authorized by the FSA under the Banking Act, the FSA could revoke the authorization, whereas art. 21(2) of the Directive refers only to provisions involving powers of the *host* Member State competent authorities.

Be that as it may, account does appear to have been taken in the UK Regulations of the European Court's case-law on national measures justified in the general good.[144] Schedule 8 paragraph 13 in principle applied the requirements of the United Kingdom deposit guarantee scheme to credit institutions authorized in other Member States which accepted deposits in the United Kingdom, but under paragraph 14(2) this could be wholly or partially waived having regard to the way in which deposits made in the United Kingdom are protected under the law of the institution's home State or by virtue of any arrangements in force there. In other words, duplication of protection was not required. However, the UK rules have now been superseded by Directive 94/19 of the European Parliament and of the Council on deposit guarantee schemes.[145]

f) Subsidiaries and consolidated supervision

Unlike branches, subsidiaries of credit institutions must be authorized in the Member State in which they are created.[146] The home Member State nevertheless has a part to play. Article 7 of the 1989 Directive provides that there must be prior consultation with the competent authorities of the other Member State involved when a credit institution is authorized which is a subsidiary of a credit institution authorized in another Member State, or which is a subsidiary of the parent undertaking of a credit institution authorized in another Member State, or which is controlled by the same persons, natural or legal, who control a credit institution authorized in another Member State. Furthermore, the relationship between

[143] Reg. 9(2).
[144] Notably Case 205/84 *Commission* v. *Germany* [1986] ECR 3755. See Chapter 4 above, pp. 101–3.
[145] OJ 1994 L135/5. See p. 146 below.
[146] The principles involved are discussed in Chapter 5 above.

parent and subsidiary is important in the calculation and monitoring of a credit institution's own funds, solvency ratio, and large exposures, as made clear in art. 3(5) of Council Directive 92/30 on the supervision of credit institutions on a consolidated basis.[147]

This Directive repealed and replaced the 1983 Directive on the same topic.[148] It applies[149] to credit institutions authorized in a Member State, to financial holding companies, defined as financial institutions (i.e. undertakings which are not credit institutions but whose principal function is the carrying on of the activities listed in the Annex to the 1989 Directive other than acceptance of deposits and other repayable funds from the public,[150] still the exclusive prerogative of credit institutions) whose subsidiary undertakings are either exclusively or mainly credit institutions or financial institutions, at least one being a credit institution as such, and to mixed-activity holding companies, defined as a parent undertaking other than a financial holding company or a credit institution, whose subsidiaries include at least one credit institution. It may also be observed that by virtue of art. 7 of the capital adequacy Directive,[151] the requirements of that Directive with regard to provisions against market risks[152] and the monitoring and control of large exposures[153] are to be applied on a consolidated basis under the consolidated supervision Directive for any institution which has a credit institution, an investment firm, or another financial institution as a subsidiary, or which holds a participation in such an entity, and for any institution whose parent undertaking is a financial holding company; however, where such a group does not include a credit institution, the consolidated supervision Directive applies subject to detailed adaptations, in particular replacing references to credit institutions by references to investment firms.[154]

The nature of the consolidated supervision varies according to the nature of the undertakings involved. The fullest form applies where a credit institution has another credit institution or a financial institution as a subsidiary, or has a participation (direct or indirect ownership of 20 per cent or more of the capital or voting rights)[155] in such institutions, and similar rules apply where a financial holding company has a credit institution as a subsidiary, except that the consolidation does not imply that the competent authorities are require to play a supervisory role in relation to the financial holding company as such.[156] However, in the case of mixed-activity holding companies with a credit institution as a subsidiary, the competent authorities responsible for the authorization and supervision of the credit institution may simply require the holding company and its subsidiaries to supply information which would be relevant for the purpose of supervizing the credit institution subsidiary.[157]

[147] OJ 1992 L110/5.

[148] Council Directive 83/350 (OJ 1983 L193/18).

[149] Art. 2.

[150] Art. 1; this is the same definition as that used in art. 1(6) of the 1989 Banking Directive.

[151] Council Directive 93/6 (OJ 1993 L141/1).

[152] Art. 4; see p. 122 above.

[153] Art. 5, which refers to Council Directive 92/121 (OJ 1993 L29/1); see pp. 126–7 above.

[154] Art. 7(3) of the capital adequacy Directive.

[155] Arts. 1 and 3(1).

[156] Art. 3(2).

[157] Art. 6(1).

Determination of the competent authorities again depends on the relationship between the undertakings involved. Where a credit institution is a parent undertaking, the consolidated supervision is exercised by the authorities which authorized that institution,[158] and the same applies where a credit institution is a subsidiary of a financial holding company.[159] However, if credit institutions in more than one Member State are subsidiaries of the same financial holding company, preference is given to the authorities who authorized a credit institution in the Member State in which the financial holding company itself was established; if there is no such credit institution subsidiary, the relevant national authorities should try to agree who is to exercise consolidate supervision, and if no agreement is reached then consolidated supervision is exercised by the competent authorities who authorized the credit institution with the greatest balance sheet total, and (in a fascinating example of a draftsman trying to envisage every possibility) if that total is the same, consolidated supervision is to be exercised by the authorities who gave the earliest authorization.

In principle the competent authorities must require full consolidation of all the credit institutions and financial institutions which are the *subsidiaries* of a parent undertaking,[160] and proportional consolidation of *participations* in credit institutions and financial institutions,[161] but proportional consolidation may also be prescribed in the parent/subsidiary relationship where the liability of the parent undertaking is limited to its share of the capital of the subsidiary because of the liability of other shareholders or members whose solvency is satisfactory.

With regard to mixed-activity holding companies, the competent authorities appear to be those who authorized the credit institution subsidiary but, as previously mentioned, their basic right is to obtain information relevant for the purpose of supervising the credit institution subsidiaries, although they may carry out or appoint external inspectors to carry out on-the-spot inspections to verify information received from mixed-activity holding companies and their subsidiaries.[162]

However, where a parent undertaking and its credit institution subsidiaries are situated in different Member States, the competent national authorities are required to communicate to each other all relevant information which may allow or aid the exercise of consolidated supervision, although such information remains subject to the obligation of professional secrecy.

Finally, while it is technically a matter of statistical information rather than prudential supervision, the European Central Bank's Regulation 2819/98 on the consolidated balance sheet of the monetary financial institutions sector[163] requires monetary financial institutions resident in the euro-zone to report monthly statistical information relating to their balance sheets to the national central bank of the Member State in which they are resident; they are also required to report further details on certain items quarterly. Monetary financial institutions are defined to include credit institutions and all other resident financial institutions whose

[158] Art. 4(1). [159] Art. 4(2). [160] Art. 5(1). [161] Art. 5(2).
[162] Art. 6(2). [163] OJ 1998 L356/7.

business is to receive deposits and/or close substitutes for deposits from entities other than monetary financial institutions and, for their own account (at least in economic terms) to grant credits and/or make investments in securities; the Executive Board of the ECB[164] is to establish and maintain a list of such institutions. The information required is set out in the second and third parts of Annex I to the Regulation, and it is in particular to be used to calculate the reserve base under ECB Regulation 2818/98 on the application of minimum reserves.[165]

g) Withdrawal of authorization

Once granted, a credit institution's authorization may only be withdrawn by the authorities who gave it, even if host State authorities may restrict or prevent activities within their jurisdiction. The grounds for withdrawal of authorization are set out in an apparently restrictive manner in art. 8 of the 1977 Directive. Authorization may be withdrawn where the institution does not make use of the authorization within twelve months, renounces the authorization, or ceases to engage in business for more than six months, unless the national legislation provides for the authorization automatically to lapse in such circumstances. It may also be withdrawn where it was obtained through false statements or any other irregular means, where the credit institution no longer possesses sufficient own funds or can no longer be relied upon to fulfil its obligations towards its creditors (in particular where it no longer provides security for the assets entrusted to it), or where the institution no longer fulfils any other condition under which the authorization was granted. While this already gives the competent authorities a wide discretion in the matter, the final ground for withdrawal of authorization is that the credit institution 'falls within one of the other cases where national law provides for withdrawal of authorization'. In this context, by virtue of art. 3(2) of the 1977 Directive, the requirements for authorization laid down by Community law are stated to be without prejudice to other conditions of general application laid down by national laws. In other words, a Member State may still apply its own rules on matters not covered by the Community legislation. For example, under the UK implementation of the Directives,[166] the Bank may revoke the authorization of a credit institution incorporated in or formed under the law of any part of the United Kingdom if it is informed by the Securities and Investments Board, or a connected UK authority having regulatory functions in relation to the provision of financial services, that the credit institution 'has contravened any provision of the Financial Services Act 1986 or any rules or regulations made under it' or 'has contravened any prohibition or requirement imposed under that Act' or 'has failed to comply with any statement of principle issued under that Act'.

[164] See Chapter 10 below. [165] OJ 1998 L356/1. See p. 122 above.

[166] SI 1992 No. 3218, reg. 28(1), amending s. 11(1) of the Banking Act 1987.

Before the entry into force of the 1989 Directive, the same criteria applied to the withdrawal of authorization of branches by the competent authorities of the host State. Under the current system, as set out in art. 21(9) of the 1989 Directive, if the competent authorities in the home State withdraw authorization, they must inform the competent authorities in the host State. The authorities in the host State are then required to take appropriate measures to prevent the institution concerned from initiating further transactions within its territory and to safeguard the interests of depositors.

The sanction of withdrawal of authorisation has subsequently been extended to other requirements imposed on credit institutions. Under art. 3 of Directive 94/19 of the European Parliament and of the Council on deposit guarantee schemes,[167] a credit institution faced with exclusion from a national deposit-guarantee scheme following failure to comply with its obligations, and which is unable to make alternative arrangements offering equivalent protection, is liable to have its authorization revoked forthwith.

However, the credit institution must be given certain minimum opportunities to defend itself and to challenge the authorities. The 1977 Directive requires[168] that reasons must be given for any withdrawal of authorization, and those concerned must be informed thereof. Furthermore, that Directive sets out a general principle of judicial review, stating in art. 13 that Member States shall ensure that decisions taken in respect of a credit institution in pursuance of laws, regulations, and administrative decisions adopted in accordance with the Directive are subject to the right to apply to the courts.

h) Confidentiality and disclosure

It is well known that different Member States have different traditions with regard to the scope of banking secrecy. Nevertheless, the 1977 Directive endeavoured in its art. 12 to set out basic criteria with regard to those concerned in the systems of authorization and supervision it established. That provision was completely redrafted by art. 16 of the 1989 Directive; it was further amended and supplemented by a series of provisions introduced by Directive 95/26 of the European Parliament and of the Council on the reinforcement of prudential supervision,[169] adopted in the wake of the collapse of the Bank of Credit and Commerce International (BCCI).

In its current version, it essentially requires[170] that all persons working or who have worked for the competent authorities, as well as auditors or experts working on their behalf, should be bound by the obligation of professional secrecy. While this term is not comprehensively defined, it is stated to mean that no confidential information which they receive in the course of their duties may be divulged to any person or authority whatsoever, except in summary or collective form so that

[167] OJ 1994 L135/5. [168] Art. 8(5). [169] OJ 1995 L168/7. [170] Art. 12(1).

individual institutions cannot be identified, without prejudice to cases covered by criminal law. The solitary exemption in favour of cases covered by criminal law represents a tightening of the original obligation of secrecy, which allowed information to be divulged where a legislative provision so required; this was interpreted by the European Court in Case 110/84 *Hillegom* v. *Hillenius*[171] as meaning that the obligation of professional secrecy could be overridden by general legislation imposing an obligation to give evidence even in civil proceedings. The limitation to criminal cases introduced by the 1989 Directive therefore at first sight appears to represent a deliberate decision by the Council to reverse that case-law. However, the case actually involved a credit institution in liquidation, and the new version of art. 12(1) adds a second sub-paragraph to the effect that where a credit institution has been declared bankrupt or is being compulsorily wound up, confidential information which does not concern third parties involved in attempts to rescue that credit institution may be divulged in civil or commercial proceedings.

It is also made clear that while the obligation of professional secrecy does not prevent the relevant competent authorities from exchanging information in accordance with the Directives, that information once exchanged is subject to the obligation.[172] Subject to the same terms, information may also be exchanged within one Member State or with another Member State between: the competent authorities and the authorities responsible for the supervision of other financial institutions, insurance companies, and financial markets, bodies involved in the liquidation and bankruptcy of credit institutions, persons responsible for carrying out statutory audits of the accounts of credit institutions and other financial institutions, in the discharge of their supervisory functions, and bodies which administer deposit-guarantee schemes to the extent necessary for the exercise of their functions.[173] The exchange of information may similarly be authorized with the authorities responsible for the supervision of bodies involved in the liquidation and bankruptcy of financial undertakings and with the authorities responsible for overseeing persons charged with carrying out statutory audits of the accounts of insurance companies, credit institutions, investment firms, and other financial institutions.[174] It may also be authorized with authorities or bodies responsible under the law for detection and investigation of breaches of company law.[175]

Disclosure may also be made to those central banks (presumably now including the ECB) and other bodies with a similar function, in their capacity as monetary authorities, and where appropriate to other public authorities responsible for overseeing payment systems, of information intended for the performance of their task[176] and, if national law so allows or requires, to other central government departments responsible for legislation on the supervision of credit institutions, financial institutions, investment services and insurance companies, and to inspec-

[171] [1985] ECR 3947. [172] Art. 12(2). [173] Art. 12(5).

[174] Art. 12(5a) added by EP and Council Directive 95/26.

[175] Art. 12(5b) added by EP and Council Directive 95/26.

[176] Art. 12(6) as amended by EP and Council Directive 95/26.

tors acting on behalf of those departments, but only where necessary for reasons of prudential control.[177] In the case of such government departments, however, disclosure may never be made of information obtained from other competent authorities or other supervisory bodies, or obtained by means of on-the-spot verification of branches carried out in the host State under art. 15 of the 1989 Directive.[178] The competent authorities may also, subject to the usual obligation of professional secrecy, communicate information to a clearing-house or other similar body recognized under national law for the provision of clearing or settlement services for one of the Member States' markets if they consider it is necessary to communicate the information in order to ensure the proper functioning of those bodies in relation to defaults or potential defaults by market participants.[179]

A further amendment made by EP and Parliament Directive 98/33[180] enables Member States to conclude agreements for the exchange of information even with non-banking supervisory authorities of third countries subject to obligations of professional secrecy similar to those applied to the exchange of information between Community authorities.

What the competent authorities may do with the information they receive is to use it to check that the conditions governing the taking-up of the business of credit institutions are met, and to facilitate the monitoring of such business, notably with regard to liquidity, solvency, large exposures, and administrative and accounting procedures and internal control mechanisms. It may also be used to impose sanctions, and in administrative appeals and judicial review proceedings relating to decisions of the competent authority.[181]

As well as this series of permissions to exchange information, EP and Council Directive 95/26[182] imposes certain obligations of disclosure.[183] Company auditors[184] carrying out defined auditing functions 'or any other statutory task' have a duty to report promptly to the competent authorities certain facts or decisions concerning the undertaking of which they become aware while carrying out that task. The facts or decisions at issue are: those liable to constitute a material breach of provisions which lay down conditions governing the authorization of financial undertakings, or which specifically govern the pursuit of their activities; those which affect the continuous functioning of the financial undertaking; and those which would lead to a refusal to certify the accounts or to 'the expression of reservations' with regard to the accounts. Auditors are under a similar duty to disclose facts and decisions affecting undertakings having 'close links resulting from a control relationship'[185] with the financial undertaking within which they are carrying our their task. In both cases, disclosure in good faith to the competent authorities is deemed not to breach the restrictions on disclosure of information whether imposed by

[177] Art. 12(7). [178] See p. 129 above.
[179] Art. 12(8) added by EP and Council Directive 95/26.
[180] OJ 1998 L204/29, adding a new art. 12(3). [181] Art. 12(4).
[182] OJ 1995 L168/7. [183] As art. 12a of Directive 77/780.
[184] Within the meaning of Council Directive 84/253 (OJ 1984 L126/20).
[185] See p. 133 above.

contract or by any legislative, regulatory, or administrative provision, and will not involve the auditors in liability of any kind.[186] Put bluntly, auditors are in these circumstances required to become whistle-blowers.

What is left of the obligation of secrecy, albeit subject to massive derogations in favour of the supervisory authorities, may be contrasted with the objectives of the Money Laundering Directive,[187] intended essentially to prohibit transactions in property derived from criminal activity undertaken to conceal or disguise its illicit origins. The importance currently attributed to this concept may be gauged from the fact that under all the Europe Agreements with Central and East European countries, the parties agree to co-operate to prevent the use of their financial systems for laundering of proceeds from criminal activities in general and drug offences in particular.[188] Under art. 3 of the Directive, credit and financial institutions must require identification of customers when entering into business relationships, in particular when opening accounts or offering safe custody facilities, and in the context of any other single transaction or linked transactions involving a sum of €15,000 or more. Furthermore, under art. 6 credit and financial institutions and their directors and employees must on their own initiative inform the authorities responsible for combatting money laundering of any fact which might be an indication of money laundering, and must at the request of those authorities supply them with all necessary information. This information must be given to the responsible authorities in the Member State in whose territory the institution forwarding the information is situated; this seems to mean that a branch in another Member State, although remaining subject to the prudential control of its home State authorities, must pass information about money laundering to the host State authorities.[189] There is a certain logic to this requirement: if the competent authorities responsible for the supervision of credit institutions discover facts that could constitute evidence of money laundering, they must inform the responsible authorities under art. 10 of the Money Laundering Directive. In principle, information supplied under art. 6 may only be used in connection with the combatting of money laundering, but 'Member States may provide that such information may also be used for other purposes', an apparently open-ended derogation.

In any event, by virtue of art. 9 disclosure in good faith to the responsible authorities by an employee or director of a credit or financial institution shall not constitute a breach of any restriction on disclosure of information imposed by contract or by any legislative, regulatory, or administrative provision, and shall not involve the institution or its directors or employees in liability of any kind.

[186] Art. 12a(2).

[187] Council Directive 91/308 (OJ 1991 L166/77).

[188] See e.g. Bulgarian Agreement art. 87, Czech Agreement art. 86.

[189] As pointed out by Dassesse in '1992: An EEC update', (1991) *JIBFL* 384 at p.387.

3. Collective and individual investments

The Directive on the co-ordination of laws, regulations, and administrative provisions relating to undertakings for collective investment in transferable securities (UCITS)[190] may be regarded as the pioneer of the system of home State control subsequently used in the Second Banking Directive and other financial services legislation. At first sight, it appears to go further, in that authorization by the competent authorities in the Member State in which the UCITS is 'situated' is stated to be 'valid for all Member States'. However, in reality the only activity by a UCITS in another Member State which seems to be envisaged by the Directive is that of marketing its units,[191] i.e. provision of services.

The bulk of the Directive is concerned with the enactment of common basic rules for the authorization, supervision, structure, and activities of UCITS and with the information they must publish: another example of increased regulation as the price for opening up the market. To the extent that a UCITS may wish to market its units in another Member State, it must under art. 44 comply with host State rules which do not fall within the field governed by the Directive, in particular host State rules on advertizing. Furthermore, under art. 45 it must, in compliance with host State rules, take the measures necessary to ensure that facilities are available in that State for making payments to unit-holders, repurchasing or redeeming units, and making available the information which UCITS are obliged to provide.

UCITS are defined in art. 1(2) as undertakings whose sole object is the collective investment in transferable securities of capital raised from the public and which operate on the principle of risk-spreading, and whose units are, at the request of holders, repurchased or redeemed, directly or indirectly, out of those undertakings' assets—entities perhaps better known in the United Kingdom as unit trusts. However, following a proposal put forward by the Commission in 1989,[192] a Directive on investment services in the securities field was adopted in 1993,[193] together with a concomitant Directive on capital adequacy of investment firms and credit institutions.[194] The investment services Directive applies to investment firms and to credit institutions whose authorization[195] covers one or more of the investment services listed in Section A of the Annex to the Directive, i.e. reception and transmission, on behalf of investors, of orders in relation to one or more of the relevant instruments,[196] execution of such orders other than for own account, dealing in those instruments as principal, portfolio management where the portfolio includes such instruments, and offering underwriting services in respect of issues of

[190] Council Directive 85/611 (OJ 1985 L375/3), to be read with Council Directive 85/553 (OJ 1985 L372/39).

[191] Arts. 44–8.

[192] OJ 1989 C43/7.

[193] Council Directive 93/22 (OJ 1993 L141/27).

[194] Council Directive 93/6 (OJ 1993 L141/1).

[195] See p. 117 above.

[196] Transferable securities, money market instruments, financial futures and options, and exchange rate and interest rate instruments.

the relevant instruments or placing of such issues. The final list is much narrower than in earlier proposals, which included giving professional investment advice, or in safekeeping and administration of any of the relevant instruments, which are now treated as non-core services.[197] An investment firm is defined as being in principle a legal person[198] whose regular occupation or business is the provision of investment services for third parties on a professional basis. Undertakings which are not legal persons may only be included subject to a long list of supplementary conditions, essentially designed to protect third parties and monitor their solvency. This may be contrasted with the earlier proposal, which appeared to include natural persons giving professional investment advice.

In essence, it follows the pattern of the Second Banking Directive, laying down a requirement of authorization[199] and making the same distinction between provision of services and establishment of branches on one hand, and establishment of subsidiaries on the other.[200] It also provides for the application of host State rules justified in the general good, but more specifically allows for the application of the conduct of business rules of the State in which a service is provided (i.e. the host State in the case of establishment of a branch or provision of services across a frontier). These rules are set out in art. 11, and are based on seven minimum principles. The principles relate to: honesty and fairness; skill, care and diligence; resources and procedures for proper performance; information about clients; disclosure to clients; avoidance or fair management of conflicts of interest; and compliance with regulatory requirements. It is suggested that some of these overlap with home State prudential control as set out in art. 10: these provisions require firms and institutions to have sound administrative and accounting procedures, to make adequate arrangements for instruments and funds belonging to investors, to arrange for appropriate records to be kept of transactions executed so as to enable the home State authorities to monitor compliance with the prudential rules, and to be so structured and organized as to minimize the risk of clients' being prejudiced by conflicts of interests—though where a branch is established in another Member State, these arrangements must not conflict with the rules of conduct laid down by the host State to cover conflicts of interest; in other words, although it is the duty of the home State to lay down such rules, the rules of the host State take priority.

Other distinctive features include variable capital requirements in the capital adequacy Directive. The minimum capital is set by art. 3 of that Directive at €50,000 for firms which do not hold funds belonging to clients, €125,000 for firms which operate according to investors' instructions, and €730.000 for other investment firms. Under art. 4, investment firms must also hold, in addition to the own funds measured against market risk which must also be held by credit institutions offering investment services,[201] own funds equal to at least three months' operating costs (referred to as fixed overheads in Annex IV of the Directive). A new Annex VII has been added to the capital adequacy Directive by EP and Council Directive

[197] Section C of the Annex. [198] Art. 1(2). [199] Art. 3. [200] Art. 14.

[201] See p. 118 above.

98/31,[202] setting out methods for calculating the market risk of positions in commodities and commodity derivatives; the resulting requirements have been described as generally lower than those applying before the introduction of the specific provisions.[203]

The investment services Directive also tackles the question of regulated and unregulated markets. Regulated markets are defined[204] as markets listed by the Member States where conditions for the operation of the market, conditions for access to the market, and conditions governing admission to listing or dealings on the market are defined by regulations issued or approved by the competent authorities. One aspect of this is that under art. 14(3) Member States may require transactions involving investors habitually resident or established in that State to be carried out in a regulated market unless the investor specifically requests otherwise.[205] Another problem was that in some Member States credit institutions could not themselves become members of regulated markets, being required to establish specialist subsidiaries; art. 15 of the Directive opens these market to credit institutions, but with a derogation until the end of 1999 for Spain, Greece, and Portugal. There was also a derogation until the end of 1996 for the other Member States involved (which appear to have been Belgium, France, and Italy). However, as noted in the context of the principle of freedom to provide services,[206] art. 15(3) and (4) appear to leave it to the host State to determine whether a physical presence is required to become a member of or have access to such a market. Article 15(3) requires as a matter of Community law access for local branches or subsidiaries of investment firms authorized in their home State, but art. 15(4) only allows access without an establishment in the host State where the regulated market of the host State so allows.

The investment services Directive also contains detailed rules about the information in relation to each regulated market which the competent national authorities must ensure is given to investors. Under art. 21, at the beginning of each market working day, information must be given as to the weighted average price, the highest price, the lowest price, and the volume negotiated on the relevant regulated market on the previous working day. For continuous regulated markets, the weighted average price and the traded volume must be published every working hour in relation to a six-hour period ending two hours before publication, and every twenty minutes there must be published the weighted average price, the highest price, and the lowest price over a two-hour period ending one hour before publication. Furthermore, where investors are given information in advance on prices and quantities of securities, such information must be available at any time, and the terms announced must be those under which the investor may carry out the transaction.

[202] OJ 1998 L204/13.

[203] See Nielsen, 'The Recent Updating of EU Financial Market Legislation' (1998) *European Business Law Review* 307.

[204] Art. 1(13) of the Directive.

[205] Art. 14(4).

[206] See p. 105 above.

It is therefore suggested that the investment services Directive has as much to do with the protection of investors as opening up the market. Nevertheless, the removal of national barriers to access under the Directive has been one of the factors leading to the development of an alliance between European Stock Exchanges instigated by the London and Frankfurt exchanges, the first stage of which, completed in January 1999, involved allowing common access to participating trading systems.[207] The second stage involves market convergence, and the third stage, in 2000, involves a single market for certain European securities which will be operated by a separate company on a single trading system.

4. Customers and consumers

The fundamental aim of the 1986[208] and 1990[209] consumer credit Directives, which have to some extent been inspired by United Kingdom consumer credit legislation, is to ensure that the consumer (defined as a natural person acting outside his trade or profession[210]) receives certain information about the credit agreements into which he enters. In particular, they require information to be given about the annual percentage rate of charge (APR), both in advertisements and offers relating to credit[211] and in the agreement itself, which must be in writing.[212] The APR is a concept which was originally left to the Member States to determine, but a Community definition was introduced by the 1990 Directive. The APR is the total cost of credit to the consumer expressed as an annual percentage of the amount of credit granted, calculated according to a formula set out in Annex II introduced by the 1990 Directive. Under art. 1a(2), introduced by the 1990 Directive, the 'total cost of the credit to the consumer' does *not* include charges payable by the borrower for non-compliance, charges other than the purchase price which would also be payable in a cash sale, charges for the transfer of funds and keeping an account to receive payment, subscriptions to associations or groups arising under separate agreements, or charges for insurance and guarantees unless intended to ensure that the creditor receives payment in the event of the death, invalidity, illness, or unemployment of the consumer.

The consumer credit Directives also deal with such matters as the consequences of repossession and early redemption. With regard to the former, art. 7 requires that the account between the parties should be made up in such a way as to ensure that repossession does not entail any unjustified enrichment; with regard to the latter, the consumer is given the right to make early settlement under art. 8, and to receive an 'equitable' reduction in the total cost of the credit, in accordance with rules laid down by the Member States.

[207] London and Frankfurt Stock Exchanges, 'European Alliance: Joint briefing and consultation document' (March 1999).

[208] OJ 1987 L42/48.

[209] OJ 1990 L61/14.

[210] Art. 1(2)(a).

[211] Art. 3.

[212] Art. 4.

It is further provided that the consumer may have a remedy against the grantor of credit when he cannot obtain satisfaction from the supplier of the goods and services, at least where the grantor of credit and the supplier of the goods or services have entered into an exclusive arrangement with regard to the supply of credit. However, Member States are left to determine to what extent and under what conditions this remedy shall be exercisable.[213]

With regard to the scope of the Directive, which in principle only extends to agreements involving amounts of between 200 and 20,000 ECU[214] it does not apply *inter alia* to mortgage credit[215] or to agreements for the purchase or improvement of land and buildings,[216] but it does apply to credit card agreements, although not to other advances on a current account granted by a credit institution or financial institution.[217] However, although the other provisions of the Directive do not apply to such advances on a current account, art. 6 still requires that the customer be informed in advance of the credit limit, the APR and other charges, and the procedure for terminating the agreement.

There is at first sight a link with the other banking legislation to the extent that art. 12(1)(a) requires those offering credit or offering to arrange credit agreements to obtain official authorization. However, this is merely an alternative to art. 12(1)(b) and (c), which allow Member States to arrange for inspection or monitoring, or merely to 'promote' the establishment of appropriate bodies to receive complaints and provide relevant information or advice.

Given the exclusion of mortgage credit from the consumer credit Directives, it must have seemed appropriate to enact special rules in this area, and a proposal was first published in 1985.[218] However, this proposal has now been overtaken by events, since 'lending' is among the activities covered by the Second Banking Directive. The result appears to be that consumers of mortgage credit fall outside the scope of specific Community consumer protection legislation, even if in reality there is protection at the national level.

While the consumer credit legislation is intended to protect consumers as borrowers, deposit guarantee legislation is essentially intended to protect them as investors. The Commission put forward a non-binding Recommendation on this matter at the end of 1986.[219] By 1992 ten of the then twelve Member States had such schemes.[220] It has already been observed that the UK implementing legislation for the Second Banking Directive treated the UK deposit guarantee scheme as an example of legislation which may be imposed on branches of banks authorized in other Member States in the 'general good'. Linked to the entry into force of the Second banking Directive, the Commission put forward a proposal for a Directive on deposit guarantees, which was eventually enacted as Directive 94/19 of the

[213] Art. 11(2). [214] Art. 2(1)(f). [215] Art. 2(3) as amended by the 1990 Directive.
[216] Art. 2(1)(a). [217] Art. 2(1)(e). [218] COM (84) 730 final; OJ 1985 C42/4.
[219] Recommendation 87/63 (OJ 1987 L33/16).
[220] According to the recitals to the initial draft of the Directive on the matter (OJ 1992 C163/6).

European Parliament and of the Council on deposit guarantee schemes.[221] The recitals to this Directive set out the need to have such a scheme in order to maintain depositor confidence, but also, no doubt in the light of American experience, indicate that it is undesirable to introduce throughout the Community a very high level of protection 'which might in certain cases have the effect of encouraging the unsound management of credit institutions'. The essentials of the Directive are that home-State deposit-guarantee schemes shall cover the depositors at branches set up by credit institutions in other Member States.[222] Until 31 December 1999, however, neither the level nor the scope, including the percentage, of cover provided is to exceed the maximum level or scope of cover offered by the corresponding guarantee scheme within the territory of the host Member State. On the other hand, branches in Member States with higher levels of protection should be enabled voluntarily to join the host State scheme.[223] With regard to branches of third-country credit institutions, art. 6 requires Member States to check that branches established by a credit institution which has its head office outwith the Community have cover equivalent to that prescribed in the Directive. Failing that, Member States may stipulate that branches established by such a credit institution must join deposit-guarantee schemes in operation within their territories.

With regard to the level of protection, deposit-guarantee schemes must stipulate that the aggregate deposits of each depositor must be covered up to €20,000 in the event of deposits being unavailable. However, Member States where, at the time when the Directive was adopted, deposits were not covered up to €20,000 could retain the maximum amount laid down in their guarantee schemes, provided that this amount was not less than €15,000 until 31 December 1999.[224] However, Member States may limit the guarantee to a specified percentage of deposits. The percentage guaranteed must be at least 90 per cent of aggregate deposits until the amount to be paid under the guarantee reaches the figure of €15,000 or €20,000, as the case may be.[225] Deposit-guarantee schemes are required to be in a position to pay duly verified claims by depositors in respect of unavailable deposits within three months of the date on which the competent authorities make the determination that the deposit is unavailable.[226]

This Directive has the distinction of having been challenged on the ground, *inter alia*, that it breached the principle of subsidiarity[227] laid down in art. [3b] of the EC Treaty, in Case C–233/94 *Germany* v. *Parliament and Council*.[228] Germany claimed, unsuccessfully, that there was no need to replace the voluntary German system of deposit guarantees by the compulsory system instituted by Directive 94/19 of the Parliament and Council.[229] However, the Court pointed out that the Directive expressly stated in its Recitals that the action the Member States had taken in response to the earlier Commission Recommendation had not fully achieved the

[221] OJ 1994 L135/5.
[222] Art. 4(1).
[223] Art. 4(2).
[224] Art. 7(1).
[225] Art. 7(4).
[226] Art. 10.
[227] See Usher, *EC Institutions and Legislation* (Longman 1998) ch. 5.
[228] [1997] ECR I-2405.
[229] OJ 1994 L135/5.

desired result; and that that situation might prove prejudicial to the proper functioning of the internal market; in its view, this showed that the Parliament and Council had acted in conformity with the principle of subsidiarity.

It may also be observed that art. 12 of the investment services Directive[230] indicated that the Commission would put forward a proposal on the harmonization of compensation systems covering transactions by investment firms, and this led to the adoption of Directive 97/9 of the European Parliament and of the Council on investor-compensation schemes,[231] which is drafted in parallel terms to the deposit-guarantee Directive.

The aim of providing information for consumers, which largely underlies the consumer credit Directive, also inspired much of the Commission's non-binding Recommendation[232] on the transparency of banking conditions relating to cross-border financial transactions, in turn replaced by Directive 97/5 of the European Parliament and Council on cross-border credit transfers.[233] This sets out a series of six principles to be followed in the context of cross-border financial transactions. The fundamental aim is that each institution should bring to the attention of its customers easily understandable and readily available information concerning such transactions, informing customers as to the fees and charges involved, and the exchange rate applied.[234] The Directive sets out time limits for effecting transfers.[235] sets out obligations with regard to refunds,[236] and requires the creation of complaints machinery.[237]

Finally, the general Directive on unfair terms in consumer contracts,[238] adopted in 1993, contains a number of provisions which relate expressly to financial service contracts. The heart of this Directive is art. 3, under which a contractual term which has not been individually negotiated shall be regarded as unfair if, contrary to the requirement of good faith, it causes a significant imbalance in the parties' rights and obligations arising under the contract, to the detriment of the consumer. A term is always to be regarded as not individually negotiated where it has been drafted in advance and the consumer has not been able to influence the substance of the term, particularly in the context of a pre-formulated standard contract. It then refers to the Annex to the Directive, which contains an indicative and non-exhaustive list of terms which may be regarded as unfair, specifically mentioning various forms of financial service contract.

Subparagraphs (g), (j), and (l) of section 1 of the Annex respectively treat as unfair: terms which enable a supplier to terminate a contract of indeterminate duration without reasonable notice except where there are serious grounds for doing so; terms which enable the supplier to alter the terms of the contract unilaterally without a valid reason which is specified in the contract; and terms which allow a supplier of services to increase the price without giving the consumer the

[230] Council Directive 93/22 (OJ 1993 L141/27).
[231] OJ 1997 L84/22.
[232] Recommendation 90/109 (OJ 1990 L67/39).
[233] OJ 1997 L43/25.
[234] Art. 3.
[235] Art. 6.
[236] Art. 8.
[237] Art. 10.
[238] Council Directive 93/13 (OJ 1993 L95/29).

corresponding right to cancel the contract if the final price is too high in relation to the price agreed when the contract was concluded. However, under section 2(c) of the Annex, none of these three provisions apply to transactions in transferable securities, financial instruments, and other products or services where the price is linked to fluctuations in a stock exchange quotation or index or a financial market rate that the supplier does not control, or to contracts for the purchase or sale of foreign currency, travellers' cheques, or international money orders denominated in foreign currency. Under section 2(a), with perhaps less obvious reason, the prohibition against terminating a contract of indeterminate duration without reasonable notice does not prevent a supplier of financial services from so doing where there is a 'valid reason', whatever that may be, provided that the supplier informs the other contracting party or parties immediately. Finally, under section 2(b), the prohibition against unilateral alteration of the contract does not prevent the adoption of terms under which the supplier of financial services reserves the right to alter the rate of interest payable by or to the consumer, or the amount of other charges for financial services, provided again that there is a 'valid reason', the supplier informs the other contracting party or parties at the earliest opportunity, and the other party or parties are free to dissolve the contract immediately.

While the reasons for the special treatment of e.g. transactions in quoted or indexed transferable securities may be self-evident, terms which would be treated as unfair in other contracts are permissible in financial services contracts, albeit with considerable safeguards.

While the general EP and Council Directive 97/7 on the protection of consumers in respect of distance contracts does not apply to financial services, leaving the matter to be governed by national rules to the extent that they are justified in the general good, at the end of 1998 the Commission did put forward a proposal for an EP and Council Directive on the distance marketing of consumer financial services.[239] This proposal would apply to any contract concerning financial services concluded between a supplier and a consumer under an organized distance sales or service-provision scheme run by the supplier, who, for the purpose of that contract, makes use of means of distance communication up to and including the time at which the contract is concluded. 'Means of distance communication' is defined as any means which, without the simultaneous physical presence of the supplier and the consumer, may be used for the distance marketing of a service between those parties. The proposed directive would provide for a 'cooling-off' period of fourteen days, in which the consumer has the right to withdraw, and this period is extended to thirty days in the case of contracts relating to mortgages, life assurance, or personal pension operations.[240] The proposal would also prohibit the distance supply of unsolicited financial services to consumers;[241] in effect therefore, it confirms the policy upheld by the Court with regard to national rules prohibiting cold-calling in Case C–384/93 *Alpine Investments*.[242]

239 OJ 1998 C385/10. 240 Art. 4(1). 241 Arts. 9 and 10.
242 [1995] ECR I–1141; see Chapter 5 above at p. 107.

5. Payments

While Directive 97/5 of the European Parliament and Council on cross-border credit transfers[243] is concerned largely with the protection of consumers in the context of cross- border financial transactions, the development of a single currency has led to the adoption of basic common rules designed to protect payments systems as such in EP and Council Directive 98/26 on settlement finality in payment and securities settlement systems.[244] Such a system is defined[245] as a formal arrangement:

- between three or more participants, without counting a possible settlement agent, a possible central counterparty, a possible clearing house, or a possible indirect participant, with common rules and standardized arrangements for the execution of transfer orders between the participants,
- governed by the law of a Member State chosen by the participants; the participants may, however, only choose the law of a Member State in which at least one of them has its head office, and
- designated, without prejudice to other more stringent conditions of general application laid down by national law, as a system and notified to the Commission by the Member State whose law is applicable, after that Member State is satisfied as to the adequacy of the rules of the system.

The transfer orders referred to in the first part of this definition are any instruction by a participant to place at the disposal of a recipient an amount of money by means of a book entry on the accounts of a credit institution, a central bank, or a settlement agent, or any instruction which results in the assumption or discharge of a payment obligation as defined by the rules of the system, or an instruction by a participant to transfer the title to, or interest in, a security or securities by means of a book entry on a register, or otherwise.

The fundamental aim of the Directive is set out in art. 3, which provides that transfer orders and netting (defined in turn as the conversion into one net claim or one net obligation of claims and obligations resulting from transfer orders which a participant or participants either issue to, or receive from, one or more other participants with the result that only a net claim can be demanded or a net obligation be owed) are legally enforceable and, even in the event of insolvency proceedings against a participant, binding on third parties, provided that the transfer orders were entered into a system before the moment of opening of such insolvency proceedings. However, where, exceptionally, transfer orders are entered into a system after the moment of opening of insolvency proceedings and are carried out on the day of opening of such proceedings, they are legally enforceable and binding on third parties only if, after the time of settlement, the settlement

[243] OJ 1997 L43/25. [244] OJ 1998 L166/45. [245] Art. 2(a).

agent, central counterparty, or clearing-house can prove that they were not aware, nor should have been aware, of the opening of such proceedings.

It is further provided that no law, regulation, rule, or practice on the setting aside of contracts and transactions concluded before the moment of opening of insolvency proceedings shall lead to the unwinding of a netting. This aim of insulating transfer orders and netting in a payments system is further reinforced by a number of specific provisions relating to insolvency. Included among these is art. 9, under which the rights of a participant to collateral security provided to it in connection with a system, and the rights of central banks of the Member States or the European Central Bank to collateral security provided to them, 'shall not be affected' by insolvency proceedings against the participant or counterparty to central banks of the Member States or the ECB which provided the collateral security. It is simply stated that such collateral security may be realized for the satisfaction of these rights. However, art. 9(2) adds that where securities (including rights in securities) are provided as collateral security to participants and/or central banks of the Member States or the ECB, and their right (or that of any nominee, agent, or third party acting on their behalf) with respect to the securities is legally recorded on a register, account, or centralized deposit system located in a Member State, the determination of the rights of such entities as holders of collateral security in relation to those securities is governed by the law of that Member State.

The fundamental aim is clearly to protect the integrity of the payments system, and effectively the rights of third parties are sacrificed to this overriding purpose. However, there is a small measure of protection for third parties: anyone with a legitimate interest may require a credit institution or investment firm to inform him or her of the systems in which it participates and to provide information about the main rules governing the functioning of those systems.

6. Conclusions

In the financial services sector the price of opening up the single internal market has indeed been increased Community legislation. Furthermore, despite the development of the concept of subsidiarity, there has been a steady movement away from soft law towards hard law rather than the other way round: in areas as diverse as large exposures,[246] deposit guarantees,[247] and cross-border credit transfers,[248] non-binding Recommendations have been replaced by binding Directives.

[246] See p. 126 above. [247] See p. 146 above. [248] See p. 149 above.

7

From units of account to the euro

1. The legal need for units of account

While a common currency for eleven of the Member States was only introduced in January 1999, the European Communities have from the outset required their own accounting units, and the euro is the direct descendant of the last version of the unit of account: Council Regulation 1103/97[1] provides that every reference in a legal instrument to the European Currency Unit (ECU) as defined under Community law is to be replaced by a reference to the euro at the rate of one euro to one ECU, and references in any legal instrument to the ECU are deemed to be references to the ECU as defined in Community law, subject to the intentions of the parties.[2]

The need for a unit of account was recognized in the Coal and Steel High Authority's Decision No. 2 of 13 December 1952[3] dealing with the levy payable under that Treaty. Article 50(2) of the Coal and Steel Treaty provided that the levies should be assessed annually on the relevant products according to their average value, and the High Authority in fact decided to fix a levy in units of account, these being units of account of the European Payments Union established in 1950. In theory, the effect of using the unit of account was that the High Authority could fix a flat-rate levy which should be the same in real terms irrespective of where in the Community the products originated, and irrespective of the currency used in any actual transaction. The levy under art. 50(2) of the Coal and Steel Treaty was intended as the 'own resource' of the Coal and Steel budget, and the modern budget of the European Communities (which in fact excludes the Coal and Steel operational budget[4]) was itself always drafted in terms of units of account.[5] The aim was to avoid using the currency of any one Member State, but one result of the introduction of the euro in place of the ECU[6] is that the Community is using the currency of eleven of its Member States for its own accounting purposes, and as far as the other four Member States are concerned, the Community is using a foreign currency as its accounting unit.

[1] OJ 1997 L162/1. [2] Art. 2. [3] JO 1952 No. 1, p. 3.

[4] Art. 20 of the Merger Treaty 1965 provides for the ECSC *administrative* expenditure to be shown in the general budget of the European Communities, and limits the amount of that expenditure to be met from the ECSC levy.

[5] ECUs have been used in the general EC budget since the entry into force of the 1980 Financial Regulations (OJ 1980 L345/23).

[6] Council Regulation 1103/97 (OJ 1997 L162/1).

Units of account were used not only in the budget itself, but also in relation to funds falling outside the scope of the budget as such. For example, successive European Development Funds, created originally for the benefit of those countries associated with the Community under art. 131 of the EC Treaty, with subsequent European Development Funds being created for the purposes of the 1963 and 1969 Yaoundé Conventions and the subsequent Lomé Conventions, were denominated in units of account, even though these funds were financed through fixed contributions from the Member States. Indeed, it was in the context of the fourth European Development Fund, established pursuant to the 1975 Lomé Convention,[7] that the unit of account calculated from the current values of a basket of currencies (the ECU) was used for the first time.

Turning to the greatest source of Community expenditure, the Common Agricultural Policy, the major common organizations are based on a common price policy,[8] in which the prices are all fixed in units of account.[9] Leaving aside the unfortunate history of monetary compensation introduced when currencies first floated in 1971, the theory since 1992 has been that there are single prices at the Community level, and exchange risks are borne at the national level.[10] However, the introduction of the euro means that Community prices are set, granted, and collected in the currency of eleven of the Member States, and there are exchange risks only in relation to the Member States which do not participate.[11]

Units of account have also been used in the context of the Common Customs Tariff. To take a well known example,[12] a price fixed in units of account was used as a method of determining which orange juice was high in natural sugar, and which orange juice should be regarded as having had sugar added to it.[13] Similarly, the system of flat-rate unit values for perishable goods also depended on the use of units of account, and now depends on the euro, although it must be said that the system originally introduced in 1981[14] involved converting prices expressed in the currency of one Member State directly into the currencies of other Member States at the rate quoted on the Brussels exchange, and that a system of converting data in national currencies into ECUs, and then converting the average values expressed in ECUs back into the various national currencies, was only introduced in 1985.[15] Following reform of the Common Agricultural Policy in the light of the Uruguay

[7] Council Decision 76/568 (OJ L176/8).

[8] See Usher, *The Law of Agriculture in the EEC* (Oxford 1988).

[9] Originally defined in Council Reg. 129/62 (JO 1962 p. 2553).

[10] Following the entry into force of Council Reg. 3813/92 (OJ 1992 L387/1), as amended by Council Reg. 150/95 (OJ 1995 L22/1), but see Council Reg. 942/98 amending Reg. 724/97 on compensation for revaluations affecting farm incomes (OJ 1998 L132/1).

[11] See now Council Reg. 2799/98 on agrimonetary arrangements for the euro (OJ 1998 L349/1), and Council Reg. 2800/98 on transitional measures under the CAP with regard to the euro (OJ 1998 L349/8).

[12] At issue in Case 135/79 *Gedelfi* v. *HZA Hamburg Jonas* [1980] ECR 1713.

[13] Under the old CCT tariff heading 20.07 B II (a) 1 and (b) 1.

[14] Commission Reg. 1577/81 (OJ 1981 L154/26).

[15] Commission Reg. 3502/85 (OJ 1985 L335/9).

Round negotiations, levies on imports of agricultural products were replaced by customs duties.[16] However, at least in the cereals sector, these tended to be at a flat rate and fixed in ECU; they are now therefore fixed in euro, which again means there is an exchange risk for imports into the four non-participant Member States.

In a different sphere, the capital of the European Investment Bank was expressed in terms of units of account, as was the amount which the Member States are required actually to pay.[17] Since the units of account must now be read as euro, again there is an exchange risk only for the four non-participants in Economic and Monetary Union. Indeed, the European Investment Bank was also a pioneer in the use of units of account in commercial transactions.[18]

More generally, Community legislation harmonizing national laws may require a common criterion of value. For example, in the context of company law the minimum capital of a public limited company was defined in art. 6(1) of the Second Company Law Directive[19] in terms of units of account, and the derogations in favour of small and medium-sized companies under arts. 11 and 27 of the Fourth Directive[20] on company accounts expressed balance sheet totals and turnover in terms of units of account. Indeed, as amended by Council Directive 90/604[21] it allowed small and medium-sized companies to publish accounts in ECU before the introduction of the euro. In the financial services sector, we have seen that the Second Banking Directive[22] prohibits the competent authorities from granting authorization in cases where the initial capital is less than €5 million.[23] Even in its original version as 5 million ECU, this caused problems for a Member State with a floating currency not within the exchange rate mechanism of the European Monetary System,[24] as seen in the UK implementation,[25] which did not convert the ECU figure into pounds, but referred to 5 million ECU 'or an amount of equal value denominated wholly or partly in another unit of account'. Similarly, the Community legislation[26] on public works contracts uses units of account to indicate the value of the contracts to which it applies, and the Directive on Product Liability[27] uses units of account to indicate the permissible limits on liability.

In the area of competition law, turnover expressed in units of account, now to be read as euros, is frequently encountered in the context of block exemptions as one of the criteria for determining which undertakings fall within those block

[16] Council Reg. 3290/94 (OJ 1994 L349/105).

[17] Decision of the Board of Governors of 13 May 1981 amending the Statute of the European Investment Bank with respect to the adoption of the ECU as the Bank's unit of account (OJ 1981 L311/1). See also the Decision of the Board of Governors of 11 June 1990 on the increase in the Bank's capital (OJ 1990 L377/1).

[18] From 1981.

[19] Council Directive 77/91 (OJ 1977 L26/1).

[20] Council Directive 78/660 (OJ 1978 L222/11).

[21] OJ 1990 L317/57.

[22] Council Directive 89/646 (OJ 1989 L386/1). See Chapter 6 above.

[23] 1989 Directive, art. 4.

[24] See Chapter 9 below.

[25] The Banking Co-ordination (Second Council Directive) Reg.s 1992 (SI 1992 No. 3218), hereinafter referred to as the UK Regs., regulation 27(4) amending Schedule 3 to the Banking Act 1987.

[26] Beginning with Council Directive 71/305 (JO 1971 L185/5).

[27] Council Directive 85/374 (OJ 1985 L210/29). See art. 16.

exemptions.[28] The concept is of particular importance in the context of the Community system of merger control introduced by Council Regulation 4064/89.[29] Under this legislation 'concentrations with a Community dimension' over which the Commission has jurisdiction are defined[30] in terms of the turnover of the undertakings concerned, subject to special rules for credit institutions[31] and other financial institutions.[32]

A final example of the use of units of account in Community law: they were also used as a measure of Community sanctions, so that one of the limits on the fines that the Commission may impose under Regulation 17/62[33] for breach of the competition rules was expressed in units of account. Similarly, the penalties that may be imposed, for example, on a witness who fails to appear before the European Court of Justice were also expressed in units of account.[34]

Perhaps even more striking was the use of Community units of account by an international organization which is not governed by Community law, even if the Community is an important participant. This resulted from the 1990 Agreement establishing the European Bank for Reconstruction and Development.[35] Under art. 4(1) of that Agreement, the authorized capital stock of the Bank is 10 billion ECU, divided into one million shares having a par value of 10,000 ECU each. The Agreement makes no attempt to define the ECU,[36] and therefore only makes sense if a reference is implied to the secondary Community legislation which defined the ECU.[37] Therefore it would appear to be subject to the general legislation requiring ECU to be read as euro.[38] These shares are subdivided into what the Agreement terms 'paid-in' shares, which had to be fully paid up in five instalments,[39] and 'callable' shares, for which payment is only demanded as and when required by the Bank to meet its liabilities. The initial value of the paid-in shares was 3 billion ECU, and each member was required to subscribe for paid-in shares and callable shares in the ratio of 3:7.

Article 6(3) of the Agreement required payments in relation to the original capital stock to be settled in ECU, US dollars, or Japanese yen, 'on the basis of the

[28] See e.g. art. 3 of Commission Reg. 1983/83 on exclusive distribution agreements (OJ 1983 L173/1), and art. 3 of Commission Reg. 417/85 on specialization agreements (OJ 1985 L53/1).

[29] OJ 1989 L395/1. See p. 86 above.

[30] Art. 1.

[31] In the absence of a more specific definition, that in Council Directive 77/780 on credit institutions (OJ 1977 L322/30) might be taken: 'an undertaking whose business is to receive deposits or other repayable funds from the public and to grant credits for its own account'. For a more detailed discussion see p. 116 above.

[32] Defined in Council Directive 92/30 on the supervision of credit institutions on a consolidated basis (OJ 1992 L110/52) as 'an undertaking, not being a credit institution, whose principal activity is to grant credit facilities (including guarantees), to acquire participations or make investments'. For more detailed consideration see p. 134 above.

[33] Council Reg. 17/62 art. 15 (JO 1962 p. 204).

[34] Rules of Procedure, art. 48.

[35] The text of which is annexed to Council Decision 90/674 concluding the Agreement on behalf of the Community (OJ 1990 L372/1, p. 4).

[36] See Louis and De Lhoneux, 'The Development of the Use of the ECU: Legal aspects' (1991) *CMLRev.* 335 at p. 343.

[37] See below p. 160.

[38] Reg. 1103/97 (OJ 1997 L162/1).

[39] Art. 6(1).

average exchange rate of the relevant currency in terms of the ECU for the period from 30 September 1989 to 31 March 1990 inclusive'. Two conclusions may be drawn from this; the first is that it was clearly the ECU rather than the dollar or yen that was the criterion of value, and the second is that the base period chosen enabled the USA to benefit from a subsequent devaluation of the dollar *vis-à-vis* the ECU.[40] Be that as it may, subsequent payments on the 'callable' stock, although they may be made in dollars, yen, or ECU, must, under art. 6(5) 'be uniform in ECU value upon each callable share calculated at the time of the call'. Finally, it may be observed that art. 6(8) provides that payment or denomination in ECU is to include payment or denomination in any fully convertible currency which is equivalent at the date of payment or encashment to the value of the relevant obligation in ECU. The essential role of the ECU can therefore be seen to have been the calculation of the sum due, which may then be paid in any convertible currency, i.e. the basic function of a unit of account.

2. Legal consequences of the use of units of account

The inevitable consequence of fixing sums in Community units of account was that whilst that sum might remain the same in nominal terms, its expression in national currency would alter if, in the days of fixed exchange rates, there was a devaluation or revaluation of a currency, or if, in the world of floating exchange rates, the market value of a currency changed. Thus, when the French currency was formally devalued in August 1957, it had a severe consequence for undertakings in France liable to pay the Coal and Steel Treaty levy, because it meant that French undertakings had to pay an additional 20 per cent levy in terms of French francs.[41] To take a more recent example, the United Kingdom has had to make additional payments to the European Investment Bank to make up the minimum paid-up capital required from the United Kingdom following the fall in value of the pound against the European Currency Unit in which the United Kingdom's obligation was expressed.[42] However, following the introduction of the euro, such risks remain only for those Member States which do not participate.

On the other hand, it has to be said that the old gold-parity units of account, the history of which is explained later in this Chapter, ceased to achieve their objectives of real uniformity irrespective of the national currency into which they were converted, when national currencies began to diverge from their official parities without being officially revalued or devalued. In the agricultural sector in particular, the logic of a single market with single prices should have meant that when the German and Dutch currencies floated upwards in value in 1971, prices expressed in those currencies would have to be reduced in order to preserve the substantive

[40] See Louis and De Lhoneux, *loc. cit.*

[41] ECSC *Sixth Report* p. 58.

[42] To pick a non-contentious year, the 1987 Finance White Paper (at p. 70) shows the sum of £33 million allocated as an additional payment to the EIB.

uniformity of Community agricultural prices. However, this was not done; rather, the system of monetary compensation was introduced,[43] followed a few years later by the system of special agricultural conversion rates, known as representative rates or more popularly as 'green' rates.[44] These remained in operation despite the introduction of the ECU into the agricultural sector in 1979, and it was only on the eve of the date set for the completion of the internal market at the end of 1992[45] that Council Regulation 3813/92[46] was enacted following the logic of what, it is respectfully submitted, should have happened in 1971. The 1992 Regulation provided for the conversion of ECU's into national currency and vice versa at an agricultural conversion rate based on representative market rates,[47] and recognized that a sum in national currency representing a Community price fixed in ECUs might have to be altered even during the course of a marketing year if the representative market rate diverged from the agricultural conversion rate by more than 2 per cent of the latter, subject to short-term transitional arrangements.[48] The problem of a possible reduction in farmers' incomes in terms of national currency if that currency increased in relative value was dealt with by permitting Member States with floating currencies to grant farmers compensatory aid in such circumstances,[49] with a possible Community contribution to that aid. For the eleven Member States participating in Economic and Monetary Union, such problems largely disappeared with the introduction of the euro. Under Council Regulation 2799/98 on agrimonetary arrangements for the euro,[50] prices and amounts fixed in legal instruments relating to the common agricultural policy are expressed in euro, and granted and collected in euro in the participating Member States. For the other Member States, however, the amounts fixed in euro are converted into their national currency, in principle at the market exchange rate, so they alone face an exchange risk, subject to general transitional arrangements where the conversion rate or exchange rate for the euro on 1 January 1999 represented an 'appreciable revaluation' against the agricultural conversion rate in force on 31 December 1998.[51]

The failure of the old gold parity units of account to maintain real uniformity when converted into national currencies at the collapse of the parities established by the International Monetary Fund led the European Court, the Council, and the Commission to treat units of account in a way which belied their role of promoting such uniformity. In Cases 41, 43, and 44/73 *Société Fénérale Sucrière* v. *Commission*[52] the European Court was faced with a Commission competition deci-

[43] Council Reg. 974/71 (JO 1971 L106/1).

[44] A system introduced with regard to the UK and Irish currencies by Council Reg. 222/73 (OJ 1973 L27/4) and generalized by Council Reg. 475/75 (OJ 1975 L52/28).

[45] EC Treaty art. 7a, originally art. 8a when introduced by the Single European Act.

[46] OJ 1992 L387/1. [47] Art. 3(1). [48] Art. 4. [49] Art. 8.

[50] OJ 1998 L349/1.

[51] Council Reg. 2800/98 on transitional measures under the CAP with regard to the euro (OJ 1998 L349/8).

[52] [1977] ECR 445.

sion, in which the Commission had laid down fines to be paid by three French sugar undertakings. These fines were expressed both in old units of account and in French francs. It was argued on behalf of the applicants that their only liability was to pay the fine as expressed in units of account, and hence that they could convert that fine, for example, into Italian lire at the old official parity, which placed a considerably higher value on the lira than the exchange markets did, and would have had the effect of reducing the real amount of the fine. The Commission, on the other hand, argued that the fine was in reality set in French francs, and that if it was to be paid in lire or any other Member State currency it should be converted at the current market rate. The Court agreed with the Commission, holding that the fine was in reality expressed in French francs, and that the reference to units of account served only to indicate that the fine fell within the limits laid down by article 15 of Regulation 17.[53] This has continued to be the view where the Commission has stated the fine in a national currency.[54] However, following the adoption of the ECU based on a basket of Community currencies[55] the Commission changed its approach, despite what the Court had said in the *Sugar* cases. The example might be taken of a Decision[56] involving Konica UK Ltd. and Konica Europe GmbH, in which fines of 75,000 ECU were imposed on each of the two companies, and these fines were required to be paid into nominated ECU accounts held by the Commission at banks in Birmingham and Cologne. There was no mention at all of a sum in national currency, and at the least the consequence was to require the undertakings to bear the exchange costs. A variation on the theme may be found in the Decision on the Helsinki Eurocheque Agreement,[57] where the fine was expressed in ECU, but it was indicated that if the fine was to be paid by the French banks in French francs then the sum in ECU was to be converted at the rate prevailing on the day preceding payment, and the same was to apply if Eurocheque International were to pay in Belgian francs. This therefore appears to be an area where the Commission's practice and the Court's statement of the law do not coincide, and the consequences could be serious for an undertaking whose national currency does not participate in the euro. In Case C–219/95P *Ferriere Nord* v. *Commission*[58] the appellant argued (in 1996) that its fine should be sharply reduced to take account of the devaluation of the lira against the ECU since the decision imposing the fine was adopted in 1989. However, its plea was held to be inadmissible on procedural grounds (since it was only raised for the first time in the Reply) and the question was therefore not considered by the Court.

In the agricultural sector, in Case 8/78 *Milac* v. *Hauptzollamt Freiburg*[59] the Court was faced with a Council Regulation[60] which effectively reduced the intervention price expressed in units of account for skimmed-milk powder in Germany. The

[53] JO 1962 p. 204. [54] Case C-49/92P *Commission* v. *Anic Participazione* (8 July 1999).
[55] For its composition see p. 160 below.
[56] Commission Decision 88/172 (OJ 1988 L78/34).
[57] Commission Decision 92/212 (OJ 1992 L95/50). See Chapter 4 above.
[58] [1997] ECR I–4411. [59] [1978] ECR 1721.
[60] Council Reg. 663/74 (OJ 1974 L85/52).

Court noted that the unity of the intervention price expressed in units of account had been broken since March 1971, and subsequently had only been formal or notional within the Community. It therefore took the view that the Council's intention was in reality to set an intervention price for skimmed-milk powder which in real terms would be as uniform as possible, and therefore to do this it was legitimate to reduce the price expressed in units of account in Germany so as to take account of the increase in real value of the German Deutschmark. Indeed, at a later stage Council Regulation 1889/87[61] provided for prices fixed in ECUs to be reduced when the conversion rate of a particular currency was devalued, so as to enable 'transferred negative monetary compensatory amounts' to be eliminated. The aim of this reduction of prices fixed in ECUs was precisely stated to be to neutralize the increase in prices in national currency, which would otherwise arise as a result of the amendment of the agricultural conversion rates. Indeed, it remained the case in the agricultural sector that units of account were in some contexts converted into national currencies at an exchange rate different from that at which they are converted for other Community purposes, until the entry into force of Council Regulation 3813/92[62] mentioned above. Under this Regulation, the amount of such divergence and the length of time for which it might occur were strictly limited.

However, in the mid 1970s it appears that some policy decisions were taken for cosmetic purposes simply to reduce the apparent size of the budget as expressed in units of account. Whilst agricultural prices expressed in units of account were converted into national currencies at green rates, the actual expenditure incurred by the national authorities was converted into units of account at official parity for budgetary purposes. In 1976 the Member States agreed that the monetary compensatory amounts paid as subsidies on imports into Italy and the United Kingdom should in fact be paid in the exporting Member State, because their costs expressed in a strong currency then converted at the old parities would produce a smaller figure in units of account than their real cost expressed in a weak currency and converted at the old parities.[63] Hence, agricultural expenditure appeared to be smaller in terms of units of account, even though in real terms it remained the same. In 1977, however, just before the ECU was finally introduced as the unit of account for the Community budget, a Council Regulation was enacted to provide for the use of a separate heading in the Community budget for the financial effect of different conversion rates applied for measures financed by the Guarantee Section of the EAGGF.[64]

Similar problems arose from the use of the old units of account as a criterion of classification under the Common Customs Tariff. An example is Case 135/79 *Gedelfi* v. *HZA Hamburg-Jonas*.[65] This involved tariff subheadings which distinguished between orange juice high in natural sugars, and orange juice which contained added sugar by a criterion of value set at 30 units of account per 100 kilos net weight. Orange juice below that value but at the relevant specific gravity was

[61] OJ 1987 L182/1.
[62] OJ 1992 L387/1.
[63] EC Commission *Tenth General Report* p. 322.
[64] Council Reg. 474/77 (OJ 1977 L64/2).
[65] [1980] ECR 1713.

deemed to contain added sugar and hence subject to a levy in addition to the customs duty. In this particular case, the price of certain orange juice imported into Germany in January 1978 expressed in Deutschmarks and converted into units of account at the official parity was less than the 30 units of account per 100 kilos, even though the current value of the Deutschmark was much higher, and the importer was able to show that if the price was expressed in any other Community currency and converted even at the official parity, the value of the orange juice would be above 30 units of account per 100 kilos. The Court held, on the principle that the Common Customs Tariff was meant to be uniform, that the levy could not be imposed if the same orange juice would be exempt from it if imported through other Member States.

However, the Court was not prepared to take *Gedelfi* to its logical conclusion in the rarely encountered context of flat-rate customs duties expressed in units of account. In Case 248/80 *Glunz* v. *HZA Hamburg Waltershof*[66] an importation into Germany of goods classified as porcelain statuettes in August 1978 attracted a specific minimum duty of 70 units of account per 100 kilos, which the unreformed version of the Common Customs Tariff then in force required to be converted at IMF parities. It was argued on behalf of the importer that, by extrapolation from *Gedelfi*, the amount payable by it in Germany should not exceed the amount which it would have had to pay if it had landed the goods and entered them for customs clearance in a port of a Member State having a weak currency. The Court nevertheless took the view that, although the imposition of uniform rates of duty on entry of goods into the Community, irrespective of the geographical location of their point of entry, was of fundamental importance to the establishment of a customs union, to impose the lowest level of duty would risk imposing entirely negative effects on a number of economic sectors in the Community and would not do justice to 'the fiscal and economic objectives of the Common Customs Tariff'; in other words, the protection of competing Community products. In fact, the basket ECU was introduced into the Common Customs Tariff at the end of 1978,[67] and while the tenor of the judgment is that it was not unreasonable for the Community institutions to have waited until then to reform the system of units of account, given the international monetary situation, it might nevertheless be suggested that the protection of Community products was already breached by imports through countries with weaker currencies.

3. Types and history of units of account

a) The gold unit

It has already been mentioned that the unit of account chosen by the Coal and Steel Community in 1952 was the unit of account of the European Payments Union,

[66] [1982] ECR 197. [67] Council Reg. 2779/78 (OJ 1978 L333/5).

which happened to correspond to the gold value of the United States dollar. At the end of 1958 the European Payments Union was replaced by the European Monetary Agreement, and the identical European Monetary Agreement unit of account became the unit of account used for Community purposes. Indeed, until the entry into force of the 1991 version, which substituted a sum of 5000 ECU,[68] the European Court's Rules of Procedure continued to contain in its art. 48 an express reference to a penalty of 250 European Monetary Agreement units of account being imposed upon a witness summoned to appear before the Court and who did not do so. Presumably the rare use of this provision explains why it was so long before it was formally amended and its relative value restored.

When the first common agricultural legislation was enacted in 1962 Regulation 129/62[69] again defined the agricultural unit of account at the official value of the United States dollar, that is a value of 0.88867088 grammes of fine gold. It also provided that where sums given in one currency were required to be expressed in another currency, the exchange rate to be applied was that which corresponded to the par value communicated to and recognized by the International Monetary Fund.

The demise of the European Monetary Agreement at the end of 1972 did not in fact lead to an immediate change in the definition of the unit of account. Indeed, the 1973 Financial Regulation[70] expressly retained the gold parity unit of account for budgetary purposes, despite the fact that currencies had by then been floating for two years.

b) The basket unit

The basket-type unit of account was first created, under the name of the European Unit of Account (EUA) in April 1975[71] as a method of calculating the amount of aid payable under the first Lomé Convention.

Despite fundamental differences in conception, the 1975 EUA was not totally divorced from the old gold parity unit of account. It was defined in Council Decision 75/250[72] as being the sum of 0.828 German marks, plus 0.0885 pounds sterling, plus 1.15 French francs, plus 109 Italian lira, plus 0.286 Dutch guilder, plus 3.66 Belgian francs, plus 0.14 Luxembourg francs, plus 0.217 Danish Krone, plus 0.00759 Irish pounds. However, in the recitals to the Decision it was made clear that the sum of this cocktail had an initial value equivalent to the value set by the International Monetary Fund on 28 June 1974 for the Special Drawing Right, otherwise known as the SDR. As then defined, this was also a basket unit, but one which gave a heavy weighting to the United States dollar which of course was not included in the European EUA basket. Until the summer of 1974 the value of an SDR was based on the gold value of the United States dollar, in other words

[68] OJ 1991 L176/1 and 7.
[69] JO 1962 p. 2553.
[70] OJ 1973 L116/1.
[71] Council Decision 75/250 (OJ 1975 L104/35).
[72] OJ 1975 L104/35.

0.888671 grammes of fine gold, which was also the definition of the value of the old EC unit of account. There is therefore a clear link between the dollar, the ECU, and the euro.

The basket SDR originally comprised sixteen currencies, the selection being changed slightly in July 1978, in particular to delete the South African rand, but in January 1981 the SDR was redefined in terms of a basket of five currencies (dollar, mark, yen, franc, and pound) in which the dollar held a 42 per cent weighting.[73] However, although the EUA and the later ECU did not refer expressly to the dollar, they were not totally dissociated from it, since the dollar was used as a method of expressing the values of each of the Member States currencies included in the basket in order then to calculate the ECU market values. This market value was apparently then converted back into the Member States' currencies at the current exchange rate for the dollar.[74]

The fundamental characteristic of the EC's basket unit was that it comprised fixed *sums* of national currencies, not fixed *percentages* of national currencies. These fixed sums did not change automatically when central rates were altered in an EMS realignment or when market values fluctuated, so that the percentage composition of the unit in terms of national currencies did change. The percentage share of a currency which rose in value would, since the EUA and now the ECU comprised a fixed element of that currency, increase, and the percentage share of a currency whose value diminished would inevitably decrease, since there was still the same nominal sum in that currency represented in the unit. For example, from 1975 to 1983, when the definition of the EUA/ECU remained unchanged, the percentage of the unit represented by the same fixed sum of German currency rose from about 27 per cent to about 37 per cent.[75] By comparison, in the last definition in 1989, its share was set at 30.1 per cent.[76]

When the ECU was created in the context of the European Monetary System, the European Council's Resolution of 5 December 1978[77] expressly provided that the value and composition of the ECU would be identical with the value of the EUA at the outset of the system, so that Council Regulation 3180/78,[78] changing the value of the unit of account used by the European Monetary Cooperation Fund,[79] defined the ECU as the sum of exactly the same currency elements as the EUA. Under the 1978 Resolution the weightings of the currencies used in the definition of the ECU could be revised within six months after the entry into force of the European Monetary System and thereafter every five years, and a revision could be requested at any other time if the weight of any currency had changed by 25 per cent or more.[80] A revision was in fact effected in September 1984 by Council

[73] See Mann *Legal Aspects of Money* (2nd ed. Oxford University Press 1982 pp. 506–9).
[74] Commission Communication on the calculation of the equivalents of the ECU.
[75] EC Commission, *The ECU* (1984) p. 12.
[76] Council Reg. 1971/89 (OJ 1989 L189/1), art. 1.
[77] EC Bulletin 1978 No.12 point 1.1.11.
[78] OJ 1978 L379/1.
[79] Created by Council Reg. 907/73 (OJ 1973 L89/2).
[80] Art. 2(3).

Regulation 2626/84,[81] which took the opportunity to include Greek drachmas in the definition, and also reduced the nominal amount of German marks, presumably because of their increase in value in the meantime, whilst increasing the nominal value of the sum of Italian lire and Irish pounds. Hence, the 1984 definition comprises 0.719 German marks, plus 0.0878 pounds sterling, plus 1.31 French francs, plus 140 Italian lira, plus 0.256 Dutch guilder, plus 3.71 Belgian francs, plus 0.14 Luxembourg francs, plus 0.219 Danish krona, plus 0.00871 Irish pounds, plus 1.15 Greek drachmas. A further revision took place in 1989, when the opportunity was taken to incorporate the Spanish peseta and the Portuguese escudo, but using rather different legislative techniques. Perhaps reflecting the confidence then felt in the ECU, Council Regulation 1971/89 was enacted on 19 June 1989,[82] defining the composition of the ECU which was to come into operation three months later on 21 September 1989. This it did firstly by determining the percentage weights to be attributed to each currency element: German mark 30.1 per cent, French franc 19 per cent, UK pound 13 per cent, Italian lira 10.15 per cent, Dutch guilder 9.4 per cent, Belgian franc 7.6 per cent, Spanish peseta 5.3 per cent, Danish krone 2.45 per cent, Irish pound 1.1 per cent, Greek drachma 0.8 per cent, Portuguese escudo 0.8 per cent and Luxembourg franc 0.3 per cent. It then required the Commission to calculate the fixed sums of national currency corresponding to these weights on the basis of ECU rates derived by the Commission from the dollar rates recorded by the central banks of the Member States on their respective exchange markets on Wednesday 20 September 1989 at 14.15. Of course, once these sums had been fixed,[83] the percentage of the unit represented by each national currency depended once again on its market exchange rate rather than the Regulation. A final consolidation of the fixed sums resulting from the 1989 calculations was published in Council Regulation 3320/94.[84]

However, it must be emphasized that, just as the 1975 EUA reflected the overall value of the SDR, and the 1978 ECU reflected the external value of the EUA, so the 1978 Resolution of the European Council stated categorically that 'revisions must not in themselves modify the external value of the unit of account'.[85] Hence, a revision in itself should have had no immediate effect on the value of the unit of account, although obviously the subsequent development of the unit might well be affected by its new composition.

c) The legal basis of the ECU

The legal basis of the basket currency unit is a matter of some interest. The 1975 Decision[86] in the context of the Lomé Convention in fact cited no Treaty provision whatsoever. Council Regulation 3180/78[87] changing the value of the unit of account used by the European Monetary Co-operation Fund referred generally to

[81] OJ 1984 L247/1.
[82] OJ 1989 L189/1.
[83] For the sums involved see OJ 1989 C241/1.
[84] OJ 1994 L350/27.
[85] Art. 2(3).
[86] Council Decision 75/250 (OJ 1975 L104/35).
[87] OJ 1978 L379/1.

the EC Treaty, and referred more particularly to article 5 of the Statutes of the European Monetary Co-operation Fund laid down by Regulation 907/73.[88] The last paragraph of this article provided that changes in the value of the unit of account should be decided on by the Council acting unanimously on a proposal from the Commission after consulting the Monetary Committee[89] and the Board of Governors of the Fund. More intriguingly, Regulations 2626/84[90] and 1971/89[91] both expressly cited art. 2(3) of the 1978 European Council Resolution on the European Monetary System, whose status is a matter of considerable debate,[92] to the effect that revisions might only be made every five years and must not modify the external value of the ECU.

They both also made reference to provisions in Acts of Accession which recognized the existence of the ECU. The 1984 Regulation cited Annex VIII to the Greek Act of Accession providing that the drachma should be included in the ECU before the end of 1985 if a revision was undertaken before that date, and the 1989 Regulation cited a Joint Declaration on the inclusion of the peseta and the escudo in the ECU annexed to the Spanish and Portuguese Act of Accession, to the effect that inclusion of those currencies could be requested on the first five-year review of the ECU after Accession. Further Treaty recognition of the ECU was given in art. 102a of the EC Treaty introduced by the Single European Act, requiring Member States to 'take account of the experience acquired . . . in developing the ECU',[93] and the ECU played a pivotal role in the monetary union provisions introduced by the Maastricht Treaty. In this context two points arise. The first is that these Treaty provisions can only be given meaning by reference to the secondary legislation which created the ECU; the second is that the Maastricht provisions have led to a fundamental change in the nature and function of the ECU, which has become metamorphasized into the euro following the commencement of the third stage of economic and monetary union.

d) Transition to the euro

Whereas one of the basic characteristics of the ECU was that its composition could be changed, even if in principle only every five years, art. 118 introduced by the Maastricht Treaty states categorically that the currency composition of the ECU basket shall not be changed, no doubt with the intention of building confidence in the international money markets. The result of this is that the September 1989 definition remained in force and could not be altered, since it could not in principle be revised until September 1994 under the previous rules, and this date was after the entry into force of art. 118. This means that the definition of the ECU could not and did not reflect an element of the currencies of the Member States which have joined since that date: Austria, Finland, and Sweden.

[88] OJ 1973 L89/2.
[89] See Chapter 8 below.
[90] OJ 1984 L247/1.
[91] OJ 1989 L189/1.
[92] See below p. 173.
[93] Wording which remains in art. 124(1).

Article 118 further provided that from the start of the third stage the value of the ECU should be irrevocably fixed in accordance with art. 123(4), which in turn lays down that from that date the Council shall, acting with the unanimity of those Member States able and willing to participate, adopt the conversion rates at which their currencies shall be irrevocably fixed and at which irrevocably fixed rate the ECU shall be substituted for these currencies, and the ECU will become a currency in its own right, albeit as the 'euro'. It is nevertheless still provided, in terms redolent of the 1978 Resolution, that this measure should by itself not modify the external value of the ECU. The irrevocable fixing of the value of the ECU related only to those currencies which it replaced, but the fundamental consequence is that from the start of the third stage of economic and monetary union the ECU/euro ceased to be a basket in which the currencies of all Member States were represented, and became the currency of the participating Member States. If non-participating Member States wish to maintain a fixed relationship with it or maintain a narrow range of floating against it within the context of the European Monetary System Mark II,[94] they will find themselves pursuing something over which they have no direct influence—unless they actually join the single currency system.[95]

e) Private use of the ECU

Whatever the nature of the ECU in the public law of the European Community, it was also used at the national level, and in the private sector, in particular as an instrument of deposit and credit.[96] While, as a basket-type unit, it had obvious attractions in spreading the exchange risk, and offered more attractive rates of interest than some national currencies, it might have been thought that the fact that its composition could be changed every five years would be something of a disincentive (albeit one which disappeared after the entry into force of the Maastricht Treaty), or at least that private contracts would refer to the composition of the ECU at the time of the contract. Nevertheless, appears that the 'open' basket, referring to the Community legislation and accepting any subsequent amendment, was generally used,[97] even though no ECU as such were issued outside the context of the European Monetary System[98] except as collectors' items in precious metals, and its value was therefore derived from its component (and until 1994 variable) national currencies. However, although the private sector might accept the composition of the ECU resulting from Community legislation, its market value depended on market forces, and at least in the period up to 1991, the market value

[94] See Chapter 8 below.

[95] Art. 122(3), (4), and (5).

[96] For a detailed discussion of the legal issues and techniques involved see Sunt, *Legal Aspects of the ECU* (Butterworths 1989).

[97] Louis and De Lhoneux, 'The Development of the Use of the ECU: Legal aspects' (1991) *CMLRev*. 335, at p. 337.

[98] See Chapter 8 below.

of the ECU appears to have exceeded the value of the sum of the component national currencies because of a gap between supply and demand.[99] It has been suggested that it represented a 'currency' resulting from the demand of economic operators,[100] but the fact that it was not a foreign currency as such led the German authorities, at least until June 1987, to treat reference to the ECU as an illegal indexation clause.[101]

In the absence of any central issuer of ECU, the banks themselves had to organize a system of payments in ECU. They initially covered themselves by holding the component currencies, but from 1986 there was a private ECU clearing system, created by the ECU Banking Association, whose aim was to permit its members to pay their reciprocal debts in ECU and set off the balance of such debts. It was open to all banks having their registered office or a subsidiary in a Member State which showed a sufficient interest in the development of transactions in ECU. They operated through the 'Swift' international payments system, which grouped payments with a view to their clearing, and the Bank for International Settlements in Basle acted as agent, opening accounts for the participating banks and supervising the clearing and daily settlement system.[102] In the result, it was perfectly possible to draw cheques or travellers' cheques, for example, denominated in ECU, although any cash payment relating thereto would have to be in a national currency.

4. The introduction of the euro

As from 1 January 1999 the currency of the participating States is the euro.[103] The euro has also replaced the ECU.[104] However, euro notes and coins will only be introduced after a transitional period of three years.[105] The aim of this section is to analyse the legislation adopted by the EC to deal with the legal problems arising from the replacement of the ECU by the euro, the replacement of the national currencies of the participants by the euro, and the continued use of national banknotes and coins until 2002.

a) Replacement of the ECU by the euro

The replacement of the ECU by the euro was not foreseen by the Maastricht Treaty, since it was only decided at the meeting of the European Council in

[99] Louis and De Lhoneux, *op. cit.* p. 353. [100] Louis and De Lhoneux, *op. cit.*

[101] Ibid. p. 338. The version of art. 102a of the EC Treaty introduced by the Single European Act, requiring Member States to take account of the development of the ECU, entered into force on 1 July 1987.

[102] Ibid. pp. 351–2. [103] Council Reg. 974/98 (OJ 1998 L139/1) art. 2.

[104] Council Reg. 1103/97 (OJ 1997 L162/1) art. 2.

[105] Council Reg. 974/98 (OJ 1998 L139/1) art. 10.

December 1995 that the the European currency should be called the 'euro' rather than the term ECU used in the Treaty. As recorded in the recitals to Council Regulations 1103/97[106] and 974/98,[107] at the meeting of the European Council in Madrid on 15 and 16 December 1995, the decision was taken that the term ECU used by the Treaty to refer to the European currency unit was a generic term, and the Governments of the fifteen Member States reached the common agreement that this decision was 'the agreed and definitive interpretation of the relevant Treaty provisions'and that the name given to the European currency should be the 'euro'. Thus, without changing the Treaty, the Treaty term was changed. The use of the term 'euro' was in fact judicially challenged by a member of the European Parliament,[108] but the action was held inadmissible since he challenged the *proposal* which eventually became Regulation 1103/97 rather than a binding legal act. In a second action, Case T–207/97 *Berthu* v. *Council*[109] he sought the annulment of Council Regulation 1103/97 itself, but this action was held inadmissible on the ground that the Regulation was not of individual concern to the applicant.

Following the decision at the Madrid European Council to use the term euro, however, Regulation 1103/97[110] was adopted in June 1997 under art. 235 of the EC Treaty to deal with the problems of conversion; it was therefore adopted contemporaneously with the Amsterdam Treaty, even if that Treaty did not make any formal amendment to introduce the term euro. Under art. 2 of this Regulation, every reference in a legal instrument to the ECU as defined under Community law is to be replaced by a reference to the euro at a rate of one euro to one ECU, and in an effort to cover the private sector use of the ECU, references in a legal instrument to the ECU are deemed to be references to the ECU as defined in Community law, subject to the intention of the parties. It is further declared, in art. 3, which is just as relevant to the replacement of national currencies by the euro as it is to the replacement of the ECU by the euro, that the introduction of the euro is not to have the effect of altering any term of a legal instrument or of discharging or excusing performance under any legal instrument, nor give a party the right unilaterally to alter or terminate such an instrument. No doubt this provision was adopted in response to worries about the possible frustration of contracts following the introduction of the euro. However, it is subject to anything which parties may have agreed between themselves, although it is highly unlikely that any contract entered into before the Madrid European Council in December 1995 will have contemplated the introduction of the euro.[111]

Note finally in this context that under art. 4(4), monetary amounts to be converted from one national currency unit into another are first to be converted into a monetary amount expressed in the euro unit, and then to be converted into the

[106] OJ 1997 L162/1.

[107] OJ 1998 L139/1.

[108] Case T–175/96 *Berthu* v. *Commission* [1997] ECR II–811.

[109] [1998] ECR II–509.

[110] OJ 1997 L162/1.

[111] The fact that the Commission had expressed a fine in national currency as well as in ECU was held to amount to a contrary intention in Case C-49/92P *Commission* v. *Anic Partecipazione* (8 July 1999).

other national currency unit. This reflects the fact that even during the transitional period before euro notes and coins are introduced, the currency unit will be the euro,[112] as will be explained below, so that there will be no bilateral exchange rates between the former national currencies except as a consequence of the conversion rate against the euro. It is further provided in art. 4(1), presumably for the same reason, that the conversion rates shall be adopted as one euro expressed in terms of each of the national currencies of the participating Member States.

b) Replacement of national currencies by the euro

In order to give the markets maximum notice as to legal rules applicable on the replacement of national currencies by the euro, even though no formal legislation could be issued until the decision had been taken on which countries should participate in the third stage of economic and monetary union,[113] the Council published a Resolution in July 1997[114] setting out what it expected to be the text of the legislation. Following the decision to move to the third stage of Economic and Monetary Union, a formal Regulation was adopted on 3 May 1998[115] which, apart from filling in the blanks, is virtually identical to the text published in the Resolution. This Regulation declares unequivocally in art. 2 that as from 1 January 1999 the currency of the participating Member States shall be the euro, that the currency unit shall be one euro, and that one euro shall be divided into one hundred cents (which again is a matter with which the Treaty does not expressly deal). The euro is to be substituted for the currency of each participating Member State at the conversion rate[116] to be set at the start of the third stage under art. 123(4) of the Treaty, and it is to be the unit of account of the European Central Bank (ECB) and of the central banks of the participating Member States.[117]

While the euro may have become the currency of the participating Member States in 1999, euro banknotes and coins will not be introduced until January 2002.[118] During the intervening period, and for up to six months thereafter, national notes and coins will remain in use, but their legal nature will change: under art. 6 of the Regulation they will become divisions of the euro rather than continuing as currencies in their own right. They will only be legal tender, however, within their territorial limits as of the day before the commencement of economic and monetary union.[119] The Regulation provides that where in a legal instrument reference is made to a national currency unit, 'this reference shall be as valid as if reference were made to the euro unit according to the conversion rates'.[120] Furthermore, the substitution of the euro for the currency of each participating

[112] Council Reg. 974/98 art. 2.
[113] EC Treaty art. 123.
[114] European Council Resolution of 7 July 1997 on the legal framework for the introduction of the euro (OJ 1997 C236/7).
[115] Council Reg. 974/98 of 3 May 1998 on the introduction of the Euro (OJ 1998 L139/1).
[116] Art. 3. The rates were set by Council Reg. 2866/98 (OJ 1998 L359/1).
[117] Art. 4.
[118] Art. 10.
[119] Art. 9.
[120] Art. 6(2).

Member State does not in itself have the effect of altering the denomination of legal instruments in existence on the date of substitution.[121]

In principle, and subject to anything the parties may have agreed, acts to be performed under legal instruments stipulating the use of or denominated in a national currency unit are to be performed in that national currency unit, and acts to be performed under legal instruments stipulating the use of or denominated in the euro unit are to be performed in the euro unit.[122] However, any amount denominated either in the euro unit or in the national currency unit of a given participating Member State and payable within that Member State by crediting an account of the creditor, can be paid by the debtor either in the euro unit or in that national currency unit. The amount is to be credited to the account of the creditor in the denomination of his account, any conversion being effected at the conversion rates.

The Regulation also empowers Member States under art. 8(4) to take measures to redenominate in the euro unit outstanding debt issued by that Member State's general government, and to enable the euro to be used as a unit of account by security and commodity markets and in systems for the regular exchange, clearing, and settlement of payments.

Banknotes denominated in euros, and coins denominated in euros or cents are to be put in circulation in the participating Member States as from 1 January 2002[123] and, subject to a changeover period of up to six months,[124] will be the only banknotes and coins having the status of legal tender in all these Member States. Nevertheless, issuers of national banknotes and coins are required to continue to accept the banknotes and coins previously issued by them against euros at the conversion rate.[125] Authority to issue notes and coins stems from art. 106 of the EC Treaty. Article 106(1) sets out what would perhaps be the most important monetary function of the ECB, going to the heart of what has been traditionally regarded as a function of the State:[126] for the participating Member States, the ECB has the exclusive right to authorize the issue of bank notes within the Community. The ECB and the national central banks may issue such notes, and the bank notes issued by the ECB and the national central banks are the only such notes to have the status of legal tender within the Community. With regard to coins, art. 106(2) permits participating Member States to issue coins subject to approval by the ECB of the volume of the issue. The Council may, acting in accordance with the co-operation procedure[127] and after consulting the ECB, adopt measures to harmonize the denominations and technical specifications of all coins intended for circulation to the extent necessary to permit their smooth circulation within the Community, resulting in the enactment of Council Regulation 975/98 of 3 May

[121] Art. 7. [122] Art. 8. [123] Art. 10. [124] Art. 15.

[125] Art. 16.

[126] See the judgment of the European Court in Case 7/78 *R* v. *Thompson* [1978] ECR 2247.

[127] Art. 252. The failure of the Amsterdam Treaty to amend any of the provisions relating to EMU means that this is the only sector where the co-operation procedure is encountered after the entry into force of that Treaty.

1998 on the denomination and technical specifications of euro coins intended for circulation.[128]

c) Practical problems

The coexistence for three years of the euro as the currency of the participating Member States with national banknotes and coins gives rise to a number of possible difficulties which the Commission has endeavoured to anticipate in a series of three non-binding Recommendations. The first[129] sets out a standard of good practice on banking charges. This provides that banks should not charge for the following:

- the conversion of incoming and outgoing payments denominated in the euro unit or in the national currency unit during the transitional period;
- the conversion of accounts from the national currency unit to the euro unit both during and at the end of the transitional period;
- the exchange for their customers of 'household amounts' of national banknotes and coins for euro banknotes and coins in 2002.

In addition, banks should not charge a different fee for services in the euro unit than that for identical services in the national currency unit.

The second recommendation[130] sets out a standard of good practice with regard to dual display of prices which would require:

- a clear indication from retailers on whether they will accept payments in euro units in the transitional period;
- a clear distinction between, on one hand, the unit in which the price is set and in which amounts to be paid are to be calculated and, on the other hand, the counter-value which is displayed for information purposes only.

This recommendation also calls for agreements, where possible, on common formats and designs for dual displays, and suggests that as a general rule dual displays can be limited to the final price which consumers have to pay and to the total on financial statements or receipts.

The third recommendation[131] is largely concerned with monitoring and information, but it does suggest that given that the changeover to the euro may pose particular challenges for small enterprises, businesses, individually or through representative organisations, should agree on principles which would help small enterprises with the changeover. In particular, it recommends that firms should give a period of notice before issuing or asking for invoices in euros in order to allow their customers and suppliers time to prepare themselves properly. In addition, where a

[128] OJ 1998 L139/6.
[129] Commission Recommendation 98/286 of 23 Apr. 1998 (OJ 1998 L130/22).
[130] Commission Recommendation 98/287 of 23 Apr. 1998 (OJ 1998 L130/26).
[131] Commission Recommendation 98/288 of 23 Apr. 1998 (OJ 1998 L130/29).

small firm requests a supplier to continue showing prices in national currency alongside prices in euros on invoices, the supplier should accept.

It remains to be seen how effective these Recommendations will be. It is merely observed that in the area of financial services there are numerous examples of non-binding recommendations being replaced by binding legislation. Commission Recommendation 87/63[132] was eventually replaced by Directive 94/19 of the European Parliament and of the Council on deposit guarantee schemes,[133] and Commission Recommendation 90/109 on transparency of banking conditions[134] has given way to Directive 97/5 of the European Parliament and Council on cross-border credit transfers.[135] However, the three Recommendations at issue here are transitional in their nature, and are likely to retain their current status.

[132] OJ 1987 L33/16. [133] OJ 1994 L135/5. [134] OJ 1990 L67/39.
[135] OJ 1997 L43/25.

8

The development of monetary union

1. Background: the Werner Report and the snake

The notion of creating monetary union within the European Community has a long history. In December 1969, at the end of the original transitional period, a meeting of Heads of State or Government (now known as the European Council) decided that a plan should be drawn up with a view to creating an economic and monetary union,[1] and in March 1970 a committee was set up under the chairmanship of the Luxembourg Prime Minister, M. Werner, to draw up a report on the basic issues by the end of May. This Report[2] reached the fundamental conclusion, repeated by the Delors Committee in 1989,[3] that in an economic and monetary union 'the Community currencies will be assured of total and irreversible mutual convertibility free from fluctuations in rates and with immutable parity rates, or preferably they will be replaced by a sole Community currency'.

They also pointed out that monetary and credit policy would have to be centralized, that external monetary policy would fall within Community competence, that essential features of public budgets would be decided at Community level, that regional and structural policies would no longer fall under exclusive national competence, and that there would need to be systematic and continuous consultation between the social partners. They observed that in the long run economic and monetary union could not do without the development of political union, and that it would be necessary to develop a centre of decision for economic policy and a Community system for the central banks. All of this seems remarkably familiar in the context of the debates following the subsequent negotiation of the Maastricht Treaty.

In March 1971 the Council and the Representatives of the Governments of the Member States adopted a Resolution[4] on the attainment by stages of economic and monetary union in the Community, declaring that at the end of that process the Community would indeed form a single currency area, but also stating that it would 'constitute an area within which persons, goods, services and capital may move freely and without distortion of competition', language strikingly similar to that used in the Single European Act in what is now art. 14 of the EC Treaty on the completion of the internal market by the end of 1992. It is tempting to

[1] *Compendium of Community Monetary Texts* (EC Commission, 1974) p. 15.
[2] EC *Bulletin 1970* Supplement 11.
[3] 1989 *Report* para. 22.
[4] JO 1971 C28/1; *Compendium of Community Monetary Texts* 1989 p. 33.

wonder whether, with hindsight, that will be seen as a step on the way to economic and monetary union. It may also be noted that the Resolution envisaged Community rules determining the uniform basis for assessing VAT, presumably the genesis of the Sixth VAT Directive.[5]

However, the assumptions underlying the resolution disappeared within a few months: the Werner Report had been drafted in a world of fixed exchange rates, where the elimination of margins of fluctuation must have appeared not to be unduly difficult, given the political will. By the summer of 1971 the system was collapsing, and the Community was faced with the rather more urgent problem of trying to prevent its Member States' currencies floating too far apart. In March 1972 the Council and the Representatives of the Governments of the Member States adopted another Resolution[6] on the application of the 1971 Resolution on the attainment by stages of economic and monetary union in the Community. As well as agreeing that a Regional Development Fund should be established, the Resolution set out the principle that, *inter alia*, the difference between the spot exchange rates of two Member States should not exceed 2.25 per cent (popularly known as the 'snake'), and that fluctuations against the dollar should not exceed the maximum allowed under the rules of the IMF, which was then 4.5 per cent under the December 1971 Smithsonian Agreement (the 'tunnel' within which the snake could wriggle). However, another year later, in March 1973,[7] it was decided no longer to intervene with regard to the dollar, leaving the snake simply as a joint float. The fundamental problem was the absence of any independent criterion of value, and by the time the snake was replaced by the European Monetary System it had in effect become a small DM zone.[8]

There were nevertheless continuing consequences of the snake and the plans for economic and monetary union in the original version of the European Monetary System. The most obvious is the original margin of fluctuation of 2.25 per cent. This has continued into the new version which came into operation in January 1999, in that while standard fluctuation band is plus or minus 15 per cent around the central rates,[9] 'on a case-by-case basis, formally agreed fluctuation bands narrower than the standard one and backed up in principle by automatic intervention and financing may be set at the request of the non-euro area Member State concerned'.[10] In fact, agreement was reached in September 1998 between the finance ministers of the Euro–11, the ECB, and the ministers and Central Bank governors of Denmark and Greece that Denmark would participate in the new exchange rate mechanism within a narrow band of fluctuation of 2.25 per cent, and that Greece would participate within the standard band of plus or minus 15 per cent.[11]

[5] Council Directive 77/388 (OJ 1977 L145/1). [6] JO 1972 C83/3; 1974 *Compendium* p. 33.

[7] Council Statement of 12 Mar. 1973 (1974 *Compendium* p. 63).

[8] Quaere whether the weighting of the DM in the ECU (see p. 162 above) had, albeit indirectly, a similar effect. For a chronology of the snake see Coffey, *The European Monetary System: Past, present and future* (2nd ed. Kluwer, 1987) p. 123.

[9] Para. 2.1. [10] Para. 2.4.

[11] *Bulletin Quotidien Europe* No. 7310, 28 and 29 Sept. 1998.

It may also be observed that the original versions of the financial mechanisms that underpinned the original EMS largely date from the period of the snake. The European Monetary Co-operation Fund (whose role was taken over by the European Monetary Institute in 1994[12] and subsumed in the activites of the European Central Bank on its creation[13] was envisaged in the 1972 Resolution, and created by Regulation 907/73,[14] and the Agreement of 10 April 1972 between the Central Banks dealing with very short-term monetary support[15] was also adopted pursuant to that Resolution. Similarly, the original measures on short-term financing[16] and medium-term support[17] also date from this period.

2. The European monetary systems

a) Legal basis

The legal basis of both versions of the European Monetary System is a matter of some debate. The structure of the original system was laid down in a Resolution of the European Council of 5 December 1978,[18] backed up by an Agreement between the central banks of the Member States of 13 March 1979 laying down the operating procedures for the EMS (hereinafter the 1979 Agreement).[19] While in one sense this merely followed the pattern set by the 1971 and 1972 Resolutions on the attainment of economic and monetary union and the creation of the 'snake',[20] a resolution is a type of act nowhere defined in the Treaties, whose legal consequences are therefore not laid down anywhere in the Treaties, although that does not mean that it has no legal consequences. The attitude of the European Court to these informal acts of Community institutions seems largely to be that while they cannot adversely affect third parties, they may be binding upon those who make them.[21] However, in Case 141/78 *France* v. *UK*[22] it was held that the Member States must, in enacting new fisheries measures, comply with the requirements of a Resolution adopted by the Council at The Hague in November 1976 pending implementation of a Community fisheries policy, on the ground that that Resolution made specific the duties of co-operation imposed on Member States under art. 10 (then art. 5) of the EC Treaty. Annex VI to that Resolution required a Member State taking unilateral fisheries measures to consult the Commission and

[12] EC Treaty, art. 117(2). [13] Ibid. art. 123(2). [14] OJ 1973 L89/2.

[15] 1974 *Compendium* p. 60. Replaced under the EMS by the Agreement of 13 Mar. 1979 (1989 *Compendium* p. 50).

[16] Agreement of 9 Feb. 1970. Revised version in 1989 *Compendium* p. 59.

[17] Council Decision 71/143 (JO 1971 L73/15).

[18] EC *Bulletin* 1978 No. 12 point 1.1.11.

[19] Revised version printed in *Compendium of Community Monetary Texts* (1989) p. 50.

[20] See p. 172 above.

[21] See Cases 87 and 130/77, 22/83, and 3 and 10/84 *Salerno* v. *Commission and Council* [1985] ECR 2523.

[22] [1979] ECR 2923.

seek its approval, and the United Kingdom was held to be in breach of its Treaty obligations by bringing into force the Fishing Nets (North-East Atlantic) Order 1977 without so doing.

It is also the case that the European Council itself, in so far as it could be regarded as distinguishable from the Council of Ministers, was a body whose existence was in no way legally recognized until the entry into force of art. 2 of the Single European Act in July 1987. It may further be observed in this context that following the Maastricht amendments, the European Council became an institution of the European Union,[23] and in the area of Community monetary policy reference is made to 'the Council, meeting in the composition of the Heads of State or of Government'.[24] On the other hand, when measures were adopted to strengthen the European Monetary System in September 1987[25] a meeting of the Council of Finance Ministers simply endorsed an agreement reached within the Committee of Central Bank governors, and it was recorded that the central banks would be able to set the new mechanisms in place without requiring any formal decision by the Council.

Any legal doubts appear to have been largely resolved by a provision introduced by the Single European Act with effect from July 1987: art. 102a of the EC Treaty (elements of which may still be found in the current art. 124). The second sentence of the first paragraph of article 102a required the Member States to take account, in the context of co-operation in economic and monetary policy, of the experience acquired in co-operation within the framework of the European Monetary System (EMS) and in developing the ECU, and to respect existing powers in this field. It is suggested that this was one of the factors which led the European Court in *Opinion 1/91*[26] to hold that, even before the entry into force of the Maastricht amendments, the Community already had the objective of achieving economic and monetary union. This sentence was retained in art. 124 of the EC Treaty until the beginning of the third stage of economic and monetary union, and that provision added to it the requirement from the original art. 107(1) that each Member State shall treat its exchange rate policy as a matter of common interest. By virtue of art. 124(2), this obligation continues in the third stage for those Member States which do not participate in the single currency system: the UK, Denmark, Sweden, and Greece.

The legal importance of the European Monetary System was further enhanced by the fact that express reference was made to it in art. 121 (formerly art. 109j) with regard to the criteria of convergence to be met before proceeding to the third stage.[27] These included (under art. 121(1)) the observance of the normal[28] fluctuation margins provided for by the Exchange Rate Mechanism of the European Monetary System, for at least two years, without devaluing against the currency of any other Member State, and the durability of convergence achieved by the

[23] Treaty on European Union art. 4 (originally art. D).
[24] See art. 109j(2), (3), and (4).
[25] EC *Bulletin* 1987 No. 9 point 1.3.1.
[26] [1991] ECR I–6079.
[27] See below p. 184.
[28] See below p. 177.

Member State and of its participation in the Exchange Rate Mechanism of the European Monetary System, being reflected in the long-term interest rate levels.

For Member States with a derogation, Member States with an opt-out which change their minds, and States which accede to the Community in the future, compliance with this criterion at first sight poses problems, because the ECU (in the guise of the euro) has become the single currency of a number of Member States, so that the original Exchange Rate Mechanism simply cannot operate. However, the Treaty fails to deal with the question of an exchange-rate mechanism in relations between those Member States which participate in Economic and Monetary Union and those which do not.

The European Monetary Institute prepared a draft framework for that relationship (a European Monetary System Mark II),[29] and this formed the basis of an agreement in principle on its structure at the Dublin European Council in December 1996. This framework was adopted in a European Council Resolution of 16 June 1997,[30] following exactly the same pattern as the 1978 Resolution of the European Council on the original European Monetary System.[31] It is thus an undefined act of an institution of the *European Union*, even though monetary policy is clearly and expressly an exclusive *Community* competence—at least for the participants in stage three.[32]

What does distinguish the Resolutions establishing the European Monetary Systems from most binding Community acts is that they do not in themselves create a comprehensive set of obligations for every Member State; in effect, it was for each Member State to decide whether to join the exchange-rate mechanism[33] under the original version, and under the current version participation in the exchange-rate mechanism is voluntary for the Member States outside the euro area, although 'Member States with a derogation can be expected to join the mechanism'.[34]

In a sense they are agreements between all the Member States that those who so wish will be bound by the rules and make use of institutions created under Community law. In this the original Resolution could be seen as an informal precedent for the Social Protocol under the Maastricht Treaty and for the concept of 'closer co-operation' introduced by the Amsterdam Treaty.[35] At the same time, it must be said that any Member State which joins the Monetary System does accept a severe limitation of its own monetary freedom, in so far as art. 3 of the 1978 Resolution and para. 2.3 of the 1997 Resolution provide that adjustments of central rates will be subject to mutual agreement by a common procedure, comprising

29 Report of the EMI to the informal ECOFIN Council, Verona, 12–13 Apr. 1996.

30 'Rapid' Information Service 18 June 1997.

31 European Council Resolution of 5 Dec. 1978 (EC *Bulletin* 1978 No. 12 Point 1.1.11).

32 See Louis, 'A legal and institutional approach for building a Monetary Union' (1998) *CMLRev.* 33 at p. 70.

33 Art. 3 of the 1978 Resolution.

34 Council Resolution of 16 June 1997, para. 1.6.

35 Art. 11 of the EC Treaty. See Usher, *EC Institutions and Legislation* (Longman, 1998) ch. 9.

all the countries participating in the exchange-rate mechanism, the Commission, and (in the 1997 version) the European Central Bank.

Finally, it might be wondered whether the 1978 Resolution was strictly a matter only of Community law: art. 5(2) of that Resolution envisaged that European countries with particularly close economic and financial ties with the European Communities could participate in the exchange-rate and intervention mechanism, so that it was not necessarily just a European Community European Monetary System. In practice it would appear that other States shadowed it rather than formally joining it, though both Norway and Sweden had participated in the 'snake'.[36] However, in 1990 the Norwegian central bank entered into a bilateral agreement with the Committee of Governors[37] of the EC central banks undertaking to take due account of the EMS agreements and exchange-rate policies and entering into bilateral swap agreements.[38] On the other hand, the EMS Mark II is expressly intended to link the currencies of Member Sates outside the euro area to the euro.[39] No mention is made of non-Member States.

As is well known, the United Kingdom did not join the original exchange-rate mechanism until October 1990, and then left it in September 1992, though it did participate in other aspects of the system from the outset. Another founder member of the system, Italy, also had to leave it in the Autumn of 1992, although it rejoined in November 1996 and was found in 1998 to have met the relevant convergence criterion.[40]

b) The ECU and the euro in the European Monetary Systems

While the details of the original version of the European Monetary System are now a matter of history, a brief outline of its exchange-rate mechanism is given to set the convergence criteria in their context. The ECU was at the heart of the exchange-rate mechanism,[41] even if the bands of fluctuation related to bilateral exchange rates between participating currencies. First, the ECU was used as the denominator of the exchange-rate mechanism, in other words the central rates of the national currencies were fixed against it and not against other national currencies; bilateral exchange rates were then calculated from those central rates. To take an example from the UK's period of participation, the central rate for the pound against the ECU was one ECU = £0.696904, and that for the franc was one ECU = FF6.89509, so that £0.696904 = FF6.89509, giving a bilateral rate of £1 = FF9.89389.

[36] Coffey, *The European Monetary System: Past, present and future* (2nd ed., Kluwer 1987) pp. 123–4.

[37] See Chapter 9 below; the functions of this body were taken over by the European Monetary Institute in 1994 under art. 117(1) of the EC Treaty, and then subsumed in the activities of the European Central bank following its establishment in 1998 by virtue of art. 123(2).

[38] *Agence Europe* 17/18 Dec. 1990 No. 5394 p. 7.

[39] See the recitals to the Resolution.

[40] See below p. 186.

[41] Art. 2(2).

Secondly, the ECU formed the basis or reference against which the 'divergence indicator' operates. In a sense these roles are, of course, linked. Basically, fluctuation margins of plus or minus 2.25 per cent were established round the bilateral exchange rates with regard to the other participating currencies derived from the central rates of a currency in relation to the ECU, although countries with previously floating currencies, i.e. those not in the 'snake', could opt for wider margins of up to plus or minus 6 per cent.[42] Initially, only Italy took advantage of this wider margin, moving to the narrow band of 2.25 per cent in January 1990,[43] but then had to leave the system in 1992. Spain when it joined in 1989,[44] Portugal, and the UK for its two years of membership also took advantage of the wider band. However, following turbulence on the money markets, in August 1993 a general margin of fluctuation of 15 per cent was adopted on a 'temporary' basis, subject to a bilateral arrangement between Germany and the Netherlands to maintain a 2.25 per cent margin between their currencies.[45] Italy was then able to rejoin the mechanism in November 1996.

Intervention was compulsory when the intervention points defined by these margins of fluctuation were reached, but as a kind of early-warning system a threshold of divergence was fixed at 75 per cent of the maximum spread of divergence against the ECU[46] calculated for each currency on an individual basis.[47] The idea behind this appears to have been that in a bilateral relationship there might be room for argument as to whether a widening gap was caused by one currency going up or by another going down. The existence of the central rate against the ECU made it possible to determine objectively which currency was moving in which direction, thus indicating which authorities needed to take action. The spread of divergence was calculated so as to eliminate the effect of the weighting of the currency in the ECU basket,[48] which in practice meant the heavier the weighting, the narrower the spread of divergence, so that the original spread for the DM was only 1.51 per cent.[49] It appears that this system of thresholds was not much used, although the September 1987 agreement on strengthening the European Monetary System provided for increased use of 'intramarginal' intervention,[50] and the widening of the band of fluctuation to 15 per cent might appear to have had the effect of virtually eliminating the need for intervention.

Under the European Monetary System Mark II, the exchange-rate mechanism is based on central rates against the euro,[51] which means that Member States outside the euro area participating in the exchange rate mechanism have to stay in a defined relationship with the euro, which is for them a foreign currency , rather than in a relationship with a basket ECU in which their currency is represented.

[42] Art. 3(1). [43] *Agence Europe* 8/9 Jan. 1990 No. 5167 p. 5.

[44] Ibid. 19/20 June 1989 No. 5039 p. 7. [45] Ibid. 2/3 Aug. 1993 No. 6034 pp. 3–4.

[46] Art. 3(5).

[47] See Coffey: *The European Monetary System: Past, present and future* (2nd ed., Kluwer 1987), pp. 22–5.

[48] Art. 3.5. [49] Coffey, loc. cit. [50] EC *Bulletin* 1987 No. 9 point 1.3.5.

[51] Para. 2.1.

Furthermore, there are no bilateral exchange rates with other national currencies with regard to which bands of fluctuation are fixed under the 1997 Resolution. Instead, the margins of fluctuation are based on the central rates against the euro itself. In other words, what matters is the relationship between the currency of a Member State outside the euro area participating in the exchange-rate mechanism and the euro, not the relationship between the currency of a Member State outside the euro area participating in the exchange-rate mechanism and the currency of another Member State outside the euro area participating in the exchange-rate mechanism. The standard fluctuation band is plus or minus 15 per cent around the central rates,[52] a figure continued from the original system after 1993, but 'on a case-by-case basis, formally agreed fluctuation bands narrower than the standard one and backed up in principle by automatic intervention and financing may be set at the request of the non-euro area Member State concerned'.[53] In fact, as stated above, in September 1998 agreement was reached between the finance ministers of the Euro–11, the ECB, and the ministers and Central Bank governors of Denmark and Greece that Denmark would participate in ERM II within a narrow band of fluctuation of 2.25 per cent, and Greece within the standard band of plus or minus 15 per cent.[54] However, it is also stated that 'the standard and narrower bands shall not prejudice the interpretation of the third indent of Article 109j(1)[55] of the EC Treaty',[56] i.e. they do not prejudice the question of what is the 'normal' margin of fluctuation.

3. The Delors Report

The Maastricht provisions on economic and monetary union find their genesis in the Report of a Committee chaired by Jacques Delors, then President of the Commission. The Committee was set up following a meeting of the European Council in Hanover in June 1988 and reported in April 1989.[57] It took as a starting point the view that the development of the single market necessitated more effective co-ordination of economic policy between national authorities, pointing out that with full freedom of capital movements and integrated financial markets, incompatible national policies would quickly translate into exchange-rate tensions and put an increasing and undue burden on monetary policy[58]—a prediction which was proved correct in 1992 and 1993. The Committee did, however, point out that economic and monetary union would be a quantum leap, implying far more than the single market programme.[59]

The Report briefly suggested that economic and monetary union would imply complete freedom of movement for persons, goods, services, and capital, as well as

[52] Ibid.
[53] Para. 2.4.
[54] *Bulletin Quotidien Europe* No. 7310, 28 and 29 Sept. 1998.
[55] Now art. 121(1).
[56] Para. 2.5.
[57] *Agence Europe Documents* No. 1550/1551, 20 Apr. 1989.
[58] Paras. 10–12.
[59] Para. 14.

irrevocably fixed exchange rates and, finally, a single currency.[60] It also expressly pointed out that it would require a transfer of decision-making power from Member States to the Community as a whole, particularly in the fields of monetary policy and macro-economic management.[61] With regard to monetary union, the Delors Report expressly referred to the Werner Committee Report,[62] and suggested that if there were an irrevocable locking of exchange-rate parities, a single currency would be a natural and desirable further development, showing that the move was irreversible and avoiding the transaction costs of converting currency.[63]

The concept of economic union was described as comprising four basic elements: the single market, competition policy, common policies aimed at structural change and regional development, and macro-economic policy co-ordination.[64] With regard to the last of these, it was acknowledged that since the Community budget would remain very small, the task of setting a Community-wide fiscal policy stance would have to be performed through the co-ordination of national budgetary policies.[65]

Finally, at the institutional level, it was recognized that a new monetary institution would be required to operate a single Community monetary policy, and the Report recommended the creation of a European System of Central Banks with the status of an autonomous Community institution.[66]

With regard to the mechanisms for achieving economic and monetary union, the Delors Committee recommended a three-stage process. The first stage did not require any Treaty amendments, and in fact the European Council meeting in Madrid in June 1989 decided that it should start on 1 July 1990.[67] In the economic field, this stage would see the completion of the internal market and the doubling of the structural funds under existing legislation, and it was recommended that the 1974 Decision[68] on economic convergence should be replaced by a system of multilateral surveillance of economic developments and policies. This recommendation was followed by the Council of Ministers in Decision 90/141 on the attainment of progressive convergence of economic policies and performance during stage one of economic and monetary union.[69] This provided for multilateral surveillance by the Council of Ministers, which was required at least twice a year to examine the economic conditions, prospects, and policies in the Community and its Member States, the compatibility of policies within Member States and in the Community at large, and the external economic environment and its interaction with the economy of the Community.[70] The Council was empowered to make economic policy suggestions; on a proposal of the Commission to issue economic policy recommendations,[71] and when potential or actual economic developments in one or more Member States threatened the economic stability and

[60] Para. 16. [61] Para. 19. [62] See p. 171 above. [63] Para. 23.
[64] Para. 25. [65] Para. 30. [66] Para. 32.
[67] See e.g. the recitals to Council Decision 90/141 on the progressive convergence of economic policies and performance during stage one of economic and monetary union (OJ 1990 L78/23).
[68] Council Decision 74/120 (OJ 1974 L63/16). [69] OJ 1990 L78/23.
[70] Art. 1. [71] Art. 2.

cohesion of the Community, the Council could, following an examination of the situation, formulate 'country-specific recommendations with a view to encouraging the necessary policy corrections'.[72]

In the monetary field, it was suggested that the first stage could see the implementation of the objective of a single financial area in which all monetary and financial instruments circulate freely, and banking, securities, and insurance services were offered uniformly throughout the Community; it is suggested that this takes a somewhat generous view of the scope of the relevant Community legislation.[73] It was further asserted that it was important to include all Community currencies in the EMS exchange-rate mechanism subject to the same rules; unfortunately, in 1992 both the UK and Italy had to leave the system, although Italy rejoined in November 1996 during the second stage of economic and monetary union. After suggesting that all impediments to the private use of the ECU should be removed, it was also recommended that the structure and functions of the Committee of Governors of Central Banks of the EC[74] should be amended in various specific ways; these recommendations were largely followed in Council Decision 90/142.[75]

However, the Committee was split[76] on whether a European Reserve Fund, rather like the European Monetary Fund envisaged in the 1978 European Monetary System Resolution,[77] should be established at this stage. One of the problems related to the interpretation of the then art. 102a of the Treaty. As well as providing, as has been noted, for recognition of the EMS and the ECU, the second paragraph stated that 'in so far as further development in the development of economic and monetary policy necessitates institutional changes, the provisions of art. 236[78] shall be applicable', i.e. the Treaty must be amended. On one interpretation it is questionable how the structure of the Committee of Governors of Central Banks of the EC could subsequently have been changed by the simple Council Decision mentioned above. However, it could be suggested that art. 102a(2) only related to institutions in the sense of the Community institutions defined in what are now arts. 7 and 8 of the EC Treaty, and that a limited body could have been created by secondary legislation.

In stage two, which the Maastricht Treaty defined as beginning on 1 January 1994,[79] the fundamental recommendation was that the institutional structure should be established.[80] This was not wholly followed in the Maastricht Treaty, which provided for the creation of a transitional European Monetary Institute[81] able to exercise some, but not all, of the powers to be enjoyed by the European Central Bank in the third stage. Finally, it was foreseen that in the third stage,

[72] Art. 5.
[73] See Chapters 2 and 6 above.
[74] The functions of this body were taken over by the European Monetary Institute in 1994 under art. 117(1) of the EC Treaty, and then subsumed in the activities of the European Central bank following its establishment in 1998 by virtue of art. 123(2).
[75] OJ 1990 L78/25.
[76] Paras. 53 and 54.
[77] See above p. 173.
[78] Now art. 304.
[79] EC Treaty art. 116(1).
[80] Para. 57.
[81] Art. 117.

which began, as required under the Maastricht provisions, on 1 January 1999, the irrevocably locked exchange rates would begin to be replaced by a single currency, and the relevant monetary and economic competences would be transferred to Community institutions, and it was pointed out that they would have to have authority to impose constraints on national budgets to the extent necessary to prevent imbalances that might threaten monetary stability.[82] Presumably this is the source of art. 104, requiring Member States[83] to avoid excessive government deficits and laying down procedures to enforce that obligation.

4. The Maastricht provisions

a) The objectives

Since the first stage of economic and monetary union began on 1 July 1990, the provisions introduced by the Maastricht Treaty are largely relevant to the second and third stages. To put these provisions in their context, it should be remembered that the Maastricht Treaty resulted from separate draft treaties respectively on Political Union and on Economic and Monetary Union, and that different solutions were adopted with regard to the achievement of those 'unions'. The provisions relating to Economic and Monetary Union took the form of amendments to the EC Treaty and therefore form an integral part of Community law;[84] on the other hand, in the context of the provisions relating to Political Union, a distinction was made between those matters which constituted amendments to the existing Community treaties, and those which fell outside the scope of the Communities, notably the provisions on a common foreign and security policy and those on co-operation in the fields of justice and home affairs.

Quite apart from its regulation of the second and third stages of Economic and Monetary Union,[85] the Maastricht Treaty added a new provision, now art. 4, setting out further Community objectives. Under art. 4(1) the activities of the Member States and the Community are to include, as provided in the Treaty and in accordance with the timetable set out therein, the adoption of an economic policy, based on the close co-ordination of Member States' economic policies, on the internal market, and on the definition of common objectives, and conducted in accordance with the principle of an open-market economy with free competition. Article 4(3) provides that these activities of the Member States and the Community shall entail compliance with the guiding principles of stable prices, sound public finances and monetary conditions, and a sustainable balance of payments. These provisions are binding upon all Member States.

[82] Para. 59.

[83] With an exception for the UK under its Protocol. However, by virtue of a reference to art. 116(4), the UK must 'endeavour' to avoid excessive government deficits.

[84] Esp. arts. 98 to 124 (formerly arts. 102a to 109m) of the EC Treaty.

[85] The capital movement provisions in effect form part of stage two: see Chapter 2 above.

However, the core of the matter is in art. 4(2), which under the Protocol[86] is not binding on the UK following the UK's notice in November 1997 that it would not participate in stage three of economic and monetary union. Article 4(2) states that, as provided in the Treaty and in accordance with the timetable and the procedures set out therein, the activities of the Member States and of the Community shall include the irrevocable fixing of exchange rates leading to the introduction of a single currency, the ECU, and the definition and conduct of a single monetary policy and exchange-rate policy, the primary objective of both of which shall be to maintain price stability and, without prejudice to this objective, to support the general economic policies in the Community, in accordance with the principle of an open-market economy with free competition. While this provision might seem to be of academic interest to the UK lawyer, it should be remembered, with regard to the United Kingdom's special treatment in the context of Economic and Monetary Union, that the EC Treaty has from the outset required, under original arts. 103 and 105, co-ordination of economic policy and exchange-rate policy, that the Single European Act added a Chapter heading on co-operation in monetary and economic policy, and that in *Opinion 1/91*[87] the European Court also suggested that the attainment of Economic and Monetary Union was *already* a Community objective. It is therefore submitted that exclusion from art. 4(2) does not necessarily mean exclusion from the objective of economic and monetary union.

b) The second-stage requirements

Turning to the more detailed steps towards economic and monetary union set out in the provisions introduced by the Maastricht Treaty: as stated above, art. 116 defined the second stage as beginning on 1 January 1994. Each Member State was by then required to have adopted appropriate measures necessary to comply with the prohibitions laid down in the new provisions on capital movements and payments[88] and in arts. 101 and 102(1). Article 101 provides, so far as relevant, that overdraft facilities or any other type of credit facility with the central banks of the Member States in favour of central governments, regional, local or other public authorities, other bodies governed by public law, or public undertakings of Member States are prohibited, as is the purchase directly from them by national central banks of debt instruments. However, this does not apply to publicly owned credit institutions which, in the context of the supply of reserves by central banks, are to be given the same treatment by national central banks as private credit institutions. Article 102(1) prohibits any measure not based on prudential considerations, establishing privileged access by Community institutions or bodies, central governments, regional, local or other public authorities, other bodies governed by public law, or public undertakings of Member States to financial institutions.

[86] Para. 5. [87] [1991] ECR I-6079. [88] See Chapter 2 above.

Member States were also required to adopt, with a view to permitting the assessment provided for in subparagraph (b) of art. 116(2), multi-annual programmes intended to ensure the lasting convergence necessary for the achievement of economic and monetary union, in particular with regard to price stability and sound public finances. Subparagraph (b) laid down that the Council should, on the basis of a report from the Commission, assess the progress made with regard to economic and monetary convergence, in particular with regard to price stability and sound public finances, and the progress made with the implementation of Community law concerning the internal market.

Article 116(3) made it clear that arts. 101 and 102(1) referred to above applied from the beginning of the second stage, as also did art. 103(1), providing that the Community shall not be liable for or assume the commitments of central governments, regional, local or other public authorities, other bodies governed by public law, or public undertakings of any Member State, without prejudice to mutual financial guarantees for the joint execution of a specific project. It also states that a Member State shall not be liable for or assume the commitment of central governments, regional, local or other public authorities, other bodies governed by public law, or public undertakings of another Member State, without prejudice to mutual financial guarantees for the joint execution of a specific project.

Certain aspects of the excessive deficits procedure under art. 104[89] also apply from the second stage, with the fundamental exception of the obligation to avoid them, and the enforcement procedure, which is replaced by the requirement under art. 116(4) to 'endeavour' to avoid such deficits, a provision which still applies to the UK in the third stage.[90] It was finally required in art. 116(5) that each Member State should, as appropriate, start the process leading to the independence of its central bank, in accordance with art. 109 which, however, does not apply to the United Kingdom following its notice that it will not participate in stage three of economic and monetary union.

Institutionally, art. 117 provided for the establishment of the European Monetary Institute at the start of the second stage.[91] However, perhaps the most important feature of the second stage was the establishment in art. 121 of the criteria determining whether progress may be made towards the third stage. This was based on a system of reports by the Commission and the European Monetary Institute to the Council on the progress made in the fulfilment by the Member States of their obligations regarding the achievement of economic and monetary union. These reports included an examination of the compatibility between each Member State's national legislation, including the statutes of its national central bank, and arts. 108 and 109 on the independence of the European Central Bank and of national central banks, and the Statute of the European System of Central Banks.

89 See p. 189 below. 90 Protocol para. 6. 91 See Chapter 9 below.

c) Convergence criteria

The reports were also required to examine the achievement of a high degree of sustainable convergence by reference to the fulfilment by each Member State of criteria which make reference mostly to factual situations and soft law, with the result that their nature could be regarded as having changed during the period between the signature of the Maastricht Treaty in February 1992 and the assessment made in May 1998. The criteria are as follows:

• *the achievement of a high degree of price stability*
This is stated to be apparent from a rate of inflation which is close to that of, at most, the three best performing Member States in terms of price stability. The Protocol on Convergence Criteria defines closeness in terms of not exceeding the rates of the best three States by more than 1.5 per cent, which in 1992 may have seemed a tight target. However, in the year to January 1998, the arithmetic average of the three best performing Member States was 1.2 per cent,[92] and to exceed that by 1.5 per cent gives a range of error of more than 100 per cent. The figure used was in fact 2.7 per cent.

• *the sustainability of the government financial position*
This is stated to be apparent from having achieved a government budgetary position without a deficit that is excessive as determined in accordance with art. 104(6). Under art. 104(2), the relevant criteria relate to the ratio of the planned or actual government deficit to gross domestic product, and to the ratio of government debt to gross domestic product. These criteria are further refined in the Protocol on the Excessive Deficit Procedure, according to which government deficit must not exceed 3 per cent of GDP, and government debt must not exceed 60 per cent of GDP, but although these limits are not absolute. A Member State which breaches the deficit ratio will not be regarded as having an excessive government deficit if the ratio has declined 'substantially and continuously' and reached a level that comes close to the reference value, or alternatively, if the excess over the reference value is only 'exceptional and temporary' and the ratio remains close to the reference value.[93] Furthermore, a higher ratio of government debt will not be regarded as excessive if the ratio is 'sufficiently diminishing' and approaching the reference value 'at a satisfactory pace'.[94] Thus both Belgium and Italy had a ratio of government debt to GDP above 120 per cent when the assessment of compliance with the convergence criteria was made,[95] yet were not regarded as having an excessive deficit. However, this is not just a hurdle to be jumped over to gain admission to the third stage of Economic and Monetary Union: the obligation to avoid an

[92] Commission Recommendation of 25 Mar. 1998, recital 6.
[93] Art. 104(2)(a).
[94] Art. 104(2)(b).
[95] Commission Report of 25 Mar. 1998 on Progress towards Convergence, 1.3.1 and 1.3.7.

excessive government deficit remains in perpetuity,[96] and its enforcement is the subject of the Stability and Growth Pact[97] discussed later in this Chapter.

- *the observance of the normal fluctuation margins provided for by the exchange-rate mechanism of the European Monetary System, for at least two years, without devaluing against the currency of any other Member State*
- *the durability of convergence achieved by the Member State and of its participation in the exchange-rate mechanism of the European Monetary System being reflected in the long-term interest rate levels.*

Before turning to the broader issues raised by these references to the European Monetary System, it may be observed that under the Protocol on Convergence Criteria it is stated that average nominal long-term interest rates should not exceed those of the three best States by more than 2 per cent. By the time the assessment was made, the figure derived from the three best States was 5.8 per cent,[98] so that again a margin of 2 per cent allows for a wide margin of error in relation to that norm, whatever may have been the situation in 1992.

As for the European Monetary System, its structure was laid down in a Resolution of the European Council of 5 December 1978,[99] backed up by an Agreement between the central banks of the Member States of 13 March 1979 laying down the operating procedures for the EMS (hereinafter the 1979 Agreement).[100] However, the European Monetary System constituted only what was meant to be its initial phase;[101] it was, for example, intended to create a European Monetary Fund within two years, but that never happened. Although its aim was to create a 'zone of monetary stability in Europe', this should be seen in the context of a world of floating exchange rates. It did not create a fixed exchange-rate system: it allowed margins of fluctuation, anticipated realignments of central rates against the ECU, and envisaged that the definition of the ECU itself could be changed. Indeed, between 1979 and 1986 there were on average nearly two realignments a year.[102] On the other hand, from then until the Autumn of 1992 the system remained relatively stable; dare one suggest that in the late 1980s the participant States had similar economic goals, whereas by 1992 the priorities of some of them had become divergent, leading to the market pressures which drove the UK and Italy out of the System?

In this context it should be observed that the criterion with regard to the exchange-rate mechanism refers to the 'normal' fluctuation margins and not to the

[96] See Hahn, 'The Stability Pact for European Monetary Union: Compliance with deficit limit as a constant legal duty' (1998) *CMLRev*. 77.

[97] European Council Resolution (OJ 1997 C236/1) on the Stability and Growth Pact, Council Regulation 1466/97 on the strengthening of the surveillance of budgetary positions and of the surveillance and co-ordination of economic policies (OJ 1997 L209/1); Council Regulation 1467/97 on speeding up and clarifying the implementation of the excessive deficit procedure (OJ 1997 L209/6).

[98] Commission Recommendation of 25 Mar. 1998, recital 9.

[99] EC *Bulletin* 1978 No. 12 point 1.1.11.

[100] Revised version printed in *Compendium of Community Monetary Texts* (1989) p. 50.

[101] 1978 Resolution, art. 1.4.

[102] Coffey, *op. cit.* pp. 126–7.

'narrow' margins. As explained above, until 1993 the normal margin was 2.25 per cent, with an exceptional band of 6 per cent. The decision taken on the night of 1–2 August 1993 by Ministers and Central Bank governors adopted on a 'temporary' basis a general margin of fluctuation of 15 per cent, subject to a bilateral arrangement between Germany and the Netherlands to maintain a 2.25 per cent margin between their currencies.[103] Leaving aside the view that such a wide band hardly represents a margin at all, it may be submitted that the 15 per cent band became the 'normal' margin of fluctuation. However, whether or not this interpretation is correct, it shows very clearly how the content of a binding Treaty provision which refers to 'soft' law may effectively be amended by a change in that soft law. The attitude taken by the Commission in its Report and Recommendation of 25 March 1998 was on one hand to say in its Recommendation[104] that the widening of the margins of fluctuation 'modified the framework' for assessing exchange-rate stability, while on the other hand stating in its Report that it had used the margin of 2.25 per cent as the basis for its assessment, and it seems to have been satisfied if a currency had 'almost always' traded within that margin.[105] However, the Treaty refers to staying within the normal margin for two years, which gave rise to particular issues in relation to Finland, Italy, and Sweden. Italy was one of the original participants in the exchange-rate mechanism of the EMS, albeit initially with a wider band of fluctuation of 6 per cent. However, like the United Kingdom, it found itself having to leave the system in September 1992, and did not rejoin until November 1996, less than two years before the assessment was made. However, in its Report[106] the Commission stated that 'although the lira has participated in the ERM only since November 1996, it has not experienced severe tensions during the review period and has thus . . . displayed sufficient stability in the last two years'. Finland, which only joined the Community in 1995, entered the ERM in October 1996, and in its Report[107] the Commission used wording virtually identical to that used in relation to Italy. However, Sweden, which also joined the Community in 1995, had not participated at all in the ERM, and was known politically not to wish to participate in stage three of EMU, but did not have the benefit (if such it be) of a special protocol like the UK or Denmark. There is no mention of this last point in the Commission's Report, which instead observes that the Swedish crown had never participated in the ERM, and that during the relevant two years it had fluctuated against the ERM currencies, 'reflecting, among other things, the absence of an exchange-rate target'. The formal Council Decision[108] uses very similar wording. Both then conclude that Sweden did not fulfil the third convergence criterion. The conclusion may therefore be drawn that while this criterion has not been interpreted literally, a Member State which does not participate at all in the ERM will not be regarded as meeting the criterion, at least if it has suffered currency fluctuation (which is very likely to be the case). The practical consequence may there-

[103] See *Agence Europe* 2/3 Aug. 1993 No. 6034 pp. 3–4.
[104] Recital 8.
[105] See e.g. Commission *Report* 1.3.11 in relation to Portugal.
[106] Para. 1.3.7.
[107] Para. 1.3.12.
[108] Council Decision 98/317 (OJ 1998 L139/30).

fore be that to the extent that membership of the ERM is voluntary, participation in the third stage of Economic and Monetary Union is also voluntary, even if no new Member States are offered the special treatment given to the UK and Denmark.

In this context, it must be emphasized that the convergence criteria are not simply a set of tests which were applied once in 1998; they remain relevant so long as there are non-participant Member States, and in the context of any future enlargement of the Community. The status of a Member State with a derogation is envisaged as being transitional rather than permanent. Indeed the responsible Commissioner, M de Silguy, has taken to referring to Member States with a derogation as 'pre-ins'.[109] Under art. 122(2), at least once every two years, or at the request of a Member State with a derogation, the Commission and the European Central Bank must report to the Council in accordance with the procedure laid down in art. 121(1). After consulting the European Parliament and after discussion in the Council, meeting in the composition of the Heads of State or of Government, the Council, acting by a qualified majority on a proposal from the Commission, is then to decide which Member States with a derogation fulfil the necessary conditions on the basis of the convergence criteria set out in art. 121(1), and abrogate the derogations of the Member States concerned.

Member States with a derogation must therefore meet the original criteria, and two of the criteria for convergence relate to the exchange-rate mechanism of the European Monetary System. This has led to the adoption of a Resolution introducing the European Monetary System Mark II,[110] given the failure of the Treaty to deal with the question of an exchange- rate mechanism in relations between Member States which participate in Economic and Monetary Union and those which do not. The main features of the European Monetary System Mark II include the fact that, as in the first version, participation in the exchange-rate mechanism is voluntary for the Member States outside the euro area, so the Swedish precedent appears to remain valid. Nevertheless, it is stated that 'Member States with a derogation can be expected to join the mechanism'.[111] The exchange-rate mechanism is based on central rates against the euro, and the standard fluctuation band is plus or minus 15 per cent around the central rates,[112] the same margin as in the original system after 1993, but 'on a case-by-case basis, formally agreed fluctuation bands narrower than the standard one and backed up in principle by automatic intervention and financing may be set at the request of the non-euro area Member State concerned'.[113] In fact, as mentioned above, in September 1998 agreement was reached between the finance ministers of the Euro–11, the ECB, and the ministers and Central Bank governors of Denmark and Greece that Denmark would participate in ERM II within a narrow band of fluctuation of 2.25

[109] Speech to Vienna Stock Exchange, 25 Sept. 1998 (RAPID documents Speech 98/182).

[110] See p. 175 above.

[111] European Council Resolution of 16 June 1997, para.1.6.

[112] Para. 2.1.

[113] Para. 2.4.

per cent, and that Greece would participate within the standard band of plus or minus 15 per cent.[114]

However, it is also stated that 'the standard and narrower bands shall not prejudice the interpretation of the third indent of Article 121(1) of the EC Treaty',[115] a singularly unhelpful provision given the doubts discussed above. It may be suggested, following the language of the Commission Recommendation of 25 March 1998 and the Council Decision of 3 May 1998, that what will really matter is whether the currency has suffered 'severe tensions', and whether it has participated at all in the exchange-rate mechanism.

The reports of the Commission and the EMI were required also to take account of the development of the ECU, the results of the integration of markets, the situation and development of the balances of payments on current account, and to examine the development of unit labour costs and other price indices.

Article 121(2) provides that on the basis of these reports, the Council, acting by a qualified majority on a recommendation from the Commission, must assess for each Member State whether it fulfils the necessary conditions for the adoption of a single currency. It must then, in one of the institutional innovations introduced by the Maastricht Treaty, recommend its findings to the Council, meeting in the composition of the Heads of State or of Government; in other words, the Council is required to make a recommendation to itself, albeit in a specified composition, which is the result of defining the European Council as an institution of the Union rather than of the Community.[116] The European Parliament must be consulted and forward its opinion to the Council, meeting in the composition of the Heads of State or of Government. Before the Council's initial assessment was made, the UK Protocol provided that the UK had to notify the Council whether it intended to move to the third stage, and unless it notified that it did intend to move to that stage it was under no obligation to do so. The UK gave notice in November 1997 that it did not intend to move to the third stage. The Danish Protocol is in similar terms, except that Denmark is treated as a 'Member State with a derogation'[117] following its notification of its intention not to proceed to the third stage.

The Maastricht provisions laid down two alternative time-scales for moving to the third stage. In both cases, the decision was to be taken by the Council, meeting in the composition of Heads of State or of Government, acting by a qualified majority, in the light of the recommendations of the Commission and of the 'ordinary' Council, and the opinion of the European Parliament. Article 121(3) provided that not later than 31 December 1996, the Council, meeting in the composition of Heads of State or of Government, must decide whether a majority of the Member States fulfilled the necessary conditions for the adoption of a single currency and decide whether it is appropriate for the Community to enter the third stage. If so, it must set the date for the beginning of the third stage. However, though this procedure was formally undertaken, a political decision had already

[114] *Bulletin Quotidien Europe* No. 7310, 28 and 29 Sept. 1998.

[115] Para. 2.5.

[116] Treaty on European Union, art. 4.

[117] See below p. 200.

been taken at the Madrid European Council in December 1995 that the third stage would actually begin on the second date envisaged by the Treaty, 1 January 1999.[118]

This overall deadline was set by art. 121(4), which provided that if by the end of 1997 the date for the beginning of the third stage had not been set, the third stage was to start on 1 January 1999. In order to achieve this, it was provided that before 1 July 1998, the Council, meeting in the composition of Heads of State or of Government, after a repetition of the procedure provided for in paragraphs 1 and 2, with the exception of the obligation to determine whether a *majority* of the Member States fulfilled the necessary criteria, must, acting by a qualified majority and on the basis of the recommendations of the ordinary Council, confirm which Member States fulfilled the necessary conditions for the adoption of a single currency. The result was Council Decision 98/317 of 3 May 1998 in accordance with art. 109j(4)[119] of the EC Treaty[120] which determined that Belgium, Germany, Spain, France, Ireland, Italy, Luxembourg, the Netherlands, Austria, Portugal, and Finland fulfilled the necessary conditions for the adoption of the single currency on 1 January 1999.

5. The Stability and Growth Pact

a) The Treaty provisions on excessive deficits

As mentioned in the context of the convergence criteria, the obligation to avoid an excessive government deficit remains in perpetuity.[121] This in itself is a clear example of the difference in treatment between monetary policy and economic policy under the provisions introduced by the Maastricht Treaty. Article 4(2) of the EC Treaty provides for the 'conduct of a single monetary policy and exchange-rate policy', and for the participants in Economic and Monetary Union, monetary policy (and the conduct of foreign-exchange operations) has become a matter of Community competence, defined and implemented by the European System of Central Banks, by virtue of art. 105(2) of the EC Treaty, with the primary objective of maintaining price stability. It will not therefore be possible, for example, for interest rates which relate to monetary policy to be fixed at the national level. Unfortunately, the Treaty does not define the concept of monetary policy, but it is evident from the Statute of the ESCB and from the ECB document entitled 'The Single Monetary Policy in Stage Three'[122] that the monetary policy instruments available to the ECB operate at the level of the wholesale money markets. It may

[118] A detailed timetable in the form of an Annex to the Conclusions of the Madrid European Council was published in OJ 1996 C22/2.

[119] Now art. 121(4).

[120] OJ 1998 L139/30.

[121] See Hahn, 'The Stability Pact for European Monetary Union: Compliance with deficit limit as a constant legal duty' (1998) *CMLRev*. 77.

[122] Sept. 1998.

conduct open-market operations, offer standing facilities, and require credit institutions to hold minimum reserves on accounts with the ESCB, and the interest rates it sets as a matter of monetary policy operate at this level.

On the other hand, although under art. 99(1), Member States are to regard their economic policies as a matter of common concern and are to co-ordinate them within the Council, they remain national policies. More particularly, government deficits and government debt remain the responsibility of national governments even if they participate in the third stage of Economic and Monetary Union, and art. 104 on the excessive deficits procedure falls under the Chapter heading 'Economic Policy'. In the structure of the Treaty it is a matter of national competence which is subject to Community co-ordination; hence the continuing obligation for Member States to meet the criteria. Under art. 104(2) the relevant criteria relate to the ratio of the planned or actual government deficit to gross domestic product, and to the ratio of government debt to gross domestic product. These criteria are further refined in the Protocol on the Excessive Deficit Procedure, according to which government deficit must not exceed 3 per cent of GDP, and government debt must not exceed 60 per cent of GDP, but these limits are not absolute. A Member State which breaches the deficit ratio will not be regarded as having an excessive government deficit if the ratio has declined 'substantially and continuously' and reached a level that comes close to the reference value, or alternatively, the excess over the reference value is only 'exceptional and temporary' and the ratio remains close to the reference value.[123] Furthermore a higher ratio of government debt will not be regarded as excessive if the ratio is 'sufficiently diminishing' and is approaching the reference value 'at a satisfactory pace'.[124]

During the second stage, Member States were obliged only to 'endeavour' to avoid excessive government deficits,[125] and this is still the case for the United Kingdom under its Protocol. Nevertheless, for Member States wishing to participate in the third stage of Economic and Monetary Union, compliance with this obligation was an absolute necessity in the third stage. The structure of the excessive deficits procedure is that it:

- sets out the obligation, applicable from the third stage to all Member States except the United Kingdom, to avoid excessive government deficits;
- establishes machinery for determining whether there is an excessive deficit, which applies to all Member States, and which was applicable throughout the second stage in relation to the obligation to endeavour to avoid excessive government deficits;
- sets out its own enforcement machinery which, however, does not apply to Member States with a derogation,[126] or to Denmark (which is treated as if it did have a derogation[127]), or to the United Kingdom.[128]

[123] Art. 104(2)(a). [124] Art. 104(2)(b). [125] Art. 116(4). [126] Art. 122(3).
[127] Danish Protocol para. 2. [128] UK Protocol para. 5.

During the first application of this procedure at the start of the second stage in 1994, ten of the then twelve Member States (i.e. all except Ireland and Luxembourg) were found to have an excessive deficit, as subsequently were the three States which joined in 1995.[129] By the time the decision on moving to the third stage was taken in May 1998, however, only Greece was found still to have an excessive deficit.[130] So far as the machinery for determining whether there is an excessive deficit is concerned, Council Regulation 3605/93[131] requires that Member States should, from the beginning of 1994 onwards, report to the Commission their planned and actual government deficits and levels of government debt twice a year,[132] before 1 March and 1 September of each year. Before 1 March they must give their planned deficit for the current year, their estimate of the actual deficit for the previous year, and their actual deficit for the three years before that. Before 1 September, they must give their updated planned deficit for the current year, and their actual deficit for the four previous years.

Article 104(3) of the Treaty provides that if a Member State does not fulfil the requirements under either or both of the criteria mentioned above, the Commission must prepare a report, which must take into account whether the government deficit exceeds government investment expenditure all other relevant factors, including the medium-term economic and budgetary position of the Member State. The Commission may also prepare a report if, notwithstanding the fulfilment of the requirements under the criteria, it is of the opinion that there is a risk of an excessive deficit in a Member State.

If the Commission considers that an excessive deficit in a Member State exists or may occur, the Commission addresses an opinion (by definition a non-binding act) to the Council, and the Council, acting by a qualified majority on a recommendation from the Commission, and having considered any observations which the Member State concerned may make, has to decide after an overall assessment whether an excessive deficit exists.[133]

If it decides that there is an excessive deficit the Council makes recommendations to the Member State concerned with a view to bringing that situation to an end within a given period. However, these recommendations are not to be made public, unless it is established that there has been no effective action in response to its recommendations within the period laid down, in which case the Council may make its recommendations public.[134] Nevertheless, under the Resolution of the European Council on the Stability and Growth Pact,[135] Member States are 'invited' to make such recommendations public on their own initiative. In any event, the Treaty itself does not lay down any time limits for the conduct of this assessment procedure.

[129] See Commission *Report on Progress towards Convergence* (25 Mar. 1998) pp. 118–19.
[130] Council Decision 98/317 (OJ 1998 L139/30).
[131] OJ 1993 L332/7.
[132] Art. 4.
[133] Art. 104(6).
[134] Art. 104(7) and (8).
[135] OJ 1997 C236/1. See below at p. 193.

As for enforcement, art. 104(10) expressly provides that the rights for the Commission or other Member States to bring actions against the State concerned before the European Court provided for in arts. 226 and 227 (formerly arts. 169 and 170) may not be exercised within the framework of paragraphs 1 to 9 of that article. However, the article sets out its own enforcement mechanism, providing that if a Member State persists in failing to put into practice the recommendations of the Council, the Council may decide to give notice to the Member State to take measures, within a specified time limit, for the deficit reduction which is judged necessary by the Council in order to remedy the situation.[136] In such case, the Council may request the Member State concerned to submit reports in accordance with a specific timetable in order to examine the adjustment efforts of that Member State. Finally, it is provided that as long as a Member State fails to comply with a decision taken in accordance with paragraph 9, the Council may decide to apply or, as the case may be, intensify one or more of the following measures:

- to require the Member State concerned to publish additional information, to be specified by the Council, before issuing bonds and securities;
- to invite the European Investment Bank to reconsider its lending policy towards the Member State concerned;
- to require the Member State concerned to make a non-interest-bearing deposit of an appropriate size with the Community until the excessive deficit has, in the view of the Council, been corrected; and
- to impose fines of an appropriate size.

In taking decisions as to the existence of an excessive deficit and in imposing remedial measures or sanctions, the Council is required to act on a recommendation from the Commission by a special majority of two-thirds of the weighted votes of its members, excluding the votes of the representative of the Member State concerned. This is a slightly lower majority than the normal qualified majority, though it is the same as the qualified majority among the participants in Economic and Monetary Union when the votes of Member States with derogations are excluded.[137]

A common thread running through the enforcement machinery set out in the Treaty text is that it is discretionary: it states what the Council 'may' do, but does not require it to take any action. This may be contrasted with the situation where the Council withdraws its measures. Under art. 104(12), the Council 'shall' abrogate some or all of its decisions as to the existence of an excessive deficit or imposing remedial measures or sanctions to the extent that the excessive deficit in the Member State concerned has, in the view of the Council, been corrected. In particular, if the Council has previously made public recommendations, it must, as soon as the decision to make the recommendation public has been abrogated, make a public statement that an excessive deficit in the Member State concerned no longer exists.

[136] Art. 104(9). [137] Art. 122(5).

In sum: although art. 104 maintains the excessive deficit criteria as continuing obligations for participants in the euro-zone, it does so by provisions which lay down no time limit for the process of assessment and which do not oblige the Council to impose sanctions This gave rise to the feeling,[138] particularly in Germany,[139] that this was not a sound basis on which to proceed to Economic and Monetary Union. The resultant political pressure led to the adoption in Amsterdam in June 1997 of a group of measures compendiously known as the Stability and Growth Pact, which has introduced an element of automaticity into the process.

b) The Pact

The Stability and Growth Pact consists of a European Council Resolution[140] on the Stability and Growth Pact, together with Council Regulation 1466/97[141] on the strengthening of the surveillance of budgetary positions and the surveillance and co-ordination of economic policies, and Council Regulation 1467/97[142] on speeding up and clarifying the implementation of the excessive deficit procedure. To the extent that reliance is placed on a Resolution of the European Council, its status is the same as both versions of the European Monetary System,[143] and the same arguments arise as in relation to the European Monetary System Mark II with regard to the legitimacy of an institution of the European Union acting in an area subject to the express competence of the European Community.[144]

The Resolution describes itself as providing 'firm political guidance to the parties who will implement the Stability and Growth Pact' and sets out what it calls 'guidelines' for the Member States, the Commission, and the Council. The Resolution states that the Member States:

1. commit themselves to respect the medium-term budgetary objective of positions close to balance or in surplus set out in their stability or convergence programmes and to take the corrective budgetary action they deem necessary to meet the objectives of their stability or convergence programmes, whenever they have information indicating actual or expected significant divergence from those objectives;
2. are invited to make public, on their own initiative, the Council recommendations made to them in accordance with art. 99(4). Such recommendations are made in the context of multilateral surveillance of economic policies where it is established that the economic policies of a Member State are not consistent with the broad guidelines for the economic policies of the Member States and of the Community adopted by the Council under art. 99(2);

[138] See Gros, 'Towards a Credible Excessive Deficits Procedure' in: Andenas, Gormley, Hadjiemmanuil, and Harden (eds) *European Economic and Monetary Union: The Institutional Framework* (Kluwer 1997) pp. 241–56.

[139] See the sources cited in Hahn, 'The Stability Pact for European Monetary Union: Compliance with deficit limit as a constant legal duty' (1998) *CMLRev.* 77 pp. 79 and 80.

[140] OJ 1997 C236/1.

[141] OJ 1997 L209/1.

[142] OJ 1997 L209/6.

[143] See above p. 173.

[144] See above p. 175.

3. commit themselves to take the corrective budgetary action they deem necessary to meet the objectives of their stability or convergence programmes once they receive an early warning in the form of a Council recommendation issued under art. 99(4);
4. will launch the corrective budgetary adjustments they deem necessary without delay on receiving information indicating the risk of an excessive deficit;
5. will correct excessive deficits as quickly as possible after their emergence; this correction should be completed no later than the year following the identification of the excessive deficit, unless there are special circumstances;
6. are invited to make public, on their own initiative, recommendations made in accordance with art. 104(7);
7. commit themselves not to invoke the benefit of art. 2(3) of the Council Regulation on speeding up and clarifying the excessive deficit procedure unless they are in severe recession; in evaluating whether the economic downturn is severe, the Member States will, as a rule, take as a reference point an annual fall in real GDP of at least 0.75 per cent.

As far as the Commission is concerned, the Resolution records that it will exercise its right of initiative under the Treaty in a manner that facilitates the strict, timely, and effective functioning of the Stability and Growth Pact, and that it will present, without delay, the necessary reports, opinions, and recommendations to enable the Council to adopt decisions under arts. 99 and 104. The Commission also committed itself to preparing a report under art. 104 (3) whenever there is a *risk* of an excessive deficit (despite the discretion implcit in the Treaty provision) or whenever the planned or actual government deficit exceeds the reference value of 3 per cent of GDP. It also undertook to present in writing to the Council the reasons for its position if it were to consider that a deficit exceeding 3 per cent of GDP was not excessive and if this opinion differed from that of the Economic and Financial Committee.

Finally, given that the Council may only determine that an excessive deficit exists on the basis of a recommendation from the Commission,[145] the Commission commits itself, if requested by the Council under art. 115, as a rule, to make a recommendation for a Council decision on whether an excessive deficit exists under art. 104(6).

The Council in turn is committed by the Resolution to 'a rigorous and timely implementation of all elements of the Stability and Growth Pact in its competence', although it also states that it will take such necessary decisions under arts. 99 and 104 'as [are] practicable'. It is 'urged' to regard the deadlines for the application of the excessive deficit procedure as upper limits; in particular, acting under art. 104 (7), the Council is to recommend that excessive deficits be corrected as quickly as possible after their emergence, and no later than the year following their identification, unless there are special circumstances. However, the heart of the matter is contained in paragraphs 3, 4, and 5 of the section of the resolution setting out the Council's commitments. These paragraphs provide that the Council:

[145] Art. 104(6).

3. is invited always to impose sanctions if a participating Member State fails to take the necessary steps to bring the excessive deficit situation to an end as recommended by the Council;
4. is urged always to require a non-interest bearing deposit, whenever the Council decides to impose sanctions on a participating Member State in accordance with art. 104(11);
5. is urged always to convert a deposit into a fine after two years of the decision to impose sanctions in accordance with art. 104(11), unless the excessive deficit has in the view of the Council been corrected.

Furthermore, if at any stage of the excessive deficit or surveillance of budgetary positions procedures the Council did not act on a Commission recommendation, the Council is 'invited' by the Resolution always to state in writing the reasons which justify a decision not to act and, in such a case, to make public the votes cast by each Member State.

This clear political commitment to use the sanctions machinery is reflected and supplemented in the legally binding obligations set out in Council Regulation 1467/97 of 7 July 1997 on speeding up and clarifying the implementation of the excessive deficit procedure.[146] In essence, this requires the Council to decide on the existence of an excessive deficit in accordance with art. 104(6), within three months of the reporting dates of 1 March and 1 September of each year established in art. 4(2) and (3) of Regulation 3605/93.[147] When it decides, in accordance with art. 104(6), that an excessive deficit exists, the Council is required at the same time to make recommendations to the Member State concerned in accordance with art. 104(7).[148] Such a recommendation is required[149] both to establish a deadline of four months at the most for effective action to be taken by the Member State concerned and to establish a deadline for the correction of the excessive deficit, a process which should be completed in the year following its identification unless there are special circumstances.[150]

When considering whether effective action has been taken in response to its recommendations made in accordance with art. 104(7)[151] the Council is required by the Regulation[152] to base its decision on publicly announced decisions by the Government of the Member State concerned, and any Council decision to give notice to the participating Member State concerned to take measures for deficit reduction in accordance with art. 104(9) is required to be taken within one month of the Council decision establishing that no effective action has been taken.[153] Any decision to impose sanctions must be taken no later than two months after the Council decision giving notice to the participating Member State concerned to take measures in accordance with art. 104(9),[154] and this decision must also be taken within ten months (which is the sum of all the periods mentioned above) of

[146] OJ 1997 L209/6.
[147] OJ 1993 L332/7. See p. 191 above.
[148] See p. 191 above.
[149] Council Regulation 1467/97 art. 3(4).
[150] Art. 3(4).
[151] See p. 191 above.
[152] Art. 4(2).
[153] Art. 5.
[154] Art. 6.

the reporting dates of 1 March and 1 September of each year established in art. 4(2) and (3) of Regulation 3605/93.[155]

With regard to the imposition of sanctions, Regulation 1467/97 provides that whenever the Council decides to apply sanctions to a participating Member State in accordance with art. 104(11), a non-interest-bearing deposit shall 'as a rule' be required, though the Council may decide to supplement this deposit by the measures provided for in the first and second indents of art. 104(11),[156] i.e. by requiring the Member State concerned to publish additional information, to be specified by the Council, before issuing bonds and securities, or by inviting the European Investment Bank to reconsider its lending policy towards the Member State concerned.

The Regulation also indicates the level of sanctions to be imposed: when the excessive deficit results from non-compliance with the criterion relating to the government deficit ratio of 3 per cent in art. 104(2) (a), the amount of the first deposit is stated to comprise a fixed component equal to 0.2 per cent of GDP, and a variable component equal to one-tenth of the difference between the deficit as a percentage of GDP in the preceding year and the reference value of 3 per cent of GDP. Each following year, until the decision on the existence of an excessive deficit is abrogated, the Council is required to assess whether the participating Member State concerned has taken effective action in response to the Council notice in accordance with art. 104(9). In this annual assessment, the Council must intensify the sanctions, unless the participating Member State concerned has complied with the Council notice; if an additional deposit is decided, it shall be equal to one-tenth of the difference between the deficit as a percentage of GDP in the preceding year and the reference value of 3 per cent of GDP, although any single deposit is subject to an upper limit of 0.5 per cent of GDP.[157] Finally, if two years after the decision to require the participating Member State concerned to make a deposit, the excessive deficit has in the view of the Council not been corrected, the deposit shall, as a rule, be converted by the Council, in accordance with art. 104(11), into a fine.

Any deposits required by way of sanction must be lodged with the Commission. However, interest on the deposits, and any fines imposed, constitute 'other revenue' of the Community under art. 269 (formerly art. 201) of the EC Treaty, and under art. 16 of the Regulation they are to be distributed among the Member States participating in the euro which do not have a deficit that is excessive in proportion to their share in the total GNP of the eligible Member States. In effect therefore, the system of sanctions leads to a transfer of financial resources from Member States which have an excessive deficit to those which do not.

More generally, Council Regulation 1466/97[158] sets out rules on strengthening the surveillance of budgetary positions and the surveillance and co-ordination of economic policies. Its aim is 'to prevent, at an early stage, the occurrence of

[155] OJ 1993 L332/7. See p. 191 above. [156] Art. 11. [157] Art. 12.
[158] OJ 1997 L209/1.

excessive general government deficits' and to promote the surveillance and co-ordination of economic policies.[159] It requires the submission of Stability Programmes by those participating in the euro, and of Convergence Programmes by the non-participants.

Under art. 99 of the Treaty, each participating Member State is required to submit to the Council and the Commission information necessary for the purpose of multilateral surveillance on an annual basis beginning on 1 March 1999,[160] in the form of a stability programme. A stability programme must present the following information:[161]

- (a) the medium-term objective for the budgetary position of close to balance or in surplus and the adjustment path towards this objective for the general government surplus/deficit and the expected path of the general government debt ratio;
- (b) the main assumptions about expected economic developments and important economic variables which are relevant to the realization of the stability programme such as government investment expenditure, real gross domestic product (GDP) growth, employment, and inflation;
- (c) a description of budgetary and other economic policy measures being taken and/or proposed to achieve the objectives of the programme, and, in the case of the main budgetary measures, an assessment of their quantitative effects on the budget;
- (d) an analysis of how changes in the main economic assumptions would affect the budgetary and debt position.

It is envisaged that, based on assessments by the Commission and the Economic and Financial Committee, the Council should, within the framework of multilateral surveillance under art. 99, examine whether the medium-term budget objective in the stability programme provides for a safety margin to ensure the avoidance of an excessive deficit, whether the economic assumptions on which the programme is based are realistic, and whether the measures being taken and/or proposed are sufficient to achieve the targeted adjustment path towards the medium-term budgetary objective. The Council is also required to examine whether the contents of the stability programme facilitate the closer co-ordination of economic policies, and whether the economic policies of the Member State concerned are consistent with the broad economic policy guidelines.[162] Where the Council, in accordance with art. 99, considers that the objectives and contents of a programme should be strengthened, the Council may 'invite' the Member State concerned to adjust its programme.

As part of multilateral surveillance in accordance with art. 99(3), the Council is required to monitor the implementation of stability programmes and the Council identifies significant divergence of the budgetary position from the medium-term budgetary objective, or the adjustment path towards it, it should, with a view to giving early warning in order to prevent the occurrence of an excessive deficit, address a recommendation under art. 99(4) to the Member State concerned to take

[159] Art. 1. [160] Art. 4. [161] Art. 3. [162] Art. 5.

the necessary adjustment measures.[163] If the Council in its subsequent monitoring judges that the divergence of the budgetary position from the medium-term budgetary objective, or the adjustment path towards it, is persisting or worsening, under art. 99(4) it must make a recommendation to the Member State concerned to take prompt corrective measures, and it may make its recommendation public.

Non-participating Member States are required to submit Convergence Programmes within the same time-scale.[164] A convergence programme must present the following information in particular on variables related to convergence:

- (a) the medium-term objective for the budgetary position of close to balance or in surplus and the adjustment path towards this objective for the general government surplus/deficit; the expected path for the general government debt ratio; the medium-term monetary policy objectives; the relationship of those objectives to price and exchange-rate stability;
- (b) the main assumptions about expected economic developments and important economic variables which are relevant to the realization of the convergence programme, such as government investment expenditure, real GDP growth, employment, and inflation;
- (c) a description of budgetary and other economic policy measures being taken and/or proposed to achieve the objectives of the programme, and, in the case of the main budgetary measures, an assessment of their quantitative effects on the budget;
- (d) an analysis of how changes in the main economic assumptions would affect the budgetary and debt position.

Apart from the references to monetary policy and exchange rates, this information is very similar to that required in Stability Programmes, and its treatment before the Council is also very similar, with provisions for monitoring[165] and for issuing recommendations in accordance with art. 99(4).[166]

[163] Art. 6. [164] Art. 7. [165] Art. 9. [166] Art. 10.

9

The 'ins' and the 'outs'

1. Introduction

With hindsight, it can be seen that the Maastricht Treaty introduced two different forms of flexibility or differentiated integration. The Social Protocol took the form of permission by all the Member States to a group of Member States to use Community institutions and legislation, which can be seen as the precursor of the general provisions on 'closer co-operation' in the Amsterdam Treaty. On the other hand, the provisions on Economic and Monetary Union provide for some Member States to receive opt-outs or derogations from binding Treaty obligations, and thus provide the model for the new Title of the EC Treaty on visas, asylum, and immigration introduced by the Amsterdam Treaty. In the case of Monetary Union, the situation arises not just from the special treatment accorded to the UK and Denmark by special Protocols, but also from the fact that it was appreciated that not all Member States would meet the strict criteria for economic convergence laid down as the precondition for participation in the monetary union; such States are referred to as 'Member States with a derogation'.[1] The EMU provisions are also different in nature from the general provisions on closer co-operation in that under art. 11(1)(a) of the EC Treaty, closer co-operation must not concern areas which fall within the exclusive competence of the Community. On the other hand, in the third stage of economic and monetary union, matters such as monetary policy and exchange-rate policy have become areas where those participating in a single currency cannot have divergent national policies and which may be regarded as a matter of exclusive Community competence irrespective of the number of Community rules introduced. Indeed, art. 4(2) expressly states that there shall be a 'single' monetary policy. It is also suggested that here, as in the fisheries sector once the deadline for the introduction of the common fisheries policy had expired,[2] participating Member States will be regarded as acting as agents of the Community: a situation effectively institutionalized in the European System of Central Banks. Intriguingly, however, it has become a matter of exclusive competence only for those who participate.

There is a further link with the general provisions on closer co-operation: in principle a decision to invoke those provisions may be taken by a qualified

[1] Art. 122 of the EC Treaty.

[2] Case 804/79 *Commission* v. *UK* [1981] ECR 1045.

majority vote in the Council,[3] and the eleven participants in the euro-zone have enough votes to constitute a qualified majority. It is therefore not inconceivable that the eleven might wish for example to use this mechanism to adopt common rules on taxation opposed by some of the non-participants.

2. Member States with a derogation

In one sense, the status of a Member State with a derogation is the obverse of a finding that other Member States fulfil the conditions for the adoption of a single currency. Since the decision was in fact taken to move to monetary union at the final deadline, the status is automatic for those Member States left out under the second sub-paragraph of art. 122(1): 'if the Council has confirmed which Member States fulfil the necessary conditions for the adoption of a single currency, in accordance with art. 121(4), those Member States which do not fulfil the conditions *shall* have a derogation' (emphasis added).

However, the status of a Member State with a derogation is envisaged as being transitional rather than permanent. Under art. 122(2), at least once every two years, or at the request of a Member State with a derogation, the Commission and the European Central Bank must report to the Council in accordance with the procedure laid down in art. 121(1). After consulting the European Parliament and discussion in the Council meeting in the composition of the Heads of State or of Government, the Council, acting by a qualified majority on a proposal from the Commission, decides which Member States with a derogation fulfil the necessary conditions on the basis of the criteria set out in art. 121(1), and abrogates the derogations of the Member States concerned. This reference to art. 121(1) could have created problems, because two of the criteria for convergence laid down in that provision relate to the exchange-rate mechanism of the European Monetary System and, as suggested above, this is the reason for creating a European Monetary System Mark II.[4]

The result of being a Member State with a derogation is that the following provisions of the Treaty do not apply to the Member State concerned: art. 104(9) and (11), which relate to the enforcement of the excessive deficits procedure, art. 105(1), (2), (3), and (5), which relate to the functions of the European System of Central Banks,[5] art. 106 on the issue of banknotes, art. 110 on the issue of secondary legislation by the European Central Bank, art. 111 on external monetary policy, and art. 112(2)(b) on the appointment of the Executive Board of the European Central Bank. The voting rights of Member States with a derogation are to be suspended for the Council decisions referred to in those Treaty provisions. In that case, under art. 122(5), a qualified majority is defined as two-thirds of the votes

[3] Though a dissentient may 'for important and stated reasons of national policy' in effect require that the matter be referred to the Council meeting in the compositions of Heads of State or Government for decision by unanimity.

[4] See Chapter 8 above.

[5] See Chapter 10 below.

of the representatives of the Member States without derogation weighted in accordance with art. 205(2), and unanimity of those Member States alone is required for an act requiring unanimity.

The exclusion of a Member State with a derogation and its national central bank from rights and obligations within the ESCB is laid down in Chapter IX of the Statute of the ESCB. Briefly, the consequence is that for most purposes in those Statutes 'Member States' means those without a derogation, and 'national central banks' means the central banks of Member States without a derogation. In other words, Member States with a derogation are largely excluded from its operation.

The practical consequences of this exclusion may be seen in the provisions governing the operation of TARGET (Trans-European Automated Real-time Gross settlement European Transfer system), the payment system for the euro. While the fear that the 'outs' would be excluded has proved to be unfounded, the price of permitting them to use it is a complex legal framework. This framework is based on a combination of an ECB Guideline[6] adopted by the Governing Council of the ECB addressed to and binding upon the national central banks of the euro–11, and the TARGET Agreement between the ECB and the national central banks of the Member States which have not adopted the euro but which wish to connect to TARGET. Effectively, the Agreement incorporates the provisions of the Guideline to apply its terms outside the euro-zone.[7]

However, art. 123(3) provides that if and as long as there are Member States with a derogation, and without prejudice to art. 107(3) of the Treaty, the General Council of the ECB referred to in art. 45 of the Statute of the ESCB shall be constituted as a third decision-making body of the ECB. Article 45.2 of the Statute provides that the General Council shall comprise the President and Vice-President of the ECB and the Governors of the national central banks, and that the other members of the Executive Board may participate, without the right to vote, in meetings of the General Council.[8] Apart from certain advisory and consultative functions, the chief functions of this body appear to be to take over those tasks of the EMI which, because of the derogations of one or more Member States, still have to be performed in the third stage, and to give advice in the preparations for the abrogation of the derogations specified in art. 122 of the Treaty.[9] In this context the General Council is to contribute to the necessary preparations for irrevocably fixing the exchange rates of the currencies of Member States with a derogation against the currencies, or the single currency, of the Member States without a derogation, as referred to in art. 111(5) of the Treaty.[10] It is also concerned with those aspects of the ECB's activity which relate to the non-participating States. Thus the ECB Decision laying down the measures necessary for paying up the capital of the ECB by the non-participating central banks[11] was adopted by the General Council of the ECB.

[6] See below p. 224.

[7] ECB *Third Progress Report* on the TARGET project, November 1998, p. 18.

[8] Its Rules of Procedure were published in OJ 1999 L75/36.

[9] Statute arts. 44 and 47.1.

[10] Ibid. art. 47.3.

[11] ECB Decision 1998/14 (OJ 1999 L110/33).

Finally, arts. 119 and 120[12] continue to apply to a Member State with a derogation, and by virtue of art. 124(2), such Member States remain under the obligation in art. 124(1) to treat their exchange-rate policy as a matter of common interest, taking account of the experience acquired in co-operation within the framework of the European Monetary System and in developing the ECU.

As far as Denmark and the United Kingdom are concerned, the effect of the Danish Protocol is essentially that Denmark is treated as if it had a derogation,[13] and the effect of the UK Protocol is that, although the United Kingdom has a small number of additional exclusions,[14] it also is treated like a Member State with a derogation, except that the provisions allowing for abrogation of the derogation do not automatically apply.[15]

3. Substantive issues

The fact that monetary policy is a matter of exclusive competence only for those who participate may lead to new aspects of the question of mixed competence in international negotiations, or to a situation in which international obligations are entered into by a 'Community' which does not include all its Members.

By way of example, the need (or hope) for an exchange-rate policy is envisaged in art. 111 of the EC Treaty; but it should be emphasized that this provision does not apply to Member States with a derogation[16] or to the United Kingdom following its decision not to participate.[17] Article 111(1) operates by way of derogation from art. 300, which sets out the general procedure for the negotiation of international agreements between the Community and non-Member States or international organizations; it empowers the Council to conclude formal agreements on an exchange-rate system for the ECU in relation to non-Community currencies—which seems to contemplate a return to something like the former IMF system—and lays down a special procedure for this to be achieved. The Council is required to act unanimously on a recommendation from the European Central Bank or from the Commission (which indicates that the power of initiative in this area is as much, if not more, with the ECB as with the Commission) after consulting the ECB in an endeavour to reach a consensus consistent with the objective of price stability, and after consulting the European Parliament. The procedure for negotiation is laid down in art. 111(3): where agreements concerning monetary or foreign exchange regime matters need to be negotiated by the Community with one or more States or international organizations, the Council, acting by a qualified majority[18] on a recommendation from the Commission and after consulting the ECB, shall decide the arrangements for the negotiation and for

[12] Original arts. 108 and 109; see Chapter 2 above.
[13] Danish Protocol art. 2.
[14] UK Protocol art. 5.
[15] Ibid.
[16] Art. 122(3) and (4).
[17] UK Protocol art. 5.
[18] Though under art. 111(1) it needs to act unanimously to conclude the resultant agreement.

the conclusion of such agreements. It is stated that these arrangements must ensure that the Community expresses a single position, and that the Commission must be 'fully associated' with the negotiations. The implication is that, whereas negotiations under the general art. 300 are conducted by the Commission, the same is not necessarily the case under art. 111, and the negotiations could, for example, be entrusted to the ECB. However, it is, clearly laid down that agreements concluded in accordance with art. 111(3) are to be binding on the institutions of the Community, on the ECB, and on Member States (but, of course, only those participating in monetary union).

What the Treaty failed to provide for is an exchange-rate relationship between the 'ins' and the 'outs'—hence the development of the European Monetary System Mark II by a Resolution of the European Council, as discussed in Chapter 8.

Although it may be a theoretical question, it is debateable that a similar problem is hidden in the safeguard measures permitted by the provisions on free movement of capital introduced by the Maastricht Treaty. Unlike all other Treaty freedoms, art. 56 provides that movements to and from third countries are to be treated the same way as movements between Member States. More specifically, art. 56(1) states that within the framework of the provisions set out in that Chapter, all restrictions on the movement of capital between Member States and between Member States and third countries shall be prohibited, and art. 56(2) states that within the same framework, all restrictions on payments between Member States and between Member States and third countries shall be prohibited. However, the safeguard clause for defending the Economic and Monetary Union in art. 59 relates only to third countries, stating that where, in exceptional circumstances, movements of capital to or from third countries cause, or threaten to cause, serious difficulties for the operation of economic and monetary union, the Council, acting by a qualified majority on a proposal from the Commission and after consulting the ECB, may take safeguard measures with regard to third countries for a period not exceeding six months if such measures are strictly necessary. There is no provision for parallel measures in relation to non-participant Member States, even though all such States may remain entitled, or be authorized, to take measures to protect their balance of payments under arts. 119 and 120. While it is perhaps unlikely that the euro–11 will need to defend themselves against the four non-participants, it is unusual to find such an imbalance in the Treaty provisions.

4. The composition of the Council

Variable participation within a single Treaty, and linkages between separate Treaties outlined above, raise the question of how far a single institutional structure may operate at all levels. Under the Maastricht provisions, it appears that the Council of Ministers varied from its basic composition under the Social Protocol; in that case it comprised representatives only of the participant governments. On the other hand, the Amsterdam provisions on closer co-operation make it clear that institutionally the non-participants would not be totally excluded. The new art. 44 of the Treaty on European Union provides that all members of the Council would be able to take part in deliberations on the matters concerned. However, only the participants would be able to take part in the adoption of decisions and to vote. This contrasts with the apparent practice of the UK not to participate in meetings under the Social Protocol, and what appears to be becoming the practice under the third stage of Economic and Monetary Union. Evidence on this last point may be gleaned from the European Council meeting in Luxembourg in December 1997. A Resolution was there agreed on economic policy co-ordination under art. 99 of the EC Treaty in Stage 3 of EMU,[19] art. 99 being a provision with regard to which there is no derogation or opt-out. Article 6 of the resolution recognizes that the ECOFIN Council (including everyone) is the only body empowered to formulate an adopt 'the broad economic policy guidelines which constitute the main instrument of economic co-ordination' but at the same time accepts that 'the Ministers of the States participating in the euro area may meet informally among themselves to discuss issues connected with their shared specific responsibilities for the single currency'. If they wish to do so in this context, it can hardly be imagined that they would wish the involvement of non-participants in discussions of what would be the participants' domestic monetary policy. Furthermore, even where ministers representative of all the governments meet in the Council, it may be observed that the eleven States participating in Economic and Monetary Union total sixty-five votes between them, which is more than the sixty-two votes required for a qualified majority; and the four 'outs' together have only twenty-two votes, which is insufficient not only to block a decision but also to trigger the 'Ioannina compromise' to delay a decision, for which twenty-three to twenty-five votes are required.[20] It is therefore conceivable that, as suggested above, those eleven States might wish, and be able, to use the closer co-operation provisions introduced by the Amsterdam Treaty to adopt legislation on issues linked to the development of Economic and Monetary Union which will be binding only on them—though it may well then form part of an 'acquis' to which those who join the Economic and Monetary Union at a later stage would be expected to adhere.

5. Other institutional issues

On the other hand, the Commission, the Parliament and the Court of Justice do not vary in their composition or their internal voting rights in the context of closer co-operation, derogations, or opt-outs. Since 1979 the European Parliament has been elected directly by the citizens of the Community, albeit not by uniform methods. The seats are nevertheless allocated to each Member State in a way which

[19] Annex I to the Conclusions of the Luxembourg European Council, 12 and 13 Dec. 1997.

[20] See Usher, *EC Institutions and Legislation* (Longman 1998) pp. 23–5.

is not directly proportionate to population but which gives the bigger Member States more seats than the smaller ones. However, in the context of economic and monetary union, representatives of the citizens of Member States which do not participate in those policy areas are involved in the decision-making process in relation to Community acts which do not apply in the geographical area they represent. Examples include art. 111(1) on exchange-rate agreements and art. 112(2)(b) on the appointment of the Executive Board of the ECB. This is not an unfamiliar problem in the UK, and is of particular importance in the context of the establishment of a separate Scottish Parliament.

The question whether the same institutions can act at all levels and for different combinations of participant States arises most clearly where the institution is not necessarily meant to be representative. While the members of the Commission must neither seek nor take instructions from any government or any other body,[21] only nationals of Member States may be members of the Commission, and the Commission must, under the Treaty in its present version, include at least one national of each of the Member States, but may not include more than two members having the nationality of the same State. There are currently twenty Commissioners, two from each of the big countries (which for this purpose include Spain) and one from each of the other Member States. However, the second paragraph of art. 213 provides that the number of members of the Commission may be altered by the Council, acting unanimously. One of the matters frequently discussed in political circles is whether the number of Commissioners should be reduced to one per State, and there have been proposals to group some of the smaller countries together to share a rotating Commissioner, which essentially is the system used for selecting Advocates-General before the Court (other than those from the four biggest countries). This debate puts clearly into focus the question whether the Commission should be regarded as a representative body or simply in terms of its operational needs.

The Treaty of Amsterdam does not directly respond to any of these proposals, but it contains a Protocol on the institutions with the prospect of enlargement of the European Union which links the size of the Commission to the weighting of votes in the Council. Under this Protocol, at the date of entry into force of the first enlargement of the Union the Commission is to comprise one national of each of the Member States, provided that, by that date, the weighting of the votes in the Council has been modified, in a manner acceptable to all Member States, notably compensating those Member States which give up the possibility of nominating a second member of the Commission. Here, therefore, the Commission is clearly treated as part of the representative equation and not as a body whose composition is determined according to its operational needs.

If the membership of the Commission is finally to be determined by its functional needs rather than (indirect) national representation, then it should clearly be

[21] Art. 213.

able to function at all levels, and it is submitted that given the legal duties of its members that should be the situation, and is the situation in the context of Stage 3 of Economic and Monetary Union. The Commission, for example, plays a leading role in the excessive deficits procedure under art. 104, and a Commission proposal may be required under art. 111 with regard to exchange-rate policy.

With regard to membership of the European Court, the Treaty is not specific as to the representation of each Member State; it merely states that the Judges and Advocates-General are to be chosen from persons whose independence is beyond doubt and who possess the qualifications required for appointment to the highest judicial offices in their respective countries or who are jurisconsults of recognized competence. However, the current Court of fifteen judges comprises one from each Member State, and if one takes the judges and Advocates General together, there have always been at least two members of the Court from the big Member States. However, following the enlargement of the Court shortly after Greek accession there has been a trend towards meeting the Court's manpower needs, as exemplified in the number of Advocates-General (in principle eight, but currently nine) rather than proportionate representation of the Member States.

In the Court of First Instance, the Treaty provisions merely required that its members should be chosen from persons whose independence is beyond doubt and who possess the ability required for appointment to judicial office, and in its initial proposals on the matter the European Court suggested that the Court of First Instance could be a small body with perhaps five judges. However, the Council eventually decided on the creation of a body with twelve judges (which turned out to have one judge from each Member State), and it has been enlarged to fifteen following the 1995 accessions, with its three new members coming from each of the three new Member States.

6. The role of the European Court of Justice

In the context of variable geometry, at the level of the Court of Justice and of the Court of First Instance serious issues arise which do not seem yet to have been addressed in the Treaty texts or the Amsterdam amendments. Put simply, can Member States which do not participate in a particular area of joint activity, and their citizens, exercise EC judicial remedies in relation to acts adopted in that area? There is a general statement concerning closer co-operation in art. 11(4) of the EC Treaty that 'the acts and decisions necessary for the implementation of co-operation activities shall be subject to all the relevant provisions of this Treaty', but that this still arguably leaves a number of issues open to debate, and in any event it does not apply to Economic and Monetary Union.

With regard to actions for annulment, in so far as rights of action are conferred upon them by the substantive Treaty provisions, and with regard to the acts susceptible to challenge under the provisions, no real problems of locus standi appear to arise with regard to actions for annulment brought by Member States, the Council, or the Commission. Indeed, Case 166/78 *Italy* v. *Council*[22] held that Italy was not barred from seeking the annulment of a Council Regulation by the fact that its representative at the relevant Council meeting had voted in favour of that Regulation; the implication is that, within its express limits, the right of action conferred upon Member States to seek the annulment of a Community act is unconditional. It is also clear that the Member States and these institutions need not show that they have an interest in bringing the proceedings,[23] although like other litigants[24] they apparently need to show that they have an interest in the grounds for annulment that they put forward, i.e. that the alleged breach made a difference to the outcome.[25]

On the other hand, a government, even the government of an area falling within the Community which is not that of a Member State as such, is treated on the same basis as a natural or legal person, as happened to the government of Gibraltar in Case C–298/89 *Gibraltar* v. *Council*.[26] The government show that the act at issue is of direct and individual concern to it. Does a non-participant government therefore have an absolute right to bring an action for annulment in relation to an act of the ECB of of a Council comprising the euro–11, or does it have to show direct and individual concern?

Serious arguments can be put both ways, but as the present author argued in his Edinburgh Inaugural Lecture[27] a related problem has already arisen in the context of references for preliminary rulings, under the 1971 Protocol on the interpretation by the Court of the 1968 Judgments Convention, where the Court took an approach not mentioned in the Treaty texts. The background is that the first reference under that Protocol, Case 12/76 *Tessili Como* v. *Dunlop*,[28] was heard in 1976, before the Member States which had joined the Community in 1973 had signed the Accession Convention to the Brussels Convention, which occurred in 1978 (and was eventually introduced into the legal systems of the UK by the Civil Jurisdiction and Judgements Act 1982). In the course of the proceedings, the question arose whether the UK and Ireland could exercise the right to submit observations with regard to the interpretation of a Convention to which they were not parties. The European Court held that under the 1972 Act of Accession, the new Member States were *legally obliged* (emphasis added) to accede to the 1968 Convention, and that they therefore had an interest in expressing their views when the Court was called upon to interpret a Convention to which they were required to become parties.

In the specific context of references for preliminary rulings, the Amsterdam Treaty deals with the matter in relation to the voluntary system of references under the revised Third Pillar in art. 35(4) of the Treaty on European Union. This provides that any Member State, whether or not it has made a declaration accepting

[22] [1979] ECR 2575, 2596.

[23] E.g. Case 45/86 *Commission* v. *Council* [1987] ECR 1493.

[24] See Case 90/74 *Deboeck* v. *Commission* [1975] ECR 1123.

[25] Case 259/87 *France* v. *Commission* [1987] ECR 4393.

[26] [1993] ECR I–3605.

[27] Usher: 'Variable Geometry or Concentric Circles: Patterns for the European Union' (1997) *International and Comparative Law Quarterly* 243–73.

[28] [1976] ECR 1473.

the jurisdiction of the Court, shall be entitled to submit statements of case or written observations to the Court. However, the Treaty is silent with regard to references in the context of other areas of flexibility.

If the test laid down in *Tessili Como* v. *Dunlop*[29] were to be applied more generally, particularly in the context of direct actions for annulment, it would produce some interesting results in the current areas of variable geometry. In the context of economic and monetary union, the 'Member States with a derogation' remain bound by the obligation to achieve that objective[30] and would therefore be able to challenge acts of Community institutions representing the participant States and ostensibly binding only on those States. On the other hand, now that the UK has given notice that it will not participate, it will not be subject to the basic Treaty obligation, and under the Court's test would not be able to exercise its special rights as a Member State, but would rather be left to show direct and individual concern. It may however be preferable for the matter to be settled in an express provision of a revised EC Treaty.

With regard to private actions for annulment, it is suggested that the requirement to show direct and individual concern circumvents the problem: there is a long history of actions for annulment brought by applicants who are neither citizens of nor resident in a Member State.[31] However, given that the third stage of Economic and Monetary Union will commence without the participation of the UK, could a UK court faced with a dispute relating to an ECB decision on the use of the euro make a reference as to its interpretation? To the extent that the decision is to be regarded as a Community act and the court is a court or tribunal of a Member State, this question should be answered in the affirmative. What if the UK voluntarily adopted domestic rules which reflected the ECB decision? While the analogy is not perfect, there are a number of instances where the Court has been willing to interpret Community acts where the issue before the national court was not the Community act as such but national legislation which made reference to or used the language of the Community act.[32]

7. Conclusion

Admiration must be expressed for the very considerable achievements of those Member States which have met the criteria for participation in stage 3 of Economic and Monetary Union. However, a structure which allows both for derogations and opt-outs creates a whole range of novel legal problems, the solutions to which have not been expressly indicated in the Treaty texts.

[29] [1976] ECR 1473.

[30] Art. 122(3) does not exempt them from art. 4(2).

[31] See, to take a couple of random examples, Case 60/81 *IBM* v. *Commission* [1981] ECR 2639, or Case C–49/88 *Al-Jubail Fertiliser* v. *Council* [1991] ECR I–3187.

[32] Cases C–294/88 & C–194/89 *Dzodzi* [1990] ECR I–3763, and Case 231/89 *Gmorzynska-Bscher* [1990] ECR I–4003.

10

Monetary institutions

1. Introduction

As well as setting out criteria and a timetable for the achievement of economic and monetary union, Maastricht Treaty also created a new institutional structure for the second and third stages of that process, involving in the second stage the creation of the European Monetary Institute and in the third stage the development of a European Central Bank and of the European System of Central Banks.[1] However, these new institutions should not be seen as a total break with the past; in many respects their functions represent the continuation and development of the activities of the institutions established under the EEC Treaty as originally drafted: the Monetary Committee (now the Economic and Financial Committee), the Committee of Governors of Central Banks, and the European Monetary Co-operation Fund.

2. The Monetary Committee

Under art. 105(2) of the original EEC Treaty, repeated as the first part of art. 114(1) of the EC Treaty as amended at Maastricht, a Monetary Committee with advisory status was set up 'in order to promote co-ordination of the policies of Member States to the full extent needed for the functioning of the internal market'. In the original version it had two tasks: to keep under review the monetary and financial situation of the Member States and of the Community and the general payments system of the Member States and to report regularly thereon to the Council and the Commission; and to deliver opinions at the request of the Council or of the Commission, or on its own initiative for submission to those institutions. The Treaty itself provided that the Member States and the Commission should each appoint two members of the Monetary Committee.

The Statutes of the Monetary Committee were set out in the first few months of the Community's life in a Council Decision of 15 March 1958.[2] With regard to the membership of the Committee, art. 5 of the Decision envisaged that 'as a general rule' each Member State should appoint one member from among senior officials of the administration, and the other member on the proposal of the central

[1] EC Treaty art. 8. [2] JO 1958 p. 390.

bank and, in effect adding to the Treaty provision, it allowed for the appointment of two 'alternate' members of the Committee by each Member State, though these could not speak or vote unless a member who was unable to attend had delegated his functions to one of them.[3] It was further provided that the Committee should meet at least six times a year,[4] which made it part of the regular round of Community meetings.

As for the functions of the Committee, the Decision repeated the Treaty provision, and drew together in its art. 4 the other Treaty provisions which required the Monetary Committee to be consulted, notably in the areas of free movement of capital,[5] changes in exchange rates which might distort competition,[6] and measures to safeguard the balance of payments.[7] Article 4 also repeated the Treaty stipulations that its opinion might also be requested in other cases by the Council or the Commission, and that it might draw up opinions on its own initiative. In practice it also drew up reports at the request of the European Council, notably a report on how the European Monetary System worked, presented in May 1993[8] and drawn up at the request of the European Council meeting held in Birmingham following the monetary turmoil in autumn 1992.

Article 114(1), inserted by the Maastricht amendments, added a third task, with a list of other provisions where the Monetary Committee was to 'contribute to the preparation of the work of the Council'. This list meant that in practice it also acquired a role in relation to the co-ordination and surveillance of economic policy (art. 99), the resolution of 'severe difficulties' (art. 100), the prohibition against privileged access by Community or national public bodies to financial institutions (art. 102), the prohibition against the Community or a Member State being liable for or assuming the commitments of central, regional, local, or other public authorities (art. 103), the excessive deficits procedure (art. 104), the measures to be taken by Member States before the start of the second stage (art. 116(2)), consultation of the European Monetary Institute (art. 117(6), compliance with the convergence criteria (art. 121(2)), and the determination as to whether a Member State should have a 'derogation' from the third stage (art. 122(1).[9] What is remarkable is that none of those provisions themselves referred expressly to the Monetary Committee.

Finally, art. 114(1) adds a fourth task: to examine, at least once a year, the situation regarding the movement of capital and the freedom of payments, as they result from the application of the Treaty and of measures adopted by the Council. This examination is to cover all measures relating to capital movements and payments. The Committee was required to report to the Commission and to the Council on the outcome of this examination. In other words, it became the monetary movements watchdog.

[3] Art. 8.
[4] Art. 9.
[5] Original arts. 71 and 73.
[6] Original art. 107(2), which does not appear to have been used in practice.
[7] Original arts. 108 and 109.
[8] *Agence Europe Documents* No. 1836, 26 May 1993.
[9] See Chapter 8 above.

However, the Monetary Committee was envisaged as continuing only until the end of the second stage. Article 114(2) provided simply that at the start of the third stage an Economic and Financial Committee should be set up, and that the Monetary Committee should be dissolved. The functions of this new Committee appear, however, to be remarkably similar to those of the Monetary Committee. The surveillance role with regard to monetary movements is expressed in identical terms, as is the duty to deliver opinions at the request of the Council or of the Commission, or on its own initiative for submission to those institutions. However, given the responsibility of the European Central Bank for monetary policy, the original duty to keep under review the *monetary* and financial situation has become a duty to keep under review the *economic* and financial situation of the Member States and of the Community and to report regularly thereon to the Council and to the Commission, but with a different emphasis: the Committee should in particular report on financial relations with third countries and international institutions.[10]

The list of Treaty provisions in the context of which the Economic and Financial Committee must contribute to the preparation of the Council's work also remains much the same, subject to the deletion of certain measures only relevant in the second stage, and with the addition of art. 105(6) on the prudential supervision of credit institutions by the European Central Bank, art. 106(2) on the issue of coins by Member States, art. 107(5) and (6) on the amendment of certain provisions of the Statute of the European System of Central Banks and the adoption of certain provisions under that Statute, art. 111 on an exchange-rate system for the ECU in relation to non-Community countries, and art. 123(4) and (5) on the irrevocable fixing of the conversion rate for the ECU and the rate to be adopted when a derogation is abrogated. Furthermore, if and as long as there are Member States with a derogation as referred to in arts. 122 and 123, art. 114(4) requires the Committee to keep under review the monetary and financial situation and the general payments system of those Member States and report regularly thereon to the Council and to the Commission.

With regard to membership of the new Committee, the fundamental change is the representation of the European Central Bank: under the last sub-paragraph of art. 114(2), the Member States, the Commission, and the ECB each appoint no more than two members of the Committee. It is further provided that detailed provisions concerning the composition of the Economic and Financial Committee are to be laid down by the Council, acting by qualified majority on a proposal from the Commission and after consulting the ECB and 'the Committee referred to in this Article', which initially meant the original Monetary Committee, but now presumably means the Economic and Financial Committee itself. Such provisions were laid down by Council Decision 98/743,[11] and new Statutes of the Economic and Financial Committee have subsequently been enacted.[12]

[10] See Chapter 11 below. [11] OJ 1998 L358/109.
[12] Council Decision 1999/8 (OJ 1999 L5/71).

3. Precursors of the European Central Bank

a) The Committee of Governors of Central Banks

While the original art. 105(2) of the EEC Treaty provided for the establishment of the Monetary Committee, art. 105(1) envisaged, *inter alia*, co-operation between the central banks of the Member States, and it was by virtue of this provision that in 1964 the Committee of Governors of the Central Banks of the Member States of the EEC was established by Council Decision 64/300.[13] From the outset there was an institutional link with the Monetary Committee: under art. 2 the chairman of that Committee could be invited to attend its meetings. There was also a link with the formal Community institutional structure, in that 'as a general rule' the Commission was to be invited to send one of its members as a representative to meetings of the Committee.

The creation of a Committee composed of governors of central banks had the initial effect of excluding Luxembourg representation, since Luxembourg had had a monetary union with Belgium since the 1920s. However, Council Decision 90/142,[14] amending the 1964 Decision in the light of the start of the first stage of economic and monetary union on 1 July 1990,[15] added the Director-General of the Luxembourg Monetary Institute to the membership of the Committee. Elevation to a more formal Community status may perhaps be assumed from the requirement in a new art. 3a added by that Decision that the members should act 'according to their own responsibilities and having due regard to Community objectives'.

A more intriguing institutional aspect of the Committee is to be found in its original Rules of Procedure,[16] adopted in Basle (i.e. outside the Community) in October 1964. Under these rules, meetings in general were to take place every two months on the same dates as meetings of the Board of Directors of the Bank for International Settlements[17] (which is based in Basle) and the Secretary-General and his assistants were in principle to be chosen from officials of the Bank for International Settlements who were nationals of the Member States of the EEC[18] (and presumably therefore themselves based in Basle). On the other hand, it may be recalled in this context that the clearing system used for the private sector ECU also involved accounts held with the Bank for International Settlements.[19]

As amended by the 1990 Decision, the tasks[20] of the Committee were to hold consultations concerning the general principles and broad lines of monetary policy, to exchange information regularly about the most important measures that fall within the competence of the central banks, to promote the co-ordination of national monetary policies with the aim of achieving price stability (i.e. low

[13] JO 1964 p. 1206. [14] OJ 1990 L78/25. [15] See Chapter 8 above.
[16] *Compendium of Community Monetary Texts* (EC Commission, 1989) p. 159.
[17] Art. 5. [18] Art. 7. [19] See Chapter 7 above. [20] Art. 3.

inflation) 'as a necessary condition for the proper functioning of the European Monetary System', to formulate opinions on the overall orientation of monetary and exchange-rate policy, and to express opinions to individual governments and the Council of Ministers on policies which might affect the internal and external monetary situation in the Community, in particular 'the functioning of the European Monetary System'. The Committee also prepared an annual report for Parliament, the Council, and the European Council, and its chairman could be invited to appear before the European Parliament or its competent committee.

With hindsight this may be seen as part of a transition towards the European Central Bank, since the Committee of Governors was dissolved at the start of the second stage, when the European Monetary Institute is established, under art. 117(1) of the EC Treaty. The Council of the European Monetary Institute, which directed and managed its affairs, comprised a President and the Governors of the national central banks—in other words the same people carried on, but under a new name and with new powers. The European Monetary Institute was in turn dissolved on the creation of the European Central Bank in June 1998, by virtue of art. 123(2) of the EC Treaty. The governors of the participating national central banks are members of the Governing Council of the ECB,[21] and the governors of all the national central banks are members of its General Council.[22]

b) The European Monetary Co-operation Fund

The 1972 Resolution of the Council and Representatives of the Governments of the Member States which created the 'snake' system[23] expressly instructed the Monetary Committee and the Committee of Governors to produce a report on the creation of a European Monetary Co-operation Fund, and this led to the enactment, under the general art. 308 (then art. 235) of the EC Treaty, of Council Regulation 907/73 establishing a European Monetary Co-operation Fund.[24] The Fund may therefore be seen as a survivor from the first plans for economic and monetary union in the early 1970s.

The Fund's links with the committees described above related not only to its genesis but also to its operation. Under the Statutes annexed to the Regulation, the Fund was to be directed and managed by a Board of Governors, whose members were to be the members of the Committee of Governors, with the addition from the outset[25] of 'a member of the Luxembourg currency authorities' able to take part in decisions whenever Luxembourg's rights and obligations were not exercised by the National Bank of Belgium. However, despite this link with the Committee of Governors, Decision 73/208 of the Representatives of the Governments of the Member States[26] set the provisional location of the Fund in Luxembourg. The

[21] See p. 218 below.

[22] See p. 221 below.

[23] Resolution of 21 Mar. 1972 (*Compendium of Community Monetary Texts* 1974 p. 33; JO 1972 C38/3). See above p. 172.

[24] OJ 1973 L89/2.

[25] Annex art. 1.

[26] OJ 1973 L207/46.

basic objectives of the Fund were to promote the proper functioning of the progressive narrowing of the margins of fluctuation of the Community currencies against each other, to promote interventions in Community currencies on the exchange markets, and to promote settlements between central banks leading to a concerted policy on reserves.

In practical terms its most important role lay in the intervention and support mechanisms of the European Monetary System.[27] In this context, Council Regulation 3181/78 relating to the European Monetary System[28] empowered the Fund to receive monetary reserves from the monetary authorities of the Member States and to issue ECUs against such assets,[29] and empowered the Fund and the national monetary authorities to use ECUs as a means of settlement and for transactions between those authorities and the Fund;[30] indeed as amended[31] it empowered the Fund to grant the monetary authorities of non-Member States and international monetary institutions the status of 'other holders' of ECUs and to fix the terms and conditions under which such ECUs may be acquired, held, and used.

However, the Fund did not become the Monetary Fund envisaged in art. 1.4 of the Resolution establishing the European Monetary System,[32] nor did the Delors Committee in its Report recommend the immediate creation of a Reserve Fund.[33] Given its close links with the Committee of Governors, however, it is hardly surprising to find it likewise subsumed into the European Monetary Institute from the beginning of the second stage, by virtue of art. 117(2) of the EC Treaty, all assets and liabilities of the Fund passing automatically to the Institute.[34] In turn, by virtue of art. 123(2), the European Monetary institute has been subsumed into the European Central Bank.

c) The European Monetary Institute

Article 117(1) provided that at the start of the second stage a European Monetary Institute ('EMI') should be established and take up its duties; it had legal personality and was directed and managed by a Council, consisting of a President and the Governors of the national central banks. However, what was only stated in the Protocol on the Statute of the EMI was that the members of the EMI were the central banks of the Member States.[35] For the purposes of the Statute, the Institut Monétaire Luxembourgeois was treated as the central bank of Luxembourg.

With regard to the members of the Council, art. 8 of the Statute took the degree of independence required by the 1990 amendment to the Committee of Governors[36] and developed it towards that required of the European Central Bank:[37] the members of the Council of the EMI who were the representatives of

[27] See Chapter 8.
[28] OJ 1978 L379/2.
[29] Art. 1.
[30] Art. 2.
[31] By Council Regulation 3066/85 (OJ 1985 L290/95).
[32] See above p. 173.
[33] See above p. 180.
[34] Statute of the European Monetary Institute, art. 1.3.
[35] Statute art. 1.2.
[36] See p. 212 above.
[37] EC Treaty art. 107.

their institutions were, with respect to their activities, to act according to their own responsibilities. In exercising the powers and performing the tasks and duties conferred upon them by the Treaty and the Statute, the Council of the EMI were not to seek or take any instructions from Community institutions or bodies or governments of Member States. It further stated that the Community institutions and bodies as well as the governments of the Member States undertook to respect this principle and not seek to influence the Council of the EMI in the performance of its tasks.

Article 117(2) and (3) divided the functions of the EMI into those concerned with the preparation of the third stage, and other more general tasks largely connected with the ECU and the European Monetary System. The general tasks were set out in art. 117(2), and required the EMI: to strengthen co-operation between the national central banks; to strengthen the co-ordination of monetary policies of the Member States, with the aim of ensuring price stability; to monitor the functioning of the European Monetary System; to hold consultations concerning issues falling within the competence of the national central banks and affecting the stability of financial institutions and markets; to take over the tasks of the European Monetary Co-operation Fund; and to facilitate the use of the ECU and oversee its development, including the smooth functioning of the ECU clearing system.

In connection with the preparation of the third stage, art. 117(3) provided that the EMI should: prepare the instruments and procedures necessary for carrying out a single monetary policy in the third stage; promote the harmonization, where necessary, of rules and practices governing the collection, compilation, and distribution of statistics in the areas in the areas within its field of competence; prepare the rules for operations to be undertaken by the national central banks within the framework of the ESCB; promote the efficiency of cross-border payments; and supervise the technical preparation of ECU bank notes. It may be suggested that promoting the efficiency of cross-border payments had more to do with the completion of the internal market than with the completion of the third stage, but under art. 7 of the Statute the EMI had to address an annual report to the Council on the state of preparations for the third stage, and under art. 117(7) the Council could, acting unanimously on a proposal from the Commission and after consulting the European Parliament and the EMI, confer upon the EMI other tasks for the preparation of the third stage. It was noted above that under art. 121(1) the EMI, like the Commission, reported to the Council on compliance by the Member States with the convergence criteria.[38]

By 31 December 1996 at the latest[39] the EMI had to specify the regulatory, organizational, and logistical framework necessary for the European System of Central Banks to perform its tasks in the third stage. This framework was submitted for decision to the European Central Bank at the date of its establishment, and appears to have been followed.

[38] See p. 183 above. [39] Art. 117(3) last sentence.

The EMI was envisaged as an interim body to be replaced by the European Central Bank on its creation.[40] The details are set out in art. 23 of the EMI Statute. In essence all assets and liabilities of the EMI passed automatically to the ECB, which had to liquidate the EMI by the beginning of the third stage.

However, art. 44 of the Statute of the Central Bank provides that the European Central Bank should take over those tasks of the EMI which, because of the derogations of one or more Member States, still have to be performed in the third stage.

4. The European Central Bank and the System of Central Banks

a) Creation and nature

The institutions described above involve representation of all the Member States and may issue acts capable of affecting all the Member States. However, a characteristic of the third stage of economic and monetary union is that it was envisaged from the outset that not all Member States would be able or willing to participate immediately,[41] and the non- participant 'Member States with a derogation', Greece and Sweden, Denmark (which is deemed to have a derogation)[42] and the United Kingdom are not fully involved in the institutional structure of the European Central Bank (ECB) or of the System of Central Banks (ESCB), and are not bound by all its acts. Its principal characteristics will therefore be considered subject to this major caveat, and the expression 'Member States with a derogation' will be used to cover all the non-participants, except where there are dispensations applying only to the UK.

The basic structure derives from art. 8 of the EC Treaty which provides for the establishment of the European System of Central Banks and the European Central Bank in accordance with the procedures laid down in the Treaty; these bodies act within the limits of the powers conferred upon them by the Treaty and by the Statute of the ESCB and of the ECB annexed to the Treaty.

The timetable for their creation was laid down in art. 123, which required that immediately after the date for the beginning of the third stage had been decided in accordance with art. 121(3),[43] or, as the case may be, immediately after 1 July 1998, the Council should adopt certain provisions required by the Statute,[44] and **the governments of the Member States without a derogation** should appoint the President, the Vice-President, and the other members of the Executive Board of the ECB. The decision appointing the members of the Executive Board was in fact taken on 26 May 1998[45] at a meeting which, although it occurred during a British Presidency of the Council, was chaired by the Austrian Chancellor (Austria being

[40] Art. 109l(2).
[41] See p. 200 above.
[42] See p. 202 above.
[43] See p. 189 above.
[44] See art. 106(6).
[45] Decision 98/345 (OJ 1998 L154/33).

the next Member State to hold the Presidency) in the absence of the United Kingdom. It is further provided that if there are Member States with a derogation, the number of members of the Executive Board may be smaller than provided for in art. 11.1 of the Statute of the ESCB (a President, a Vice-President, and four others) but may in no circumstances be less than four. However, the full complement of appointments was made, though even with an Executive Board of six, five of the participant States have no member, never mind the Member States with a derogation. In this respect, the Executive Board of the ECB may be regarded as the first Community institutional body with a membership designed to meet its operational needs rather than the representation of the Member States.[46] As soon as the Executive Board was appointed (the appointments took effect from 1 June 1998) the ESCB and the ECB were established and prepared for their full operation as described in the Treaty and the Statute of the ESCB. However, the full exercise of their powers did not start until the first day of the third stage, 1 January 1999. As soon as the ECB was established it took over the tasks of the EMI, which went into liquidation upon the establishment of the ECB.[47]

The move towards a single currency was envisaged in parallel with the creation of the ECB. It was provided in art. 123(4) that at the starting date of the third stage the Council should, acting with the unanimity of the Member States without a derogation, on a proposal from the Commission and after consulting the ECB, adopt the conversion rates at which their currencies shall be irrevocably fixed and at which irrevocably fixed rate the euro should be substituted for these currencies. This was effected by Council Regulation 2866/98 on conversion rates for the euro.[48]

A requirement of independence similar to if not stronger than that imposed on members of the Commission by art. 213(2) of the EC Treaty is laid down by art. 108 (which, however, does not apply to the United Kingdom[49]). When exercising the powers and carrying out the tasks and duties conferred upon them by the Treaty and the Statute of the ESCB, neither the ECB, nor a national central bank, nor any member of their decision-making bodies may seek or take instructions from Community institutions or bodies, from any government of a Member State, or from any other body. Conversely, the Community institutions and bodies and the governments of the Member States undertake to respect this principle and not to seek to influence the members of the decision-making bodies of the ECB or of the national central banks in the performance of their tasks. Linked to this, art. 109 (which also does not apply to the United Kingdom) obliges each Member State to ensure, at the latest at the date of the establishment of the ESCB, that its national legislation including the statutes of its national central bank is compatible with the

[46] See with regard to the Commission, Usher 'EC Institutions and Legislation' (Longman 1998) pp. 35–6.

[47] Art. 123(2). See p. 216 above.

[48] OJ 1998 L359/1.

[49] UK Protocol art. 5.

Treaty and the Statute of the ESCB. This strong statement of independence has led to critical comment as to the lack of democratic control over the ECB.[50]

More specifically, art. 14.2 of the Statute (which does not apply to the UK[51]) requires that the statutes of the national central banks should, in particular, provide that the term of office of a Governor of a national central bank shall be no less than five years. Furthermore, a Governor may be relieved from office only if he no longer fulfils the conditions required for the performance of his duties or if he has been guilty of serious misconduct. A decision to this effect may be referred to the Court of Justice by the Governor concerned or the Governing Council of the ECB on grounds of infringement of the Treaty or of any rule of law relating to its application—a unique example of a national official becoming subject to Community jurisdiction.

b) Institutional structure

The basic framework is set out in art. 107 of the EC Treaty, under which the ESCB, the Statute of which is laid down in a Protocol annexed to the Treaty, is composed of the ECB and of the national central banks. It is to have legal personality, and the ESCB is to be governed by the decision-making bodies of the ECB which are the Governing Council and the Executive Board. This should be read with art. 123(3): if and as long as there are Member States with a derogation, the General Council of the ECB referred to in art. 45 of the Statute of the ESCB shall be constituted as a third decision-making body of the ECB.

This framework is fleshed out in art. 112 and the Statute. The Governing Council of the ECB comprises the members of the Executive Board of the ECB and the Governors of the national central banks of Member States without a derogation.[52] The Executive Board comprises the President, the Vice-President, and four other members. Under art. 112(2)(b), which does not in any event apply to Member States with a derogation,[53] the President, the Vice-President, and the other members of the Executive Board are appointed from among persons of recognized standing and professional experience in monetary or banking matters by common accord of the Governments of the Member States without a derogation[54] at the level of Heads of State or of Government, on a recommendation from the Council, after it has consulted the European Parliament and the Governing Council of the ECB. Their term of office is to be eight years and may not be renewed. Under the Statute[55] the initial appointments were to be staggered, so that in the future members would not all be replaced at the same time; thus the President was appointed for eight years (whatever may be the political understand-

[50] Gormley and De Haan: 'The Democratic Deficit of the European Central Bank' (1996) *EL Rev.* 95. For a detailed comparative analysis see Amtenbrink 'The Democratic Accountability of Central Banks' (Hart, Oxford, 1999).

[51] UK Protocol art. 8.

[52] Art. 112(1); Statute art. 10.1 with art. 43.4.

[53] Art. 122(3).

[54] Art. 122(4).

[55] Art. 50.

ings relating to that appointment), the Vice President was appointed for four years, and the other members were appointed for terms of, respectively, five, six, seven, and eight years.[56] It must finally be emphasized again that only nationals of Member States without a derogation[57] may be members of the Executive Board.

Formal links with other Community institutions are established under art. 113. This provides that the President of the Council and a member of the Commission may participate, without the right to vote, in meetings of the Governing Council of the ECB, and that the President of the Council may submit a motion for deliberation to the Governing Council of the ECB. Conversely, the President of the ECB must be invited to participate in Council meetings when the Council is discussing matters relating to the objectives and tasks of the ESCB. It is further provided[58] that the ECB must address an annual report on the activities of the ESCB and on the monetary policy of both the previous and current year to the European Parliament, the Council, the Commission, and also the European Council. This report is to be presented by the President of the ECB to the Council and to the European Parliament, which may hold a general debate on that basis. The President of the ECB and the other members of the Executive Board may also, at the request of the European Parliament or on their own initiative, be heard by the competent Committees of the European Parliament. Although the legal obligation is to report to the Parliament once a year, when the first President, Mr Duisenberg, appeared before the Parliament when it was being consulted as to his appointment, he apparently undertook to report to the Parliament four times a year.[59]

The responsibilities of the decision-making bodies are set out in art. 12 of the Statute. Under art. 12.1, which does not confer any rights or obligations on Member States with a derogation,[60] the Governing Council must adopt the guidelines and take the decisions necessary to ensure the performance of the tasks entrusted to the ESCB under the Treaty and the Statute. It is to formulate the monetary policy of the Community including, as appropriate, decisions relating to intermediate monetary objectives, key interest rates, and the supply of reserves in the ESCB, and must establish the necessary guidelines for their implementation. Under the Rules of Procedure of the ECB,[61] there must be a quorum of two-thirds of the Governing Council's members in order for it to vote,[62] and a secret ballot may be initiated at the request of three members.[63] Decisions may also be taken by written procedure unless at least three members object, though this normally requires at least five working days for consideration by every member.

The Executive Board, on the other hand, is to implement monetary policy in accordance with the guidelines and decisions laid down by the Governing Council. In doing so the Executive Board must give the necessary instructions to national

[56] Decision 98/345 (OJ 1998 L154/33). [57] Art. 122(4). [58] Art. 113(3).

[59] Speech by the President of the European Parliament, Mr Gil-Robles, at the University of Edinburgh, 3 Dec. 1998.

[60] Statute art. 43.1. [61] Rules of Procedure as amended on 22 Apr. 1999 (OJ 1999 L125/34).

[62] Art. 4.1. [63] Art. 4.6.

central banks of the Member States without a derogation.[64] The Executive Board may have additional powers delegated to it where the Governing Council so decides. Under the Rules of Procedure[65] such a delegation of powers must be notified to the parties concerned, or published, if appropriate, in matters having legal effects on third parties. It is further provided that acts adopted by way of delegation must be promptly notified to the Governing Council.[66] The Executive Board also has responsibility for the preparation of meetings of the Governing Council;[67] in particular, the Executive Board draws up a provisional agenda for Governing Council meetings.[68] As for its own proceedings, the Executive Board also requires a quorum of two-thirds in order to vote, though an extraordinary meeting may be convened at which decisions may be taken without regard to the quorum.[69] Decisions may also be taken by written procedure unless at least two members object.[70]

The distinction between the Executive Board and the Governing Council is blurred by the fact that the members of the Executive Board are also members of the Governing Council. Aparticulary striking example of the legal consequences of this may be seen in Council Regulation 2532/98 on the powers of the ECB to impose sanctions.[71] Under this Regulation it is for the Executive Board to adopt a reasoned decision as to whether an undertaking has committed an infringement, and as to the sanction to be imposed, if any.[72] The undertaking concerned then has the right to request a review of the Executive Board's decision by the Governing Council[73]—which of course includes the members of the Executive Board. At first sight the nature of this proposition is perhaps startling but it is to some extent mitigated by the fact that it is clearly intended only as an administrative remedy:[74] the decision of the Governing Council is subject to judicial review, and the Executive Board's decision is subject to judicial review if the Governing Council does not take a decision within two months of the request.[75] Even so, it is suggested that it is less than desirable even for an administrative review to be conducted by a body which includes the people who made the original decision.

As for the 'System', i.e. the relationship with national central banks, art. 12.1 provides that to the extent deemed possible and appropriate and without prejudice to the other provisions of art. 12, the ECB shall have recourse to the national central banks to carry out operations which form part of the tasks of the ESCB. More particularly, under art. 14.3 of the Statute, which also does not confer any rights or obligations on Member States with a derogation,[76] the national central banks are an integral part of the ESCB and must act in accordance with the guidelines and instructions of ECB. It is for the Governing Council to take the necessary steps to

[64] Statute art. 43.4. [65] Art. 14. [66] Art. 14.1. [67] Statute art. 12.2.
[68] Rules of Procedure art. 5.1. [69] Rules of Procedure art. 7.1.
[70] Art. 7.2. [71] OJ 1998 L318/4. [72] Art. 3(4). [73] Art. 3(6).
[74] Rather like the requirement to seek an administrative remedy under the Staff Regulations in disputes between officials and their employing institution. The matter is discussed in more detail below at p. 228.
[75] Art. 3.7. [76] Statute art. 43.1.

ensure compliance with the guidelines and instructions of the ECB, and to require that any necessary information be given to it. However, under art. 14.4 national central banks may perform functions other than those specified in the Statute unless the Governing Council finds, by a majority of two-thirds of the votes cast, that these interfere with the objectives and tasks of the ESCB. Such functions are to be performed on the responsibility and liability of national central banks and are not to be regarded as part of the functions of the ESCB.

While there remain Member States not able or willing to participate immediately in the third stage of economic and monetary union, the only decision-making body of the ECB in which they are represented is the General Council referred to in art. 123(3) of the Treaty and art. 45 of the Statute. Under art. 45.2, this consists of the President and Vice-President of the ECB and the Governors of all the national central banks. The other members of the Executive Board may participate in its meetings without the right to vote. Apart from certain advisory and consultative functions, its principal role is to take over those tasks of the EMI which, because of the derogations of one or more Member States, still have to be performed in the third stage, and to give advice in the preparations for the abrogation of the derogations specified in art. 122 of the Treaty.[77] With regard to the latter function, the General Council is to contribute to the necessary preparations for irrevocably fixing the exchange rates of the currencies of Member States with a derogations against the currencies, or the single currency, of the Member States without a derogation, as referred to in art. 123(5) of the Treaty. Otherwise, under art. 47.4 of the Statute 'the General Council shall be informed by the President of the ECB of decisions of the Governing Council'. The General Council has enacted its own Rules of Procedure[78] under art. 46.4 of the Statute; again a quorum of two-thirds of the members is required for a vote to be taken, and decisions may also be taken by written procedure unless at least three members object.[79]

Given the structure outlined above, it may be understood why the ECB could not be established on a provisional basis during the second stage.

c) Functions

The basic objectives and tasks of the ECSB and the ECB are set out in arts. 105 and 106 of the EC Treaty (neither of which apply to the UK)[80] with one exception, and most of which do not apply to other Member States with a derogation,[81] with two exceptions. There is one exception in common, i.e. a provision which applies to all Member States: art. 105(6), which is of considerable importance to the commercial banking community. Under this provision the Council may, acting unanimously on a proposal from the Commission and after consulting the ECB and receiving the assent of the European Parliament, confer upon the ECB specific

[77] Statute arts. 47.1 and 44.
[78] OJ 1999 L75/36.
[79] Art.4.1 and 4.3.
[80] UK Protocol art. 5.
[81] Art. 122(3).

tasks concerning policies relating to the prudential supervision of credit institutions and other financial institutions with the exception of insurance undertakings. If this power is used, it could have considerable consequences for the 'general good' provisions of the Second Banking Directive, for example.[82] In any event, it is suggested that legislation enacted for purposes of monetary policy may have consequences for prudential supervision. Thus, Council Regulation 2533/98 on the collection of statistical information by the ECB[83] and ECB Regulation 2819/98 on the consolidated balance sheet of the monetary financial institutions sector[84] may be intended to provide information to drive monetary policy, but such information would also be useful for prudential purposes. Similarly, Council Regulation 2531/98[85] and ECB Regulation 2818/98 on the application of minimum reserves[86] in principle require credit institutions in the participating Member States to hold 2 per cent of their reserve base (deposits, debt securities, and money market paper, subject to certain exceptions) in a reserve account with the national central bank in each participating Member State in which they have an establishment, in relation to their reserve base in the corresponding State.[87] This may be intended as an instrument for the performance of money market management and monetary control functions[88] but it also has a palpable prudential effect.

The provision from which only the UK is excluded is art. 105(4), under which the ECB is to be consulted on any proposed Community act in its fields of competence and by national authorities regarding any draft legislative provision in its fields of competence;[89] it further provides that the ECB may submit opinions to the appropriate Community institutions or bodies or to national authorities on matters in its fields of competence. As fleshed out in Council Decision 98/415 on the consultation of the ECB by national authorities regarding draft legislative provisions,[90] the duty to consult extends to currency matters, means of payment, national central banks, the collection, compilation, and distribution of monetary, financial, banking, payment systems, and balance of payments statistics, payment and settlement systems, and rules applying to financial institutions 'in so far as they materially influence the stability of financial institutions and markets'. Non-participating Member States bound by this obligation must also consult the ECB on any draft legislative provisions on the instruments of monetary policy (which is no longer a matter of national competence for the participant Member States).[91]

Otherwise the objectives and tasks listed are of direct interest only to Member States without a derogation. Under art. 105(1) the primary objective of the ESCB is to be to maintain price stability; without prejudice to that objective, the ESCB is also to support the general economic policies in the Community with a view to

[82] See Chapter 6 above.
[83] OJ 1998 L318/8.
[84] OJ 1998 L356/7.
[85] OJ 1998 L318/1.
[86] OJ 1998 L356/1.
[87] ECB Regulation arts. 4.2 and 6.1.
[88] Recitals to the Council Regulation.
[89] But within the limits and under the conditions set out by the Council in accordance with the procedure laid down in art. 107(6).
[90] OJ 1998 L189/42.
[91] Art. 2.

contributing to the achievement of the objectives of the Community as laid down in art. 2. The ESCB must act in accordance with the principle of an open-market economy with free competition, favouring an efficient allocation of resources, and in compliance with the principles set out in art. 4.

The basic tasks[92] to be carried out through the ESCB are: to define and implement the monetary policy of the Community; to conduct foreign exchange operations consistent with the provisions of art. 109;[93] to hold and manage the official foreign reserves of the Member States, without prejudice to the holding and management by the governments of Member States of foreign exchange working balances; and to promote the smooth operation of payment systems. The ESCB may also[94] contribute to the smooth conduct of policies pursued by the competent authorities relating to the prudential supervision of credit institutions and the stability of the financial system.

Article 106(1) sets out what is perhaps the most important monetary function of the ECB, going to the heart of what has been traditionally regarded as a function of the State,[95] though as seen in Chapter 8, it is subject to transitional arrangements for three years: for Member States without a derogation, the ECB has the exclusive right to authorize the issue of bank notes within the Community. The ECB and the national central banks may issue such notes, and the bank notes issued by the ECB and the national central banks shall be the only such notes to have the status of legal tender within the Community. With regard to coins, art. 106(2) permits participating Member States to issue coins, subject to approval by the ECB of the volume of the issue. The Council may, acting in accordance with the co-operation procedure (despite its replacement by the co-decision procedure in other areas of Community activity by the Amsterdam Treaty) and after consulting the ECB, adopt measures to harmonize the denominations and technical specifications of all coins intended for circulation to the extent necessary to permit their smooth circulation within the Community. This was initially done by Council Regulation 975/98 on euro coins.[96]

Although it is a prohibition rather than a task, art. 101, which appears to apply to all Member States, forbids overdraft facilities or any other type of credit facility with the ECB or with the central banks of the Member States (hereinafter referred to as 'national central banks') in favour of Community institutions or bodies, central governments, regional, local or other public authorities, other bodies governed by public law, or public undertakings of Member States, and also forbids the purchase directly from them by the ECB or national central banks of debt instruments. However, this does not apply to publicly owned credit institutions which, in the context of the supply of reserves by central banks, are given the same treatment by national central banks and the ECB as private credit institutions.

92 Art. 105(2). 93 See Chapter 11 below. 94 Art. 105(5).
95 See European Court judgment in Case 7/78 *R* v. *Thompson* [1978] ECR 2247 (p. 6 above).
96 OJ 1998 L139/6.

d) Legal acts

Although it may be a bank, it is foreseen in art. 110 (which again does not apply to Member States with a derogation[97]) that the ECB may issue binding legal acts similar in nature to those listed in art. 249 which may be issued by the Council and Parliament together, by the Council, or by the Commission. It is provided that in order to carry out the tasks entrusted to the ESCB, the ECB shall, in accordance with the provisions of the Treaty and under the conditions laid down in the Statute, make regulations to the extent necessary to implement certain tasks defined in the Statute in the acts of the Council;[98] it may take decisions necessary for carrying out the tasks entrusted to the ESCB under the Treaty and the Statute; and it may make recommendations and deliver opinions.

In terms remarkably similar to those of art. 249, art. 110(2) states that a regulation shall have general application and shall be binding in its entirety and directly applicable in all Member States; recommendations and opinions shall have no binding force; and a decision shall be binding in its entirety upon those to whom it is addressed. It is further provided that arts. 253 to 256 of the EC Treaty (on reasoning, publication and notification, and enforcement) shall apply to regulations and decisions adopted by the ECB. While under these provisions publication is only obligatory for regulations, the ECB may decide to publish its decisions, recommendations, and opinions. However, these are not necessarily the only legal acts which may emanate from the bank: art. 12 of the Statute refers to the governing Council adopting 'guidelines' and to the Executive Board giving 'instructions' to the national central banks. It has been suggested that these may give rise to third-party rights and that they may be regarded as reviewable acts.[99] Indeed the legal importance of Guidelines may be illustrated by the fact that the legal framework of TARGET (Trans-European Automated Real-time Gross settlement European Transfer system), the payments system for the euro, is set out in an ECB Guideline adopted by the Governing Council of the ECB addressed to and binding upon the national central banks of the euro–11. However TARGET also illustrates the consequences of the fact that the ECB legislative acts are only binding within the euro–11: the national central banks of the Member States which have not adopted the euro but which wish to connect to TARGET have had to enter into the TARGET Agreement with the ECB. Effectively the Agreement incorporates the provisions of the Guideline to apply its terms outside the euro-zone.[100]

While the Treaty refers to these legal acts generically as acts of the ECB, each of the decision-making bodies of the ECB in fact adopts acts separately within the limits of its competence. This is clear from the Statute of the ECB, which refers in art. 12 specifically to the Executive Board and to the Governing Council and in

[97] Art. 122(3); UK Protocol art. 5.

[98] See art. 107(6).

[99] See e.g. Louis, 'A legal and institutional approach for building a Monetary Union' (1998) *CMLRev*. 33 at pp. 54–8.

[100] ECB *Third Progress Report* on the TARGET project, Nov. 1998, p. 18.

art. 47 to the General Council. It is also clear from practice: to take some random examples, ECB Regulation 2818/98 on the application of minimum reserves[101] was adopted by the Governing Council, as were the ECB's Rules of Procedure,[102] but Decision 1998/14 on the paying-up of the capital of the ECB by the non-participating national central banks,[103] and indeed the Rules of Procedure of the General Council,[104] were adopted by the General Council. The distribution of legislative responsibility is set out in some detail in art. 17 of the general Rules of Procedure.[105] The hierarchy adopted in this provision mixes the acts defined in the Treaty and those mentioned (but not defined) in the Statute. Thus it is provided that:

- ECB Regulations shall be adopted by the Governing Council and signed on its behalf by the President;
- ECB guidelines shall be adopted by the Governing Council and signed on its behalf by the President. They shall state the reasons on which they are based. Notification of the national central banks may take place by means of telefax, electronic mail or telex, or in paper form.

In principle therefore, Regulations and guidelines (which may arguably be regarded as similar to Directives under the EC Treaty) may only be adopted by the Governing Council. However, art. 17.3 provides that the Governing Council may delegate its normative powers to the Executive Board for the purpose of implementing its Regulations and guidelines. In such a case, the Regulation or guideline concerned must specify the issues to be implemented, as well as 'the limits and scope of the delegated powers'.

On the other hand, art. 17.4 recognizes that ECB Decisions and recommendations may be adopted either by the Governing Council or by the Executive Board in their respective areas of competence. In both cases they are to be signed by the President, and must state the reasons on which they are based. However, where art. 42 of the Statute refers to 'recommendations' (meaning in effect proposals) for secondary Community legislation, such recommendations are to be adopted by the Governing Council. Similarly, ECB opinions are in principle required to be adopted by the Governing Council, although in exceptional circumstances, and unless not less than three Governors state their wish to retain the competence of the Governing Council for the adoption of specific opinions, 'ECB opinions may be adopted by the Executive Board, in line with comments provided by the Governing Council and taking into account the contribution of the General Council'.

The ECB 'instructions' referred to in the Statute are adopted by the Executive Board in its own right, and signed on its behalf by the President or any two Executive Board members. Notification of the national central banks may take place by means of telefax, electronic mail or telex, or in paper form.

[101] OJ 1998 L356/1. [102] OJ 1999 L125/34. [103] OJ 1999 L110/33.
[104] OJ 1999 L75/36. [105] OJ 1999 L125/34.

e) Sanctions

Finally, like the Commission in the context of the general competition rules, the ECB is given a policing role by art. 110(3): within the limits and under the conditions adopted by the Council[106] the ECB is to be entitled to impose fines or periodic penalty payments on undertakings for failure to comply with obligations under its regulations and decisions. This role is exercised by the Executive Board in co-operation with the national central banks under procedures laid down in Council Regulation 2532/98.[107] Sanctions relate to infringements, defined as any failure by an undertaking to fulfil an obligation arising from ECB regulations or decisions.[108] In this context undertakings mean 'those natural or legal persons, private or public, with the exception of public persons in the exercise of their public powers, in a participating Member State, which are the subject of obligations arising from ECB regulations and decisions, and shall include branches or other permanent establishments located in a participating Member State, the head office or registered office of which is outside a participating Member State'.

The decision whether to initiate an infringement procedure may be taken either by the Executive Board of the ECB or by the national central bank of the Member State in whose jurisdiction the alleged infringement has occurred. The Executive Board of the ECB may act on its own initiative or on the basis of a motion addressed to it by the national central bank of the Member State in whose jurisdiction the alleged infringement has occurred, and a national central bank may act on its own initiative or on the basis of a motion addressed to it by the ECB. Article 3(1) of the Regulation requires that written notification of the decision to initiate an infringement procedure be given to the undertaking concerned, to the relevant supervisory authority, and, depending on who initiated the proceedings, to the national central bank of the Member State in whose jurisdiction the alleged infringement has occurred or to the ECB itself. The notification must disclose the details of the allegations against the undertaking and the evidence on which such allegations are founded. Where appropriate, the decision to initiate the procedure should require the termination of the alleged infringement and give notice to the undertaking concerned that periodic penalty payments may be imposed.

If an undertaking is required to submit to an infringement procedure, the ECB or the national central bank, as the case may be, has the right to:

(a) require the submission of documents;
(b) examine the books and records of the undertaking;
(c) take copies or extracts from such books and records; and
(d) obtain written or oral explanations.[109]

When an undertaking obstructs the conduct of the infringement procedure, the participating Member State in which the relevant premises are located is required

[106] Under the procedure laid down in art. 107(6).
[107] OJ 1998 L318/4.
[108] Art. 1(4).
[109] Art. 3(2).

to afford 'the necessary assistance', including ensuring access by the ECB or the national central bank to the premises of the undertaking, so that the rights listed above can be exercised.

The undertaking has the right to be heard by the ECB or the national central bank, as the case may be, and it must be given no fewer than thirty days to present its defence. However, whether the infringement procedure has been conducted by the ECB or by a national central bank, it is the Executive Board of the ECB which has the power to take a decision concluding that procedure. Under art. 3(4) the Executive Board of the ECB is required to adopt a reasoned decision as to whether an undertaking has committed an infringement, setting out the sanction to be imposed, if any, as soon as possible after receiving a submission from the national central bank which initiated the infringement procedure or after having consulted the national central bank of the Member State in whose jurisdiction the alleged infringement has occurred. The upper limit for a fine is set at €500,000; the upper limit for periodic penalty payments is set at €10,000 per day of infringement. Periodic penalty payments may be imposed in respect of a maximum period of six months following the notification to the undertaking of the decision to initiate the infringement procedure. Unlike the competition rules, there is no express relationship to turnover, though the ECB is expressly required, in determining whether to impose a sanction and in determining the appropriate sanction, to be guided by the principle of proportionality.[110] It is also required, *inter alia*, to take account of the economic size of the undertaking. No sanction is to be enforced against the undertaking until the decision has become final, because: the period (thirty days)[111] for making a request for review to the Governing Council of the ECB has elapsed without the undertaking requesting a review; the Governing Council has notified the undertaking of its decision on such a request for review; or the period allowed for the Governing Council to respond to such a request (two months)[112] has elapsed without the Governing Council having taken a decision. In any event, the proceeds from sanctions imposed by the ECB belong to the ECB[113] (whereas under the competition rules fines fall within the Community budget) and the regulation requires an undertaking to bear the costs of the infringement procedure if it has been decided that it has committed an infringement.

The Executive Board's decision must be notified in writing to the undertaking concerned, and it must also be informed of its right of review. Notification of the decision must also be given to the relevant supervisory authorities and to the national central bank of the Member State in whose jurisdiction the infringement occurred. The Regulation then provides[114] that the undertaking has the right to request a review of the decision of the Executive Board by the Governing Council of the ECB. Such a request must be made within thirty days of the receipt of the notification of the decision and must be addressed in writing to the Governing Council of the ECB.

[110] Art. 2(2). [111] Art. 3(6). [112] Art. 3(7). [113] Art. 3(9). [114] Art. 3(6).

Such internal review mechanisms are not unknown in Community law, perhaps the best known being the requirement under art. 90 of the Staff Regulations for an official to make a complaint to his or her appointing authority before bringing an action before the Court of First Instance,[115] but what is particularly striking about this review procedure is the relationship between the Executive Board and the Governing Council of the ECB: all the members of the Executive Board are also members of the Governing Council. While it may be acceptable for administrative review procedures not to display the degree of independence required of the judicial process, it is suggested that this procedure falls between two stools: it is neither a method of inviting the body which took the decision to reconsider the matter (which effectively is the situation under the Staff Regulations), nor a review by a genuinely separate body. Be that as it may, written notification of the Governing Council's decision must be given to the undertaking concerned, to the relevant supervisory authority of that undertaking, and to the national central bank of the Member State in whose jurisdiction the infringement occurred, and it must inform the undertaking of its right of judicial review. In any event, if no decision has been taken by the Governing Council of the ECB within two months of the request, the undertaking concerned may request a judicial review of the decision of the Executive Board in accordance with the Treaty. The question must be asked whether the Regulation may restrict the undertaking's Treaty right under art. 230 to seek the annulment of a decision addressed to it. In the context of the Staff Regulations, art. 236 of the EC Treaty gives the Court jurisdiction in any dispute between the Community and its servants 'within the limits and under the conditions laid down in the Staff Regulations or the Conditions of Employment', but there is no such limitation on the Court's jurisdiction over ECB decisions under art. 230. The only Treaty reference to limits and conditions in this context relates to the powers of the ECB itself under art. 110(3), as mentioned above. Even under the Staff Regulations, it has long been established that the internal complaints procedure does not have to be used where an official invokes general Treaty remedies rather than the specific staff remedies.[116] There is also an express exception in art. 91(4) of the Staff Regulations, which allows an official to bring an action before the Court immediately after submitting his complaint to the appointing authority if the application in this action is accompanied by a request for interim measures. Effectively, this is merely a device to allow interim measures to be requested, since the proceedings in the main action are suspended until an express or implied decision is taken on the complaint, and the President of the First Chamber in Case 75/72R *Perinciolo* v. *Council* said[117] that the admissibility of the main action must not be prejudged. However, there is no parallel provision in the Regulation concerning the powers of the ECB to impose sanctions.

As for the powers of the Court, the Regulation makes it clear that in this instance the European Court has unlimited jurisdiction within the meaning of art. 229 of

[115] See Usher, *European Court Practice* (Sweet & Maxwell, London, 1983) pp. 81–6.

[116] See e.g. Case 33/80 *Albini* v. *Council* [1981] ECR 2141.

[117] [1972] ECR 1201, 1203.

the Treaty with regard to penalties. The Court may therefore substitute its own view for that of the ECB as to an appropriate remedy.

Finally, the Regulation lays down time limits for the initiation of proceedings, for taking decisions in such proceedings, and for the enforcement of such decisions.[118] The right to take the decision to initiate an infringement procedure expires one year after the existence of the alleged infringement first became known either to the ECB or to the national central bank of the Member State in whose jurisdiction the alleged infringement occurred. There is, in any case, an overall limit of five years after the infringement occurred or, in the case of a continued infringement, five years after the infringement was terminated. The right to take the decision to impose a sanction in respect of an infringement expires one year after the decision to initiate the procedure was taken, and the right to start an enforcement procedure expires six months after the decision has become enforceable.

Regulation 2532/98 clearly sets out general rules, which may be subject to more specific provisions; art. 6 provides that 'in the event of a conflict between the provisions of this Regulation and the provisions of other Council Regulations enabling the ECB to impose sanctions, the provisions of the latter shall prevail'.

f) Judicial review

The power to issue binding legal acts, and its involvement in the more general legislative process, no doubt helps to explain why the ECB is made subject to, but also able to benefit from, the full range of judicial remedies under the EC Treaty;[119] it may be said that one of the characteristics of the European Central Bank is that it should be both subject to and able to seek judicial review.

The result is that, in the context of actions for annulment under art. 230, the Court of Justice may review the legality of acts of the ECB, other than recommendations and opinions (which appears to mean decisions addressed to national central banks) in the same way as acts adopted jointly by the European Parliament and the Council, and acts of the Council and of the Commission. The use of the generic term 'acts' appears to cover the 'guidelines' and 'instructions' discussed above[120] to the extent that they produce binding legal effects.[121] So far as seeking review is concerned, the ECB is treated like the European Parliament in that it may bring an action for the purpose of protecting its prerogatives. Actions for failure to act may be brought against the ECB under art. 232, but the Bank itself may only bring such actions in the areas falling within its field of competence. If an act of the ECB is annulled, or if it is found to have failed to act, then under art. 233 it is

[118] Art. 4.

[119] For a fuller discussion, see Craig, 'EMU, the European Central Bank, and Judicial Review' in *Legal Framework of the Single European Currency* ed. Beaumont and Walker (Hart, Oxford, 1999) pp. 95–115.

[120] See p. 224.

[121] See e.g. Case 294/83 *Les Verts* v. *European Parliament* [1986] ECR 1339.

required to take the necessary measures to comply with the judgment of the Court of Justice.

With regard to references for preliminary rulings under art. 234, the validity and interpretation of the ECB's acts may be considered by the Court. More striking still, is the fact that the ECB can invoke a special enforcement procedure against national central banks under art. 237 paragraph (d). This gives the European Court jurisdiction in disputes concerning the fulfilment by the national central banks of obligations under the Treaty,[122] and this provision contains no express exemptions or derogations. It provides that in this connection the powers of the Council of the ECB (which presumably means the Governing Council) in respect of national central banks shall be the same as those conferred upon the Commission in respect of Member States by art. 226. If the Court of Justice finds that a national central bank has failed to fulfil an obligation under the Treaty, that bank is required to take the necessary measures to comply with the judgment of the Court of Justice.

Under the revised version of art. 288, the established rules on non-contractual liability apply under the same conditions to damage caused by the ECB or by its servants in the performance of their duties, although, given the structure of the System of Central Banks, art. 35.3 of the Statute makes it clear that natioanl central banks are liable according to their respective national laws. Contractual liability, on the other hand, is dealt with in the Statute: art. 35.2 provides that disputes between the ECB and its creditors, debtors, or any other person, shall fall within the jurisdiction of the competent national courts, save where jurisdiction has been conferred upon the Court of Justice. However, it is envisaged that the Court of Justice will have jurisdiction to give judgment pursuant to any arbitration clause contained in a contract concluded by or on behalf of the ECB, whether that contract be governed by public or private law.[123]

Procedurally, a decision of the ECB to bring an action before the Court of Justice will be taken by the Governing Council.[124]

While the Treaty refers generically to actions brought by and against the ECB, the ECB actually acts through its decision-making bodies.[125] While it can hardly be doubted that an act of the appropriate decision-making body is an act of the ECB—indeed the Treaty envisages no other way for the ECB to act—the Treaty provisions do not expressly envisage a dispute between the decision-making bodies (unlikely though this may be). Since the ECB itself enjoys legal personality,[126] it is questionable whether its internal bodies may be regarded as legal persons able to bring an action for annulment or failure to act. On the other hand, the Court did recognize a right of action for the European Parliament to bring actions to protect its prerogatives,[127] before the Treaty was amended to allow for such actions, even though it is the Community rather than its institutions which has legal personality.[128]

[122] And the Statute of the ESCB.
[123] Art. 35.4.
[124] Art. 35.5.
[125] See above pp. 224–5.
[126] EC Treaty art. 107(2).
[127] Case C–70/88 *EP* v. *Council* [1990] ECR I–2041.
[128] Art. 281.

11

External monetary relations and influences

1. Capital movements and current payments

a) General issues

In the modern world the Community cannot be treated in isolation in respect of monetary policy. Although many of the amendments to the EEC Treaty effected by the Single European Act were intended to facilitate the completion of the internal market by the end of 1992, a more outward–looking view is discernible in the amendment of art. 70(1) of the EEC Treaty by the Single European Act. This enabled the Council to enact legislation concerning the movement of capital to and from non-Member States by a qualified majority, except in so far as such measures might constitute a step backwards from the existing level of liberalization, in which case unanimity would be required. It further stated that the Council should 'endeavour to attain the highest possible degree of liberalization'. However, to the extent that Community measures left differences between the exchange rules of Member States, art. 70(2) still permitted a Member State to take unilateral measures to prevent its residents from taking advantage of the internal free movement of capital so as to benefit from the more liberal rules on transfers to and from non-Member States in another Member State. In many ways this resembled art. 134 (then art. 115) of the EC Treaty,[1] under which a Member State could prevent the import of goods in free circulation in another Member State where it itself was a beneficiary of a quota, and the importation would enable the quota to be circumvented. However, under art. 134 the Member State must have authorization from the Commission to protect that quota, and no such permission appears to have been granted after the end of 1992, whereas under art. 70(2) control was to be by the Council after the event.

The principal result of the revised art. 70(1) was art. 7 of the 1988 Capital Movements Directive,[2] under which Member States were to 'endeavour' to attain the same degree of liberalization in their treatment of transfers in respect of movements of capital to or from third countries as that which applied to operations with residents of Member States. It may be submitted that the use of the word 'endeavour' in both art. 70(1) of the Treaty and art. 7 of the Directive meant that neither

[1] See Green, Hartley, and Usher, *The Legal Foundations of the Single European Market* (Oxford University Press, 1991) pp. 24–7.

[2] Council Directive 88/361 (OJ 1988 L178/5).

the Council nor the Member States were under an unconditional obligation, capable of being relied on by individuals, as was held by the European Court in relation to the similar terminology used in the original art. 71 (the standstill provision) in Case 203/80 *Casati*.[3] On the other hand, the original art. 72 imposed a clear obligation on Member States to keep the Commission informed 'of any movements of capital to or from third countries which come to their knowledge', an obligation which hardly seems practical given the scale of movements on modern monetary markets.

At first sight the situation is different under the current provisions, which entered into force on 1 January 1994. Was observed in Chapter 2, the basic provisions appear to treat internal and external monetary movements in the same way. Under art. 56(1) all restrictions on the movement of capital between Member States 'and between Member States and third countries' are prohibited, and art. 56(2) prohibits all restrictions on payments between Member States 'and between Member States and third countries'. However, in the terms of art. 56(1) and (2), these prohibitions only operate within the framework of 'the provisions set out in this Chapter' (i.e. Chapter 4 of Title III of the EC Treaty on Capital and Payments), and art. 57(1) provides that the provisions of art. 56 are to be without prejudice to the application to third countries of any restrictions which existed on 31 December 1993 under national or Community law adopted in respect of the movement of capital to or from third countries involving direct investment (including investment in real estate), establishment, the provision of financial services, or the admission of securities to capital markets. The result appears to be that with regard to monetary movements to and from third countries relating to those matters, art. 56 only in fact prohibits the imposition of new restrictions, and does not require the elimination of restrictions legitimately adopted before its entry into force.

However, art. 57(2) empowers the Council, acting by a qualified majority on a proposal from the Commission, to adopt measures on the movement of capital to or from third countries involving direct investment (including investment in real estate), establishment, the provision of financial services, or the admission of securities to capital markets, 'whilst endeavouring to achieve the objective of free movement of capital between Member States and third countries to the greatest extent possible'. The two paragraphs of art. 57 may thus be seen as interrelated: the Council is given power to legislate only in those areas where the Treaty itself does not automatically require existing restrictions to be eliminated by the Member States, and the requirement merely to endeavour to achieve free movement 'to the greatest extent possible' implies that the measures adopted by the Council need not amount to total liberalization. This is confirmed by the last sentence of art. 57(2), which, repeating the terms of the former art. 70(1) as amended by the Single European Act, states that unanimity shall be required for measures under this paragraph which constitute a step back in Community law as regards the liberalization

[3] [1981] ECR 2595. See p. 16.

of the movement of capital to or from third countries. This necessarily implies that measures taken under art. 57(2) may increase restrictions as well as relax them.

Be that as it may, to the extent that a payment or capital movement is not excluded, art. 56 has been held to be directly effective even with regard to capital movements to third countries such as Switzerland and Turkey.[4]

This is an interesting development given the Court's reluctance in earlier case-law automatically to extend concepts developed in the context of the internal market to situations governed by similar language in relations with third countries. For example, Case 270/80 *Polydor* v. *Harlequin*,[5] in the context of the free movement of goods, held that even where a free trade agreement expressly prohibits not only quantitative restrictions but also measures having effects equivalent to quantitative restrictions, the same interpretation of that phrase need not be given in the context of trade with a non-Member State as will be given in the context of trade between States, since there is no intention to create a single market under free trade agreements.

A synthesis of the approach to the direct effect of provisions of international agreements was given in the context of an agreement between the Community and Portugal in the *Kupferberg* case[6]. The Court started from the principle that it is open to the Community and a third country to agree what effect the provisions of the agreement are to have in the internal legal order of the contracting parties, and that the matter fell to be decided by the court only in the absence of express agreement on the point, although emphasizing that it was open to the courts of one contracting party to consider that certain provisions were directly effective even if that view was not shared by courts of the other contracting party. It went on to consider whether the provision at issue could be regarded as unconditional and sufficiently precise to have direct effect in the light of the object and purpose of the agreement, concluding that the provision at issue imposed an unconditional rule against discrimination in matters of taxation, dependent only on a finding that the products affected were of like nature, so that it could be applied by a court and produce direct effects throughout the Community. However, the Court emphasized that, although the provision at issue had the same object as art. 95 (now art. 90) of the EC Treaty, each of these provisions should be interpreted in its own context, and that the interpretation given to art. 90 could not be applied by way of simple analogy to the corresponding provision of an agreement on free trade. However, in the judgment *Sanz de Lera* does not discuss these issues, and simply holds art. 56 to be directly effective in itself and on its own terms.

[4] Cases C–163, 165 and 250/94 *Sanz de Lera* [1995] ECR I–4821.

[5] [1982] ECR 379.

[6] Case 104/81 *Hauptzollamt Mainz* v. *C. A. Kupferberg & Cie KG* [1982] ECR 3641, [1983] 1 CMLR 1.

b) Specific restrictions

Despite this directly effective application of art. 56 to movements to and from third countries, restrictions specific to monetary movements to or from third countries are envisaged in arts. 59 and 60. Under art. 59, where, in exceptional circumstances, movements of capital to or from third countries cause, or threaten to cause, serious difficulties for the operation of economic and monetary union, the Council, acting by a qualified majority on a proposal from the Commission and after consulting the European Central Bank, may take safeguard measures with regard to third countries for a period not exceeding six months if such measures are strictly necessary.

Article 60(1) relates expressly to art. 301 (introduced by the Maastricht Treaty as art. 228a) which provides for Community implementation of policies agreed by the European Union[7] in the context of foreign and security policy, stating that where it is provided, in a common position or in a joint action adopted according to the provisions of the Treaty on European Union relating to the common foreign and security policy, for an action by the Community to interrupt or to reduce, in part or completely, economic relations with one or more third countries, the Council is to take the necessary urgent measures, acting by a qualified majority on a proposal from the Commission. Article 60(1) applies this to monetary movements to or from the third countries concerned, providing that if, in the cases envisaged in art. 301, action by the Community is deemed necessary, the Council may, in accordance with the procedure provided for in art. 301, take the necessary urgent measures on the movement of capital and on payments as regards the third countries concerned.[8]

Similar unilateral action by Member States is envisaged in art. 60(2), without prejudice to art. 297 (formerly art. 224, which provides for consultation between Member States in the event, *inter alia*, of war, or serious international tension constituting a threat of war) and as long as the Council has not taken measures pursuant to art. 60(1). Under this provision a Member State may, for serious political reasons and on grounds of urgency, take unilateral measures against a third country with regard to capital movements and payments. The Commission and the other Member States must be informed of such measures by the date of their entry into force at the latest. Nevertheless, the Council may, acting by a qualified majority on a proposal from the Commission, and subject to informing the European Parliament, decide that the Member State concerned shall amend or abolish such measures.

[7] See Usher, 'Maastricht and English Law', (1993) *Statute Law Review* pp. 28–45.

[8] In the context of trade sanctions, foreign policy decisions have in fact been implemented under art. 133 (formerly art. 113) as a matter of common commercial policy. See Council Regulations 3300/91 (OJ 1991 L315/1) and 1432/92 (OJ 1992 L151/4) with regard to sanctions against Serbia and Montenegro.

It is clear from this context that the unilateral restrictions which a Member State may impose on monetary movements to or from a third country must relate to a dispute with, or disapproval of the conduct of, that third country, and may not be taken to protect the economic situation of that Member State.

c) Taxation

To the extent that monetary movements to and from third countries do fall within the general principle of free movement laid down by art. 56, they also appear to be subject to the restrictions which may be imposed under art. 58 on monetary movements within the Community,[9] since in its terms art. 58 is not limited to movements within the Community. While art. 58 may allow Member States to distinguish between tax-payers who are not in the same situation with regard to their place of residence or with regard to the place where their capital is invested, and to take all requisite measures to prevent infringement of national law and regulations, particularly in the field of taxation and the prudential supervision of financial institutions, or to take measures which are justified on grounds of public policy or public security, this is subject to the overall caveat that such measures must not constitute arbitrary discrimination or a disguised restriction on the free movement of capital and payments as defined in art. 56. Nevertheless, in the context of monetary movements to and from third countries, the caveat may not be interpreted in the same way as in the context of monetary movements between Member States, in effect leaving it possible to impose a wider range of restrictions.

It was suggested in Chapter 3 above that discriminatory tax treatment apparently authorized under art. 58(1)(a) may conflict with other Treaty freedoms, and that a simple way of avoiding that conflict would be to say that a situation governed by another Treaty freedom does not fall within art. 58(1)(a). This is a possible explanation of the decision in Case C–118/96 *Safir* v. *Skattemyndigheten i Dalarnas Län*,[10] where it was held to be a breach of art. 49 for Sweden to impose a different tax regime for insurance policies purchased from providers outside Sweden which would have the effect of deterring Swedish residents from taking out such policies, even though it was intended to achieve tax neutrality between policies purchased inside and outside Sweden. It was there stated that the decision on this point made it unnecessary to determine whether the legislation was also incompatible with arts. 56 and 58—even though under the express terms of art. 50 services are only services within the meaning of the Treaty to the extent that they do not fall under one of the other Treaty freedoms. However, monetary movements outside the Community are highly unlikely to constitute an economic activity governed by one of the other Treaty freedoms, since all the other freedoms apply only to activities or transactions within the Community, so such an interpretation leaves art. 58(1)(a) to apply in full in situations involving monetary movements outside the Community.

[9] See p. 27 et seq. [10] [1998] ECR I-1899.

Be that as it may, art. 58(1)(a) only entered into force on 1 January 1994 and, as noted in Chapter 3, there is attached to the Maastricht Treaty a Declaration in the following terms:

> The Conference affirms that the right of Member States to apply the relevant provisions of their tax law as referred to in [Article 73d(1)(a)] of this Treaty will apply only with respect to the relevant provisions which exist at the end of 1993. However, this Declaration shall apply only to capital movements between Member States and to payments effected between Member States.

While a mere Declaration may not amend the terms of the Treaty, it has long been established in other areas of Community law that it may be binding upon its author.[11] If the Member States are bound by their Declaration, it is submitted that its effect is that with regard to monetary movements between Member States, the only discriminatory measures which may be maintained under art. 58(1)(a) are those which were lawfully in force at the end of 1993. On the other hand, it also means that art. 58(1)(a) applies in full to situations involving monetary movements outside the Community.

Article 58(1)(a) is drafted in very broad terms. It allows Member States to apply the relevant provision of their tax law which distinguish between tax-payers (with no mention of nationality) who are not in the same situation with regard to their place of residence or with regard to the place where their capital is invested. However, it is still subject to the general requirement in art. 58(3) that the measures in question should not constitute arbitrary discrimination or a disguised restriction on the free movement of capital and payments. The particular question arises here how to reconcile a provision which expressly allows differences in treatment on the basis of residence or place of investment with a provision which prohibits arbitrary discrimination.

It is submitted that, in order to avoid being characterized as 'arbitrary', the discriminatory tax treatment must be shown to be objectively justified, even in the context of monetary movements to and from third countries, since the Treaty freedom applies to such movements. It may also be suggested that in this context the criteria laid down by the Court in Case C–204/90 *Bachmann* v. *Belgium*[12] continue to be relevant: the measures must be intended to protect the coherence of the national tax system, and must be shown to be necessary for the achievement of that objective. It is also questionable whether, as in the context of the internal free movement of goods, in order to justify differential tax treatment under art. 58(1)(a), not only must the measure be justified to protect the coherence of the tax system, but it must also be shown that effective measures are taken at the domestic level in the national tax system to deal with the perceived problem.[13]

[11] In the context of declarations under Regulation 1408/71 on social security, see Case 35/77 *Beerens* [1977 ECR 2249, 2254.

[12] [1992] ECR I–249.

[13] Case 4/75 *Rewe-Zentralfinanz* v. *Landwirtschaftskammer Bonn* [1975] ECR 843 and Case 121/85 *Conegate* v. *HM Customs and Excise* [1986] ECR 1007.

It is also interesting to examine how far possible tax discrimination under art. 58(1)(a) fits in with the Community's wider obligations. In the context of the European Economic Area, art. 40 of that Agreement provides that there shall be no restrictions between the contracting parties on the movement of capital belonging to persons resident in EC Member States or EFTA States 'and no discrimination based on the nationality or on the place of residence of the parties or on the place where such capital is invested'. Article 41 provides that current payments connected with the movement of goods, persons, services, or capital between contracting parties within the framework of the provisions of the Agreement shall be free of all restrictions. Article 40 is implemented in Annex XII, which effectively reproduces the 1988 Directive. This, as indicated in Chapter 3, contains no equivalent of art. 58(1)(a); on the other hand the Treaty freedoms clearly do apply in the EEA. It is therefore suggested that the discrimination allowed under art. 58(1)(a) is not permissible in the EEA context—unless art. 58(1)(a) is to prevail over the EEA Agreement. As to this, both provisions entered into force on 1 January 1994, and unless arts. 40 to 45 of the EEA are to be regarded as of no effect, they must be treated as the special rules which apply in the EEA context in place of the general rules for third countries which flow from art. 56 *et seq.* of the EC Treaty.

As for the Europe Agreements with Central and Eastern European countries, payments must be authorized in freely convertible currency to the extent that the transactions underlying the payments concern movements of goods, services, or persons between the parties which have been liberalized pursuant to the Agreement.[14] Furthermore, the Member States of the Community have undertaken from the entry into force of the respective Agreements not to introduce any new foreign exchange restrictions on the movement of capital and current payments connected therewith between residents of the Community and the relevant Central or Eastern European State, and not to make existing arrangements more restrictive.[15] However, they have not undertaken (except to the extent of holding consultations) to eliminate previously existing restrictions, and it is therefore suggested that to the extent that lawful tax discrimination is possible on the basis of residence or place of investment in relation to relevant Central or Eastern European States at the time of the entry into force of their respective Agreements, such discrimination may continue where justified under art. 58(1)(a).

Turning to the more general framework of international obligations, the General Agreement on Trade in Services[16] art. XVII only requires non-discrimination to the extent that specific commitments have been entered into. However, even there, art. XIV provides that, subject to the requirement that such measures are not

[14] See art. 60 of the Agreements with Bulgaria, the Czech Republic, Romania, and Slovakia, and art. 59 of the Agreements with Hungary and Poland.

[15] See art. 61(2) of the Agreements with Bulgaria, the Czech Republic, and Slovakia, art. 61(3) of the Agreement with Romania, and art. 60(2) of the Agreements with Hungary and Poland.

[16] To which both the Community and its Member States are parties within their respective spheres of competence.

applied in a manner which would constitute a means of arbitrary or unjustifiable discrimination between countries where like conditions prevail, or a disguised restriction on trade in services, 'nothing in this Agreement shall be construed to prevent the adoption or enforcement by any Member of measures: . . .

(d) inconsistent with Article XVII, provided that the difference in treatment is aimed at ensuring the equitable or effective imposition or collection of direct taxes[17] in respect of services or service suppliers of other Members;
(e) inconsistent with Article II, provided that the difference in treatment is the result of an agreement on the avoidance of double taxation or provisions on the avoidance of double taxation in any other international agreement or arrangement by which the Member is bound.

A footnote indicates that 'measures that are aimed at ensuring the equitable or effective imposition or collection of direct taxes' include measures taken by a Member under its taxation system which:

—apply to non-resident service suppliers in recognition of the fact that the tax obligation of non-residents is determined with respect to taxable items sourced or located in the Member's territory; or
—apply to non-residents in order to ensure the imposition or collection of taxes in the Member's territory; or
—apply to non-residents or residents in order to prevent the avoidance or evasion of taxes, including compliance measures; or
—apply to consumers of services supplied in or from the territory of another Member in order to ensure the imposition or collection of taxes on such consumers derived from sources in the Member's territory; or
—distinguish service suppliers subject to tax on worldwide taxable items from other service suppliers, in recognition of the difference in the nature of the tax base between them; or
—determine, allocate, or apportion income, profit, gain, loss, deduction, or credit of resident persons or branches, or between related persons or branches of the same person, in order to safeguard the Member's tax base.

This again seems to indicate a series of justifications for tax discrimination which might fall within art. 58(1)(a). It is therefore suggested that a dividing line be drawn between the situation concerning monetary movements within the EC and the EEA on one hand, and movements involving other countries, including those with Europe Agreements, on the other, though in the latter case it would appear that no new discrimination amounting to a restriction on monetary movements may be introduced.

[17] For the purpose of this Agreement 'direct taxes' comprise all taxes on total income, on total capital, or on elements of income or of capital, including taxes on gains from the alienation of property, taxes on estates, inheritances, and gifts, and taxes on the total amounts of wages or salaries paid by enterprises, as well as taxes on capital appreciation.

2. Competition rules

While arts. 81 and 82 of the EC Treaty only prohibit conduct 'which may affect trade between Member States', it has long been accepted that this concept may cover the conduct of undertakings outside the Community which produces effects inside the Community,[18] agreements entered into outside the Community which are implemented within it,[19] and conduct which largely affected exports from the Community.[20] These principles apply fully in the financial services sector, and it may be observed, for example, that the 1985 Eurocheques Decision[21] involved a large number of banks outside the Community and that the 1992 Decision on the Eurocheque Helsinki Agreement,[22] as its name implies, involved an agreement entered into outside the Community—but which in fact concerned the operation of the system in one Member State.

Without setting out detailed rules, it may be observed that the General Agreement on Trade in Services recognizes the problem of distortions caused by anti-competitive practices. Article IX states that Members recognize that certain business practices of service suppliers, other than those falling under art. VIII on monopolies and exclusive service providers, may restrain competition and thereby restrict trade in services. It was therefore agreed that each Member should, at the request of any other Member, enter into consultations with a view to eliminating such practices. Each Member is required to accord full and sympathetic consideration to such a request and to co-operate through the supply of publicly available non-confidential information of relevance to the matter in question. The Member addressed is also required to provide other information available to the requesting Member, subject to its domestic law and to the conclusion of satisfactory agreement concerning the safeguarding of its confidentiality by the requesting Member.

3. Cross-border financial services

a) General issues

The Community's own legislation shows external international influence in two ways: some of it seems to have been influenced by developments in other international fora, and some of it is expressly designed to deal with third country undertakings (or, more accurately, their Community subsidiaries). The former situation is most clearly shown in the Solvency Ratio Directive.[23] This largely follows the

[18] Case 48/69 *ICI* v. *Commission* [1972] ECR 619.

[19] Cases 89, 104, 114, 116, 117, and 125–129/85 *Ahlstrom Osakeyhtio* v. *Commission* [1988] ECR 5193.

[20] Cases 6 and 7/73 *Commercial Solvents* v. *Commission* [1974] ECR 223.

[21] Commission Decision 85/77 (OJ 1985 L35/43). See pp. 65 above.

[22] Commission Decision 92/212 (OJ 1992 L95/50). See pp. 68 above.

[23] Council Directive 89/647 (OJ 1989 L386/14).

criteria, notably the 8 per cent ratio, laid down in 1988 by the Cooke Committee set up by the Bank for International Settlements in Basle,[24] with the major difference that whereas the Cooke proposals were intended to apply to banks carrying out international business, the Directive applies to all relevant credit institutions in the Community, even if they only operate locally.[25]

Special provisions dealing with the problem of third country undertakings and their subsidiaries may be found in arts. 8 and 9 of the Second Banking Directive.[26] This Directive, as has been seen,[27] sets out the principle that a credit institution authorized in one Member State may establish a branch or offer services in any other Member State. The perceived problem was that under art. 48 of the EC Treaty the benefit of the provisions on establishment and services extends to 'companies or firms formed in accordance with the law of a Member State and having their registered office, central administration, or principal place of business within the Community', a formula which could include a company incorporated and operating in a Member State which was the wholly-owned subsidiary of an undertaking based in a third country, so that a credit institution which was such a subsidiary could take advantage of the EC banking 'passport'.

When the proposal for the Second banking Directive was being drafted, Commissioner De Clercq said on record that the Community saw no reason why the benefits of its internal liberalization should be extended unilaterally to third countries, but that the Community would be ready and willing to negotiate reciprocal concessions,[28] and the original proposal[29] insisted on reciprocity in the context of the acquisition of participation in credit undertakings and the establishment of European Community subsidiaries by third country undertakings. In their final form, arts. 8 and 9 require notification to the Commission by the national authorities of their authorization of a direct or indirect subsidiary of a third-country undertaking or of the acquisition of a holding in a Community credit institution by such an undertaking. They further provide a channel of information through the Member States to the Commission with regard to difficulties encountered by Community credit institutions in establishing themselves or carrying out banking activities in third countries, and the Commission itself is required to draw up periodic reports on the treatment accorded to Community credit institutions in third countries.

Where it appears to the Commission that a third country is not granting Community credit institutions effective market access, comparable to that granted by the Community to credit institutions from that third country,[30] the Commission is given power, subject to obtaining a mandate by qualified majority

[24] Dufloux and Karlin, 'La Réglementation Prudentielle des Banques: Les travaux récents du Comité Cooke', *Banque* 1988 p. 1246 and 1989 p. 77.

[25] Blandon, '1993: No Time for Risks', *Banker*, January 1993 pp. 24–7.

[26] Council Directive 89/646 (OJ 1989 L386/1).

[27] See pp. 128–32 above.

[28] Levitin, 'The Treatment of United States Financial Services Firms in Post–1992 Europe', (1990) *Harvard International LJ* p. 507 at p. 521.

[29] OJ 1988 C84/1.

[30] Art. 9(3).

from the Council, to enter into negotiations to remedy the situation. Similarly, where it appears to the Commission that Community credit institutions do not receive national treatment offering the same competitive conditions as are available to domestic credit institutions and the conditions of effective market access are not fulfilled,[31] the Commission is itself given power to enter into negotiations to remedy the situation, and a mechanism is provided under which the Commission may issue decisions requiring Member States to limit or suspend authorizations, or approvals of acquisitions of holdings, sought by parent undertakings governed by the laws of the third country in question, initially for a period of three months, which may be extended by the Council by qualified majority. However, this does not apply to credit institutions or their subsidiaries already authorized in the Community, so only those trying to enter the Community market for the first time are affected.

Where one of the situations exists which would enable it to open negotiations or limit or suspend authorizations, the Commission may request the Member States to inform it of any request for authorization by a direct or indirect subsidiary of parent undertakings one or more of which are governed by the laws of the third country in question; the Commission may also request to be notified whenever Member States are informed[32] that such an undertaking proposes to acquire such a holding in a Community credit institution as to make it its subsidiary.

It is submitted that this is hardly a requirement of reciprocity as such, and indeed art. 9(6) makes it clear that any measures taken must comply with the Community's obligations under any international agreements governing the taking up and pursuit of the business of credit institutions, which provision anticipates the outcome of the GATT negotiations. On the other hand, the Community has, for example, entered into a bilateral agreement with Switzerland on non-life insurance.[33] Be that as it may, the provisions set out in the Second Banking Directive form a model subsequently followed in the investment services Directive,[34] art. 7 of which uses substantially identical terminology in the context of the authorization of investment firms which are the direct or indirect subsidiary of a parent undertaking governed by the law of a third country, or of the acquisition of a holding in a Community investment firm by such a parent undertaking which had the effect of making the firm its subsidiary. One apparent difference, however, is the involvement in decisions whether to limit or suspend authorizations of a committee on transferable securities, the creation of which is envisaged in the investment services Directive.

b) General Agreement on Trade in Services

Both the Community and its Member States are parties to the Uruguay Round General Agreement on Trade in Services, a situation which arises from the scope

[31] Art. 9(4).

[32] Under art. 11; see p. 124 above.

[33] OJ 1991 L205/1. This agreement entered into force on 1 Jan. 1993 (see OJ 1993 L33/16).

[34] Council Directive 93/22 (OJ 1993 L141/27).

of that agreement. Under that Agreement, trade in services is defined as the supply of a service:

(a) from the territory of one Member into the territory of any other Member;
(b) in the territory of one Member to the service consumer of any other Member;
(c) by a service supplier of one Member, through commercial presence in the territory of any other Member;
(d) by a service supplier of one Member, through presence of natural persons of a Member in the territory of any other Member.

The view taken by the European Court in its *Opinion 1/94*[35] on the competence of the Community to conclude the Uruguay Round Agreements was that cross-frontier supplies under (a) involved a situation where the supplier was established in one country and the consumer resided in another, and neither moved to the other's country; it was therefore 'not unlike' trade in goods, and could be regarded as falling within the common commercial policy under art. 133. It was therefore a matter of exclusive Community competence. On the other hand, the other three headings involved the movement of natural or legal persons and did not therefore fall within the common commercial policy. In so far as they fell outside the scope of common commercial policy, the Court took the view that it was only to the extent that internal common rules had been adopted, including provisions relating to the treatment of nationals of non-Member countries or expressly conferring on its institutions powers to negotiate with third countries, that the Community had exclusive external competence. In fact, the specific example of internal common rules including such provisions which the Court gave was the Second Banking Directive,[36] the relevant provisions of which are discussed earlier in this Chapter.

Given the resultant mixed competence, the Court stressed the need for close co-operation between the Member States and the Community institutions, and it may be observed from the recitals to successive Council Decisions giving effect to the successive Protocols setting out the results of the WTO negotiations on financial services[37] that the commitments were negotiated by the Commission 'on behalf of the European Community and its Member States'. Indeed, the annexed Schedule of Specific Commitments sets out more limitations on behalf of Member States than it does on behalf of the Community.

The GATS distinguishes between general obligations (set out in Part II) and a framework for specific commitments (set out in Part III). The basic general principle set out in art. II is that of most-favoured-nation treatment, a concept which may differ in the context of mixed competence depending on whether it relates to treatment by the Community or treatment by a Member State. This is clearly shown in the exemptions from this principle invoked by the EC and its Member

[35] [1994] ECR I–5276.

[36] Council Directive 89/646 (OJ 1989 L386/1).

[37] Culminating in the Fifth Protocol, concluded on behalf of the Community by Council Decision 1999/61 (OJ 1999 L20/18).

States under art. II(2): an exemption is claimed both by the Community in relation to the non-life insurance agreement with Switzerland discussed above[38] and with regard to Italy in relation to the national 'offshore' tax regime discussed in Chapter 3[39] giving tax concessions to profits derived from business with or concerning the countries of Eastern Europe. There is also a general exemption in art. V:

This Agreement shall not prevent any of its Members from being a party to or entering into an agreement liberalizing trade in services between or among the parties to such an agreement, provided that such an agreement:
(a) has substantial sectoral coverage, and
(b) provides for the absence or elimination of substantially all discrimination, in the sense of Article XVII, between or among the parties, in the sectors covered under sub-paragraph (a), through:
 (i) elimination of existing discriminatory measures, and/or
 (ii) prohibition of new or more discriminatory measures,
 either at the entry into force of that agreement or on the basis of a reasonable time-frame, except for measures permitted under Articles XI, XII, XIV and XIV bis.

This is clearly appropriate to allow for the internal rules of the European Community, and is linked to art. Vbis, stating that:

This Agreement shall not prevent any of its Members from being a party to an agreement establishing full integration of the labour markets between or among the parties to such an agreement, provided that such an agreement:
(a) exempts citizens of parties to the agreement from requirements concerning residency and work permits;
(b) is notified to the Council for Trade in Services.

More generally, art. XI also provides that, subject to restrictions to safeguard the balance of payments under art. XII, no Member shall apply restrictions on international transfers and payments for current transactions relating to its specific commitments. This is declared not to affect the rights and obligations of the members of the International Monetary Fund under the Articles of Agreement of the Fund. There are also general exceptions set out in art. XIV, to the effect that nothing in the Agreement shall be construed to prevent the adoption or enforcement by any Member of measures:

(a) necessary to protect public morals or to maintain public order;[40]
(b) necessary to protect human, animal, or plant life or health;
(c) necessary to secure compliance with laws or regulations which are not inconsistent with the provisions of this Agreement including those relating to:
 (i) the prevention of deceptive and fraudulent practices or to deal with the effects of a default on services contracts;

[38] See p. 241. [39] See p. 41.
[40] The public order exception may be invoked only where a genuine and sufficiently serious threat is posed to one of the fundamental interests of society.

(ii) the protection of the privacy of individuals in relation to the processing and dissemination of personal data and the protection of confidentiality of individual records and accounts;

(iii) safety.

This provision also allows, subject to requirements discussed earlier in this Chapter,[41] for measures inconsistent with specific commitments of national treatment under art. XVII in relation to direct taxation of services or service suppliers of other Members.

As for specific commitments, the Agreement provides for market access and national treatment. With regard to market access, art. XVI(1) provides that each Member shall accord services and service suppliers of any other Member treatment no less favourable than that provided for under the terms, limitations, and conditions agreed and specified in its schedule. It may be observed that limitations set out in the Schedule of Specific Commitments of the EC and its Member States annexed to Council Decision 1999/61[42] relate almost exclusively to limitations on market access imposed in individual Member States; the exception is a Community-wide limitation relating to the requirements of Council Directive 85/611 on undertakings for collective investment in transferable securities (UCITS).[43] With regard to national treatment, art. XVII(1) provides that 'in the sectors inscribed in its schedule, and subject to any conditions and qualifications set out therein, each Member shall accord to services and service suppliers of any other Member, in respect of all measures affecting the supply of services, treatment no less favourable than that it accords to its own like services and service suppliers'. Again, it is suggested that national treatment at the Community level is not necessarily coterminous with national treatment at the Member State level, but in fact there are relatively few limitations set out in the Schedule of Specific Commitments of the EC and its Member States, and they appear to be entirely at the national level.

Finally, under the Annex on Financial Services annexed to GATS, the 'services supplied in the exercise of governmental authority', which are excluded from the definition of 'services' in art. I(3)(b) of the Agreement, are stated to include activities conducted by a central bank or monetary authority or by any other public entity in pursuit of monetary or exchange rate policies. The Annex also provides that, notwithstanding any other provisions of the Agreement, a Member shall not be prevented from taking measures for prudential reasons, including for the protection of investors, depositors, policy holders, or persons to whom a fiduciary duty is owed by a financial service supplier, or to ensure the integrity and stability of the financial system.[44] On the other hand, under para. 3.1 a Member may recognize prudential measures of any other country in determining how the Member's measures relating to financial services shall be applied.

[41] See pp. 238 above.

[42] OJ 1999 L20/38.

[43] OJ 1985 L375/3. See pp. 141 above.

[44] Para. 2.1.

4. Exchange rates and units of account

When the three Community Treaties entered into force in the 1950s all the Member States participated in the system of fixed exchange rates established under the International Monetary Fund. It was noted above that the unit of account chosen by the Coal and Steel Community in 1952 was the unit of account of the European Payments Union, which happened to correspond to the gold value of the United States dollar, and that when in 1958 the European Payments Union was replaced by the European Monetary Agreement, the identical European Monetary Agreement unit of account became the unit of account used for Community purposes.[45] Similarly, when the first common agricultural legislation was enacted in 1962, Regulation 129/62[46] again defined the agricultural unit of account at the official value of the United States dollar, and it was also there provided that where sums given in one currency were required to be expressed in another currency, the exchange rate to be applied should be that which corresponded to the par value communicated to and recognized by the International Monetary Fund.

Following the collapse of the system of fixed parities in 1971–2, it was still belived to be necessary to find an external criterion of value when the Community started the joint float known as the 'snake'.[47] The founding Resolution[48] set out the principle that, *inter alia*, the difference between the spot exchange rates of two Member States should not exceed 2.25 per cent (the 'snake'), but it also provided that fluctuations against the dollar should not exceed the maximum allowed under the rules of the IMF, which was then 4.5 per cent under the December 1971 Smithsonian Agreement (the 'tunnel' within which the snake could wriggle). However, another year later, in March 1973[49] it was decided no longer to intervene with regard to the dollar, leaving the snake simply as a joint float.

Nevertheless, when in 1975 the basket-type European Unit of Account (which later became the current European Currency Unit[50]) was created for the purposes of the Lomé Convention, it was still deemed to be necessary to find an external marker, and the overall value of the EUA was derived from the value in June 1974 of the 'Special Drawing Rights' (SDR) of the International Monetary Fund,[51] based on a basket of currencies which gave a heavy weighting to the United States dollar, the original value of the SDR being, in turn, based on the gold value of the US dollar.[52] Hence, a link can be traced between the original unit of account and the basket ECU which has evolved into the euro.

While the ECU as a basket of national currencies might have been able to operate in a relatively self-contained way without need for a further external criterion of value, the possible need (or hope) for an exchange-rate policy following the

[45] See Chapter 7 above.
[46] JO 1962 p. 2553.
[47] See Chapter 8 above.
[48] JO 1972 C83/3; 1974 *Compendium* p. 33.
[49] Council Statement of 12 Mar. 1973 (1974 *Compendium* p. 63).
[50] See Chapter 6 above.
[51] As stated in the recitals to Council Decision 75/250 (OJ 1975 L104/35).
[52] See above pp. 160–1.

introduction of the euro is envisaged in art. 111 of the EC Treaty as introduced by the Maastricht amendments; it should however be emphasized that this provision only entered into force at the beginning of the third stage[53] and that it does not apply to Member States with a derogation[54] or to the United Kingdom.[55] Article 111(1) operates by way of derogation from art. 300, which sets out the general procedure for the negotiation of international agreements between the Community and non-Member States or international organizations; it empowers the Council to conclude formal agreements on an exchange-rate system for the ECU in relation to non-Community currencies—which seems to contemplate a return to something like the former IMF system—and lays down a special procedure for this to be achieved. The Council is required to act unanimously[56] on a recommendation from the European Central Bank or from the Commission (which indicates that the power of initiative in this area is as much, if not more, with the ECB as with the Commission) after consulting the ECB in an endeavour to reach a consensus consistent with the objective of price stability, and after consulting the European Parliament. The procedure for negotiation is laid down in art. 111(3), which provides that where agreements concerning monetary or foreign exchange regime matters need to be negotiated by the Community with one or more States or international organizations, the Council, acting by a qualified majority[57] on a recommendation from the Commission and after consulting the ECB, shall decide the arrangements for the negotiation and for the conclusion of such agreements. It is stated that these arrangements must ensure that the Community expresses a single position, and that the Commission must be 'fully associated' with the negotiations. The implication of this is that, whereas negotiations under the general art. 300 are conducted by the Commission, the same is not necessarily the case under art. 111, and the negotiations could, for example, be entrusted to the ECB. However, it is clearly laid down that agreements concluded in accordance with art. 111(3) are to be binding on the institutions of the Community, on the ECB, and on Member States (but, of course, only those participating in monetary union).

Although the Council may only conclude such an agreement by unanimity, art. 111(1) provides that within the exchange-rate system, it may adopt, adjust, or abandon the central rates of the ECU acting by a qualified majority on a recommendation from the ECB or from the Commission, and after consulting the ECB in an endeavour to reach a consensus consistent with the objective of price stability; the role of the European Parliament in these situations is merely to be informed by the President of the Council of the adoption, adjustment, or abandonment of the ECU central rates.

In the absence of an exchange-rate system negotiated under art. 111(1) and (3) in relation to one or more non-Community currencies, art. 111(2) provides for the

[53] Art. 116(3).

[54] Art. 122(3) and (4). See Chapter 8 above.

[55] UK Protocol art. 5.

[56] I.e. by unanimity of the members of the euro-zone.

[57] Though it will be recalled that under art. 111(1) it needs to act unanimously to conclude the resultant agreement.

Council to formulate general orientations for Community exchange-rate policy in relation to these currencies, though these general orientations must be without prejudice to the primary objective of the ESCB to maintain price stability. To do this, the Council may act by a qualified majority either on a recommendation from the Commission and after consulting the ECB or simply on a recommendation from the ECB, which again shows the power of initiatives of the ECB in this area.

On matters other than exchange-rate policy, provision is made in art. 111(4) for the Council acting by a qualified majority, on a proposal from the Commission and after consulting the ECB, to decide on the position of the Community at international level as regards issues of particular relevance to economic and monetary union and, acting unanimously, to decide its representation in compliance with the allocation of powers laid down in arts. 99 and 105. These respectively require Member States to regard their economic policies as a matter of common concern and to co-ordinate them within the Council, and set out the objectives of the European System of Central Banks and the tasks of the ECB. Against this background, it was decided at the Vienna European Council in December 1998[58] that with regard to the external representation of the Community, the President of the ECOFIN Council, or if the President is from a non-euro area Member State, the President of the euro–11, assisted by the Commission, should participate in meetings of the G7 (Finance) and that the ECB, as the Community body competent for monetary policy, should be granted an observer status at the IMF board. The views of the European Community/EMU on other issues of particular relevance to the EMU would be presented at the IMF board by the relevant member of the Executive Director's office of the Member State holding the euro Presidency, assisted by a representative of the Commission. The European Council invited the Council to act on the basis of a Commission proposal incorporating this agreement. It also declared that the coherence and effectiveness of the Community require that it should be able to speak with one voice on issues of particular relevance to economic and monetary union. The European Council therefore encouraged the Commission, the Council, and the Member States to take the necessary action to ensure a timely and effective preparation of common positions and common understandings which could be presented to third parties in international fora.

Finally, art. 111(5) affirms that, without prejudice to Community competence and Community agreements as regards economic and monetary union, Member States may negotiate in international bodies and conclude international agreements. Since, unlike art. 174(4) on external competence in matters of environmental policy, this does not purport on the face of it to preserve national competence in matters where the Community has competence,[59] it is submitted that it does no more than repeat the truism that Member States retain competence in matters which do not fall within Community competence; in any event, as part of art. 111, it is

[58] RAPID Information Service, 13 Dec. 1998.

[59] See Usher, 'The Source and Structure of EEC Environmental Law' in: *Environment and Planning Law* (ed. Vaughan, Butterworths, 1991) pp. 1–15.

relevant only to those Member States participating in monetary union in the third stage. However, precisely because of that, what is novel about art. 111, but nonetheless a characteristic of the third stage of economic and monetary union as it results from the Maastricht Treaty, is that international agreements may be entered into in the name of the Community which will be binding on some but not all of the Member States.

Index

The manufacturer's authorised representative in the EU for product safety is Oxford University Press España S.A. of el Parque Empresarial San Fernando de Henares, Avenida de Castilla, 2 – 28830 Madrid (www.oup.es/en or product.safety@oup.com). OUP España S.A. also acts as importer into Spain of products made by the manufacturer.

www.ingramcontent.com/pod-product-compliance
Lightning Source LLC
LaVergne TN
LVHW011748200926
848484LV00003B/653

9780198298779